COUVERT

Clive Shong Ho

Copyright © 2018 (Clive Shong Ho)
All rights reserved worldwide.

Scriptures taken from the HOLY BIBLE, NEW INTERNATIONAL VERSION®. Copyright © 1973, 1978, 1984 by International Bible Society. Used by permission of Zondervan.

No part of the book may be copied or changed in any format, sold, or used in a way other than what is outlined in this book, under any circumstances, without the prior written permission of the publisher.

Publisher: Inspiring Publishers,
P.O. Box 159, Calwell, ACT Australia 2905
Email: publishaspg@gmail.com
http://www.inspiringpublishers.com

 A catalogue record for this book is available from the National Library of Australia

National Library of Australia The Prepublication Data Service

Author: Clive Shong Ho
Title: Couvert
Genre: Philosophy / Religion
ISBN: 978-0-6483864-6-9

Foreword

This work was not intended as a Bible study, although I have quoted many Scripture passages. The Bible is the central reference of this work because I want to stay on the right track. This has been the maxim of my faith from inception. Those that love the Lord will find it of some interest, but it is imperative to maintain a personal thriving walk with Christ because faith is a personal thing.

This book has two sections, the first part being mainly drawn from practical experience. The second part is about the Holy Spirit's input into my life and my spiritual walk. Many things are intertwined, and large parts are drawn from my observation of behaviour in ministry and the events that have crossed my path. The Scripture references set the standard and different people may find certain parts easier to handle than others. Nevertheless, it is the target that all believers must work towards without exception.

Freewill permeates this entire work and it will invoke the reader to assess their position in relation to Jesus. The practice of freewill always has a bearing on the question: Why can't I do this or that? In most if not all cases, we know that our choices are not always godly. I know what the Bibles says, but the self-driven nature within procrastinates because it is torn between self-interest and God's interest.

I have used the pronoun 'you' fairly frequently because it delineates responsibility. You have to decide how you want to relate to God. No matter what happens, the action has to emanate from you because the Lord judges each person individually. People don't like to be coerced into choosing, but it has to be done as God will assess each and every human that has ever lived on this earth. There are fervent believers, casual believers and those who think that they are passionate believers. You have to find out where you stand with Christ.

This book is my personal testimony to Jesus Christ who I believe and trust in. I have strived to live according to all that I have written, but there's still much to be improved. This is a continuous reminder that I am but a mere student that depends on the grand Master for illumination. It is an account of how I had progressed in spirit and it works for me. I hope that you may be encouraged to discover your own way to spirituality in living fellowship with Jesus.

There are Christians that have been believers for a very long time, yet they may still be holding out on Jesus. They may be almost at the point of denying self, but not quite there. I struggled with this so many times in the past. The idea of exchanging the corporeal for the incorporeal just seems too risky and distressing. Personal-will determines a person's fate before God and the risk or benefit is shaped by your own hand.

Much thought has gone into the writing and even more from the inspiration of the Holy Spirit from time to time, especially the parts relating to the Bible and the applications that I have written about. One aspect that I was quite pleased with was that the Spirit brought to mind an incident in the mid-1990's that had a bearing on my choice to serve abroad. I had clean forgotten about it as it wasn't important enough for me to keep in mind (at the time). However, it carried valuable personal guidance because it was pertinent in my career changing decision.

I hope that you may gain something from reading this book. It could be anything that provokes action or adds to spiritual motivation. As far as the Bible is concerned, there's no new revelation, but the Holy Spirit is there to open up the joy of discovering new ways to view and apply spiritual truths in your personal interests. These ideas may be relevant to both internal and external application. In my opinion, the greatest value lies in the internal transformation because real private co-development with Jesus is the ultimate security. The mind of Christ is available to all believers if we allow him to take possession of our spirit. I thank God to have had this opportunity to pen my thoughts because it means so much to me.

The two great determinants of one's destiny i.e. freewill and the Holy Spirit are elements that each person must seriously deal with as early in their Christian life as possible. Interactive relationship with God hinges upon it so a greater awareness ought to be placed here. Every decision that we make has an outcome for which we are responsible. Bad spiritual choices are something that no normal person would choose, but self-determination often throws caution to the wind.

My foremost desire is to comply with all the morals in this book and not fall into hypocrisy. It's no simple feat because the destroyer is always looking for opportunity. This means that I will have to cover my back until the end of my days. I know full well that if I stay close to Jesus, he will keep me on the right path. In Christ there's nothing to worry about, but we allow the material to hinder our faith.

I wish that you will have as much enjoyment in reading this book, as much as I had in compiling it.

All the best,
Clive

Contents

SECTION ONE

Chapter 1. Naturally 3
Chapter 2. Self-made 19
Chapter 3. Identity 39
Chapter 4. Unnaturally 51
Chapter 5. The start 59
Chapter 6. Conduct 69
Chapter 7. Confusion 79
Chapter 8. Cultural Influences 85
Chapter 9. Pre-emptive favour 97
Chapter 10. You did not choose me 107
Chapter 11. A perspective of freewill 111
Chapter 12. What is the purpose of freewill? 115
Chapter 13. The Focus of dependent-will 121
Chapter 14. The Consequences of freewill 129
Chapter 15. Caution 137
Chapter 16. The turning point 141
Chapter 17. The transformed life 145

SECTION TWO

Chapter 18. The way forward 157
Chapter 19. Cycle 167
Chapter 20. Invitation 177
Chapter 21. Self-control 183
Chapter 22. Knowing and walking 191

Chapter 23. Servant and serving 205
Chapter 24. Paradox 211
Chapter 25. Spiritually 215
Chapter 26. Vexation 221
Chapter 27. Intrinsic Nature 227
Chapter 28. In the beginning 235
Chapter 29. Heaven 239
Chapter 30. Always a child 243
Chapter 31. Spiritual child 261
Chapter 32. Spiritual child-adult 283
Chapter 33. Self-denial and humility 317
Chapter 34. Self-help 349
Chapter 35. The road ahead 359

SECTION ONE

Chapter 1
Naturally

Self-will is the paramount asset that a human being possesses because it gives an identity to a person. Freewill is the greatest faculty that God has bestowed upon humankind. It is the right to act independently from everybody else. However, it is not the right to act independently of God as you will see later on in Section Two. Since people are social beings, much of our freewill is shaped by the influence of peers. However, the lives of some of the greatest achievers in history are evident that they took intuitive risks that resulted in significantly moulding world events. They looked beyond the immediate and exercised their imagination and initiative. Recorded human history only goes back about 6,000 to 8,000 years. It's really strange that it's only in the last century; in particular the latter half of the 20th century that ground-breaking intelligence has given us the progressive technology and standard of living of today. From the beginning of the 21st century, technology has developed at an unprecedented pace.

The astounding rate at which new technology is emerging is far too great for any single person to master, hence the birth of a wave of new field specialists. Up till the mid-1970's it was possible for an accountant to learn and know a sufficient amount of knowledge to become a reliable expert. After the 1980's that was no longer the case and the 21st century information blow-out has forced accountants to specialise in one particular discipline. A similar analogy would be true of other trades and professions.

Over the past six thousand years, progress in science has been very slow. The reality is profound as all the state of the art technology and information has been packed in only the last fifty years after World War 2. Now, it looks like there's no stopping what humans may be capable of. Certain things that were impossible twenty years ago are now reality, especially in medical research. The drawback is the lack of knowledge, but once researchers know what causes the problem then finding the solutions are only a matter of time and money. One has to wonder why it is so. It seems like something was holding human advancement back for so long in the past and now suddenly it has been unleashed. Progress is only limited by finance and avenues of research.

Your will determines your very being. You are an individual that has a unique make-up. Your character, personality, creativity, mannerisms, emotions etc. are expressed through your will. In highly assertive people, self-direction is all too evident. Society, culture, education and habits affect people's thinking and behaviour. Western culture advocates the view that you are the captain of your own ship and you have the right to choose accordingly. Culture and religious practices in certain societies are so intertwined that it is extremely difficult for an individual to break out and go their own way. Despite how enslaving the system may be, you are still an individual who has feelings and are able to expound your own views, unless you don't want to change. Self-will expresses the freedom that we have to make personal choices. Each person is ultimately responsible to God and will be scrutinised along the lines of all the decisions that they have made. I'm referring primarily to western culture.

Contributory negligence arises when a person (injured party) through their own negligence had suffered loss that they could have prevented. Even though a third party had actually caused the loss (accident), the injured party would not be entitled to collect any damages (money) from the party that supposedly caused the mishap. This spells out freewill and responsibility in that a person is liable to care for the accuracy and correctness of their decisions/actions. Personal negligence contributed to the loss and this is their own responsibility. Therefore, a person cannot blame Satan or anybody else for temptation or misdeeds because they could have avoided it by proper and correct exercise of self-will.

Everybody who is in an advisory position must take great care that the advisee understands very clearly their personal responsibility. Advisors must always allow the advisee to freely make their own decision; in this way, the latter is accountable for their own actions. It's common knowledge that councillors should never cross the line and become personally involved. It may be due to zealousness, affection, bonding too close, ego or some other reason that the councillor takes on the client's problem in a personal way. This is not the correct ethical position to be in and it's violations are open to abuse of the moral code. Freewill can get a person into a lot of unnecessary trouble.

All the more reason not to get involved in some else's sin no matter how attractive the gain may appear. You have the freewill to resist. In the garden, Eve ate of the fruit first and was guilty, and then she gave it to Adam. He knew the rules and he didn't even try to stop her. He greatly respected his companion and didn't interfere with her freedom to choose. Adam became equally guilty when he also ate. He tried to blame his companion (Gen 3:12) but that was a lame excuse. His duty was to stop her from doing wrong or just walk away from the scene to escape guilt because he had freewill. It's a classic case of being too close to someone and falling into the same sin.

In close relationship situations, a person's judgment may be impaired because of the friendship, trust and the physical presence of that person. Face-to-face interaction is very powerful persuasion as there are many words, gestures and emotions that may impact a person's decision. People have to depend on their personal beliefs and convictions so as to do the right thing. More to the point, they have to rely on their own independent judgment. It requires even greater resolve to place total trust in God when the external factors strongly go against your moral beliefs.

My mother taught me to be sensitive and not to impose on others, so I always show respect and avoid being a nuisance. I learnt to handle my problems by myself and not to pass them onto somebody else. However, I absorbed all of the moral principles from the Bible which I read regularly. As I observed events over time, I noticed that certain folk that I classified as good didn't quite fit in that category. In my teenage years, I thought that if a Christian read the Bible, they should automatically adopt and follow those precepts because that was what I was doing. It seemed logical to me that everybody should be thinking and acting in an orderly manner and giving due respect to all concerned. Naturally I was most disappointed as my theory of Christian behaviour was totally shattered by the reality. It exposed the ubiquity of self-determination in all walks of life that is not as friendly as I thought.

It didn't take me long to realise that people naturally choose paths according to their personal values. Much if not all of it is driven by self-interest. At times it appeared that as long as they had what they wanted it was okay, and if they didn't then they would take all steps to get it. It was everybody for themselves. I wrestled with the concept of friendship and what kind of a relationship I held with my friends. Between the ages of five to ten, I valued friendship very highly. It was an adventure where I found great enjoyment and satisfaction from bonding with my peers. We had fun and laughs and also took the punishment together when caught in mischief. Comradeship was real to me and relationship was personal. I had regular playtimes with my mates, and always looked forward to seeing them. Our gatherings were an unwritten arrangement that was regularly adhered to. There are some things that I will never forget as they will remain in the recesses of my mind because of their impact.

However, after the age of ten there was a sudden change and those play-time schedules were all turned upside down. I used to go to our old haunts at the usual time expecting to see my friends, but nobody turned up! The explanations that came out of that were that they had things to do. I also realised then that they had other interests and other circle of friends that I wasn't a part of. Although I was disappointed, I accepted that the circumstances had changed. At that stage, I didn't give it much thought, but it forced me to change my habits as I had no choice. This was the very first occasion where I was acutely aware that outside influences had determined my lifestyle choices. They had chosen to do other things for their own pleasure, and too bad that I was left out. I had to entertain myself and get accustomed to the fact that friends will only meet when it suits them. Nothing was fixed and arrangements could change suddenly. Societal behaviour was unpredictable and I had to get accustomed to the fact. It was a coarse introduction into the realm of freewill and reality. My friends had their own priorities and interests. It suddenly catapulted me into the adult world and manner of doing things. It was so different from the sheltered situation of early childhood.

Perhaps some of my friends were under instructions from their parents to do other things (homework or other domestic duties). Perhaps their personal desires led them to other interests. People simply grow up and discover different attractions. Everybody has the right to choose what they want to do. There's nothing more natural than being yourself and expressing your personality. Usually this would be manifested through a person's inherent talent. Your actions tell the world what you are and it's all triggered by freewill.

Self-interest is a natural instinct. Whenever people have other interests that they consider more attractive they will break or postpone a pre-arranged engagement. For a kid, this is hard to swallow. There's nothing wrong with pursuing personal desires but as youngsters grow into teenagers, self-satisfaction quickly become acts of selfishness. You are the most important person in the world and you do what pleases self. Being free to choose your own way is a God-given privilege because freewill was created to be part of the human makeup. Right in the beginning, God gave Adam the task of selecting the names of all the animals. In addition, God permitted Adam and Eve to choose what they wanted to do, whether good or bad. The right to self-determination is inalienable.

When I started studying accounting at university, I was into sharing information and helping my friends in whatever way that I could. In preparation for the Accounting 2 exam, I was doing revision with a friend on some multiple-choice questions. We worked on the difficult problems had decided on a certain approach. However, just before entering the exam hall on the Monday morning, he came over and told me that the method we had worked on was wrong because he had discussed it with another friend over the weekend. I was devastated and felt betrayed. He didn't even have the courtesy to phone me. I resolved to be careful about who I trusted from then on. My sharing with him was done in good faith and after that I felt that I could only trust myself. It was a bitter moment but I managed to get a supplementary exam which I passed and that was a relief. It does indicate that people will enrich themselves at the expense of others, even one who may appear to be a sincere friend. Self-will can be insensitive and uncaring.

Self-gain if left unchecked would lead to greed and then to unethical behaviour. Self-centredness tends towards extreme actions whereby nothing and nobody matters except personal goals. People would trample on others, use them and hurt their feelings just to get what they want. Broken friendships come about because of personal bias. Self-centeredness is idolatry because you either worship the Creator or the creation; there's nothing in between. Each person has a unique personality and character, and an individual's sinful nature may be classified under particular types. That certain group of sin would torment you for life because it's character/personality based. Money, sex, power, popularity, prestige, pride, gambling, alcohol and status are some of the categories. Normally, a person would be captured by one or two main types but some of the effects may even overflow to a lesser type and thereby creating new problems. The contagion must be tightly controlled so that one need only concentrate on the primary difficulties.

We all are in the same spiritual dilemma regarding sin, and the spiritual has eternal ramifications so it warrants careful attention. There are so many options and forms that distract us from the simple decision: is it going to be Jesus or self? We build the forms up around us to the point where it is extremely hard to give it all up. Our habits, mindset and enjoyment of what we possess act against the spiritual direction that God desires of us and it upsets the fellowship that is so essential to spiritual growth. Unbridled freewill is anti-God, yet the accepted view is that every person has the right to do what's best for self. Selfishness makes us rationalise and justify our comfortable position and the material objectives that we are moving towards. This insidious line of thought bears undesirable consequences and some of us will regret our past decisions on that day. Normative secular criteria consider self-satisfaction as harmless and natural; but God views it as sin. Sin whether sizable and miniscule is still sin. What a nightmare – what are we supposed to do with freewill?

Individuality is a natural endowment but we misconstrue this to be the main criteria in life, so much so that we rebuff our spiritual being that make up our true self-will. The greater the attention given to the outward person, the more insignificant the spirit becomes. Individuality is seen in a person through the actions that they carry out. Everybody sees the material things and so we pay much attention to our physical appearance and presentation. The outer person is a barrier to the inner spirit. Over time it can grow so hard that the conscience is suppressed to such a degree that it can be easily manipulated in favour of the material things. Many people in the West are not even aware that they have a spirit within. Satisfaction of the material need is the only thing that matters.

Humans communicate through the physical but God communicates with people through his Spirit. The 'inside out maxim' that Stephen Covey talks about in his book 'The Seven Habits of Highly Effective People' is a character grounded principle. It's similar to the process of regeneration in the Christian life which is godliness centred and character based; whereby the new self under God's law has to be demonstrated outwardly via the body. Clearly, God has placed himself at a disadvantage because he works through a person's spirit and the inner self is hidden and easily ignored. Human preference will always have the propensity towards self. Christians have the same inclination until they reach a turning point in sanctification. This is when you reverse your old sinful behaviour and put God first in life. Initially, each step forward is a great effort because you have to first get rid of the outward malpractices and then claw back righteousness to get on the path of holiness; adhere to its precepts and advance in the image of God (holiness). The Lord didn't place all the odds in his favour to gain an advantage in his battle against the evil one. There's an overwhelming sense of fair-play for all. The freewill to choose was fairly endowed and people have to make up their own minds. Unfortunately, many will fit into Matthew 7:13-14.

The Creator made human-beings for companionship, but human personal aspiration alienates them from God. Character quality becomes apparent through the exercise of self-will and independence. It either goes God's way or more likely in the opposite direction that is self-oriented. Once the hardness of self-will is broken, the spiritual life is able to break free and express itself in Christ. Union with the Father can only be achieved through sincere, consistent and continual submission to him. Christ has so much to teach us if we would only allow him to take control.

Misdirected self-will is a disease birthed by sin that plagues a believer right to the grave because it's a struggle against one's own spirit. Unbelievers don't have this dilemma because their actions have no relationship to God. Whatever they do is outside of Jesus Christ and all their commendable acts are worthless under the Lord's scrutiny (Isaiah 64:6). Misdirection arises through personal desire and self-justification and is self-inflicted.

Believers have to be very careful never to do any work that stems from their own creativity. Personal ideas must always be subjected to prayer and waiting for the Lord's direction. The Creator is not a random being and hence the kingdom work and eternal rewards are interconnected and this only comes via Jesus Christ. Ephesians 1:11 tells of a predetermined framework that God has laid out for each Christian to fit into in their time on earth. The actual detail is not revealed as the Lord operates via the Spirit and his will is revealed through personal relationship. Worldly individualism that encourages freewill has to be replaced by God's will in the spirit.

The achievements of high profile personalities in Scripture are examples God's power demonstrated through them. By the same token, an obscure believer is likewise chosen for a specific purpose that is suitable at their level. All believers have a part to play albeit in a non-spectacular manner. The calling may be to missionary endeavour, charitable work, teaching or kingdom engagement. However, most Christian work would fit into the builder category whereby gifts are applied in a group endeavour towards a bigger picture in kingdom expansion.

Teamwork is founded on a common goal that every member agrees upon and contributes towards. The individual has to decide whether they fit the mould or not. The group exists solely for the sake of the pre-set goals determined by the governing body. There are different ways to attain those targets and concomitantly, members have various talents and each person need to be effectively used. Team attention shouldn't be solely focussed on those that possess strong communication skills and experience otherwise useful options may be inadvertently ignored. The inexperienced members would normally assume the subordinate status. It is correct to capitalise on the thriving parts of ministry, and this aspect in its ordinary course of development would have built-in support, repair and maintenance and contingency plans. In this way the work becomes self-sustaining and will grow over time. The inconspicuous members of the team should never be ignored by the majority because every part is important to God. This is more than mere lip-service and warm greetings. There ought to be active exploration of possible opportunities and ways to employ their talents in ministry. This is not always straightforward and sometimes, the openings just aren't available. However, it does get all team members engaged and working together. Leaders are in a position where they have to exercise their judgment, but even they are susceptible to error of self-will if they do not manage the ministry righteously and fairly.

Acts 13:2 tells of the church in Antioch being an expanding ministry with lots of work yet to do. However, Paul and Barnabas were extracted and sent out for a different work. At first glance, it seems untenable and perhaps illogical to be sending the best talent away, but God was using them to realise his own goals. Potential opportunities may take a member away from the team, and it may affect comradery, but prayer and impartiality will invite the Spirit's guidance.

The Antioch church was into local kingdom work and Paul and Barnabas were called to cross-cultural ministry. The aim does not change, but the tools do. If the Antioch church had ignored the call and concentrated solely on the local objective, they would have missed out on this ground-breaking work. Most probably Paul and Barnabas would have gone anyway because they believed in God first. Differing opinion and judgment calls may arise and upset this team decision process, but self has to be denied and godliness must reign. The undergirding principle of the verse mentioned in Acts (above) is found in 1 Corinthians 12:12 that stresses common membership in a body that is striving towards the same purpose. The Corinthians passage uses bold terms to describe the incorrect behaviour amongst members. Although the actual words may not be uttered, attitudes tell the intention of the people concerned and that may lead to division.

Although Paul and Barnabas were not officially labelled as experts or specialists, they possessed gifts that were particularly suited to this specific task. Fortunately, they didn't have the problem of isolation in their fellowship. In any team situation, there may be a minority that don't seem to fit in with the rest because they have a different trade, profession or role. There's a real danger that these people may be 'silently excluded' by the majority.

When people are too accustomed to one aspect of ministry, they assume it to be normal. They lose their perspective of the greater vision, and may feel threatened by a new aspect of ministry that appears on the scene of which they have no direct input in. This may become an impediment to team cohesion and it may cause complications where the majority feel that they are losing control because they have no understanding in a different discipline. When a new possibility appears that is outside of the comfort zone, it is easy to overlook it and not give it appropriate thought and prayer. The Lord may be trying to introduce a new work and we let it go unnoticed because it's too unsettling to contemplate. It may be something similar to what Paul and Barnabas were called to. It's helpful to bear in mind that the overall objective remains the same but new and unfamiliar procedures have to be adopted. Members should not be afraid to explore things that are outside of the square. The Lord will approve or denounce that idea, but we won't know if we don't try.

Each person has to be sure of their calling because they have to follow what Jesus is leading them to do. The crux of the matter is that Christ heads the individual and not the team because that is where the calling originated from. If a clash of interest arises, that person must be clear on God's calling upon them and not allow team philosophy to dominate. Should an amicable position not be agreed on within the team, then departure would be the most appropriate course of action. Sometimes, members get so engrossed in the team/comrade concept that they manipulate circumstances in order to maintain the status quo. This would not be correct if an honest assessment of spiritual direction indicates the contrary. The evaluation process merely requires a person to pray and to exercise a free and unfettered discretion regarding the team and all the alternatives on a fair and honest basis. Inside a person's heart, the Holy Spirit will tell them what's right and honourable. In fact, if all concerned are tuned in to the Spirit, they will all come to the same conclusion.

There may be strong-willed people that make a rather abrupt decision to withdraw from a project and that may seem counter-productive and even discouraging. If no reasons are offered then only that person knows their own motive. During my teenage years, I was playing basketball and our team was in the process of development. One day when I arrived on court, I was told that a key player had left to join another team. I expressed my great disappointment and how unfair it was that we had worked so hard to build up this team over many months. The coach gave an honest and practical retort; that we don't own that player and he could do as he deemed fit. That's freewill.

I have faced this dilemma twice that I can remember clearly. The two situations involved departing from ministry positions. On both occasions, the build up to withdrawal took several months and much deliberation. After the event, I had always looked back and looked out for signs from the Lord that may indicate the contrary. Maybe I made a mistake, in which case I would have renounced my decision as an error and taken a course of action to redress the issue. What's done is done and there may be very little that can be applied to rectify or compensate. However, it is vital not to hide your mistakes and to recognise where you went wrong (for future reference). It's not a matter of rationality, pride or self-determination but rather in keeping with the Lord's will. I'm glad to say that for months afterwards, I had seen not the slightest signs that my decisions were wrong. Moreover, the results produced all the joys and excitement of improved fellowship with Christ, and the positive indicators were convincing and a relief. There was no element of doubt whatsoever. The responsive relationship from the Lord's encouragement was all the assurance that I needed. God was with me and it showed through inspirational thoughts from the Bible, as well as motivation to complete this book.

When all the hype is channelled in a single direction, it would unwarily promote the isolationism of those who have no direct input. The oddball feels out of place and is not in a position to contribute to the team's activities. Early exit is the ideal decision, but in ministry it is not always this simple due to the initial calling. Since it is God who called that person to ministry; it is God who has to order or bring about a change of direction. This may require a period of waiting for the right signs to appear. When it is hard to appease one's feelings, each passing day is a test of patience and perseverance. You know what you want to do, but you can't do it. Continuation with the group seems so pointless and a waste of time, yet the waiting continues as the answers are not forthcoming. Minutes can feel like hours, and days like months. It's very hard to stand alone at the best of times, and the one thing that will get you through this dilemma is faith in what you believe in. Rationality points to the quick way out, but faith restrains and brings with it a certain degree of peace amidst the mental turmoil. The question of how long to put up with this situation plays on the mind time and time again. The succinct repetitive question is: what am I doing here? Nothing much, but I can't leave until I receive further guidance from the Lord. Trusting God to respond and waiting patiently while standing alone takes a lot of courage. The feeling of redundancy when everybody is sharing and enjoying common ground is depressing and damaging to self-confidence.

Patience is a virtue and it may even be a test from the Lord. The uplifting part is that the Holy Spirit will always give direction and encouraging signs to the needy seeker. Normally it comes from exhortation from Scripture and small things in life that just seem to work it-self out. A sure direction unfolds and much needed joy follows. To walk alone on the basis of faith alone is unpalatable, and it makes lonesomeness feel more pronounced. However, it opens one's spiritual life to new insights. Over time, small faith grows rock-solid as God puts the pieces together. If you keep your attention on God, you may actually enjoy your predicament knowing that he is with you all the way. True victory comes when a person's spiritual aspirations have overcome the physical urges of self-will. The longer the testing time, the greater the spiritual benefit. The best education comes from going through trials with God, and you will discover that the spiritual gain is the most cherished benefit. The material is temporal and happiness or personal satisfaction is short-lived. This is the truth that the Bible is trying to convey to us all along, yet we have to learn it the hard way.

There is only one way: God's way or no way. When an idea is formed, we pray about it and apply our technical know-how to handle it. In the initial stages there may be few obstacles. As we progress and more variables get added into the mix, we are apt to rely on personal exertion and outside assistance rather than on God's direction. Don't get me wrong, everybody needs information from those in the know. Caution must be exercised so as not to over-rely on human resources. This diversion occurs time and time again. When a task grows in magnitude, it would be accompanied by enthusiasm or trepidation or a mixture of both. Inevitably human input and advice come into play. Competition in the spiritual realm is always present. Wherever the Lord has a hand in something, Satan will always be standing in the wings ready to fill the gaps with imitations, fakes and incongruous information. The latter has tremendous appeal to our personal senses in one way or another. This is when we rationalise our motives and actions to conform to what we want to believe are the Lord's directives.

If you are aware of this ploy, then you will be less likely to fall out of line with God. You can know with total confidence that if you stay in close contact with the Holy Spirit's guidance, you will never be wrong. The competing ideas in those situations are real and momentarily very comforting, reasonable and appealing. The Bibles tells us that we don't know how God works and this means that despite having well laid out plans, it is still imperative to commit each individual phase to God's guidance in the event that something needs to be changed.

Normally, once the management agree on a ministry objective, it becomes fixed. However, if the field conditions alter, then an immediate assessment has to be made as to whether the current directions are still valid. More often than not, the methodology would have to be modified or changed to suit the field situation. Targets are fixed but there may be various ways to approach the work. Sometimes field conditions are highly restrictive and there is no direct path to the target people group. When the access point favours peripheral ministry, there is a danger of distraction from the main objective. A certain opening may be easily accessible but does not reach or target the intended group. It is okay to go this way, but there must be regular assessments of the dangers of continuing down this path. The results may clearly display that this method is ineffective or it may even work towards the wrong goal (reaching an unintended people group).

This is the critical time to re-think strategy and methodology. It would be an error to become so engrossed in the periphery and forget about the primary aim because it has become too difficult to redirect effort that way. It's comfortable to stay on the easy road and talk about alternative ministry that comes readily. Diversion is just what the evil one wants. This situation is goal-inefficient and could evolve into a bad habit that creates a comfortable operating environment. It's effortless then to slip into a false sense of satisfaction. The core objectives are what a ministry exists for and they must take centre-stage in everything that the group does. To do otherwise would amount to unfaithfulness to supporters and the calling. Easy access points that are not directly associated with the organisation's core interests are distractions that drain energy and resources. If there is no other alternative, then there must be much prayer and thought going into how to get back to the main target group under such restrictive conditions. This priority must never be forced to the sidelines. Indirect entry points make ministry uncomfortable and breeds uneasiness in the mind because the largest portion of time and effort is placed in a secondary matter. This problem pertains to ministry to a minority group when visas are granted for work with the majority.

The only way forward is to keep the peripheral activities under control at the minimum level possible, and great effort and planning has to go into breaking into the 'too hard basket'. This is actually double-work because the assigned work activities have to be done and at the same time, the worker has to find ways to develop strategies that are aimed at the primary target group. This is often frustrating with no visible signs of development for months on end. The thought of hopelessness plays on the mind because the core objectives are clear, but there's no effective way to achieve them. The worker's resolve on the commissioned objectives is tested every day on the field. It's hard to stay focussed on the intended mission, but other organisations are also going through similar frustrations. It depends on how comfortable you have made yourself. If you allow yourself to concentrate on non-core ministry because it is what you encounter daily, then you will by default set less time aside for the core objectives because they are just too hard to pursue. A frank check on your average ministry activities and time spent will tell you where you stand in terms of your mandatory objectives.

For those that go in as tentmakers, duty has to be fulfilled because of the employee obligation. The associated time and effort spent in the workplace are an immediate handicap. However, progressive thinkers will always have a clear definition on the top priority and constantly strive in that direction. This requires great discipline and self-control. The main aim ought to be brought to the fore on every appropriate occasion, even though little may be done at the time. This constant reminder keeps the members on track. Unadulterated focus sharpens the senses and prompts people into action. When the progress is slow or stagnant, it is the time to be looking at different approaches. Innovation brings the best out of a person, and who knows, a breakthrough may be found where there was none previously. Prayer is the key to getting ahead as this is a spiritual contest.

Such limitations should not be allowed to dominate one's psyche, but rather, spur creative ways to get around them. Indirect ministry means burning the candle at both ends whereby all spare time and effort must also be applied in the main task. At the end of the day when it's time for relaxation, who wants to spend time on things that have little or no result and appears to be going nowhere? Any normal person needs a balance between work and rest. In order to be faithful to the calling, a worker has to be abnormal in a manner of speaking. If minimal effort is directed to the main purpose, then progress will be slow and carelessness will lead to regression. It may be more disheartening where every possible thing has been done and still no positive leads emerge. It's a tough call, but smart persistent people work things out. A friend of mine from a different mission organisation working in the same area became so frustrated at the slow progress that he left the ministry and returned home.

It is wise to find out what others are doing in the field. Networking is essential in cross-cultural work as others may have useful knowledge and practices that one is unaware of. The most up to date position may only be ascertained where the current state is known of all the present work in progress. There may also be opportunity to partner with others and learn through synergistic means. It's advantageous to learn from the mistakes of others rather than to go through that torturous process yourself.

The simple maxim is to stay in close proximity to the Lord and not allow the work to be derailed. The difficulty is that sometimes diversions are brought about by the advice and influence of friends and peers. But it still comes back to the basic tenet: to trust God more than anything or anyone else. This would truly challenge whether one places the Lord above influential friends, family and circumstantial pressures (Luke 14:26-27). Some people may assert their complete dependence on God, but certain actions may indicate that self-indulgence is still very much alive within.

God created nature to be harmonious, beneficial and complimentary within creation, but human nature was gifted with intelligence and hence carries a latent element of bias towards self. Once unleashed, the domination of selfishness is swift, uncompromising and extremely hard to eradicate. This was not the way God meant it to be and sin has caused our dysfunctional relationship with him to be blatantly obvious, yet we don't appear the least concerned. We encourage the damage to proliferate to the stage where we are powerless to extricate ourselves, and only the Lord can redeem our dire predicament. We have brought about disharmony with our Creator, and we have to do something about it.

The fall demonstrated human prejudice towards self. Adam and Eve thought that they could personally benefit from knowledge outside of God. Since then, human beings have assumed self-will as a natural part of life. Everything that a person does has some direct or indirect bearing on self-will. You can will to do good or bad. This is a human prerogative and is therefore subject to human error. No matter how arguments are framed, the onus of self-determination remains a personal struggle when relating to God. We have to choose righteously and its only Jesus that can reinstate us to correct spiritual standing with our Father.

Chapter 2
Self-made

Prior to the fall, humans were only capable of doing good, but after that people had the option to do evil as well. Sin made humans enemies of God. Humans perpetrate evil acts through the mind and body. Generally speaking a human being is made up of:

Body – that interacts in the physical world.

Mind – that that express intelligence and creativity.

Spirit – that gives rise to conscience, faith and the ability to relate to God.

The spirit is also applied as the soul or the heart, but sometimes the Bible refers to the soul as the whole person (body, mind and spirit).

All three parts are tied into a person's freewill. In order to make decisions and get things done one must have the will to do it. Should there be a conflict between any of the above, a decision would normally be postponed until enough information comes to light or when the time is ripe. They are separate parts and have different functions, but they form a syzygy and are not mutually exclusive.

The Body.

In some instance a person will make a decision despite uncertainty. A certain degree of risk is involved and a decision is made with that in mind. The body may gain an immediate benefit but the mind/spirit may oppose it on ethical or moral grounds. In this case, the person may feel that they are able to live with the consequences so it's a comfortable risk.

We are born into sin and the likelihood of making poor decisions based purely on physical conditions, logic and conscience is high. In fact, it is to our disadvantage because we tend to concentrate on the material and ignore the spiritual. Sometimes we only become aware of our spiritual side much later after the horse has bolted. Our upbringing prioritizes the concept of self-reliance. We would rather trust our own intuition than place faith in God. Self-reliance is a good thing but it can cross over into pride very quickly. We make bad decisions and it's only after our backs are up against the wall, and in desperation do we turn to Jesus. Old habits that we have grown up with from childhood lead us into fixed behaviour patterns. We get ourselves into trouble and then ask God to get us out. When there's a delay, we feel that God is not listening or answering. Of the three elements, the most attention is given to the body. This is a habit because we look into the mirror every day and sometimes several times a day and self-attention is subconsciously heightened in the mind.

The body experiences all the senses that a person possesses: the enjoyment of eating; the satisfaction of relaxation; aestheticism to appreciate the fine things in life; the pain of suffering; the fulfilment of work; the fun of physical activity and sports; the enjoyment of relaxation etc. However, if we concentrate too much on the body then we become selfish and personal gain (self-fulfilment) would be the main priority in life. From birth you are taught to take care of yourself and to obtain the best for yourself. Two children arguing over who has the biggest, the best, the smartest, the most and all those things that promote pride and self-importance show how much people value self-esteem. No doubt, many of us have indeed experienced this first hand during our time on earth. Our natural inclination is to make decisions based on the superficial elements in life that benefit self before others.

The brain initiates all the thought processes and the conditioning starts in the home and continues to the early stages of school. In the west, the culture and the free enterprise system encourages freedom of thought and creativity, and very young children may be conditioned to make decisions on their own. In those formative years, the instruction is always to care for self. This bias thinking will encourage selfishness. However, wise parents always teach their children good manners and to consider others as well. Unfortunately, some parents nurture independent thought in their children at the expense of self-discipline. The latter is necessary to establish moral and ethical principles in a child's mind that lead to mature responsible behaviour. The world loves creative and intelligent individuals who astound people with new ideas and breakthroughs in emerging innovations and technology. A person would naturally want to excel and get ahead of the pack. People want to be different so they think, act, dress and behave in ways that set themselves apart from the ordinary. It's acceptable because they are merely making use of their freedom to think outside the box. The world tells you to look into yourself and find your hidden self. One interpretation is that each person may have a special talent that's waiting to be released. You are encouraged to be the best that you are able to be. Get out there and squash the competition at all costs.

You may wonder which part actually initiates the decisions. It depends on the individual's nature and whether they desire to satisfy the body, mind or spirit at that particular point in time. The expression of self is usually made with regard to outward conditions combined with rational thought, but sometimes it's just pure fancy and nothing else. When certain people have succeeded and achieved something desirable, everyone wants it. The body and mind are the prime movers because material satisfaction is the all-important motivation. The majority of decisions are made towards satisfying the mind and body. We don't usually prioritise spiritual gratification because this places God first and others closely after. It is an alien concept and we must turn our habits around.

The world tells you that you have rights. They encourage you to be different, to be yourself! You are unique and you should live out your dreams. This is what it is to be human, after all, that's life. The Creator on the contrary is telling us that the present human state is unnatural and abnormal, and he is trying to bring us back to his original design. The idea is not to destroy our freewill, personality, character or uniqueness, but to nurture an intimate relationship that is motivated by agape. The purpose is not to remove freewill but to train it to choose justly. The extent that a person values God would determine the depth of commitment.

Culture is what makes people different. Cultures that infringe on basic human rights and decency should be approached with care. Human rights advocate that traditional festivals need not be lost in a cross-cultural situation, and it also upholds the freedom to practice one's religion. It would be a pity to do away with practices that have formed an ethnic group's history through blind assimilation. Undesirable traditions do not bode well with decency and fortunately there are very few in the developed countries. Western nations are apt to separate the state from religion and culture. The government's main aim is to provide the highest stand of living that it is able to achieve. Some nations may integrate the state, religion and culture to a greater or lesser degree. However, religion may transcend borders in our globalised world and exist alongside the local traditions. People have the right to choose and practice their particular faith or non-faith.

The creation account in Genesis says that God created everything in an orderly and harmonious fashion. God was pleased with his handiwork and called it good and very good (Genesis 1:21 and 31). Human beings enter the scene with the ability to think and make decisions. Freewill is a unique endowment from God that was given at creation. Adam and Eve were dependent on God for companionship, holiness and eternal life even though they may not have been aware of it. God was in charge and he made all the major decisions because he was in full control of their lives. The Lord has set all the executive rules that govern the metaphysical, the laws of nature and the rules that people are supposed to operate within. Creativity cannot progress and succeed without intelligence, reasoning and freedom of expression. However, humans cannot control nature or create life, so freewill is limited because executive sovereignty belongs to God.

Freewill comes under the executive authority of God because Adam and Eve did not have the ability or power to create rules of their own that have a binding effect on God. Self-will is merely the ability to select from a range of options. Self-determination is only a secondary privilege as freewill is only relevant at the operational level and not at the creation level. It has no power base to back it and cannot challenge the authority of God. Satan also has freewill as humans do and he too is a created being.

Operational freewill is subservient to executive management control (God's freewill) because it lacks impetus. The fall demonstrated human opposition against sovereign management. It was imitating Satan's rebellion and ejection from heaven and the presence of God. Thus, he made the earth his home and preyed on humans. Adam and Eve found out how painful it was to fall outside the protection and fellowship of God when they were expelled from the Garden of Eden. God left them because they had become unholy. They must have spent the rest of their lives seeking after the Lord because they once knew him personally and it was the greatest highlight of their lives, but there was no way to relive those glory days. In the garden, they had meaning and purpose in life through intimate fellowship with God. After the fall, they had no purpose in life except to survive and reproduce. The rest of their days were probably spent trying everything to get back to God, but he gave them little or no response. It conveys a strong message regarding the gravity of sin.

Before the fall, dependence on God was seamlessly woven into their lives by merely being in favour with the Lord and he gave them everything that satisfied their deepest needs. It was all centred on spiritual purity and the bodily appearance didn't matter (Genesis 2:25). Their fellowship with God was perfect. Spiritual righteousness is the foremost concern that God has for the human race and the physical body is a secondary issue. While in the garden, Adam and Eve were spared the need to learn how to depend on God for their existence. This dependence had the potential to unlock and learn all the characteristics of God that a human being is designed to cope with. It's an intriguing feature that humans were created with the ability to imitate God and be like him in personality and character i.e. spiritual perfection in Christ. God can only accept a perfect being into heaven.

Post-fall, they had to learn what dependence meant and how to go about getting it. Unfortunately, they had very few guidelines because the New Testament only came several millennia later. The first lesson on dependence was that God provided skins to cloth themselves (Genesis 3:21). The Lord kept in touch with humanity as in the case of Cain and Able. Adam could use his own survival skills to stay alive but it was the spiritual education that remained elusive. It was impossible for him to forget the harmony that he enjoyed with the Lord in the garden. He learnt the bitterness of the absence of intimacy with God.

The sinful behaviour around him was a constant reminder of his greatest mistake. It would be logical for Adam to crave those flawless days of the past. Once bitten twice shy, and he would have tried very hard to stay pure and sin-free. There are no other significant sins written about Adam subsequently and it is fair to say that he must have tried hard to imitate the goodness of God that he had learned pre-fall. In his 930 years on earth, God would have interacted with Adam in some way as assurance that he wasn't totally forgotten. I don't think that God ever taught him about repentance, but it's a non-issue as God will judge Adam by the spiritual condition of his heart (Romans 2: 14-15). God loved Adam, a sinner, just as he loves you and me. After all, Adam was the 'firstborn' of human kind that was made perfect and holy.

Adam and Eve's off-spring had never known what first-hand intimacy with God was like. Their main source of knowledge was through the oral tradition and practice passed down from Adam. God may have given them signs of his presence from time to time. Thus, over a short time span, people's thinking grew bolder and broader and their actions fell deeper into sin, hence the Great Flood in Genesis Chapter 6. People came to despise the idea that they are created beings, and the aim of the tower of Babel was birthed see Genesis Chapter 11. The objective was self-deification through the unity of the entire human race to build its own kingdom and shake off its dependence and accountability to God.

Freewill has focussed significance upon self and God is ignored. It is inward-looking and naturally goes against the Lord's intentions. We must know the downside about ourselves and make the corrections in the light of our knowledge of Christ. Only then is God able to make use of us. The New Testament teaches us what dependence on God means and how to work it out in our lives. It isn't hard to come to the realisation that we need Jesus actively functioning in our lives. Indeed, our words of confession become mechanical and cheap when we utter them each time we sin. The greater challenge is to attain the level where Jesus becomes part of our mundane lives where we commit everything to his leading. It's easier said than done but it does display the degree of self-centredness and the depth of sin that has pervaded our lives. The question is how much of the damage is one willing to rectify?

Of the three elements mentioned, the body is the first base where the most problems are manifested. Since the body is tangible it is the means of all our outward communication. People pay careful attention to external appearances. Attention to self is a conditioning process that begins developing right from childhood. The basic teaching on personal hygiene is essential for good health, but undue interest should not be placed on facial good looks as this could fuel the growth of pride. Pride is a personal over-rating of self and it's all reflected superficially with the root perilously established in the heart.

You are strongly influenced by the society and the environment that you were raised in. If that system is corrupt, then your upbringing will be influenced by those behaviours as well. Humans are social beings and naturally desire the acceptance and respect from peers and associates. In most instances, their aims become our aims; their habits become our habits and their perceptions became our perceptions; that is if you are that way inclined. Most people have realised this at some stage of their lives. Society makes you what you are. When I was in my early teens I truly believed that, but as I started my working career I discovered that I had a choice in the manner that I wanted to run my life. I had freewill to shape my life in all major decisions. I didn't have to conform to society and I was the captain of my own ship.

There were times in my early working life when self-help gave me mental resilience to get through some depressing times. Things just seemed so overwhelming and crushing down on me. I felt so helpless at the time and life appeared pointless because everybody was getting ahead of me and I seemed to fade in comparison. At that point, I took a hard look at myself. The conclusion that I came to was that I had a brain, a sound body and a will to determine my own path in life. It's intriguing how the assent of the will can be so powerful in the face of adversity. In fact, my situation did not change and I had merely adopted a positive paradigm shift. Although the problems didn't disappear overnight, my approach was much more optimistic. I was a nominal Christian and believed that God was out there somewhere but I did not seriously petition his assistance. After praying for a period of time, I gave up because no noticeable change came about.

A young friend in China told me of similar concerns and my advice was to maintain his trust in the Lord to direct his path. He was facing all the difficulties that all young people in China faced i.e. work, home ownership, marriage, financial security etc. I had gone through all of that and he was just starting. The road ahead always looks harder and rockier at the starting line. His position was not unique and he just had to apply himself one step at a time.

The Mind.

The body and mind interact in partnership but they function separately. The mind controls a person's thoughts and actions. It may behave rationally or irrationally (knee-jerk reaction). Psychological tendencies come into play whereby certain dominant thoughts make a person choose a particular action. A fellow student in the Mandarin language class was always making the same written mistakes because his mind perceived the Chinese characters in a fixed manner. It was a mental impediment that he had to correct, if not it will remain as a bad habit.

The Bible mentions that thoughts come from a person's heart (Matthew 15:19, Luke 2:19). However, the thought processes happen in the mind. The heart houses all feelings, emotional state and forms the attitudes that a person stands for. These feelings prompt the brain to process thoughts and ideas that works out in bodily actions. After some deliberation, a decision is made in a person's mind but at the same time, deep-seated feelings in the heart affects the person as a whole. The mind is able to learn the technique of logical thought and reasoning. A person's heart posture and rational thinking work harmoniously to communicate speech, actions and intentions.

The heart is the source of a person's will. Faith, hope and love are matters that form deep within a person's being. Feelings are sourced from the heart and then processed in the mind. Normally, when a decision is made in the mind, it relates directly to the attitude in the heart. Careless errors are excepted since normal people do not habitually and purposefully conceive foolish behaviour. Freewill is a finite concept and is inextricably bound in the heart.

A free-thinking human being has the ability to change. However, in certain situations there is an unwillingness to change. This resistance is driven by the will, and fixed ideas are the hardest to change. During the Cold-War, the greatest fear was an all-out nuclear confrontation. Both sides were sensible enough to steer clear of that alternative, hence the term 'Cold-War'. Conventional war was not encouraged so it became a spy versus spy game. By and large it was a stale mate and a waste of time and money, yet it had to be done because of the two opposing economic systems. As the West kept on making advances in lifestyle and the standard of living, the communist bloc nations were stagnating. Essentially it was a battle of ideologies. The USA was convinced that if they could show the Soviet Union that capitalism was a better way of life for all people; then the Russians would give up their quest for communism, and vice versa. It was clear that the USA and the West had the better lifestyle which kept on improving. Capitalism meant that the sky was the limit and people could live out their dreams. Communism had the welfare of the people as its main objective, but it had deep-seated set-backs because human central planners make mistakes.

The Eastern Bloc nations watched in envy at the ever-advancing standard of living in the West, and many people tried to defect in pursuit of their dreams. The idea of individual freedom, satisfaction of personal needs, improved lifestyle and wealth creation continuously dogged those living under socialism. Generally, the western nations believed that if everybody had a good quality lifestyle, there would be no need for war. This line of thought is partially correct as wars may be triggered by military aircraft straying into restricted air space, economic greed, religious difference or some other reason. The collapse of the Berlin Wall in 1988 subsequently caused a series of independence movements and the breakup of the Soviet Union. The unified Germany gave East Germans a way to integrate into the higher lifestyle of their West German counterparts.

For decades the two sides were at odds and it was thought that friction would continue indefinitely. However, the Soviet Union finally gave in. The transition from communism to capitalism was possible and workable. The breakaway republics weakened the Russian influence around the world and free enterprise took hold in all those newly found nations. There were many teething problems that Russia had to contend with including discontent with the changeover to capitalism because economic controls were not in place at the time. Some even yearned to return to the days of communism because the government couldn't control the transition in a proper and orderly manner. They didn't have the experience and the change was too rapid. Free enterprise opened gaps in the economy that were quickly filled by undesirable elements as there weren't appropriate laws to guard against them. After a long struggle, free enterprise prevailed. This clearly demonstrates that change is possible even from seemingly unyielding rigid thinking and years of dogmatic adherence to inefficient ideologies. A change in the direction of freewill brought about a tectonic shift in lifestyle for hundreds of millions.

North Korea is the only major communist nation that has not taken measures to embrace the free enterprise system. Recent talks between Donald Trump and Kim Jong-un have hinted at the possibility of denuclearisation and trade ties. His recent visit to China and South Korea had opened the possibility for warmer relations with the South. A high delegation officer visited the South and offered a rare apology over a minor error. It's a good sign of rebuilding relationships between the two states. A diplomatic apology is of great value and it paves the way for a potential healing process to begin. If things run smoothly, then the north could possibly follow China's route of economic reform. If they become a trading nation with the rest of the world, then their reliance on their trading partners will greatly diminish their ambition of war. There's a strong possibility that Kim Jong-un will change his rigid communism economic policy.

China has adopted a 'one country two systems' approach, so they have a socialist government running a largely capitalist economic system. So far, it has proved to be extremely successful. This policy has brought immense wealth into the country and markedly raised the nation's standard of living. Explosive growth has propelled them to the number two spot in world economic rankings; a truly remarkable feat in such a short space of time. Staunch communists party members were highly critical of Deng Xiaoping's move to liberate the Chinese economy, but history shows that he was right. The right change does wonders for the ensuing generations.

Both Russia and China's spectacular breakaway from their past was earth-shattering, yet it was relatively quick and easy. It merely involved money and a different economic discipline. However, where religion is concerned, wealth is no catalyst and it makes change extremely difficult because people hold on to what they have been taught. Humans have a strong internal resistance to change in regard to religious matters. Under normal circumstances (freedom of religion), the attraction of wealth, and human comforts have no power to alter a person's faith. The spiritual motive in a human being is more powerful than the material. Where freewill is uninhibited, one person can never change another person's faith no matter how hard they try. If that person does not accept the proposal before them, then nothing will bring about a change of mind. There is a stubborn force within that willingly gives up all material comforts to satisfy a person's beliefs or they will do anything to uphold their faith. This spiritual power is personal and is something that no other human being can touch. It is inexplicable in worldly terms, but readily accepted by those that believe in the Bible; as the spirit is given to each human being by God. The Christian faith is solely dependent of the Lord.

Self-elevation supresses fear and give raise to self-confidence and innovation. Deep-thinking people develop theories that ordinary people have never considered. People like to hear new things and to know new ways to deal with problems. Smart entrepreneurs become billionaire over-night. Pragmatic thinkers are highly respected in all fields and they become leaders in their area of expertise. Public acclaim will boost the ego and over time it will lead to a point where people are so engrossed in their own theories that they talk as if their word is truth. When this happens, they don't feel any trepidation because they are so accustomed to people following their theories without question. People willingly and fervently believe in evolution despite there being no evidence that a single living cell appeared from nowhere and then transformed to plant, to animal and to human being functioning perfectly in a complex world that we still don't fully understand. If God is not respected as Creator, then people will find other substitutes to believe in. Desperation or blind bias will stoke their hunger to find anything that is remotely plausible to pursue. Where there is no fear; God becomes nothing but a myth and freewill becomes god.

Learning to fear the Lord is simple. The cardinal requirement is submission; if there is no submission then there will not be a fear of God. You will never be intimidated by anything that you think or feel has no authority because it cannot harm you. The pleasure and freedom of self-centredness is temporal. It is more important to look beyond self to see the greatness in creation. Psalm 36:1-2 talks about the wicked who have no fear of God. They are blinded by their personal success and see no sin in their behaviour. Conceiving evil is a human decision and not from God. Psalm 39:12 says we live as aliens to God instead of friends or sons and daughters. Notwithstanding the fact that we may be Christians, we are still strangers to God and have to learn to know him much more closely. Fear only manifests itself after a person realises the power and majesty of God. When fear finds its proper place in life, the Lord will add intelligence and better understanding about himself and your spiritual development on earth (Psalm 111:10).

There is a fear that is destructive and is directed by a kill or be killed scenario such as we find in war. The Lord does not treat us in this manner and neither should we. It drives a relationship apart and there is nothing wholesome about it. People would avoid this kind of situation because it's too hard to live with. When fear plays on a person's nerves too often, then a form of hatred will develop.

There is also a constructive fear that hates sin and wrong-doing. It is one that is associated with reverence, respect and humility. This is a refined form of trepidation that seeks to get closer and closer to God in life. The milestone must be reached where the bond with the Lord is so good that you fear for anything that will upset it. You will do all that is necessary to preserve and enhance this wonderful status that you so desperately desire and cling to. Real spiritual fear is when you will do anything so as not to displease the Father. An intimate bonding with the Lord carries no fear. God is God and must be duly honoured as such. The fear is in your own actions whereby you avoid doing anything that is contrary to the Lord's commands. By fearing your ungodly actions, you are fearing God. Merely speaking about the fear of the Lord may be distant and theoretical, but the reality of self-indulgence must be earnestly redressed. God encourages this kind of fear because he wants to draw people to himself.

Love is the greater force and 1John 4:18 states that there is no fear in love. Perfect love removes the fear of judgment. The love for the Lord is centred on the love for righteousness, and this path accumulates reward and not punishment. The one who fears is made perfect in love. It is the point of stability where you know God sufficiently to trust him unconditionally; that he is a rewarder and not a punisher because of his love. Reward is only given to those that abide by the will of God. In Christian life, there is an opposing maxim; that you have to live in love and fear of God at the same time. Favouring one above the other is unhealthy as it would lead to extremism. The correct balance is necessary so as to build up a meaningful bond with Christ. God's love for a person happens in this lifetime and endures into eternity; he never goes back on his word. The fear of the Lord ends at the judgement because there is no fear in heaven. However, the fear of Satan will take up where God left off on earth and it will be continued forever in hell. Love grows naturally as we respond to God. However, there's a lot to do in regard to fear because self-will must be submitted to the Lord. Ranking self above God means that a person has no fear of the Judgment. We are the cause and effect of our own problems and even worse, maybe for others as well. It is preferable to cultivate cautious behaviour in fear than to over-rely on the love of God to cover our shortcomings. The former entails a positive and progressive relationship building process with God and the latter falls back on the grace of forgiveness to get us out of trouble cheaply. Healthy fear is an essential part of Christian life and ought to be duly regarded.

At the time of writing, there was an international cricket scandal brought about by the Australian cricket team playing the fourth test match against South Africa in Johannesburg. It involved three major players in the Australian team that had resorted to ball-tampering (cheating). Applying sandpaper to the ball would bring about an advantage through reverse-swing. There are so many cameras following each player's movements and they caught the actions of the culprit. These scenes were televised worldwide. The umpires were notified and an investigation revealed the evidence and a prompt admission of guilt followed. Cricket is a gentleman's sport and is known for fair-play. In fact, every sport abides by rules that set the scene for fair competition that is based purely on talent.

A representative from Cricket Australian (CA) flew to Johannesburg immediately and the three were suspended. Three other players came over to replace them for the remainder of the match. The culprits were handed suspensions of one year each for two players and nine months for the third. CA felt that they had to be heavily dealt with otherwise it would convey a very poor moral message to the young people that idolise the players and the game of cricket.

A public survey at the time of the verdict showed 60% agreeing to the suspensions meted out and 40 % opposing. After the players' tearful confession at the various press conferences, public opinion had changed to 50.4% agreeing and 49.6% disagreeing. In the space of a week, such a big turn-around had come about. It seemed as though public opinion is based on emotion and personal interest and moral values are forgotten or considered as valueless. Furthermore, they only looked at this situation from their own selfish viewpoints. They did not consider the fact that the rest of the cricket world was watching very closely. Loose morals breeds chaos and bitterness.

My view is that the suspensions must stand in order for justice to take its course. Transgressions have been committed and the guilty have to pay the price. I'm an avid cricket lover and would love to see those young men attain their full potential. One particular player is reputed to be able to match or better the performance of Sir Donald Bradman. It would be a privilege to witness such a player emerge in the modern game of cricket. My support for them starts immediately, but they must serve out their time. They are not criminals, but a wrong is a wrong and the price must be paid. Similarly, in the Olympic Games, drug abuse is not a criminal act, but offenders are punished according to their misdeeds.

People that do not believe in Christ behave mainly through reasoning in their mind. Conscience can be suppressed or rationalised away and their spirit has no moral check that restrains them from misdemeanour. I don't know what each individual's religious affiliation was or whether they had any religious beliefs at all. Why would they take such a high risk knowing that the other cricket nations are also watching and the chances of being caught were inevitable? I think that their self-image and pride were at stake because they appeared to be the first Australian team that would have lost a test series in South Africa since 1969/70. South Africa was banned from international cricket during the apartheid years and the two nations resumed sporting ties in 1992. It would have been an unenviable mark on their reputation, so they threw caution to the wind and did the unthinkable. No doubt, the thought of losing to such bitter rivals also had a part to play. One player commented that he was a bit hesitant, but he allowed it to happen. A 'win at all costs' mentality may also have contributed to this process.

Self-will can do so much damage. On the other hand, self-will could have chosen the right path, but that would have been too hard on their self-esteem. Lucrative international contracts worth about $2.5 million p.a. were lost to the top two players. In addition, several sponsors have cancelled their commitment citing that the violations were not in keeping with the values of their corporate image. Selfish actions that get out of hand will invite a reaction from third parties. The foolish exercise of freewill by the few brought about a demoralising defeat for all their team mates. Losing by such a wide margin (492 runs) was no shame against an in-form side, but it may not have been that way. The top players could have rallied the team, boosted morale and played for a respectful draw. Self-determination that goes haywire is no good for anybody. Each person ought to think carefully about any possible collateral damage that may affect innocent by-standers, particularly those close to you. Selfishness is often viewed as confined to one person alone, but the ripple effect will always breach the confines of our personal stronghold.

There were altercations between players and spectators because these two rivals were not particularly fond of each other. Whatever psychological or personal hurt that came out of those encounters did not warrant unfair play. Proper protest should have been lodged with the appropriate authorities and due process followed through. Sledging is part of cricket and quality players have to be able to handle comments that cross the line. Emotions on the personal front and particularly those regarding winning or losing must be kept in check. We are taught in the Bible to maintain self-control and a person's true worth is tested under high stake circumstances as the above. There are some valuable points that Christians may extract from this saga. We face the same principles in our spiritual walk and the stakes are high as far as God is concerned. A flippant approach will indicate a weak desire to be right with the Lord. Only foolish people will say that 'it's a small matter; don't lose any sleep over it'.

A person can change their mind if they want to. They can change any part of their life if they so desire because of freewill. Some people adhere immovably to their ideals and change is almost impossible. It is something deeply entrenched in their inner being that assumes this stance. It's called self and its bastion is in the spirit.

The Spirit.

Everybody wants to look their best outwardly and win the respect of others. We will do everything in our power to enhance that. Onlookers have an impact on our behaviour to a certain extent. It is right to take care of our body and to keep it healthy (1 Corinthians 6:19-20). God loved what he created except for the contamination of sin. Humans in particular occupy a special place in the order of creation. Self-care must be practiced appropriately; undue attention fuels the problems of pride, selfishness and egotism, whereas proper care for the spirit leads to humility. The spirit is hidden from sight and humility in the soul is apt to lead a person to withdraw from public attention. Self-care is more appropriately addressed as self-control in regard to sanctification. Both humility and self-control have to be nurtured in order to progress in regeneration. Humility counteracts pride and needs a lot of attention to develop after God's purpose. Pride ought to be eradicated and all effort concentrated on humility.

We lavish consideration on biological life. This is contrary to God's expectations because he views the soul as the most important thing in life (Matthew 10:28 and 16:26). Paul advises believers to rather place emphasis on the intangible things that have eternal value and not on the temporary comforts of this world. He used the word 'unseen' which is associated with heaven and the spiritual part of human nature. We are conditioned to place excessive value on the wrong things. However, if you view the body as merely a tool to be used by the Lord, then you are stepping in the right direction. Self-satisfaction must yield to delayed gratification. The spiritual dimension ranks above the body and the mind. The body will die but the spirit endures in infinity either in heaven or in hell.

People neglect their spiritual lives and it is shoved back behind the scenes in daily routine. In most cases it is completely forgotten and disconnected from the actions of the body/mind. Lifestyle in the western countries is such that it habitually exaggerates the attention given to the outward form and people forget or don't even realise that they have a spiritual identity within themselves. However, the New Age

Movement has drawn the public's attention to the spirit within, and more people have become aware of it. Unbelievers apply their spirit to worship idolatry.

Conscience is the ability to distinguish between what is acceptable and what is not; between right and wrong based on what that person believes in. However, conscience not only discerns laws and regulations but also morals and ethics. A person may confine their conscience to the body/mind and appear be a good person in the eyes of others. This stance will nurture the propensity to worldly values. People usually turn their attention to their spiritual lives late in life or not at all. Some Christians are willing to maintain a certain level of religion but have little desire to improve their spiritual standing.

The higher morals and ethics come from the teachings in the Word of God. Jesus is the centre of Christian life and without him there is no life. There are many passages calling upon people to consider the afterlife that will either lead to heaven or to hell. The process of knowing God may come gradually or suddenly, but the initial dilemma is whether to submit to a higher morality or to maintain trust in self and personal conviction alone.

To change from self-reliance to faith in God is a big step to take. Old habits are hard to reform. The spirit yearns for attention but is ignored as the material takes precedence. Spiritual reform is a process that calls for a reversal of priority; to put the soul first and the physical last. It goes against the grain and is most unsettling for those who are self-reliant and accustomed to providing for themselves in financial and material matters.

Hans Peter Royer was speaking at the Keswick Convention at Mt Tambourine in 2006 and he raised the point that the request for safety in travels was a recurring priority in prayer. He felt that it was secondary and whenever he went away on speaking engagements or for work related purposes, his request was for God's will to prevail and for the work to be done properly. Only after all the kingdom purposes have been petitioned then safety may be mentioned as the last item or not at all. It may be argued that if God has chosen a person for a work, then he will ensure that that person is kept safe to get the job done. It's easy to misplace priorities if the spirit is not given wholesome consideration. Hans Peter ranked the spiritual above the material, right in line with the Word of God.

Steven Covey posed 'the inside out' principle for business management. He felt that management had to initiate healthy change from the inside (at the top level) and then the effect would be filtered down to all levels of staff. If sound business principles and procedures are instilled in the mind and behaviour of the staff, then healthy practices and better results would emerge in the entity's operations. In this way, greater effectiveness, higher achievement and stronger growth will be added to the business.

In his DVD titled 'It all goes back in the box' John Ortberg talks about the inner person and the outer person. He mentions the value of the 'inside game' that is able to lift a person's performance to new heights and win a closely contested match. The 'inside game' is analogous to the human spirit. It is the development of godliness through the faithful foster of the fruit of the Spirit (Gal 5:22-23). God wants to rework the inner person to become a place where he may rightfully reoccupy as he originally intended. John Ortberg mirrors the same inside out principle that the Bible teaches and that Steven Covey alludes to. Ortberg mentions comparing self with others so that improvements may be made. This is mostly applied in the secular sense and is a useful tool for personal advancement. However, it's the spiritual dimension (godliness) that is the relevant to God and that has to be given due consideration. The 'inside game' is godliness and the outward reflection is evidence of the fruit of the Spirit in one's personality. I believe that this is the most significant task in Christian life on this earth. The intrinsic nature of the spirit is unknown to the public and one may only observe a person's output and hope to apply self to match or better it. The notion of comparing the quality of one person's soul with another is unheard of and there is no means to do it either.

The inside out principle isn't something new, and God has been applying this concept right in the Old Testament (Ezekiel 11:19-20, 36:26-27). It's the only way to fightback the hold that sin has over the human spirit. Sin has invaded the purity of the human soul and God wants to change it. The unregenerate spirit is desperately ill and the Holy Spirit must repair the damage. The Christian endeavour is to get back to righteousness in the core of one's spirit.

After the fall, the dominance of sin in the heart caused all human action to be alienated from the Lord. The waywardness of the Israelites in the Old Testament was primarily caused by material attraction because they wanted to be like the heathen nations around them. They wanted a human king and the freedom to worship other gods just like everybody else. Unfortunately, this is not normal or acceptable according to the Lord. The New Testament tells people explicitly to change from material desires to spiritual priorities (Galatians 5:16 and Romans 7:6). More detail is given through the incarnation of the Son of God and the new covenant that he brought to the world. People in the Old Testament only knew that they had to obey the law and to maintain relationship with God and that was all physical procedure. The human will is a spiritual unction of faith that is directed at spiritual renewal from the inside out. The Holy Spirit must be invited in to impart holiness and train one's spirit so that the process of renewal may get under way.

Conscience in its entirety has to be submitted to God and only then may the Holy Spirit do a thorough work. Conscience is that part of a person's spirit that informs the brain of right and wrong. It is the spiritual processor that interacts with the Holy Spirit from which it learns holiness and distinguishes sin and unrighteousness. Conscience processes the spiritual information and comes up with a final decision that it sends to the brain for action. Conscience can be bias in favour of self but it can also be renewed in holiness and become selfless. The human spirit is the receptacle of all the spiritual knowledge that a person absorbs (righteous and unrighteous). Thus, it is a person's conscience that makes the decisions as it knows the difference between right and wrong. I view conscience and the spirit as being the same.

I have already mentioned in the previous section that the heart is where a person's belief and essential posture is stationed. The fundamental nature of the heart equates to the spirit. This inner self is really a person's spirit, the human core that never dies (the biological heart deteriorates and dies with the body). Freewill is based in the spirit and it makes the final decisions whether good or bad. Our actions tell of our spiritual condition in relation to the Lord.

The spirit is the most essential part of a human being because God is Spirit. The Holy Spirit relates to people through their spirit. It is the spirit that is made in the image of God and not the body because God is Spirit. Self is embedded in a person's spirit and selfishness may be allowed to share a place in a believer's walk to sanctification. This may be unwittingly or purposefully introduced despite all our good intentions of faithfulness to Christ. All behaviour that is connected to self is derived from the spirit. Renewal aims at ridding the spirit of self and putting the Holy Spirit in charge.

A pastor once mentioned in his sermon the enigma in cross-cultural relations where a person says yes when they actually mean no. One cultural reason is that the speaker says yes meaning that 'I have heard what you are saying' and it's not necessarily indicating approval. The other reason is the speaker has a divided mind and spirit. The mind says yes verbally, but the spirit (true intention) disapproves and wills to act contrarily. This occurs in Christian behaviour too, but the informed believers will greatly reduce this double-mindedness. It must delight God to no end; seeing his objective being realised. It's not perfect, but it's a long way from the unregenerate state where no Christian should linger in.

Certain people have an uncontrollable disposition in the spirit that favours a particular thing or person. When dealing with unrelated people, all is said and done in a logical manner. However, when confronted with the obsession, the person behaves according to bias (self) even if it blatantly contradicts logic and reason. This is not necessarily hypocrisy but rather non-consensus of mind and spirit. It's a kind of double standard where mental assent is different to spiritual intentions. It shows that the spirit controls the will and may act contrary to the mind. A great deal of patience is required when working with such people, and you have to find out what makes them tick and avoid making hasty judgment.

Fortunately, God does not have a split-personality and we can be sure of his promises. Humans have this dysfunctional behaviour and we create problems for ourselves and for others. The importance of self in the spirit has to be thoroughly cleansed by the Spirit's holiness and a complete remake in righteousness put in place that will enable a close fellowship with Jesus.

Both conscience and spirit/soul are intangible elements, so they can't be proved empirically. The Holy Spirit ministers to the spirit, and this puts the conscience at rest. In the scientific realm, conscience falls under the study of psychology, whereas the Bible does not make a clear distinction between the spirit/heart/soul/conscience. The brain exercises common sense in the logical thinking process, whereas the spirit exudes sanctified common sense from the Holy Spirit.

Self-determination may raise more dilemmas than we care to admit because so many things may go awry within our complex make-up. The spirit and mind are hidden from public scrutiny and sins are birthed in those deep recesses. By the same token, a regenerate person expresses righteous acts from the very same base. When dealing with others, we make allowance for the following: rationalised thinking, personal feelings, avoidance of shame, outward appearance, public image, pretence and other subconscious elements that project what we want to convey to others. Unwholesome acts may be produced and the challenge is to yield to the Spirit's searchlight on our spirit (heart) and submit to doing what is right. We know the correct action clearly but doing it at the crucial moment when it really counts is something else. It is not a matter of us mastering our bad habits, but for the Master to master us. This is the only way we will ever get out of the rut that sin has landed us in. The Master's will is the only thing that is flawless and carries value for our spiritual wellbeing.

The changes that are necessary to progress towards an enhanced spiritual lifestyle are relatively simple to identify, but it is the hurdle of the will that has to be overcome within one's spirit.

Chapter 3
Identity

Human beings are the only created species that have the ability to imagine and dream and make those dreams come true. It's a remarkable thing that people wield so much power in the world today and some have the capability of making great strides on the technological front. Things that were seemingly impossible a few years ago have become reality. The recorded history of humankind is about 5,000 years. It's only after the Second World War that the increase in knowledge and technology has compounded exponentially. Why has there been such phenomenal change in such a relatively short space in time? On the Biblical time scale, this period is about 1.5% of human history; and on the evolutionary time frame it's about .0001% for the first 1 million years. The infinitesimal time estimate in the latter leave gaping questions in the evolution of human intelligence; why the sudden jump after being around for millions of years? Besides, there must have been some kind of communication or recording of human history during the past one hundred thousand years, but, where is it? It defies contemporary history and logic that humans were dumb for millions of years.

The present situation shows that humans suddenly started inventing things and then even more abruptly, became multi-talented going into the digital-age. Looking to the future, evolution does not make sense based on the gradual millions of years theory because the human being is still just a human being with all its limitations. People have been dreaming about staying alive forever in this earthly body, but nobody has found the solution and nobody ever will. Human beings have not physically evolved into a super-being, but intelligence has gone through the roof.

I once gave a class of students this example. Evolution implies that the entire animal kingdom evolved at an equivalent pace for millions of years; and there is a great variety and a balance of ecology in diversity. I fail to see how this is possible, unless God purposely directed it that way. If development was not simultaneous, fair and equal for each category of life, it would be a case of survival of the fittest and the early extinction of many animal and plant species. How can one explain the quantum-leap of human intelligence in the last fifty years (after the deployment of the first atomic weapons on Japan)? From the beginning of the 21st century, the employment of human intelligence has sky-rocketed with no end in sight. Yet the intelligence of animals has remained the same. In fact, they only have an inbred animal instinct and may only perform intelligent acts after they have been trained by human beings. Free thinking fuels the imagination and science fiction projects images of human hybridisation with animals and with alien beings. However, this is just fanciful imagination because human and animal genetics are incompatible and there have been no discoveries of alien life.

Human ingenuity appears to have no limits, except for temporary set-backs and certain apparently impossible things. On the other hand, the rest of creation remains confined to the limitations that God had framed about it at the time of creation. Even the most intelligent animals cannot break out of their mould and advance their status to a higher and more dominant position, thus an ape will always be confined to being an ape. From Biblical history, animals have remained the same with no advancement in capability since creation. In order to avoid extinction and to maintain the ecological balance, all living things had to develop at the same pace and at the same time. If apes were given the privilege to develop into human beings, then why didn't the rest of the animal kingdom develop additional and advanced skills to ward off and dominate their natural enemies? It means that all creation operates under the regulations set by a higher authority. It is only human beings that are able to effectively apply research and technology to obtain ever greater power and dominance on earth and to continue advancing into the future. Sounds familiar?

God exercises executive freewill in relation to humans who are limited to operational freewill. Similarly, humans have executive freewill over animals whose operational freewill is strictly confined to their natural instinct and physical make-up. In their natural state, it is impossible for animals to gain intelligence and rise up to challenge human beings. Human intelligence is a God-given virtue, but if left to unbridled freewill it becomes a vice.

In view of the superior position that humans occupy on earth, the question: 'who am I' is significant. In the beginning, human was a special work that God had brought into being (Ge. 1:26). Adam and Eve were given the nous to dominate the beasts, birds and fish. From the Scripture we glean that human possesses certain moral, spiritual and character traits that mimic God. This is demonstrated by our acts of worship, prayer, the fruit of the Spirit and our capacity for fellowship with God. However, the New Testament indicates that believers are already in a higher status; that of family and we share in Jesus' inheritance (Romans 8:17). The human being is a special instrument of God and believers will receive the ultimate decoration for their obedience. Human beings are set apart from the rest of creation. Human intelligence surpasses all of that in the animal kingdom and it keeps on expanding at a staggering pace. The ability and scope of human thinking has no boundaries. This perceptiveness had always been part of the human makeup. At the Tower of Babel in Genesis 11:6 "The LORD said,

> "If as one people speaking the same language they have begun to do this, then nothing they plan to do will be impossible for them."

For the first time, God stated the stark reality of human's creativity and brilliance. We have been living in the age of information overload since the beginning of the 1990's. New innovations have developed so rapidly and made earlier inventions obsolete. Things are changing so quickly that it's impossible to keep up to date with all of it. During this period, advancements in the internet were particularly acute. The increase in population from 1billion in 1800 to 7 billion in 2012 provided more researchers that lifted the rate of new inventions. The human brain is still the same, but multiple intelligence can be applied in new and very powerful ways. Progress will always generate new data. Ordinary people will just have to use those systems without understanding the operational detail. Human curiosity can never to bridled, and there's no stopping the capability of human ingenuity, except for God.

When I qualified as a Chartered Accountant in 1988, we were expected to know everything in our profession, and the exams ensured that we kept abreast of the latest developments. By the mid-1990's any accountant worth their salt would openly admit that it was impossible to know everything in the accounting profession. The body of information continues to expand into the future and specialization is the only way forward. Our rules of professional conduct dictate that we seek the help of specialists when the situation calls for it. Complex financial instruments and legal requirements mean that a person can't go it alone no matter how good they position themselves.

Developments in science, technology and computerization are mind-boggling. The days of the 'impossible' appear to be waning.

When I was young, I used that word a great deal in different aspects of life, but today it doesn't carry the same weight and I certainly am wary when I apply it. Much of what seems to be impossible today is due to the fact that researchers don't have the necessary information on how things work and the required finance to carry out the related research. The onslaught of breakthroughs marches on and it's only a matter of time before solutions to the 'impossible' emerge. This line of thinking only applies to the material world and not to the metaphysical. However, certain natural phenomena will always be impossible to control such as the creation of life, ocean tides, tectonic plate activity, weather patterns, volcanic action etc. because they fall under the domain of the Creator.

Today, the word 'impossible' should be substituted by the word 'delayed'. You are a highly intelligent being even if you don't feel like it because your peers expose your inadequacies. The positive approach is to take up the challenge and make a difference. This intelligence is God-given because humans are special. God gave humans the power to rule over all of the animals, birds and fish, but not over nature. There are many natural phenomena that we still don't understand because God did not give humans the authority to control those. The executive control remains with the Lord and people are left with the operational ability to work with nature. This freedom may be very destructive if rash and unwise decisions are made by those in positions of authority. This merely demonstrates the awesome power of God over all creation. No matter how far we are allowed to progress, humans will always be subject to the parameters put in place by the Lord. In this respect, all things beyond that border will always be impossible for humans. People overstate material progress because it's directed at self and they forget about the metaphysical where we are one hundred percent dependent on God.

Fellowship with the Lord is a function that was purposely bestowed for our benefit. No other creature or created being has the privilege and access to this resource. During my early Christian life, I heard friends saying that the purpose in life is to glorify God. I set out trying to work out what this means and how to go about it. At the time it seemed to be that I should tell and show others of the greatness of God and to praise him for his majesty. My actions as a Christian must point to Jesus as the source and caretaker of my renewed life. We know that it is the Holy Spirit working in and through us that demonstrates Jesus to the outside world. What can I do to glorify God? The fact that I am created in the image of God already glorifies him. Therefore, everything that I say and do must follow after God. If not, then I would be working against God's design.

The purpose of life starts back in the Garden of Eden. Fellowship with God is the primary purpose in this world. This makes the procedural part clearer for me and I can set out a structured path to follow. Fellowship means having a closer growing relationship with the Lord such that he enjoys and responds to us appropriately. It's a natural two-way thing, one that Adam and Eve did without even thinking about it.

Adam was like a friend and personal companion of God. They were glorifying God by remaining in righteousness and fellowship and this was their act of worship, just as God originally intended. Holiness is a requisite for worship because it takes after the image of God. After the fall, personal transformation to sanctification became necessary because believers have to return to holiness. The sanctified life will blend into intimate fellowship with the trinitarian aspect of the godhead and all the fruit of the Spirit will develop with it. In a sense, God wants believers to follow after him within the intended limitations of the human framework. Worship becomes a concomitant part of a believer's behaviour as it is taught and directed by the indwelling Holy Spirit. From our fallen position it is very hard to comprehend because ever present sin highlights the distance that we have to make up to reach an acceptable state of holiness. This is the point where the Spirit consistently incites you in fellowship.

It was only after the fall that the concept of worship took on significance. Humans had forgotten their Creator and had to be repeatedly reminded to depend on him for eternal life. God had to introduce the law that Israel had to have. The speed at which sin separated people from God was astounding. Sin turns a person against God, but can it reach the point where a person loses the image of God? No, because a person who loses the image of God (if that is at all possible on earth) cannot be a human being anymore because all humans are made in God's likeness. God's image is the inalterable link that humans have in relation to God. Nothing in all creation can change, destroy or tamper with the image of God in any way. No matter how deep a person is in sin, they have every opportunity to return to the Lord and it only depends on self-will. Directly related to the image is the salvation process and the reward system that were only intended to benefit humans. Can you expect anything less from a loving Father and his ingenious design?

The Lord didn't allow death to triumph because humans are far too precious to him. Obeying the law was the primary means of worshipping God in the time before Christ. It was a forced procedure because people had to comply and it bore the connotation of salvation by ritualistic effort. The law set Israel apart for God and told the world of the only true God. Christ introduced the new covenant that has eliminated the need for compliance with the law to fellowship with God. We need to get back to the position that Adam and Eve had with God prior to the fall. Meaningful worship necessitates a close fellowship with God and that in turn requires holiness. This coincides with the goal to be more Christlike. Jesus is trying to bring us back to God and Satan is trying to keep us captive in sin. God is trying to restore his original plan for humankind and Satan is trying to thwart it. God is trying to save his precious creation and Satan is trying to destroy it by capturing people in their secular desires and pleasures. The evil one cannot launch an assault on the Lord but he can wreak havoc on the thing that is most precious to him; an indirect offensive. Even though fellowship with God was a natural part of human behaviour, sin has turned it around to be unnatural. We would prefer to wallow in sin because it makes us feel independent and self-sufficient rather than to walk humbly in the light. Obeying God is unnatural and very uncomfortable, and freewill has everything to do with it.

Heaven will be one continuous act of worship. Does it sound tenuous? God wasn't bored in the Garden of Eden as he interacted with Adam and Eve and vice versa. When people have to shift their perspective away from self to God, they feel out of sorts. What appears entertaining to humans is boring to God. It points to the fact that we don't know God as we ought to. We have yet to learn and experience the true nature of worship. It's not merely singing praise and worship songs, verbalising and performing acts that glorify God. Those are superficial manifestations and are useful for witnessing to the unsaved. It goes far deeper than that and strikes at the core of the spirit that bears the image of God. The image of God has to be enhanced through righteousness because people have allowed sin to permeate their lives and forgotten their roots.

Holiness and obedience are the true elements of worship and the way we glorify God. Jesus never taught us how to do this because he was already one with the Father and the miracles that he performed exalt God. On the other hand, we have to learn how to become one with the Father and thereby worship God in spirit and in truth (John 4:23). The intention to become like Christ at the spiritual level is burdensome because freewill is a loose-cannon that could give rise to all sorts of problems.

The Torah specifically describes how the nature, method and objects used in worship ought to be performed. The Israelites kept falling foul of the law and the need for regular sacrifices was consequential. The law that was supposed to bring Israel closer to God in fact didn't. Instead of keeping sin under control, humans allowed it to get out of control. This problem was solved by the indwelling Holy Spirit coming to earth after Jesus' ascension. Nevertheless, Christians still have internal clashes with the Holy Spirit. Paul wrote about struggling with sin in Romans 7:7-8 and we all wrestle with the same issues today. We may be aware that we should be enquiring of God on every decision that we make, yet we don't always do it earnestly. The idea of worship is to keep our attention focussed on God as our director in life. Since we are born into sin, we don't know how to worship God naturally.

Tony Campollo wrote a book in which he said that there are many things in life that are of value. However, people have incorrectly valued all these things and mixed up all the price tags. All the things that are of great value to God have no material value in the eyes of people. The material world makes Christians susceptible to this sort of corrupted thinking and practice. The Bible tells us to pay attention to the unseen eternal things instead of the material temporal comforts (2 Corinthians 4:18). The exercise of one's choice is a personal right which is very flattering at the time but it carries implications that may turn out to be embarrassments when we face the Lord.

No matter how much freedom you have or how dynamic you may feel, it doesn't change the fact that you are a created being that is subservient to an all-powerful Creator. The majority of people exercise their freedom too liberally and that endangers their spiritual growth. The lamentable aspect is that we don't realise it and our actions sometimes show that we don't care much.

In the New Testament context, our relationship aspect takes a U-turn back to what is was in the beginning. There's work to be done in the kingdom of God and I have to be a useful instrument that fits into God's plan for his people. The choices that I make must coincide with the over-arching scheme and this calls for personal discipline. The prominence of this personal task cannot be sufficiently accentuated. Since the Lord has chosen humans to complete his plans on earth, each worker plays a very significant part albeit an apparently minor one from a popularity perspective. Ultimately, the future reward would tell us just how important a part each one of us has performed during our limited time on earth. Who are you? You are of inestimable value to God. The full value may only be realised under his terms because he shapes a person's worth and provides the building blocks to spiritual dynamic. In the same breath, it ought to be borne in mind that a person cannot become holy by their own exertion because they cannot regenerate their spirit without God. The Lord can use anybody for his purposes but it is primarily believers that he uses to construct his kingdom because of the associated rewards that he attributes to each part of the operation.

We mainly view work as an income earning task that fends for our existence on earth. Regardless how we feel about it, work is a necessity. Humans were created for work as evidenced in the Garden of Eden. Prior to the fall work was a normal part of life and there was an element of enjoyment in it. That's a question that we all ask today: do you enjoy your work? Adam's fellowship with God harboured no strife and he was happy with what he was doing. Work is a normal part of life but the curse has made it laborious and unpalatable. Adam's work in the garden was mainly physical, but after the fall our main work is in our spiritual revival. Secular business puts food on the table, but that ought to yield to our spiritual wellbeing. Adopt the position that your vocation is your ministry and your spiritual aims will be favourably placed to succeed.

Apart from work and family, what do we do with the rest of our lives on earth? Jesus placed no value on finances and the comforts of life. It was easy for him because earthly retirement was not on his agenda, unlike mere mortals who have to face this reality. The decision to follow Jesus' example and take the low-income route is not an easy one. As the world advances in all respects, this choice becomes increasingly harder to make. In a progressive society, everyone likes to have the latest technology and gadgets and that cost money.

The suggestion in Matthew 6:19 – 20 is familiar to most believers. The unsettling fact is that treasure in heaven is unlike a bank account where you can physically observe the deposits and withdrawals. If the withdrawals start increasing then you top up the deposits or reduce spending in order to stay in the black. In the kingdom business there is no means of gauging the extent of the savings in heaven and we don't have full understanding of what forms they are going to take. It's a matter of that big word 'faith' all over again; if you believe that Jesus would make good his word to get you into heaven then you also have to trust him to provide the treasure to enjoy for eternity, if you have earned it. Under secular circumstances, it's clear that you can't serve the Lord and fulfil your own desires simultaneously. God is a jealous being and wants all of you and all of your attention. Good friends of mine have lamented their right to freewill and wished that they didn't have it. That thought has also occurred to me as well, but this is not reality. God sees this as a test of your faithfulness; are you going to pass or are you going to fail? Whatever you may view as important is what your mind and body will strive towards. Nothing can be more pure and honest than that. Your value system determines your actions.

What happens in the case where you know the will of God and yet behave in the opposite manner or only act in partial fulfilment? One's life span on earth is the time allowed for you to prepare and accumulate benefits in eternity. This life is the only chance that you will have. The stakes are so high and mistakes are often irreversible. The most distasteful part is that the status is not visible, tangible or measurable by human standards. It must be worked out by faith. Some people tend to accept the justification by faith part but go on to neglect their preparation for everlasting existence with the Father. The case of 'out of sight and out of mind' is exacerbated because all those around us are mainly concentrating on material things, and that has a definite impact on our direction as well. If we get lost on this assignment, then our lives on earth would be defeated and we end up with spiritual failure. It is not only personal loss, but God would also have been robbed of the worship and appropriate glorification that would have emerged through our obedience, and fulfilment of his desire to re-make us into the ideal spiritual being that he had in mind before we were born.

We usually think that self-centredness only affects those that we associate with. The visible is our primary reference point for our decisions. Yet, any selfish action affects God as well. He is invisible and we often ignore him. Selfishness is offensive to God because he advocates a love for others and to consider them first. The moral duty encompasses not only material gain but also the accompanying feelings, comfort and emotions. We displease the person that we ought to be pleasing the most.

A sober reminder is that kingdom work will always be accomplished by somebody (besides self), but spiritual loss is an individual reality that is irrecoverable. At the end of earthly life, there is no means of making up for loss. Potential loss of time and opportunity have permanent ramifications at the time of that decision. God's plans are predetermined for a specific person at a certain time. There is no suggestion that declined opportunities may be reintroduced at a later date (Ephesians 1:11). If a person turns down an opportunity then the only course available is to continue to do good and hope that God will be compassionate and give a second chance. Freedom of choice is everybody's privilege. It will reveal where the heart or the love is; if it's not drawn to the Creator then it's with the creation.

The words 'well done good and faithful servant' (Luke 19:17) suggests a proper completion of a task. Each task carries its own reward and the person that fulfils that job will obtain the benefit. We tend to isolate applause with a specific task. This is a flawed approach because a good servant is assessed as a whole. The consistent delivery of quality service stems from character. Everything that they do is at the standard and taste that meets with the highest approval. That accolade is not only for one job well executed, but for the person's proven performance over time. They are trusted in whatever they do that the result will satisfy the Lord's expectations. It implies that improvement has to be ongoing and every milestone must be motivation towards a higher moral. God has more to offer than any person is able to contain. People judge incorrectly that they have reached their spiritual peak and they stop growing further. You can never know more than the Master.

Romans 2:6 God "will give to each person according to what he has done". Also see Psalm 62:12 and Proverbs. 24:12. A task may form part of a large assignment that is broken up into multiple sub-tasks whereby many people contribute to its success. Kingdom work is the blueprint that God recognises as relevant to all believers. If a person rejects the calling then God will find somebody else to do it. The calling always involves personal sacrifice and it's up to the individual to run with it. The Bible does not praise people for work that is incomplete. Colossians 4:17, 2 Timothy 4:7, Revelation 2:7, 2:26 urge readers to persevere and remain faithful in their lot in life.

If Paul placed such importance on the consummation of the task then it must rank as a high priority. In Revelation 2:4 Jesus rebukes the church in Ephesus for having neglected their first love. Their core concerns had drifted away from Jesus to other things. The exhortation is to overcome those distractions in order to gain the prize. Revelation 2:26 conveys a similar tone. Jesus warns the church in Thyatira not to be enticed by immorality. Each person will be evaluated according to their own acts. The advice is to remain faithful to Jesus right until the end. Again, there is the motivation to rise above your own predispositions and it is reinforced by the words 'and does my will to the end'. It's an individual's freewill versus God's will scenario. Ultimately, it's self-determination that raises animosity with God.

The question remains: how much reward would be allocated to partial obedience? Where a person has done a work part way through and gone off to do personal business in good faith, then fair judgment would suggest that God would give a partial reward. However, the lost portion would be sorely felt in eternity. If partial obedience is accompanied by self-direction and injected into kingdom work, then there will be no reward and judgment will ensue. Nobody can tell God how to do his work. Personal interference in God's plans is considered as mutiny (1 Samuel 13:13) and is not a wise risk.

The question: 'Who am I' if viewed in isolation will lead to an introverted worldview and selfishness will be encouraged. Humans are social beings and this necessarily requires a proactive mindset. Relational behaviour is ingrained in the social fabric and everybody fits in some place or another. Those that do not assimilate will develop anti-social and reclusive habits. Relationships are built on needs both secular and spiritual. If needs are limited or confined to the social realm, then spiritual development will be severely curtailed.

The question: 'Who am I' ought to be considered at the highest level which entails the spirit. People may aid and facilitate our material needs, but it is only God who can revive our spirit, and there is no place for interference by self. Our spiritual self that we are the least acquainted with is like an open book that the Lord knows best. Spiritual education must be approached with a perspective to God's purpose and relationship to people. Self-determination can easily interject where it is not wanted.

We may feel that our fellowship with the Lord is acceptable. We have been doing it this way for a long time and things have turned out okay. Jesus showed his connection with his Father as being united as one (John 17:11) and his prayer was for his disciples to have the same unity with the Father. It's a supernatural bonding. Personal standards are not good enough and a major overhaul has to take place. This requires concentration to keep active communication with the Lord throughout the day. Fellowship with Jesus must be revitalised to the level where the Holy Spirit is pleased to interpose at will. Each person has to find the way that works for them. The bond that Jesus had with his Father was spontaneous, but we experience periods of extended silence. The effort needed to attain harmony with the Lord is enormous. Obviously, Jesus was perfect and therefore had a faultless relationship with his Father, but this is no excuse for not trying. Determined and unbroken engagement will get you there. The establishment of a solid connection with the Spirit is the key to a prolific future relationship. Frivolity shows disrespect for God and long intervals of silence will resume. There must be heartfelt commitment and not mere ritual. Although there is no visible evidence, you will know without a doubt that the Spirit is active in your spirit. This is a unique feature that God passes on to each individual that he connects with. Nevertheless, others will notice the difference in you (Matthew 7:16-20).

The Spirit's direction, tuition and fellowship will give kingdom work spiritual meaning to the worker. People like to see results and the natural inclination is to place physical work as the first thing that has to be done. The notion that spiritual enhancement comes automatically as part of the kingdom work or that it would grow with the work is misplaced. Spiritual growth and ministry are separate disciplines. Each believer has a designated place in God's kingdom work. Does your self-will fit into God's plans? Does your personal comfort and ambition matter? It's better to get these things straightened out before embarking on a journey with the Spirit. Self-made problems occur when we try to follow the Spirit and satisfy personal ambition at the same time.

Grace has its limits as there is a point where procrastination may be viewed as rejection. When God gives up on you (rather that you have ignored him for too long), it will be a poor eternity waiting. Who said that the Christian life was easy!

Chapter 4
Unnaturally

Our habits are ingrained in our conduct and they shape us into what people see on the outside. They are so compelling that we find it very difficult to change. Some people adopt this view: 'that's me and I'm not changing my style'. It's a mark of self-expression that conjures up an image of uniqueness and personal status. It may be merely an excuse to continue the way they are. Of course, it begs the question: why don't they want to change? It may be driven by an array of reasons. Some may be stubborn and just refuse to change; some don't want to concede to the other view to see the position from a different perspective; some do it out of spite; some out of a sense of pride that shuts out other alternatives; some out of peer pressure, cultural or family background; some need much more time to work through the issues; some because of religious beliefs; some because of the lack of information and incomplete knowledge; some merely because they don't wish to try something new and prefer the comfort of old habits, and the list goes on.

This phrase tells of a person's good and bad characteristics that are summed up in their assertions. People size up a person by looking at their good and bad points and then an opinion is formed. It's human nature that we always seem to recall the bad things first and maybe later on consider the better side of another's behaviour. We have to be careful how we make assessments about others and we ought to make every attempt to apply a fair and equitable approach. The statement 'I don't want to change my style' may also convey the message that I don't want to change my habits (bad or good). What at first seems to be an expression of individuality and personal identity may also expose a flawed nature. If 'my style' is acceptable, it wouldn't cause too many problems, but if it's corrupted then invariably the outworking would divide the opinion of others somewhere along the line. You may assume 'my style' to be a personal footprint that identifies you as unique, that's your personal choice. However, you have to be equally responsible to accurately vet your style so that it builds others up and does not cause aversion. Personal style should only be maintained if it meritoriously wins the respect of others.

If you don't want to change your style, it means that you don't want to improve your old/current outlook and habits. Your methodology and mindset are perfect for yourself, but it ignores the concerns of others. Partiality is prejudice and is subject to error. However, only Jesus is complete and there's a reason if he prompts you to consider a change. In the fallen human state, change is largely directed at the defective side of our spiritual life. Nevertheless, the good elements of the spiritual are always open to improvement by the Holy Spirit as well. The godly attributes have to be continually enhanced. The old adage: 'if it ain't broken; don't fix it' only applies to the physical world. The evil one will always attempt to break down the godly characteristics in a person's life. Christians have to be constantly on-guard and the spiritual tenet is: 'if it's good; make it better' (Ephesians 1:17 and Hebrews 11:40). The exhortation is to know God better and stay with his plan to attain completeness. There may be a mental blockage that must be removed; a person may understand correctly, yet the actions do not accompany the mind (spiritual intentions in the heart).

It is my view that we have different styles at various stages of our lives because we adopt new methods and ideologies. If something better comes up, we take them on and our lives are enriched as our style adapts to the changes. The hope of improving is everybody's intention in this life, because this is the obvious thing to do. Mature folk would look back on their lives and although some mistakes were made, they would have attempted to become better people along the way. Character improvements would have been made in one way or another as the conditions allowed.

Does kingdom work contribute any spiritual benefit to personal spiritual development? The answer is only indirectly, if at all. The worker has to be purposely looking for the spiritual morals in the work and practicing them, otherwise they will be overlooked. The benefits of an evangelical conference or winning converts to Christ do not make a worker more spiritual. It is God who gives the enlargement and the workers merely get the wheels turning (John 6:44 and 65). Rather, the success is supposed to inspire people to search deep within themselves to seek after the originator of those causes and effect. Work and personal introspection go hand in hand. If this has been neglected then precious lessons would have been missed. There may be a part of a person's old nature that has never quite submitted to Jesus, and thus has not been enhanced by regeneration. This is usually the last stronghold that a person values and wants to hang onto for as long as possible. Negligence breeds carelessness and over-confidence, and this weakness retards the process of renewal.

Many years ago, a Christian friend was recommended a book to read about people relations by another Christian friend. Yet, the giver didn't reflect most of those principles in their own life - so much for practising what you preach. It sounds strange that a person can read a piece of writing on morality and not apply it in life. Perhaps they didn't actually read the book, then why recommend it to a friend? Most probably they had other ideas and didn't accept the contents in the book because it clashed with their style. Personal bias has a strong influence over the will. It takes great conviction to get the immovable self to give in. Trying something different can teach a person a lot about themselves and also uncover some pleasant surprises.

People change their habits or mind in pursuit of something better. Even though they may not feel entirely comfortable with the decision, they would do it for a purpose. People have the freewill to change even the most deep-seated habits. Various reasons may complicate matters but each element will have a right or wrong answer. An intricate problem may be worked through strata by strata and then whittled down to a final conclusion. Perplexing legal cases process through a long hearing of prosecution and defence that seem unending, but ultimately a final assessment always brings the case to closure. Christians ought to be constantly weeding out the bad habits and converting weaknesses to personal advantage. The aim is to reduce or eradicate the undesirable tendencies and to keep on improving the good that is in spiritual character.

Why don't people want to change? Change is awkward and people don't like moving out of what they are comfortable with. If you think about it, we have all been changing right from birth until the present time, so change is not so unnatural after all. It's the force of habit that has to be beaten. Our value system changes over time and our behaviour adapts accordingly. A young Muslim believer asked me about life-changes very early on in our association. I had no hesitation in saying that my core objectives in life had switched from the material to the spiritual. We have freewill and the ability to adopt different attitudes. We are able to assess the facts and then choose what we want. Change goes against all that a person has come to accept and that may be unsettling. If you have all the information before you and are able to accept the underlying logic then why is it so hard to change?

Muslim believers have a more realistic understanding of change because they have to overcome the rigidity of their Islamic background. They are compelled by the Holy Spirit to transform their entire being and go through the process of allowing Christ to change them from the inside out. They emerge as renewed people for having gone through a greater struggle. Along the way, they have to deal with social behaviour that is entrenched in religious practice. It's not simple to live with such discord in Islamic society but their walk with Christ in faith liberates them. The need to witness for Christ and the desire not to alienate family creates an unending dilemma. They cannot express their new-found faith openly as we do in the west.

When I was helping out at the English Corner at ETC in China, I always endeavoured to get the young students to 'think outside the box'. This phrase was coined by Edward De Bono and has been a great inspiration to me throughout my adult life. There was a need for this because the education system in China was based on rote learning. On the other hand, the west advocated the form of liberal arts education whereby the student is taught various disciplines and encouraged to do research work. The goal is to search for answers as opposed to being taught a method with a set written solution. Lateral thinking is a useful tool for problem-solving in the business environment but also in many aspects of social behaviour. It gets you out of tunnel-vision and opens a broader thinking approach to life. The ability to incorporate factors outside of the immediate problem to generate ideas will open up other alternatives.

When you apply this concept to your spiritual life, you will tend to develop an inquiring mind. As the Holy Spirit gives understanding, relationship to Jesus becomes more meaningful. Hidden inspiration from the Bible comes with the passage of time and the unmistakable stimulus from the Spirit will be very clear. The principal doctrines of Scripture may be understood from books, but that is mere head knowledge. Only the Holy Spirit can bring new insights and make that knowledge come alive through different application. This privilege comes to those that yield their spirit to the Holy Spirit.

In daily life, people are smart to recognise the benefits and then take appropriate action to obtain those. It's a mechanical reaction to change to more attractive options because we all want to get ahead in life and enjoy a better lifestyle. This life is very short and we must be looking to eternity. Now you are talking; the spiritual is more important than the material and we have to be caring for our future spiritual existence above everything else. This entails giving up freewill which is unpalatable to most people. Surrendering your freewill to Jesus involves a fundamental change that shakes the core of your being. Even after following Jesus for many years, many of us still find it quite difficult to submit completely to the Lord. When you put your life in someone else's hands, you lose control as decisions are being made for you and that is distasteful. It's only unpalatable because you are not accustomed to it.

People say: 'I must have more faith'. This is a relative concept as each person measures faith differently. At the end of the day, a person's acts would usually tell of the extent of their faith (Matthew. 7:16). It's more important to have a means of measuring your actions that are directly linked to the faith process. The restated motto ought to be: I must have more action. I thought that my faith was exemplary when I gave up my career to serve on the mission field. It was a challenging decision that I didn't take lightly. After I completed my service, I emerged with a refined faith that was a notable upgrade from the previous milestone. Enhanced faith resulted in visible as well as intangible responses from the Lord that were plain and undeniable. Better spiritual fellowship was the best outcome that I could have hoped for.

The faith that God develops in a person is indestructible. It is outside of self and so compelling that a person can't give it up. The thought of ever walking away from God is a ridiculous notion and downright inconceivable. The person that asks the Lord for more faith is truly blessed when they receive the response.

God doesn't present a sketch of the procedures that he wants for each task. Since we are brought up in a material world it is natural to be looking out for a game plan before taking on an assignment, but the Lord doesn't work that way. We are led by the Spirit and each step is revealed as we go along. A large project may require a business to be set up. Things don't just automatically work out just because we are doing kingdom work. The normal set-up procedures have to be put in place and the business and operating procedures have to be learnt and implemented. Mistakes may be made but careful planning should keep those to a minimum. There may be costly lessons that emerge, but we learn from those and move on as the Spirit leads. Faith is the trust that we place in Jesus to direct our path. It's okay when things are running smoothly but in the opposite scenario, circumstance can cause us to do things that are unfaithful. It requires great discipline to refrain from self-action and continue trusting God in the face of uncomfortable situations. If you get it right, it's so rewarding for your spirit and your physical outlook glows.

Loss of income and uncertainty are abrasive to the senses and unsettling to the mind as it is considered as unstable and risky, so people will shy away from the calling. God responds likewise and then we wonder why the Spirit is so silent. If the Lord is kind, he would sometimes force us out of our shell to get on with his work. Although this may be unpleasant at first, it is actually a blessing. On the other hand, he will leave us to our own devices and find someone else to do it.

The departure from loving oneself to loving Jesus and others as a priority is a palpable challenge for most of us. This is apparent from the way we make our choices. We would always reserve the best for ourselves and pass the lesser things to others. When you consider all the selfishness within, we know that we value ourselves way out of proportion to what Scripture requires of a Christian. However, shifting the importance from self to others is not impossible but why is it that only a few are able to do this and most cannot? Selflessness is not a one-off approach in selective situations but a sincere gesture to all under all circumstances, especially to those that we don't like. If you have strong convictions about personal perceptions and are readily upset by negative comment then you will find this an enormous obstacle to overcome. This will probably be one barrier that's negating your spiritual refinement. There are two sides to any situation, and this moral is merely asking you to consider both sides of the contention.

The goal is to give up freewill and allow God's will to take over. We all know how to do this; and that is to love God unconditionally and others equally as ourselves (Mark. 12:30-31). Familiar passages are easily committed to memory and that's where they will stay. Over time they just become noble words that stay in the mind. We are to love the Lord above everything else. Nevertheless, when we engage daily life, we allow other things to occupy that position. They interfere with our priorities and we live a parallel life where the mind loves God unreservedly but the body goes for self-satisfaction.

Paul talks about the unselfish love of God in 1 Corinthians 13, and John describes the agape love of God in 1 John 4:10. We can read these passages over and over again and still be unable to fully implement them. The meaning of love is sacrifice. Then again, each individual defines this relatively and the extent of committing to that sacrifice is limited to personal perception. If we believe the Scripture then why don't we do it? We are slaves to freewill to the detriment of our spiritual wellbeing. We make our spiritual growth an uphill battle.

All our natural virtues and characteristics, no matter how good they may appear to be have been tainted by inherent sin. In reality, God cannot use the natural person because it is completely out of order. The process of death to the 'old person' and the ushering in of the 'new person' can only be done from the inside out. Works only have longevity in Christ and a believer must imitate Christ's personality. Jesus uttered the words in Mark 12:30-31 and he made good his word. New spiritual virtues in righteousness are the key to rewarding service. God's mindset comes into the new thinking and the old dries up and is hopefully forgotten for good. Freewill derails good intentions and old habits are easily resurrected. The secular notion is that we live in a free world but the spiritual maxim tells us otherwise (Romans 6:22).

The new person is soundly positioned for the Holy Spirit to fully develop and to be utilised by the Father. God's endorsement on these works (in the individual) is largely unseen but they carry great reward which may not be immediately apparent. Those with charismatic gifts are able to capture the attention and respect of the public and they receive due attention for their efforts. On the other hand, the works of the new person are mostly hidden but they always exhibit some aspect of God's grace and character. When the Spirit works in a person, there is no selfish ambition. It is odd that works are carried out in a selfless manner but the reward is self-purposed in that it cannot be shared with anyone. God requires that workers operate in full unselfishness and then he follows up by awarding an apparent selfish bounty to the faithful. Believers cannot purposely aim to work to selfishly accumulate eternal rewards because the Lord looks at the heart and unwholesome ambition will be penalised.

Discipleship is not an invention of the human mind. Only the Teacher has the power to turn you into one of his disciples. The unnatural call of God demands that we completely discard the inherent values of the natural person within us and replace it with the character of Jesus. It's a simple concept yet so cumbersome for many, and we know very well why.

Chapter 5
The start

As we mature in our thinking and broaden our value systems, we gradually fix certain habits in our mind. It's a subconscious thing that prompts impulsive actions. Often, we assume the influence of our peers as a yardstick by which we establish our values. After all, you can only gauge your standing by comparing yourself with others. The grass is always greener on the other side. We set our goals and these targets become the core values that a person holds, and we apply our judgment to make decisions to meet those goals. If you harbour the thought that you should win at all costs then the probability of offending others is very high. The fundamental notion is that you are exercising your freewill to please yourself. The world sees nothing amiss because one is merely doing the best for oneself - the right of every human being on earth.

Adam was given the freedom to eat from any tree (Genesis 2:16-17), and he could name all the animals (Genesis 2:19). He had freewill to do as he desired in this respect. However, he could not eat of the tree of the knowledge of good and evil. This was an imperative and not a matter of freewill. Since God owns all creation, we are merely stewards of his handiwork and therefore, human freewill is restricted to the wishes of the Creator.

God is at the sovereign level and humans are at the operations level. Thus, Adam had freedom to use his discretion in everything in the Garden of Eden, including working the fields. It was unrestricted freewill to operate and care for the garden because the Lord didn't dictate or interfere in any way. Adam must have roamed the garden freely and enjoyed the magnificence of a perfect world when he wasn't meeting with God. Adam had a perfect brain and it must have been a pleasure for both God and Adam that they understood each other when they were walking in the garden during the cool afternoons and talking about various things. Their fellowship was harmonious and natural.

It's quite astounding really when you consider that the Creator regarded intimacy with his creation as a high priority. Fellowship with God was incidental and Adam didn't have to learn how to do it; he wasn't awkward in God's presence nor did he have any fears about being with God. This person-to-person relationship was the ultimate bonding that any human being could ever experience. It demonstrates that God is ordered and purposeful because he created human above everything else, a special creature for his personal enjoyment. Humans are made in the image of God and given autonomy to act in their own interests. In our present fallen state, we are just a little lower in status than the angels. Prior to original sin, Adam and Eve were higher than the angels because they were friends of God and not mere servants or messengers as the angels are.

Everything appears to be concentrated on the material side of life. There was no need to raise the spiritual because Adam was holy in the same way as God. Original sin broke that synchronicity and God could no longer be an intimate part of the human experience. The spiritual link was severed and corrupted to the point of no return. Human beings cannot reconstruct their way back to God because we have neither the capability nor the means. Satan won and the human spirit was lost forever. Nonetheless, as the Bible mainly describes Adam's physical relationship to God, it is of the least importance because Adam died spiritually that day. Adam didn't need to learn spiritual discipline while he was holy, but everything changed. Suddenly, he was lost and clueless as to how to reinstate his former glory. Holiness can only be taught and imparted by the Lord and humanity's dependence on God has been unconditionally built into our make-up at creation.

After the fall, we behave and think that self-help is our first port of call due to worldly influences. This is the most effective delusion that Satan implanted in the human mind. God sees it very differently and the priority of spiritual training is the foremost objective. It is not optional and the associated outworking of the physical is merely incidental.

The ever-present corruption of sin defeats our best efforts to obey Jesus. It is a constant hurdle to get our spiritual selves in submission to the Lord. Inherent sin has made friendship with the Lord an arduous uphill battle. Opposing backgrounds between God and humans can only be reconciled through God's initiative. Revival is an internal thing and it must remake the spirit first before it can be of any value in outward actions. Harmony will only come when the spirit is re-born of God (John 1:13). Jesus opened the way to reconciliation and he is the link for humans to return to God. The remoulding of the spirit is the hard part that we have to choose and act upon.

When the Lord addresses believers as his children it implies a reinstatement of the position prior to the fall and thus restoring the full spiritual relationship. This re-connection is intimate and personal because the believer is given the status as a son or daughter of God. Most notably, our rebirth is a spiritual one and a person is a spiritual child of the Father. The body of Christ is essentially a spiritual family but interacting in material form. The church building is just a physical structure to facilitate the spiritual development of the family of God. It renders the biological kinship invalid because all children must fellowship with the Father personally in undivided allegiance (John 4:23-24). Biological connections are meaningless and Jesus made it clear in Matthew 12:48 and it specifically designates those that are obedient to Father's will as the family of God (John 19:26-27). Our relationship with Father is a spiritual one as he is Spirit.

Jesus explained that our basic problem comes from the heart and then the wicked motives go to the brain that conjures up evil schemes (Mark 7:20-23). It has to be cleaned out so that it can be fruitful. You have to will (self) to be remade by the power of the Spirit. Once the vessel has been refilled with sanctified information, you still have to apply it in reality to embed it in the personality. Your freewill is very much alive after this awakening, but it takes on a totally different posture. Self-will will always yearn to be under submission to Christ in the regeneration framework. It's uncanny when you think about it; self-will is still the same as it was before you became a Christian, yet it willingly yields and is subservient to Jesus. There must be a supernatural reason for it. The adage: 'you can take a horse to the water but you can't make it drink' is one that most of us have come across at some point of our lives. Despite sincere well wishes and honest beneficence, nothing will change the mind of the obstinate. Yet, God can cause a believer to do that which they had never desired to do before.

Once a person gets to know God personally, their response is overwhelming and overpowering to the extent that sacrifice of personal will becomes quite natural. The perfection of God is able to win over the most stubborn spirit. Millions of born-again Christians have proved this fact. When a person reaches the point of openness and hunger for closer contact with God, it becomes an unfair dual and God always wins. The obstinacy of self-will that keeps challenging God is what people mistake for human power (that God cannot control). The strength of God's perfect attributes confidently allows him to grant humans freewill knowing that he is well and truly able to win over all those whose hearts are inclined towards goodness. Even the most-evil person may be won over if they approach Christ honestly and justly.

However, not everybody's heart is pliable and sensitive to the Holy Spirit. This is why there has always been and will continue to have a certain number of God-haters, that are vacuous and frivolous in the world at any given time, whose idolatry of self-will will keep them against Jesus and salvation. Whatever time is spent with them in the Word will be wasted. Their spirit is dull and unreceptive to righteousness because unrighteousness is too deep-rooted.

Unlimited atonement advocates that salvation is for every person in the world that is alive at any given moment. The passages in John 1:29, John 3:16, 1 Timothy 4:10, Hebrews 2:9, 1 John 2:2, and Isaiah 53:6 are inclined towards unreserved expiation. This indicates that all sin has been properly dealt with by Christ's death on the cross. Salvation is open to each and every person alive in the world at any given time. However, it does not translate to automatic salvation for all because the essential ingredient for this is that a willing and able spirit has to make a free and unfettered choice to accept Jesus Christ as the only means to reach God. The case for unlimited atonement may be understood in terms of freewill. Since the Lord has opened the way to heaven, it's still dependent on the individual to accept God's terms of their own volition. This invitation stems from the love and grace of God. Therefore, any form of negligence, ignorance, rejection or misuse of the divine invitation means contempt of God and grave loss for that person. The Lord regards his Word sternly and he will uphold all that he has said.

The 'elect' is simply those who have sensitive spirits and will exercise a decision in submission to Jesus. The elect will choose Christ therefore the Lord can safely elect them because he knows their hearts, even of all those who are yet to be born. Nothing is hidden from God so why can he not elect all those who have a part in his family? All those who do not follow after the heart of God will never be elected because they don't have the right spiritual inclination. Nobody can blame God because the Bible is there to explain enough about him for entry into heaven. Election is not a bias procedure at all. It is grounded in God's omniscience and his foreknowledge. The blame always lies in the individual's choice. Personal attitude either leads to faith in Christ or expulsion from eternal life.

The greatest value that Christians may gain is when we start to relate freewill from God's angle. There has been so much controversial material written on freewill from the human standpoint, but we have to assess it according to God's outlook in order to gain a correct understanding for personal direction. God's view ranks above the human opinion. From the Scripture we can see what the Lord has planned for the human race. He simply wants a spiritual bonding with all his people. We can start by renewing our minds according to Romans 12:2. This is actually the reconstruction of the spirit (that instructs the mind) because it is the spirit that interacts with God, and his will must be instilled in a person's spirit.

The human-will ought to be subjugated to God not by any means of coercion but by a genuine desire to volunteer. The kingdom of God is a perfect piece of work and only God can fit all the pieces together to his own satisfaction. Humans have no power to dictate to the Lord how his kingdom is to be formed. The Bible tells us what God's demands are. John 7:17,1 Thessalonians 4:3, 5:18, give insight into a few aspects of God's will. However, John 15:4 states clearly that Jesus is the only means to fulfil the role that the Lord has given each one of us on earth. If you get your relationship with Christ right, then everything else will fall into place and God will give you a pass mark when you come up for assessment. The ease of understanding the simple words may fool people into thinking that their spirit is growing in holiness. The information in the mind has to reach the spirit so that it assimilates into character which then must be displayed in daily life. It's a spiritual unction from the brain to the spirit. It's only a light veneer that separates the two, but the shortest route is often the hardest path. Christians will be spending all their lives attempting to maintain correct standing with Christ.

Freewill chooses what's best for self, but the revamped spirit will choose God's will. The unregenerate person is never correct because God only accepts human actions that are grounded in the person of Christ. Anything that a person does that is self-driven and outside of Jesus' authority has no eternal value (John 15:6). Jesus' leadership is critical in everything that we do. This passage indirectly negates freewill. Everything must be done through the guidance and direction of Jesus. This thought must be given serious consideration. We must be in Christ at all times to ensure the proper completion of the works that God pre-planned for each of us. It is not worth wasting your time on earth doing things that will just be a great disappointment when Jesus assesses it on that day. Time is limited and personal satisfaction is temporary; but those things that carry over to perpetuity are what truly count.

In Chapter 2 we looked at the human make up and the relevant parts are the mind and the spirit. The Bible mentions the heart when talking about a person's innermost being. God looks at the heart whereas people look at the outward appearance. The heart is a vital organ for human life. We also know that the heart is incapable of thinking, making decisions or doing anything other than keeping the blood circulating and maintaining life support. It will degenerate and die with the body. The referral to the heart means the most intimate part of a person that is unseen and unique to each individual. It is the spirit that exists in every human being – the real you. It is the real being that will never die. The body will decay and return to dust but the spirit will return to God for judgment because it will either exist in heaven or in hell (Ecclesiastes 12:7).

The Holy Spirit must work to clean out the old internal mess and transmit the holiness of God. This is the process of on-going sanctification. We are all too aware of how difficult this is as our old nature is in constant strife with the indwelling Spirit. Once our spirit is in submission to the Holy Spirit, we are able to direct our minds in accordance with God's will. That is, the spirit (heart) directs the mind (1Corinthians 2:11, Ephesians 3:16). Then Romans 12:2 comes into effect and the mind will direct the body to perform those actions initiated by the Holy Spirit. The cycle will be complete once the spiritual concepts are assimilated and embedded into one's character. People will be able to see Jesus through our behaviour. It is the Holy Spirit working in a person to point to and magnify the goodness of the living Christ.

The renewed mind brings peace in knowing how to correctly discern and implement God's will. The mind can only be transformed after our spirit has been surrendered to God. The greater challenge is to keep that transformation growing until we reach the end of our natural lives. Undisciplined thinking patterns can quickly work against the regeneration process.

I was in an ethics seminar and the speaker presented the following case. A student asked his ethics lecturer for advice on a practical ethics problem. It was a particularly difficult matter as it involved a great deal of money. The lecturer gave the perfect theoretical answer and then the student asked what he would do personally. The reply was that he would not follow ethics but avail himself of the substantial monetary gain. The student was perplexed at this contradiction and asked why. His reply: 'what I teach and what I do are two different things'. As Christians we struggle with a similar thing in our walk with God. Although we have the enlightenment of a renewed mind, yet we falter in action on occasion.

The Spirit filled life means complete yielding to the guidance of the Holy Spirit. It requires all aspects of one's life to be submitted to the Lord. Small sins could catch you off-guard but confession and the urge to please Christ must be present so that renewal continues as the priority. It irks me when that happens but it also tells me that I'm human and that I'm capable of slipping. The good that is in me is the goodness from God and reminds me how much I really need Christ. Keep counting the changes that the Spirit has brought about and don't give up any hard-fought ground. The sanctified life is also a habit that you nurture and become accustomed to in due course. Transformation must be permanent and vacillation indicates that this process is incomplete. Allegiance to Christ will strengthen and sacrificial living will get easier.

A fundamental redirection of your thinking habits and behaviour patterns are a prerequisite to the renewing of your mind. Moreover, it requires that you stay in line with the Spirit and never look back. The obstinacy of self-will will be the obstacle that returns to haunt you over and over again. Self-determination and the Holy Spirit cannot exist harmoniously as they are always at loggerheads. The Spirit must be central in our lives and this requires constant attention. James 4:1 says that strife is birthed from within a person. One has to be wary of upsetting others but also not to undermine the Spirit's work because vexation is caused by self. The pertinent issue is the spirit's role as the primary mover. Spiritual regeneration in the heart directs renewal to the sanctified mind.

Morals and ethics also enter the mix. At times, we either uphold or infringe these principles in different ways. It's a battle within our minds and hearts that we face whenever we encounter discord. Whatever we crave for and hanker after takes a lead position in our ranking order and we will utilise all things at our disposal to realise our desires. Disputes don't always get resolved in the real world. If no compromise is reached, separation becomes the only option. Marriage breakups arise mainly because of irreconcilable differences and sometimes it's just unworkable and it's all caused by divided personal values.

Our external expression is merely a reflection of our internal commitments and beliefs. God moves directly to the core of our being as this is where the crinkles have to be ironed out. The private place of our will is where we must contend with the reality of God. It's a confrontation between our aspirations and the Lord's holiness. The work of regeneration to holiness is God's wish for us. Without renewal, our value before God is severely undermined and unfavourable. A decision must be reached and we must wrestle with God's imposition on our values. This has to take place in the deepest niche of our spirit because that is where it counts. After all is said and done, each person still has freewill to accept or reject God's advances.

There's only one acceptable outcome: God must win and self must lose. The loss of self-determination is really a win for self and for the Lord. The change from the inside out is so rewarding that joy overflows. This instant upgrade genuinely cleans out the old unhealthy habits and ushers in the new spiritual qualities that stay with a person forever. You will begin to savour a faint glimpse of what it is to be more like Christ. Over time it keeps on getting easier because there's no major struggle regarding conflict that was so problematic when we first began. The more you get rid of the old, the easier it is to comply with the new. You would actually want to give more and more to Jesus – something that was inconceivable before. Jesus gave humankind his best and we face the challenge of returning the favour.

Similarly, our dealings with others ought to be constantly groomed towards a submission of self-will to God's will. Self never dies but the change of character becomes the new norm. The making of a saint is a lifetime process. We all find this tiring and somewhat discouraging because we can't seem to get to the place where we are satisfied. God's standard of holiness is out of reach yet that is the destination that we must be heading towards. The initial laborious steps of chipping away at our favourite fancies won't stop until all is surrendered. However, some will take much longer to give up their final strongholds. As long as we faithfully honour our commitment to progress, God will be pleased and help will come. A point of personal encouragement is to think that I have given up so much for God already that I'm not stopping now. This is a constructive tool each time you face a hurdle.

The final things that we truly struggle with are character related and it's very stubborn to dislodge. During times of carelessness and negligence, it's easy to make the wrong choices. This often occurs when secular things over shadow our minds and occupy an excessive amount of our time. Even though we know that Christ comes first and we have our regular devotions, sometimes these beleaguered things seem to impose themselves disproportionately on our time and attention. If we move in the wrong direction, we may feel that it was okay because God will forgive. Insensitivity can set in very quickly and you can stealthily revert to self-will yet thinking that you are still making positive headway in sanctification. This subtle invasion of sin can undo all that you have worked so hard to attain. Rationalisation of any sort must not be entertained.

When we reach a reasonably mature level, regression in any manner will hurt the Lord immensely. It's like betraying a bosom friend and infinitely more. We have travelled with him for so long and undergone and overcome all the hurdles to get to where we are. Then we let carelessness destroy it all. The Lord's view is to get us renewed in holiness and any form of backsliding will mean a loss to God and a victory to Satan. The odd thing is that we satisfy ourselves via rational reasoning and we often take the spiritual (unseen) too lightly. It may mean nothing or precious little to our mind but it is a serious matter for God. Going back to self-satisfaction hurts God more than we care to think. His happiness and desires are broken due to our indiscretion.

He is so gentle, always allowing us to err and then to bring us back, without prejudice and fully loving. Understand that even a little sin at this higher stage of regeneration is more hurtful than the big sins at the start of your journey. Personal weaknesses vary from individual to individual, and we have to be particularly mindful of the hidden weaknesses in our latter Christian years because it can stop us from achieving our maximum regeneration capacity. It will be a great shame to fall short on the home straight. We are precious to God and ought not to disappoint him or ourselves.

Chapter 6
Conduct

The concept of relationship, obedience and love is interdependent and all three parts have to be seamlessly coordinated. The absence of or inadequacy of any element displays a weakness in the tripartite and would subsequently be reflected in the association. God is a relational being and humans were made with the same desire for relationship. If you wish to be productive in the Lord's work you must have the desire to love people. People that can't get along with others hold a powerful stance on self-interest and personal opinion.

Good intentions are just that, the behaviour that emerges may not be in line with the good intentions because bias may interfere with fair judgment. Unfair practices tarnish the attitude of love. Personal feelings may get the better of fair judgment and this fools a person into thinking that they have an unfettered loving demeanour. Love is shown to the favoured ones and hostility to those out of favour. All of God's work deals with people because people comprise the kingdom of heaven. Fair-play towards all parties involved is essential in order to maintain trust and personal integrity.

The worker has to be disciplined in all three parts. It is only after you have trained yourself can you then disseminate it to others. Regular self-examination is the control mechanism whereby improvements are made in morality. There must be no letting up until the last fault is beaten. At this point in our walk with the Lord we realise that being a follower of Jesus is not easy at all. In our disciplined walk to sanctification, the conflicting decisions that we face; the hardship and difficulties that confront us; personal and people disappointments that sap our confidence and emotional strength will test our truthfulness. Yet, we keep striving to maintain constant guard of our moral high ground.

Self-will can do so much harm and nobody can stop us. The tendency to sin is part of our being and we have to make deliberate efforts to remain faithful to Jesus so that we stay on the right trajectory. The order is: love; obedience; relationship, but just thinking and saying the word 'love' does not make it happen. You have to put the mechanism in place and then act resolutely.

Relationship.

The ranking is: God - people - self, and this is the basic principle in forming any relationship. Christians may be seen as instruments that the Lord uses at specific times to connect with others. Kingdom expansion is structured on people to people interaction. In the kingdom work, the work-in-progress is people. This is the most important thing to God and hence it must be the same for each member of the body of Christ. God uses people to form his kingdom on earth and accomplish his work. It's wonderful that he has chosen this medium because it gives us purpose in life and reward in the hereafter. The focus on people must be constantly before us otherwise we retreat to self-interest. The priority should be God's direction first, then the benefit of people next and self in the rear.

However, freewill largely places self before God and people secondary. This mindset can break up relationships. If we are to function productively, then we must realign our vision to the way the Lord sees things. This puts people ahead of self but freewill always sticks its foot in the wrong places. The reorientation is never easy, even when you are at the place where you have most things correctly positioned, self always has to be kept in check in order not to slip-up or revert to selfish habits.

Motivational words can be cheap and inert and giving free advice is easy but experience tells us that sound relationships have to be nurtured because they don't come easy. The positive side is that the Holy Spirit brings out the good in you so that taking the right steps are not so hard. This process is not tiresome but it demands relentless effort to make the right decisions on every occasion. Winning over difficult personalities and getting the other party to the position where friendship can take root may require much patience and perseverance. At every stage we have to bear in mind that the relationship is more important than self-gratification and that's not always easy to apply.

Genuine attempts ought to be made to put others first. The question is whether you like the person that you are working with and would you sacrifice your time and put the procedures in place that will lead to a lasting relationship. Knowledge of the opposite party is fundamental in building a meaningful association. What if you don't like what you have discovered? When things are going smoothly, Satan often introduces unpleasantries to irritate a person. In order to initiate a change in others, you have to be sufficiently equipped in righteousness and the unpalatable issues won't be problematic. Building a harmonious friendship is doable if you are serious about the work and you love people. It may be a bumpy ride, but Jesus will help you succeed (John 14:21-22). The attitude: 'I will change only after he changes' won't arise in the sanctified mind as compromise and the determination to get around the problems will be the priority. Failure is attributable to the absence of self-abasement or humility and self is always to blame. It questions the veracity of one's regeneration.

Relationship with people varies depending on how much common ground there is. The nurturing of a friendship is a two-way process, and the parties have to be likeminded to develop. Normally, if constructive engagement is sought from both sides, positive growth will make inroads. When a relationship begins to mature, initial dislikes and aversions can and normally does convert to understanding and an amicable bond may be developed. However, if the worldviews disagree or cannot be reconciled, then it would be pointless pursuing that association. Personality clashes and impasse have to be sorted out upfront to avoid wasting time and resources. Not everybody may get along with one another, even among Christian circles. Hence, getting the right people together would save much frustration.

Relationship basics are birthed when we come to Jesus (John 5:40, 6:37, 7:37). We start our walk with God by learning from Christ. The consistency, length, dependency and intensity really depend on how much and how far we allow the Holy Spirit to take us. In theory we understand this to be a learning exercise like school. Therefore, if we study the Scripture and do the walk, we should get there after a certain period of time. However, the Bible is so rich in spiritual knowledge that we can dedicate the major part of our time on earth studying it and still not profit from all its secrets; the reason being that the Word of God is spiritually discerned (1 Corinthians 2:14). Only the Holy Spirit can impart the mind of Christ to the learner who is imbued with fresh illumination. Spiritual understanding and development is the priority in life-education because they are directly affixed to God's will and work, and pays handsome dividends in the everlasting kingdom.

There are other factors in life that we allow to interfere with this aspect of our relationship with the Lord. Unfortunately, it is a time-based choice. If you give your time to things concerning secular life then you can't give your time to God and vice versa. Paul exhorts us to give uninterrupted devotion to the Lord (1 Corinthians 7:35). It's a real issue for many of us.

You may conceive the idea that you will give a certain period of your life to work, raise a family and build security on earth, and then dedicate the rest to God. If this decision is driven by self-interest then it will not yield the optimum spiritual benefit because God requires the best from you and passing the leftovers to him is more of an insult. The Spirit transmits discernment according to his timing and not human's. Life is so short and even a lifetime is insufficient to know God adequately. The open invitation 'to come' is always available but it should not be unduly delayed because of self-indulgence. The opposite half is 'to go'. After we have been walking with Jesus and digesting the spiritual input, then we become usable tools. Matthew 10:7 and 28:19 tells us that our life and knowledge can be applied to bless others. Reaching the lost, making disciples, encouraging those in need and teaching them to follow Christ are the main purposes. Conversion of the willing is very quick and simple, but it's the discipleship that requires so much energy and commitment.

The Holy Spirit works to enhance the body of Christ using each individual's talent and capacity. And the body works collectively and individually to glorify the Father. The trainees learn skills and then pass them on to others that are willing to learn. This is a self-perpetuating cycle that is powered by the Spirit. However, there is a time constraint and you have to be willing go at God's timing. This is often accompanied by some inconvenience, discomfort or other cost, so it's not a simple decision. However, self-discipline and introspection are crucial to one's personal connection with Jesus. This relationship is the basic work that has to be placed first at every turn and the guidance of the Spirit will ensure that no mistakes are made. It delights God to no end when you dedicate all of yourself to him. In return, he is all too willing to give you all the teaching that you are competent to handle. In the absence of pride and other hurdles, this nourishing process can be maintained right until the end of one's days on earth. It's easier said than done. Relationship on earth is just the beginning and the full impact of your pursuit on earth will be fully realised in eternity. The Trinity depicts a relationship that is in complete accord and that should be our aspiration as well with Christ.

Obedience.

The path to sanctification requires a great deal of effort and determination on our part. The biggest obstacle that each has to overcome is to bring individual freedom under God's control. We must abandon freewill and allow the Lord to assume the leadership and complete control over our decisions. Once this is properly in place, then training in holiness can take root and grow. When we first received Jesus into our soul, we earnestly repented and had the firm desire to follow him. The metamorphosis towards the new life wasn't hard because we had the drive to do the right thing – to be more like Jesus. However, after the easy bits were taken care of, the struggle still remains. It's the ingrained personality and character trait shortcomings that we seem to battle with all our lives. When we sincerely take stock of our character we find that there is always something that needs to be improved. This is actually a good place to be because your relationship with the Lord has come a long way to be where it is at present. The easy things have been dealt with and no Jesus-loving soul would want to go back to the old life. The further we progress, the more attention and effort we need to exert to get over the remaining stubborn obstacles that regularly stain our behaviour. This work never comes to a halt, our recurring pitfalls ought to be a challenge to overcome self.

In the same manner that Jesus had done when he emptied himself of his glorious status and became a human being, we have to get rid of self. The kenosis procedure saw Jesus relinquish omnipotence and became a humble servant of the Father. The incarnation is one of the most reassuring realities for me as a human being. Now instantly there's a direct link between humans and God. The transcendence of God was removed by his immanence in Jesus; what was out of reach became reality that was corporeal. The Holy Spirit remains in us to bring the mind of Christ into our lives. God's immanence is the most helpful part in our fellowship with him. The Spirit's services are available to everyone who loves Christ and he will help rid us of our pernicious self.

It calls for the total death of freewill and living closely with the Lord so that all daily decisions are automatically passed by the Spirit before we take any steps forward. This is far easier said than done. Who can sincerely say that they want to give up all rights to self; that they no longer want to captain their own ship? Even so, there are many minor decisions that we make as a matter of course that we consider as inconsequential and do not warrant prayer. Nonetheless, involving the Lord in everything is conducive to developing a sound relationship instead of trying to partition our spiritual and secular lives (Philippians 4:6, Ephesians 6:18). Ministry is reflected through a person's occupation in the secular sphere. This is not necessarily telling the gospel (may be objectionable to some hearers) but the crucial display of the spiritual morals of the sanctified life. A dualistic lifestyle will invariably reveal certain shortcomings that have not been corrected. Worldly ways are deceitful and often make a person feel confident and capable of dealing with those personal faults. Yet, we do little to rectify our ways.

Freewill is driven by instinct and self-interest, but Jesus goes against all of that. The problem lies in our thought processes and background. Believers are morally dysfunctional and need to be realigned to godliness before God can work with us. When God and humans come together there's an inevitable personality clash and freewill is our biggest headache.

Jesus gives knowledge but you have to make the choice to change. Obedience is of greater value to God than sacrifice (ritualistic compliance with religious forms). Sanctification is a process to become more like Christ and it requires the absence of freewill. You were bought at a price. God wants all of you. We all understand the theory but when it comes to practice, I'm afraid the application doesn't quite stack up to the knowledge. To a large extent, we as committed believers are only partially to blame because sin is intrusive and pervasive. The Apostle Paul said that he wants to do the right things but somehow ends up doing the wrong things. However, we have a big role to play when we are called to partner in the kingdom work. We have to set self aside and be led entirely by the will of the Lord. It's a conscious effort that each of us must purposefully choose and execute and we are responsible for our choices.

Obedience is not forced on a person but rather prescribed and encouraged. God respects human freewill. Normally, the Lord never forces people to do anything. There are certain exceptions like Jonah and possibly Moses. After Pentecost, believers are in partnership with the Holy Spirit, but he is supposed to assume the lead and this makes him the senior partner.

God clearly lays down the standards that humanity ought to abide by. There are grave warnings for non-compliance and also pledges of rich rewards for obedience, but the ultimate decision still rests with the individual.

Love.

Love is the element that holds the other two parts together. Love keeps everything in God's kingdom in coherence (Colossians 3:14). Selfishness opposes the ideology of sacrifice and it must be completely removed so that love can operate properly. Love makes a person do things that they detested before. It's a wonderful experience because deep down you know that it's right. The habit of love grows on you as you draw nearer to Christ and consideration for others becomes a natural part of life. If outsiders can see your sensitivity and concern for others, then you are well on the right track.

Respect for others, good manners, being a nice guy etc. is not love. People in reputable positions in ministry may display competence and ability and yet show few signs of love. Love is not normally talked about and people would rather study the more interesting theological topics where they can debate and hold intellectual discussions on. Love must be demonstrated and sometimes it's very hard to see the evidence in Christian behaviour. It would be interesting to see how the average believer answers the question on how to demonstrate love to non-believers and to fellow Christians in action and commitment. The essential aspect of love is practice. The Spirit can teach you everything you need to know about agape. It's easy to understand but not simple to implement because you are the problem.

John 15:17 commands us to love each other and this is not a choice. We don't give it enough attention because it always calls for sacrifice of some sort. Those who wish to attain the fullness of God's love will soon discover that this objective will clash head-on with self-will. The love that we have is sub-standard and will remain that way until we have agape in spirit and in action. That's why sanctification is an on-going process in this life. Self-interest is always going to torment and frustrate your regeneration advancement until you do something about it.

1 John 4:19 states that God loved us first therefore we are enabled to return that love to him. This initiative never comes from the human will. The Spirit conditions a believer so that God's love flows through that person, this is not human love. God's love existed before creation

and humans would not know love if God did not reveal it first. Humans are conduits through which God establishes and manifests his character. Humans follow after the Lord and were designed with an ability to love. Love cannot be compelled or conditioned into a person such as in a workplace situation. Kind actions may be taught and habitually formed but it may still lack the element of love. Love is a personal choice and each person has the right to choose to exercise love or to withhold it. Love is a universal concept known to all in different ways, bar exceptional cases. Freewill allows a person to accept love but not return it. This is a very selfish and uncaring demeanour.

Normally, a loving act stirs a person to action. It is a proactive tool that seeks to connect those concerned. Some people return love as an obligation, but this is just returning a favour in keeping with good etiquette. Agape is loaded with feeling and it comes from the renewed spirit. It knows no limit and acts with great concern for others. Nothing is too precious to be sacrificed for the beneficiaries.

In a situation where the recipient is aware of love being shown and still does not respond then something is wrong. This person either doesn't like the giver or thinks that the act is their right to receive or they may not respect the giver or they are selfish or a combination. Such behaviour points to self-gratification as well as disrespect for the relationship. It's probably viewed as within their rights that they can just keep on accepting and have no duty to return the complement. This may be due to selfishness, disrespect or plain stinginess. Idolatry is extremely offensive to God and putting money before godliness is unconscionable.

God has gone through great lengths and made sacrifices beyond the norm, and such love must be reciprocated. The recipient cannot keep accepting the enrichment without feelings. If so, the hardness of heart is caused by the evil one and they have capitulated. Self-elevation, insensitivity and callousness do not come from the Lord and such an attitude will get what it deserves. A person may serve admirably in ministry but that may not be an act of love. Some people work out the concept of love in the brain in terms of self, money or whatever a person values and their spirit may be blinded by self-interest. External acts may hide the lack of sincerity and self-interest in their heart.

Jesus gave to the human race the ultimate act of love on the cross and every human being is obligated to him. This was not merely a good deed, but a priceless sacrifice where unquantifiable spiritual transactions were passed. God does not expect us to do the same as Jesus did, but he does demand an appropriate response. A sincere attempt to try will invoke the Spirit's assistance, and we will be able to satisfy the Lord's expectation of us. Unfortunately, it will require sacrifice of some sort, just as Jesus did. The reward is maturity in holiness and an improved bonding with Jesus Christ. It would be so much easier if we didn't have a choice, but our fate is in our own hands. Those that like to be in control and want to make executive decisions on their own have the opportunity now to make a seismic decision for their eternity.

Chapter 7
Confusion

While studying at Bible College, I came across the subject of Process Theology. I had never heard of it before. I was amazed at how many books were written on this subject and upon reading some of them I felt that the concept had too many flaws. I want to briefly touch on some of the main points.

Process theology asserts that the material world is not static, so both God and humans are progressively changing and growing in knowledge. God's interaction with the world and humans is in a 'constant process of change' and is never finished, only in the event of death. Human beings are continuously channelled in a forward direction that enhances the quality of life. Process theology is dedicated to harmonising the vast amounts of new knowledge with the contemporary understanding of how things are today. It resembles a kind of chess game where humans keep on changing their minds and God reacts accordingly. The theory is that God cannot decide until a person has made their final decision. Process theology conflicts with the traditional concept that God is immutable. It is based on the current state of affairs whereby God has to harmonise with the expanding contemporary understanding of 'how things are'.

The following is an extract from the Stanford Encyclopaedia of Philosophy: First published Thu. July 29th, 2004. Substantive revision Mon. Oct 6th 2008 (published on the internet).

> Process theism is not based on religious doctrine or theology and it is not a scientific theory; it is product of metaphysics, or what Whitehead calls 'speculative philosophy'. It is an attempt to explain human experience in a coherent, logical and systematic way. Process theism advocates that God is the supreme or eminent creative power, but not the only creative power. Thus, process theists speak of God and the creatures as co-creators. Human beings, however, do not always will their own good or the good of other people. In those cases on the classical view, God brings it about that people freely decide not to will the good of others. Process theists argue that this makes God responsible for evil and suffering in a way that contradicts divine goodness. On the classical view, for example, the crimes that disfigure human history are the fault of human beings, but they are also God's doing.

The above and many other writings on this subject make me shudder because it goes against all that I know of a perfect God. Speculative philosophy is merely an attempt to explain human behaviour in the real world and should not be ranked above Biblical precepts. If human behaviour is explained logically as we desire it then it makes God out to be illogical. How can humans be co-creators? Creation was complete at the end of day six of creation week in Genesis. The concept of co-creators can only mean that humans are free to decide which course of action we want to take here on earth. 'Co-creators' is a misnomer because freewill cannot create matter in the physical or spiritual worlds. It only relates to our decision-making. Billions of people making different decisions each day is a very complex thing for the human mind to comprehend, but God already knows the conclusion of every decision. To be a co-creator with God is just wishful thinking. It is a poor attempt to elevate self-will to challenge the Almighty.

Those who claim that God is a cohort in their sinful behaviour are just trying to appease their conscience and to escape the judgement. If God is partly to blame then he must punish himself for those sins as well! This is not referred to anywhere in the Bible. Every person is responsible for their own sin and God is incapable of sin.

Along the above lines, process theists are contradicting themselves. On the one hand they say that they have freewill to act apart from God; and on the other hand, they say that when it comes to evil deeds, God cooperated in their actions to carry them out. They want to get away scot-free from all their personal sins. This means that there is no freewill when evil deeds are being perpetrated. They make God to be capricious because he may contradict himself at any time. It defies logic and reasoning.

Process theology views were conceived as early as 1917. Certain theologians and philosophers in the 1930's felt that the social gospel was losing attraction so they embarked on scientific means to study religion. Psychology and sociology were the tools applied to this new method of study. Henry Wilson Wieman and Bernard Meland were the fore-runners in promoting the concept of radical empiricism i.e. the doctrine that all knowledge derives from experience. Alfred North Whitehead was one of the earliest thinkers to embody the ideas of process theology in comprehensive form.

This theory is purely a human theological construct. It shifts the individual's responsibility back on to God. How can they say that they have freewill to do anything and simultaneously claim that God is a co-perpetrator in all their evil actions? Thus, freewill only pertains to the good deeds but not to sin. This negates the basic tenet of freewill.

Process theists and other proponents take the dynamic of freewill as an absolute determinant and they erroneously apply that to God. Since we don't even know what we are going to do, therefore God doesn't know until we actually do it. God is in a 'constant state of learning'. This suggests that human will has power over the Almighty. It's a self-elevating theory and portrays self to be arrogant and brazen. You can't out-play God by any stretch of the imagination. This theory does not support the kingdom concept because servants will be doing the work yet God does not know what they are doing and effectively will have no control over his own kingdom.

When a decision is made it brings about a process that excludes outside interference as it progresses to a conclusion. Outsiders are prevented from adding or excluding anything during the process. The decision maker then takes full ownership of the consequences. All of creation is dependent on God for its existence. Human beings cannot find their own way to heaven. Our faith and love come from God alone to assist us to find Christ and without it we will still be completely lost. Then we have to follow the path of discipleship to righteousness because others cannot act as our substitute to do it for us. Hence, we are directly responsible for our own results. This is a universal principle – if you break the law, you suffer the consequences. Discussion on metaphysical things does not negate this principle. Life is full of decisions that an individual has to make and normally, people are aware of the ramifications of their worldly decisions.

The final decision always rests on that person alone. In fact, I can have faith or love today and sincerely admit it to everyone; and then turn around and renounce all of that and return to a position of unbelief. The ultimate decision is in my own hands and nobody else's. There may be many uncertainties at the time the decision is made, but God sees into the future and already knows which path I am going to take. In this respect you cannot out-think or out-smart God. It is not inconceivable that he is able to select beforehand those who will enter his kingdom.

These views are explained in a roundabout way and I have to read all their convoluted notes and still have to summarise what they actually mean. In most if not all cases, they could have said all they want in a fraction of the writing. Perhaps all the words in between are designed to confuse rather than clarify. After all that painstaking reading, I usually end up asking myself what has this got to do with the practical Christian life of following Christ? It's very little or nothing at all.

The writers have put in a big effort and much thought into their work. Never allow the interesting bits to get hold of you because the disjointed parts are dangerous (1 Timothy 1:6-7, 4:1-2, Acts 17:21). Usually, these writings disregard systematic theology and concentrate on one aspect in isolation. The Bible must be the sole source of reference. Based on the principle that each person is accountable to God, then nothing else matters except the Word of God. Human ideas may be accepted only if they accurately illustrate some point in Scripture as a whole. Anything else can be happily rejected as a waste of time. If you are not in God's will then personal effort counts for nothing. Sound Biblical analysis and writings are useful to broaden a person's knowledge and understanding of God. However, a positive relationship only materialises via practice.

Some argue that God is the primary mover and since sin is a created thing (from creation week), therefore he must be responsible for sin as well. However, prior to Satan's rebellion in heaven, there was no sin anywhere. Thereafter he was cast out and heaven remained sin-free and will be so for all eternity. The Garden of Eden was sin-free until disobedience entered the human experience. In this regard, there is no chicken and egg argument because sin came after all creation was completed on day six. God did not include any trace of sin in his perfect creation. Sin was created by Satan and it came into existence after a perfect world was put in place. At this stage, sin was confined to the metaphysical realm. However, disobedience in Adam gave rise to human-sin in the material world. This was Satan's attempt to corrupt perfection and it has marred the human race until the Judgment. The Lord cursed the entire creation because of sin. Through this act, God would be contradicting himself if he had created sin in the first instance. Therefore, the Lord is not responsible for sin in any manner or form.

How did sin actually come into existence? We are not told the details of Satan's fall (together with his conspirators). However, both Satan and Adam acted against God's decree. Sin means missing the mark that God has set. Thus, sin arises outside of the realm of God's perfection and it is caused by created beings. All created beings have freewill and are capable of sin and turning against the Lord. The originator of sin was Satan and it flowed on to Adam and the rest of humankind. Satan was also created as a holy and perfect being prior to his rebellion.

Sin is outside of God's tolerance and his nature. It is unwarranted to say that God created sin in the first place because he is good and he cannot sin. Sin was not created by God to inflict pain upon himself or anyone else. It's an absurdity to think that God would create sin that he cannot stand and thus offend himself! If God could sin then he would be a capricious being where nothing is stable and many things could and probably would contradict themselves. If God created sin then why doesn't the Bible tell of him using the medium of sin to do everything that he wants fulfilled (sinning is far easier than doing good)? Wouldn't it be good if we could all get to heaven without having to pass any form of faith or trial? We could live any way we desire and God could merely take all those nasty parts out of our record and give us the green light all the way.

The disturbing question is that when you die, will you really get into heaven? How do you know whether everything was just an amusing game and that he may change his mind unexpectedly? If there is no guaranteed method of entry into heaven then what's the point of adherence to good? The logical choice would be to 'eat, drink and be merry'. God is righteous and immutable and believers can trust that he will stand by all that he has said in his Word. The only sure way to remove doubt is faith from God through close fellowship with Jesus. This is a personal friendship with God where a person learns to think the way God wants people to and the Holy Spirit will assure you of the truth. This is a realisation of your faith in spiritual terms and is cemented through your association with Christ. God's care and interaction with a person removes all uncertainty because he makes his Word a reality in your spirit. Millions and millions of believers have a faith in Christ that they will never surrender.

Perhaps some may think that God had everything worked out from the start and his plan to sacrifice himself (in the person of Jesus) was actually meant to incorporate an element to atone for his own wrongs. This is ridiculous as God committed no sin and Jesus was perfect. There is no proof that the Lord ever sinned. The Bible makes it clear that Jesus' redemptive work is only for human beings, not for spirits or angels or for himself. Only humans have the unique privilege of regeneration. Nowhere in the Bible has God ever admitted or confessed to sinning nor is he guilty of any because he is holy.

We know that sin comes about through an actual action or procedure. What action or procedure has God performed that shows that he actually committed sin? The Lord has laid down all the rules that constitute his commands and moral code for righteous and holy living. If he then goes and performs some action that makes him responsible for sin then he is a hypocrite by breaking his own rules, and that is definitively impossible.

It was Adam's sin that was so hurtful to God. He hates Adam's actions but he loves Adam so much that he is constrained to save the human race. The Lord looked upon his creation as very good, and he wasn't going to allow Satan to subtract from it. God did not cause Adam and Eve to sin and they did it themselves.

I have never deliberately gone out to conjure up a scheme to mislead or to propagate selfish ideas. It was the unintentional things that bothered me. If I wanted to maintain a clean slate with God then accountability was paramount. What about the inconspicuous things that have passed unnoticed? How do I know what indirect negative consequences have resulted from my interaction with those around me? This issue really played on my mind for a very long time. A correct understanding of atonement has put my mind and spirit at ease. Keep short accounts with God and he will work everything out (Romans 8:28).

Self-image in a person's spirit can be inflated to raise self-esteem, and freewill can be allowed to go overboard with theological ideas that don't hold water. Self-expression in the wrong context can be misleading and people do it because of their right to personal opinion. Self-control is an honourable trait yet it is easily forgotten when it comes to self-assertion.

Chapter 8
Cultural Influences

Part 1

In my late teens a friend quoted: 'society makes you what you are'. I had never given it much thought before and it was an interesting statement. Parents, family, friends and the environment had some input into shaping my ideals and to a certain extent my temperament. There was a certain truth to it and my feeling was that I'm here and I am me. In those early years, life was just a routine and I had no aspirations apart from completing my studies.

The Renaissance began spreading culture throughout Europe starting in Italy. This campaign covered approximately the 14th to the 17th Century, the former known as the Late Middle Ages. The advent of the printing press (Johannes Gutenberg, 1450) and the effective use of paper facilitated the propagation of information and ideas and this became a reality in the later 15th Century. The cultural content was based on the knowledge, studies, literature and paintings from the 14th Century. The foremost boon was for the person in the street because it was the beginning of wide-ranging education. The demand for books and for variety grew steadily because they were more affordable than before, first for the middle class and then to the masses. The accumulation of knowledge by an individual was made easier and learning was expedited. Those who were hungry for information were only limited by the sources and language barriers.

Martin Luther's works set in motion the Protestant Reformation in the 16th century. He opposed the system of selling indulgences for the freedom from punishment for sin; to reduce the amount of time the soul spends in purgatory. He advocated the notion of salvation through faith alone, thus the phrase 'justification by faith'. Sin is forgiven through trusting Christ because he died for all people's sin. It cannot be purchased by financial or any other means. He opposed certain practices of the Roman Catholic Church, and he promoted the Bible as the sole authority on living the Christian life. Martin Luther nailed his Ninety-Five Theses to the door of the All Saints' Church in Wittenberg on 31st October 1517, and this gave the green-light for the subsequent reformation. Naturally, this upset the church authorities to no end. He wanted ordinary people to be able to read the Bible so he translated it into German (from Latin). This broke the people's reliance on the church as the sole repository of the Word of God.

In January 1518, Luther's Ninety-Five Theses were translated from Latin into German. This was the first significant application of the printing press for the dissemination of educational data (apart from the news). His theses were printed, copied and circulated in Germany in the space of two weeks and the rest of Europe within two months. Martin Luther was excommunicated from the church because he refused to withdraw his convictions. His apparent loss has resulted in our gain. The pertinent issue is that people should decide for themselves and not rely on others to make those decisions for them and correctly so because faith is a personal commitment to the Lord. You must think and conduct your faith in personal relationship to Jesus Christ.

Greek philosophy is the cornerstone of Western thinking and it emphasises the individual person. Critical thinking may be traced back to Socrates (470BC – 399BC). His work 'Socratic Questioning' is one of the earliest and finest instructions on critical thinking. His method of questioning concentrated on the need for the thinking process to be applied with clarity and logic. His ideas were further developed by Plato, Aristotle and others. All these early thinkers supported the view that superficial presentation may have alternate meaning and only the informed thinker would be able to discern its value. First appearances are often deceiving.

In the Middle Ages, Thomas Aquinas suggested in his writings that reasoning had to be systematically processed and that it had to be cross-examined. During this period (15th to 16th Centuries) rational thinking took a major leap forward when a number of European scholars researched critical thinking in law, arts, religion etc. Francis Bacon (England) examined the area of misuse in exercising the mind and thought process. In his book 'The Advancement of Learning' he stressed the importance of applying empirical means in the thinking framework. His book may be considered as the forerunner in the field of critical thinking. It may be viewed as a vertical thought process that builds up step by step until it reaches a coherent conclusion.

Approximately fifty years after Francis Bacon, Rene Descartes (France) produced his book 'Rules for the Direction of the Mind', possibly the second pioneering work in critical evaluation. He dealt with the essential elements by utilising the principle of 'systematic doubt'. His assertion was that foundational assumptions had to be sound and well founded in the thinking process. Furthermore, every part of the thinking routine had to be questioned, doubted and tested. His methodology placed doubt before trust; one does not accept a notion until it has been justified. All the assertions in an argument had to analysed, verified and placed in logical order. Propositions are not posited until proved to be true. His other claim to fame was the statement: Cogito cogito ergo cogito sum — "I think that I think, therefore I think that I am". Only Descartes really knows what he meant by it, but at face value, there's a strong suggestion of free thinking and self-assertion as to who you are. The free mind is a place where nobody can enter unless you allow them, and you alone decide what comes out.

The Age of Reasoning (the Enlightenment) took root in the 18th century in Western Europe and England. Its core was scientific rationalism and method. Faith had to be proved and the Bible came in to question. People wanted material data to show that God exists. However, this question of proof was already posed by Moses in Exodus 33:20. He asked to see God's glory, but the reply was that no one may see God's face and live. Philip also asked Jesus to show them the Father and that would be enough for them (John 14:8). A physical appearance was denied in both cases, yet they still believed. It was a matter of faith overshadowing the need for visible evidence.

Prior to Babel, all the people were related in some way, they all spoke one language and they only knew the one true Creator/God. Nobody asked to see the visible form of God because they had faith in the Lord. God was real and active to them. Even the rebels that concocted the idea of the tower were well aware of God and wanted to elevate themselves to challenge the Lord's sovereignty over their lives (didn't want to be scattered all over the earth, Genesis 11:4). After Babel when all the nations were distributed throughout the earth, only Abram's line knew the true God. The rest of the ethnic groups were left to develop their own culture, practices and religion. The distance between humans and God widened; faith diminished and the need for physical evidence arose. Critics who have no faith want scientific or empirical analysis as proof before they believe anything.

Rene Descartes developed the 'method of doubt' and secular thinkers required sufficient evidence through scientific analysis before an argument could be accepted as valid. The exploration of doubt became standard procedure in critical thought. It was science versus faith and human being was the judge. Marxism and Nazism were two political philosophies that were used to propagate atheism on mass. There were two schools of thought that became popular. The libertarian view that was prevalent in the middle class; which led to classical liberalism whereby people were aspiring to be god. This stream was drawn towards capitalism because it gave the entrepreneur power and influence. The egalitarian view appealed to the industrial class and this facilitated the birth of socialism and communism. Ideas proliferated during this period, but many lacked coordination and harmony as a whole.

The Enlightenment was an optimistic age that elevated self-confidence. It accelerated free thinking to new heights. Capitalism was birthed in the Middle Ages, well before the Enlightenment. The earliest form was merchant capitalism when the increase in trade spurred traders in London and Amsterdam to form the first chartered joint-stock companies. It then led to the formation of the first stock exchange and banking and insurance establishments. Modern capitalism emerged during the 16th to the 18th centuries when mercantile principles were improved and refined by Josiah Child (England) and Jean-Baptiste Colbert (France) among others. In the mid-18th century, Adam Smith led a new band of economic writers and during this time, industrial capitalism took root. Mechanisation was the order of the day together with the division of labour and the standardisation of work tasks. The resulting industrial revolution that transpired saw the decline of traditional artisans, guilds and journeyman because of mass production.

Capitalism is centred on personal gain. It is the process of individual or private wealth accumulation through profit making. Where the laws and law-enforcement are inadequate, profiteering poses a dilemma. I work for myself and my gains are my own and I have no obligation to share it with anybody. The sky's the limit and you are free to earn as much as you are able to or be as greedy as you want. Extreme capitalism is very destructive towards the environment and it obstructs those who do not have the means to compete. Monopolies wield great power and encourage greed and are a barrier to free healthy/fair competition. Extreme capitalism seeks to eliminate all competition. However, at any point in the capitalism continuum, idolatry will be lurking because there's money and power at stake and self-enrichment may be expressed in so many forms that people find attractive.

All of the abovementioned has a bearing on the individual's thought processes. It's easier to understand how history and culture shape a person's behaviour. The common denominator is 'me' or 'I' and this has significant influence on decision-making. Secular influences urge you to do things and how good or bad it turns out depends on how far you want to push it. It's good to innovate and move forward for personal or social benefit but often consciously or unconsciously it encourages self-interest to the extreme. Understandably, when the individual starts the thinking process, self becomes judgmental, proud, dogmatic and ambitious. This is good for research and development and social justice, but bad when it concerns wealth because people always tend towards greed and selfishness. You are not your brother's keeper, so it's each person unto their own. I have self-will and I can do whatever I please. Since you are the most important person in your frame of reference it's not hard to figure out why you make decisions the way you do. Even under communism, self-concern is the priority; if we are all getting the same pay, then why should I work harder? It's actually selfishness because the person will do the least amount of work that they could possibly get away with. Socialist countries that have switched over to the free-market system are experiencing the same selfish attitudes as the west nations.

Critical thinking had stamped its mark in the western world and gradually evolved into what we have today. An interesting development was by Edward De Bono who introduced the concept of 'lateral thinking' to the world in 1967. It may be applied as a problem-solving aid that utilises inconspicuous elements and diffuse factors to finding possible solutions that are not apparent using the chronological logic approach. Horizontal analysis seeks to generate as many related ideas as possible in the hope of finding an optimum solution. In the thinking process, the mix of ideas may lead to the birth of new possibilities that were never thought of.

In the 1970's and 1980's management consultants came up with the term 'think outside the box'. The origin is said to have come from the USA in the late 1960's to early 1970's. However, many consultants claimed to have coined the phrase during that time. The approach is to consider the issue at hand as if there are no constraints or inhibitions and to produce some unusual answers. Executive advisers and coaches encouraged their clients to apply lateral thinking to explore situations outside of the immediate subject. The objective is to find a possible answer that may be hidden. It was a problem-solving tool and often led to innovative ways of doing things through the flow of new approaches. The objective was to nurture unimpeded resourceful imagination to come up with novel ideas and fresh input. The most common example that they used was the 'nine dots puzzle'. All the random dots had to be joined with one pen stroke and without crossing the same line twice.

Eastern philosophy that is grounded in Confucianism paints an opposing view to the West. Eastern history also has its great thinkers who espoused a softer form of critical and rational thinking than the West. The East have their share of entrepreneurs, business leaders and religious thinkers. They also had their great inventors and dynamic minds, but their cultural thinking approach is different. The universe is so vast and humans are so small in comparison. Nature functions perfectly and everything fits in and works harmoniously and in a complementary manner. Human beings are born into the world and must live in a way that promotes harmony with nature as well as to live in peace with each other. The individual is a small cog in the wheel when relating to the whole (universe), and the whole is the more important because it sustains life, therefore the individual is secondary. A person would relate to their environment rationally and with emotions but they have to toe the line and fit in and not disrupt the overall mechanism. Collectivism is the way of life that restricts the freedom of the individual.

The order is to start with the biggest element and work down to the smallest unit. Philosophically speaking the order may be represented as: the world; nations and national sovereignty; the wider area where you live; home town; community; family and finally self. Ordinary people's lives are mostly inter-twined with the latter three elements. The head of the house will do everything to benefit his dependants and the president would do all in their power to enrich their countrymen.

A person has to find their role in life and balance it in such a way that the harmony in the system/society is maintained. The establishment of strong relationships is a primary way to promoting peaceful co-existence and development. Individual rights have to be sacrificed for the greater good.

In China where the hometown concept or place of birth signifies identity and ownership, relocation is grossly repulsive despite compensation from the government. In the modernisation process, the government would often tear down old dwellings and replace it with new infrastructure or buildings, and the residents would have no choice but to relocate. Usually, there are no protests because of the in-grained mentality of sacrifice for the greater good. However, in the large cities where capitalism has assumed certain western traits, personal rights have become more assertive. As China continues with the policy of urbanisation, no doubt there will be more changes in the political and socio-economic arena in future years.

The eastern mind gives priority to collectivism and the western approach focusses on individualism. The western education system encourages personal expression but also promotes criticism and discussion of personal opinion as part of the learning process. One has to be prepared that others may question and challenge one's views. In China, the rote learning system was still in place at the time of writing and challenging elders and teachers was still taboo. One should not cause another to lose face, so contrary opinions have to be manoeuvred in an indirect manner. An Australian businessman operating in China told me that he made a decision one day and something went wrong. He asked the local supervisor in charge whether he saw that a problem brewing, and the answer was yes. The businessman was furious and retorted 'why didn't you tell me?' It was a cultural issue, the supervisor didn't want his boss to lose face, and he wouldn't approach him directly. He couldn't find the right words or manner to tell his boss that he had made a wrong decision. The businessman further added: 'when I see a problem, I immediately lateral out, but they don't do that here'.

Critical thinking in China was mainly confined to the first-tier universities in the early 2000's. However, modernisation and the internet have prompted students and individuals to think more broadly. The west experiences extreme personal selfishness and the east advocate group-selfishness. The form in which the eastern and western mind makes decisions is quite different. The former would make money for the broader benefit of the unit (family) and the latter would be driven mainly for selfish reasons. The western approach is guilty of driving individual selfishness to the extreme, where self-will is king. Self-will in the eastern mindset must subjugate to collectivism. In the volatile big end of business, glimpses of selfishness appear occasionally but tradition is still upheld.

I arrived in China in October 2004 and the internet had already begun to impact public opinion. At that time, Premier Wen Jiabao made a public statement that the government could no longer keep the public in the dark. The government couldn't restrict freedom of thought, and this opened the way to more government related information being released to the public. However, the public also knew that it was wise to refrain from freedom of speech because the authorities would always react to perceived threats. When Xi Jinping took over the presidency from Hu Jintao, he cleaned out corruption and there was a greater openness to information disclosure. The new approach was a form of consultative-democracy whereby representatives from all major sectors of society were invited to participate in the annual CCPC meetings to bring suggestions and input to government policy. It was a form of social democracy with Chinese characteristics, meaning that the socialist government was still the ruling authority whereby they chose the limit and manner of freedom allowed to the public.

A decade later, every student at university had a smart phone and all were connected to 'QQ' (social media) within their group because of the need to share information. Personal blogs mushroomed all over the country and personal opinion went through the roof. The government introduced tighter internet security monitoring procedures. I bumped into a neighbour in my complex and he just started talking about the weaknesses in government right outside the police sub-office at the entrance of our complex! I felt very uneasy. He did all the talking and said that this was not permitted twenty years ago and anybody caught making negative statements about the government would be thrown in prison immediately. However today, things have changed. Freedom has tremendous power when supported by the masses. However, it all starts with the individual because somebody has to invent the initial thought and promote it.

At the time of writing, the Chinese government was on the verge of introducing a social credit system for every household. Points are added for meritorious behaviour and deducted for unruly attitude. This is all made possible through 'big data' because there were about 800 million smart phone users. Smart phone technology had developed at break-neck pace and 5G was already being tested in certain areas. The points system has key implications for education, work placement and other essential social services. Big Brother was thinking ahead looking after its own interests and the mass urbanisation plans that they want to implement. Self-will makes a person accountable to God first and the government also introduce regulations to limit unsavoury actions, and social norms provide a guide to acceptable behaviour. These things show that freewill is not absolute and people have to heed their conduct as there are responsibilities attached.

In John 12:32 Jesus said that he will draw all men to himself. The significance lies in the word 'myself' because the Christian faith is founded on a personal relationship with Jesus. Believers who have taken the time and developed a genuine bonding with Christ will never leave him. Jesus responds by working through the intimate things in life that the believer knows can only come from God because Jesus gives that inimitable sensation. This is a personal thing that the Spirit does when a believer deepens their trust in him. The bonding process is perpetual because getting to know Jesus is a lifetime endeavour. Instead of self-satisfaction, self must yield to the Holy Spirit.

Christians in the west must comprehend how their thinking has been influenced by their background. The matter of self-will has decisive connotations on matters of faith. Self is not king and it can do grievous harm to a person's spirit.

Part 2.

Religion and culture are intertwined. The children are taught by their parents and peers how to behave in society. They learn very quickly to adhere to societal etiquette. Everybody does the same things so everybody lives in agreement and conformity. If something is out of place or inconsistent with the norm, people take notice and start asking questions. Thus, everybody knows not to rock the boat because this can bring embarrassment and shame to self and one's family. With the passage of time, behaviour becomes a habit and a neighbourhood watch enters the system seamlessly. The mature section of society usually assumes a police function that would enforce conformity. This gives them an unlegislated authority to deal with situations according to their customs and traditions. Mob rule is extremely powerful and frightening and it can be stirred up in an instant.

Children are conditioned from a very young age to follow the customs. They know no other and this is what they take into adulthood. There is no option. Customary religious forms become the norm. The group identity encourages the notion of religious birthright of which Islam is the leading protagonist. However, there are other cultures where the family members are allowed to choose their religion. Cultural and religious constraints are hard to unshackle because freewill has been denied or quashed.

However, in a society that is based on human rights and individual freedom, the individual is empowered to make their own decisions in life. The most unusual things may be done (provided that it's within the law) and nobody has the right to impose upon that person. People are encouraged to seek and find out what they want in life and to do it. This is the spirit of freewill.

Human rights are an inalienable right for every human being living on earth. It makes a lot of sense if you have been brought up under western values. If a society suppresses this vital part of human thought, how then are they expected to accept change or consider other religions or philosophy? Even under oppressive regimes, citizens have some form of civil rights otherwise anarchy will prevail. The restriction on their actions is mainly because they haven't been given other choices.

Western thought fosters exploratory thought in all things that do not transgress the laws, morals and social criteria. It is founded on the principle that a just society allows its citizens to think and assess matters independently. You have the choice to believe what you want. Freedom of religion is a fundamental right of every citizen in the western society.

The attractiveness of western values is that it affords access to information that a person needs to know about any religion that they may choose or not to have a religion at all. A person may change their mind at any time and nobody blinks an eyelid. This is the ideal state of human existence. God gave Adam freedom to exercise his mind and to choose what he wanted. It was an unrestrained endowment with the power to even go against God. Alas, Adam exercised his right incorrectly, and it put all of humanity in his position as independent thinking and free acting people on the wrong side of God. The mind has the capability of thinking and contriving anything it wants. Christian society is tolerant in that harmonious co-habitation is promoted and respected. Everybody has the right to choose what they wish to believe. Some merely believe in themselves.

In God's system, culture is unimportant and a faithful relationship is the only thing that matters to him and it is vital for people in this life. The Christian faith is not an inherent element acquired at birth; nobody is born a Christian. It is a voluntary personal commitment to Jesus Christ by an assenting mind and spirit. There is absolutely no need to alter the culture when cross-cultural ethnic people come into relationship with Christ unless that culture opposes Biblical precepts.

However, religious undertones may be embedded in the local culture and Christians have to be aware of this danger because syncretism is harmful to constructing a positive relationship with Jesus.

Western culture is based on Biblical principles but the evidence is found in the Christian actually living out their faith in Christ. This means that a person can inter-migrate to any culture and still maintain a faithful relationship with Jesus Christ. Your strength is grounded on a personal relationship with Jesus and not on your environment or the target culture that you are entering. Christian culture is based on all the commands for godly living from Scripture. We practice them regularly and it becomes enmeshed in our lifestyle. The outside world can see who we are from our conduct. Most religions have a similar transferability feature.

In the secular context, via calculations, physical evidence, logic, experimentation and verification, one is able to prove theories. In this way, people accept proven systems and normative principles. However, in the realm of religion you can't physically prove anything. You can show people the logic in the Bible and why Jesus is the way to heaven, but if they don't want to accept it then nothing that you say or do would be sufficient proof for them. Christianity is not founded on proof but on faith, and stubborn people that refuse to exercise faith will remain in their unbelief.

Enslavement by culture, habits and religion is a fact of life. Where people do not adopt Biblical principles, society will keep the people captive to the ways of tradition. Group behaviour enforces compliance through the watchdog mentality. Everything is carried out in a straitjacket manner through works and ritual. Ingrained habits make them insensitive to the Word of God. No amount of reasoning or Scripture references can soften their hearts or make them consider. Hardliners restrain those who show an interest in something new. They elevate loyalty and distinction; this is us and this is what we do that defines our identity.

Christianity is about the kingdom of God and we can't take a human approach to it because we come under God's rules. The foremost objective is to maintain close relationship with Jesus. The next task is to bring self under control, and then to renovate our character to conform to Jesus' requirements. Proper self-control can make the right things happen. The spiritual remake is one where God makes you into what you truly ought to be; after his own image and identity.

Chapter 9
Pre-emptive favour

The elect is chosen by God to become adopted children of God before the creation week even started. The love of God predestined these privileged people to become sons and daughters of the Father through Jesus Christ (Ephesians 1:5, Romans 8:29). It presupposes that the elect will choose Christ as saviour after they are introduced to him. The Lord knew the elect in a personal way before creation. Furthermore, he was sure that they would choose Christ and commit their lives to him. Who is able to make such a bold statement knowing that freewill can be unpredictable as the best of times? The level of confidence must be perfect and the source of intelligence must be faultless. This is no empty claim because the spirit world is watching even though humans have no means of verification. If this tenet is false in any manner, the Creator will be accused of an untruth. The countless witnesses in the spirit world to God's Word and actions have no case against him whatsoever. There is absolutely no need for humans to seek proof of God in any way. All prophecy both past and future are being monitored very closely by all the good and evil spirits alike.

How does predestination fit in with the freewill of humankind? God can't change the past therefore he has to work with foreknowledge and predestination. Humans can debate, surmise, theorise, synthesise and imagine all sorts of things but eventually some action must be taken. Freewill is a personal initiative. Nobody knows how each person is going to decide until the decision is actually made. However, freewill is not a knee-jerk reaction and is directed by instinct as well as inherent values. God is an orderly being and is never caught by surprise even though some people may have that fanciful imagination. God has foreknowledge and knows what the final decision that each and every person alive on earth will make, so he is able to foretell with full accuracy what the future will be. No matter how complex or how many options are available to a person, the final choice is known to God before it is even made.

In some of the writings on predestination, the authors have tended to isolate the topic and ignore the pertinent attributes of God. They comment on the subject without reference to the overall sovereignty of God's foreknowledge and many serious anomalies arise. In attempting to understand God, it is a gross error to apply this kind of straightjacket thought process to a Being whose character and attributes rise way above human understanding. The general conclusion is that predestination and freewill are at odds and incompatible. If freewill is supreme, then God does not have foreknowledge and he has to follow billions of people very closely every second of the day to see what they have decided. This portrays God as dependent on the behaviour of humans and he cannot claim to be sovereign above all creation i.e. human action dictate how God reacts. This gives humans a certain degree of leverage over the Lord's reactions. The Bible says that people are puny beings under God's might (Psalm 8:4, Isaiah 40:6-7). Self-will encourages a person to think otherwise.

How can a loving God be as uncaring as to judge people to eternal damnation? How can he forgive some and then destroy others? How can he be sensitive to his followers and also allow them to go through suffering? If we read these anomalies in isolation then we end up with a capricious god. There are valid reasons for everything that God does because he is an orderly being. In order to make sense of it all, we must analyse the reasons for each apparent irregularity and understand why the Lord behaves in that way. A reasonable conclusion cannot be reached without careful study. In most cases, you would have to consider one or more attributes of God that are inter-related in order to make sense of it. The same analogy applies to the freewill versus predestination debate.

The greatest challenge in my spiritual walk was to take up the calling to go to the mission field. I was fully aware of all the implications and it was either going to be Jesus or me. When you are faced with this sort of thing, you don't forget it easily. The trivial alternatives were not hard to decide on but big ones always carried a substantial cost.

I knew without a doubt that once I made a choice for Jesus, the alternative will be lost i.e. a great job that I enjoyed very much. It was a dream-job unlike anything I ever had before. It will be gone for good because the time and opportunity cannot be re-called. I made the choice to quit and I had to live with it. The cost in terms of earnings, security, ambition and comfort plagued me for days on end. I went to Bible College and that took my attention away from this dilemma. I have no doubt that the Lord knew every move that I would make before the event.

According to predestination, God knew before I was even born what choice I would make at that specific moment and there was no need to 'fix any circumstances' to manipulate me into doing anything. It was simple, he led and I followed by making the decisions that he led me to. When I look back at each step that I had taken, the ensuing circumstances tell me that I had made the right choices. It's easy to read a lot of words about what someone else has written but the uncertainty, anxiety and loss of control was very real to me during those two years of Bible study. My academic achievements, career and the values that I had held all my life were uprooted. What God was calling me to do was diametrically opposed to all that I stood for in the secular world. Yet, God never for one moment forced me into doing anything. I could have walked away from it all and gone back to work and continued with my previous lifestyle. I had worked all my life since leaving high school and the first month or two at college was a most unfamiliar feeling. I used to pause from time to time and think about what I would have been doing at work because the motions were still very fresh in my subconscious mind. Nevertheless, I persisted and finished my course and left for the field.

Predestination does not mean that God is essentially responsible for who is saved. Rather, it shows that God's foreknowledge enables him to select those believers because he knows who will choose Jesus. Salvation is open to all, but it is only those who have faith and repent of their sins that will seek after Jesus. When the gospel is preached, it is up to the individual to make their own decision for Christ. God has to draw the person to Jesus, not the evangelist whose job is merely to declare the Good News. God must draw that person, but at the crucial moment, the individual must exercise self-will to accept Jesus as Lord and saviour. God knows each person's heart and all the elect who will be saved.

Double predestination suggests that God has a list of all those he wants to save and another roll of all those that will be condemned. In theory this makes him responsible for both. However, the process of predestination is an ordered one and not a random list of the elect. We only have certainty after the event has taken place. God makes a predetermined list (because he is omniscient) of those that he allows into heaven, but that list is determined by the individual themselves. God does not manipulate the individual's actions so that he decides exactly who has faith and who doesn't. The Lord draws a person near through faith. The heart that is pliant and responsive will grab at the encouragement (faith) that Jesus has to offer but the stubborn hearts won't. Impartiality and fair-play gives predestination credibility from both the divine and human perspective. No person may lay claim to the notion that God forced them to believe or disbelieve. They alone had to make the crucial decisions. The Lord will never manipulate a person's freewill. Self-will determines who goes on the predestination list and who doesn't and God knows this beforehand. The decision-maker decides their own fate and God does not interfere.

Foreknowledge.

Predestination works because of foreknowledge. God knows the beginning and the end of everything and he can make an exact judgement before creation because the outcomes are already clear to him. God cannot change the past which is reserved for judgment. The past is a result of human freewill and so humans will be judged according to their works. The only way for the Lord to get his kingdom work done (by humans) exactly according to his plan is to know what will happen in the future. He knows what everybody is going to do and is able to choose the right people to complete those particular tasks.

The following passages allude to God's unrestrained and perfect view of all future occurrences: Romans 8:29, Acts 2:23, I Peter 1:2 and John 6:64. It's utterly erroneous to even think that human freewill can outsmart God. Yet this is what some of the writings appear to suggest. Obedience is the critical issue for each of the elect and not so much individual skills because the Spirit will equip. God knows each of us intimately and how we will choose, so his plan can never go wrong. It's a foregone conclusion.

Fatalism.

Fatalism often carries negative connotations because we tend to think of it in terms of chance, surprise, uncontrollable events, fortune, horoscope and other fortuitous occurrences. Certain religions advocate fatalism because they have no rational explanation for such events. People just accept it as a matter of reality when such events occur and they call it fate. Buddhism and Islam have this concept embedded in their practices. Things just happen and there's no logical or systematic reasoning for it.

The Bible does not support fatalism because God is omniscient and omnipresent so he knows all that is happening in the world. He is a

God of order and design. There's no uncertainty with him, although people do not understand the situation at the time. The Lord is fully in control and he will guide Christians to do the right things to complete his kingdom work. Specifically, his kingdom plan will be accomplished at the right time and place and no accidental or unforeseen event will derail the process. When disaster occurs, we know that God is aware of our plight and we trust him to help us get through it. Suffering is a time to draw near to Jesus and learn the valuable spiritual lessons that are associated with it.

James 4:13-14 tells us that freewill leads to strife because it is selfish and does not take God's directions for us into account. People may die before they even get to finish what they have planned. James is referring to boasting about personal ambition. Self-determination is antagonistic towards God and cannot exist in a fruitful relationship with him. God's will is paramount yet he allows people to pursue their desires. Whatever happens whether good or bad may be a mystery to us but the Lord sees it clearly. We follow the leads that he lays before us and all will be made clear as time goes by. There is no need to refer to fatalism as there is a reason for everything, and we will find out when we get to heaven. Faith in the face of uncertainty is a great honour to God. If you can't trust your Father, then who can you trust?

The Lord demonstrated in King Nebuchadnezzar that he is in control of all the kingdoms of the world. The latter reigned between 620BC to 539BC and he was the most powerful and longest reigning king in the Neo-Babylonian empire. The events in Daniel 4:33-37 tells that God can interfere with the highest authority on earth at any time that he desires. Nebuchadnezzar was punished because of his sin (verse 27). He had freewill and complete power on earth to do anything that he pleased. However, all earthly authority exits by the will of God (Romans 13:1-2) and freewill is limited by God's will (James 4:15).

Human beings will never learn from history and will make the same mistakes as Nebuchadnezzar. Fortunately, he repented and his kingdom was restored to him and he became even greater. He specifically said that human will is futile against the power of God who is able to humiliate the proud at will. He praised, exalted and glorified God because he is righteous and just (verse 37). There's a real possibility that we will see Nebuchadnezzar in heaven but I wonder what kind of reward he will receive?

Christians can learn from every good and bad thing in life. The good induces us to praise and worship God and the bad occurrences aid understanding by helping us to discover God's purpose and guidance in misfortune. The best gain is when you impregnate in your mind and soul with constant spirit-prayers to God. There is no greater form of persuasion than when God meets you under personal circumstances of deep uncertainty and desperation. The spiritual enlightenment from him makes a person want more, and for him to keep on delivering such insights forever.

In a confounding situation where emotions may lead to panic due to utter helplessness, it's best to attribute that event to the will of God. Nothing can be done about it and all you can do is watch and wait. This is not fatalism but faith. With God there is no such thing as fatalism because he will show us a way out. The outworking may not be the way that we want it, but we have to accept and work with what has transpired. It's a win-win scenario all the way as he has supreme authority. Even though there may be no tangible gain on earth, you can be sure of the reward that is waiting in heaven for your faithfulness.

Prophesy.

We are in the last days and it's only the final parts of prophesy in Revelation, the Minor Prophets and Daniel that await the world. Satan had countless opportunities to discredit God after the fall. As prophesy materialised his chances diminished substantially and now he can only do as much damage as he can in the last days. The evil one had thousands of years to prove God wrong but he couldn't make things go against the Word of God. All prophesy in the Bible about the Christ gave Satan insight, knowledge and opportunity to devise his schemes. Yet, the Prince of the World in all his power and craftiness was powerless to stop God from doing what he said. The Lord's sovereignty is indisputable. The greatest joy would be when we meet Jesus face-to-face and he takes us to our heavenly home. Satan cannot change God's promises and this means that he cannot alter predestination (John 10:28-29) and human self-will is equally impotent. If Satan can do nothing to defame predestination, then self-will is likewise incredulous because the evil one is far more potent than any human being.

The freewill versus predestination debate is certainly thought provoking. It has no practical spiritual value and it does not promote a person's standing with the Lord. Human philosophy gives much head knowledge but only God gives beneficial spiritual increment. Wise theories can easily become a form of idolatry. Humans are capable of producing admirable works; but only the Holy Spirit can deliver spiritual fruit that endures.

Other aspects of human nature.

God is perfect: His omniscience, omnipresence and immutability put predestination and foreknowledge above human intelligence. Granted that there are many things that we don't have answers to because we don't have complete knowledge. This raises uncertainty and doubt and the unsanctified mind would immediately choose to trust in personal experience and visible evidence. Freewill will come to the fore, but without divine guidance even the most sensibly schemed course of action is susceptible to error. It is erroneous to place predestination on the same level as freewill. There is nothing that people can do to refute or discredit God's pre-emptive favour.

From Adam's time to Noah's descendants, there was just one people group in the world and all the people just knew the one true Creator/God. The fact that people were not satisfied with the Lord as their God tells of the potency of free-thinking. At that time, the world was confined to the Middle-East region. The people wanted to band together and unite their strength and talents. It was a blatant demonstration of freewill and self-gratification. They were aiming for self-reliance instead of dependence on God. It was the beginning of a revolution; rebellion against God's supremacy and leadership. This group wasn't satisfied to be led, but they wanted to become leaders that were free of God's authority and judgment. Unbelievers who hold self in high regard would have the tendency to challenge God's supremacy. Believers would not normally confront God directly, but they will do it indirectly through selfishness.

After Babel, the ethnic groups migrated to the other parts of the entire globe. In this respect, the Lord allocated territories for each group and timed it so that each group grew to own and dominate their territory. Within the safety of their own borders, the nations developed their particular culture and customs. Each nation knew exactly where they lived and the extent of their authority. On a micro-level, individuals were also allocated (by the Lord) to the exact places where they should live. Christians believe that God is in control and he leads each person to the exact place where they should live, minister and to build relationship with him (Acts 17:26-27). The account of Babel in Genesis 11:4 states that the people wanted fame and strength in numbers. Unity gave them tremendous power.

However, the Acts passage says that this separation was done for people to search for God. This appears to be ironic because only Israel had the full revelation of the true God that was on-going until the New Testament was compiled. The scattered peoples were left with a notion of the true God and no further revelation. This void led them to develop their own ideas of god and worship. Over the millennia, the dispersed people become entrench in their customs and beliefs, and it's very difficult to get them to accept a foreign religion. All they know is what has been handed down from generation to generation which they believe is true. It seems unfair but that's history. Babel didn't offer the people a lifeline to stay in touch with the Creator but had the opposite effect of aiding them to drift away from God. It's a logical progression because the people of Babel had already rejected the Lord and exercised their freewill to self-determination. God respected their freedom and it just became harder for them to find God, even today. Nonetheless, they still have the duty to seek after the God of their ancestors. They can start by comparing what they have with the Bible. Missionaries have encountered isolated tribes that have believed merely upon hearing the gospel. Yet, there are many that won't submit because they carry the hardness of their forefathers from the time of Babel.

The negative effect of Babel was compensated by Jesus Christ who opened the kingdom of God to all peoples of the world through faith in him. God is close to each person and it behoves us to seek after him first before he will meet our needs. Those who hear the gospel have the opportunity to find God through Jesus. However, the human psyche doesn't change and after thousands of years many peoples' hearts are still as hard as it was then. When people make decisions without reference to God, they become self-reliant and inter-dependent on other people or things. Everything is focussed on the material and it's very difficult to exercise faith in God because it's outside of their frame of reference. God loves all humankind regardless of their place of birth, but peoples' customs and beliefs have caused a self-made gap between them and God. When freewill goes bad, it really goes bad and the fault lies solely with that person. I have witnessed to people in cross-cultural ministry and most acknowledge the gospel message, but they just won't let go of their tradition and belief.

There was a young Muslim university student who had developed a strong friendship with four different missionaries. He was the target of their efforts because of his ethnicity. They prayed with and for him (and for his family's needs), gave him a contextualised Bible, explained Scripture to him readily, gave him much needed financial assistance, kept in touch regularly even while he was studying abroad, and after five years he had still not budged from his religious background. They said that he was very close, and all they could do was just to press on. Islam is a community practice and a person is born a Muslim. Potential converts to Christ always fear excommunication from their family and their society. Tradition and customs are formidable deterrents that keep people captive. On the other hand, I know of other Muslim students that have chosen to be authentic followers of Jesus Christ, contextualised their faith and never gone back to Islam. They are the privileged elect. People who have been in the business long enough develop a gut-feel for the industry. They may sometimes make decisions that are not the most rational to the untrained eye, but it's the 'logic of the trade'. If you don't have the related intuition, then you will never make the same decision as they do.

The freedom to choose can be a very complex issue but we have sufficient information in the Bible to do the right thing. God exists in the metaphysical realm and is able to circumvent all the uncertainty and unknowns to see exactly what the decision-maker will finally do as well as the related result. It's an unassailable position because God is omniscient. The reality that the Lord is fully aware of everything in the spiritual dimension and on earth, and humans cannot access anything in the metaphysical tells of the human limitation. The futility that freewill can challenge the supernatural raises serious doubts even for the most open-minded reasoning.

Chapter 10
You did not choose me

It seems illogical that humans have been given freewill; the ability to choose or reject God or do anything at will. We know that the Father has prepared us to enter and work in his kingdom before creation took place. The only way this can be possible is if God has precise knowledge of each and every person who has ever walked this earth. He must know our character, mindset, emotions, and values intimately in order to predict with accuracy what actions we will take in any given situation. The bottom line is that he can confidently trust us to fulfil a specific niche in His kingdom when called to do so (John 15:16).

Since appointment or membership into his work did not originate from our initiative, we must treat freewill very cautiously in relation to God. It's an astounding thing that God knows us thoroughly and is able to entrust us with things that he needs done. He can take the useful part in us and remake so that it fits the job exactly; all the while we know that we have freewill to accept or reject the path he has allocated to us. It may seem like very high risk but risk only exists in uncertainty. Randomness never forms part of kingdom work because God has order and complete knowledge.

Although we are conscious of the warnings in Scripture of the entrapment of pride, it is inbred in human nature to want to do things that others would notice and applaud. Most Christian workers are able to keep it in check. However, the moment when other people are present, be they co-workers, associates or other, the opportunity for pride to emerge is very real. It may enter in a subtle manner and then run out of control if left unsupervised. The odd thing is that people are always conscious to avoid going down this road, yet it still happens. In most cases, it's the people who look up to you that fuel the drive to egotism. Conversely, when you are working alone, there is no reason or cause for pride yet it's always there. If your objective is to prove something to others or to show that you are right, then the spectre of self-elevation will always be following you around.

The secular expression 'take pride in you work' encourages people to take possession of their assignment and to make it a personal matter that they can boast about. It's an occasion to show-off one's flair, intelligence, creativity and skill. This is me, I did it and I take full credit for it. This is useful when seeking promotion or trying to impress the boss. The secular system rewards talented workers and pride becomes attached to that work. This is more so if there is an added reward and recognition system in place to motivate staff. Some people guard their space jealously and intruders are not welcome. It's all motivated by self-will and self-interest. The better approach is to maintain responsibility and fulfil your duties and it will dampen the urge to project self because that is not the objective.

When doing kingdom work, it must be borne in mind that this work does not belong to you and you have no ownership of the result. The worker is merely a steward who is looking after God's interests. God is the inspector and he has to be satisfied that the task has been performed according to his wishes. Hence, there is no cause for vaunting one's ability. The worker must exercise due care and do the work accurately to the best of their ability. There is no personal possession because the kingdom belongs to the Lord and workers only receive a reward in heaven for their role. One cannot put a personal mark on the work done and there is no promotion system in kingdom work. Only God can be proud of his own design and formation of his kingdom. Christians in ministry have to be very careful to keep a tight rein on their secular habits in kingdom matters. God expects the work to be done appropriately and that's the limit of one's involvement. It is inappropriate to take some of the glory that belongs solely to God. Therefore, new work cannot originate from personal creativity and everything must be committed to prayer for guidance.

Generally, God's work does not require a great deal of intelligence. It's usually mundane service that is connected to people relationship. There is no need for self-motivation but patience and persistence are required to finish the job. It may be tempting to break away from the routine and introduce some personal ideas but this is encroaching on sovereign territory. One has to examine one's motives and be prayerful to see how the Lord directs.

Freewill not only elevates self, but also dulls the spirit to what is eternally precious. You have to get your mind and attitude in line with God. I have found this to be a huge hurdle to get over and only after that was I willing to submit. This was a major turnaround and I placed self-interest last. I was very pleased with my genuine revised attitude and was earnestly seeking the Lord's will. After many hours of prayer and patient waiting, I was expecting some announcement from the Lord. Months and years passed and there was still no answer. All the time, I was wondering why the silence. During those times, the influences all around me provided great impetus to get ahead; to keep up with the Jones's; to make my mark in life. I knew very well what was at stake and a close friend even asked me whether this was what I really wanted to do. Time was ticking away and I managed to keep the materialism instinct at bay. It was no easy task I might add because my subconscious mind kept reminding me of the loss of earnings.

In hindsight, there was nothing wrong and God just wanted me to wait. When you have to wait several years for a response, it truly tests your freewill. I just kept doing what was right albeit monotonous and uneventful. Silence can be deafening to a soul desperately seeking answers. On the other hand, it is also spiritually fulfilling to learn patience before the Lord. Silence cleanses the mind from external noise and settles the spirit as one focusses attention on Christ. Eventually when the door opened I knew beyond doubt that my self-will was beaten and God was in charge. There were still a few bits that needed attention but that was quickly brought in line. Some friends have asked me how I knew that what I was doing was in the Lord's will. I had five points that I wanted confirmation on and all were met. There was no doubt and I went ahead as the way unfolded into the mission field.

Chapter 11
A perspective of freewill

"The greatest power that a person possesses is the power to choose."
- J. Martin Kohe

The ability to choose gives meaning to life. A person has self-esteem, value and identity when given a right to choose. In government polls, meetings, opinion polls and the like, the voter has a certain degree of persuasion. This is freewill, the unrestrained ability to make a decision based on personal values. We make decisions on everything that we have to do for the day. Most of the choices are constrained by circumstance, but we still have a choice.

Choices are made with a specific goal in mind. The brain draws on background information and works out the reasons before making a decision. Each person has a set of values that determines the desired standard that a decision seeks to achieve in the outcome. When freewill is exercised, a person satisfies a need or desire. Freewill carries ownership of a decision that the decision-maker has to live with. On the human level, an outcome can never be known with precision until the actual decision is made and the results clearly displayed. Uncertainty prevails over the entire human race as the multiplicity of decisions is taken every second of the day. It's mindboggling for a human being to follow but very clear to God.

Some writers incorporate the ideas of uncertainty, determinism, causality (randomness), coercion, predictability and non-controllable factors in their thesis on freewill. It makes for interesting reading, but they tend to lose themselves in the complexity. The Bible does not present God as a puppeteer that makes people do certain things. Writers have linked freewill with predestination and proposed that God has already determined who will go to heaven and therefore, freewill is not really free and we have no responsibility for our actions. It can get quite confusing and they always leave out other related parts of Scripture that have a bearing on the subject. Getting into a quagmire like that does no good. Ultimately, we are all going to meet God and fine sounding theories will have no support or credibility. The only sure way be right with God is to apply what is written in the Bible. It sounds boring so people like to theorise. There will be a judgment and it's your neck on the line.

In the worldly sense, freewill is a precious possession. It's an expression of the inner self and it nurtures self-identity. This gives people control over their own lives and the direction that they want to pursue in life. Notably, high profile businessmen like to leave their mark in history. When people die, they like to be remembered for what they have done on earth. Subsequent generations will notice their achievements and remember their name. The idea of their name written in the history books and living forever (so to speak) is appealing to these people. Of course, it is only confined to this life on earth. The urge to make an impression is driven by self-esteem. Self-importance means everything to them. They forget (purposefully or unwittingly) that they have a personal appointment with God at the end of their days on earth.

Freewill was given to Adam and Eve and all humans have the same prerogative. Judgment was imposed on them for their defective choices, and the same analogy goes for the human race. It's imperative to stay on the right side the Lord. People have a responsibility to seek after and follow God's decrees as a matter of duty (1 Corinthians 7:24), and things have to be done according to his criteria. We have to please God and we can't apply our own standards in life. Personal opinion is not allowed to interfere with God's requirements. This straight-jacket approach is claustrophobic for the unbeliever. As for the one who loves Jesus, it is a privilege and a pleasure.

Each person will be called to account for their actions (Matthew 12:36, Romans 3:19, 14:12). Believers will be judged for the validity of their actions and the net result will be reward or loss. Unbelievers will face Judgment Day and there will just be condemnation. Complicated theories concocted by renowned thinkers have no credit in God's sight. There is no reason to be spending time and effort on things that don't matter. The rules are simple and every human being has the ability to follow them. People that are under some restriction will be dealt with fairly and considerately because the Lord is impartial. There will be no excuse or valid reason that anybody may be able to raise in their defence. It's either wrong or right, and self is accountable. On that day, every person will be stripped of all their pride and self-esteem and they will bow to the Lord. Getting things right on earth will save untold embarrassment.

Self is only important on earth and this relates to the material world and the physical body. The praise of men is the aim of many who love pride. Self will be a nobody on that day. The remedy is here on earth and is available to all right now. It starts with trust in Jesus Christ, and obedience to follow the precepts in the Bible, then the Holy Spirit will lead a person to glory. It's better to admit one's error now and be able to initiate corrective measures than wait until it's too late. Freewill is not free and it must be submitted to God. If not, it indicates that the love for self is ranked before the love for God. Freewill affords apparent power to self, but not superiority over the Lord.

The quote by J. Martin Kohe suggests that the greatest power is the freedom to choose. This ought to be read in context as it only applies to the secular world. God gives no choice but himself and self-will has no persuasion over him. Self-determination is subject to a higher authority and the boundaries within which humans are limited to. In daily life, choice is merely routine and carries no significant influence over another person bar family responsibilities. Adolescents that transition to adulthood have to live their own lives and follow their own personal ambitions. It's a soft power that pertains to that person only. Civil and human rights give a person self-esteem and unleashes the latent potential within. Regardless of how any person chooses, it has no control over the Divine.

Freewill is quite simple and should be kept that way. The devil has a way of raising doubt and introducing complexity where there's no need. The Bible puts our responsibilities down very simply. It is self that wills to go off the rails and to delve into areas that the Bible doesn't approve of. Self-deification creates its own brand of theology and creates ideas that elevate theory to the same authority as Scripture. Freedom of expression may hold good for people, but not for God. Freewill is a remarkable honour and it can either result in a grave loss or gracious reward. It must be exercised correctly. If you (like me) care about your spirit, you must rethink how freewill is shaping your life right now. Don't leave it too late because even the abundant grace of God has a limit.

It is inaccurate for a regenerated Christian to have freewill because this is a worldly expression. The Christian-will should not be independent because self operates in submission to Christ and plays a secondary role.

Chapter 12
What is the purpose of freewill?

The secular purpose of freewill is to please yourself. Generally, a person has the freedom to act to fulfil their desires and to maximise self-gratification. Frank Sinatra's song 'My Way' was very popular in the early 1970's. It was a bold expression of personal freedom to live according to your own desires. It made the public think about self-determination. At Bruce Lee's funeral this song was his signature theme. He had lived a short but self-directed way of life. When celebrities say or do something, the public will take more notice. From time to time, we come across things that we know little about, so we seek knowledge from the available sources. After some thought, we make a decision and assume responsibility for the outcome. This is a common daily occurrence. Sometimes, we are forced to make a decision on the spur of the moment without adequate time to think, and afterwards we realise that we have made a mistake. Everybody at some stage of life had admitted to self or others that 'I made a mistake'. We learn from our errors and as long as the good decisions outweigh the bad, we can reconcile our actions and find a balance. The aim is always towards self-betterment in wealth, education, business, relationships etc. Freewill in the worldly sense is mostly selfishly skewed. There are exceptions where certain people really care for the welfare of others. These people are mainly involved in social programs that pay very little or nothing at all and it's a labour of love.

The freedom of expression is a basic happiness driver. People choose a lifestyle within their means that delivers maximum fulfilment. Finance is the yardstick that determines the choices that are available and those caught in the poverty trap have limited choice to maximise their happiness. Westerners that visit a third world village often find that the people there are happy despite their simple lifestyle. They are free from all the problems and complexities that a wealthy society creates. Nobody interferes with their lifestyle and they are free to follow their own customs. Generally, residents in the slums and lowest levels of society in the big cities all over the world face a desperate plight to escape destitution. Financial freedom is their main ambition, but they can't get out of the poverty trap due to lack of education, opportunity, financial assistance or inherent circumstances. They make do with what they have, but their limited freedom will always leave a void in their happiness aspirations.

Western lifestyle enhances personal freedoms. In other parts of the world, freewill may be restricted and some severely. One such example is the caste system that exists (existed) in various forms in India, Africa, Korean, Latin America, Yemeni, Japan, Sri Lanka, Nepal, Pakistani, and Bangladesh. Most countries have outlawed this culture. On 15th August, 1947, the Indian government abolished the caste system and declared such practices as legal offences. However, this law is difficult to police as discrimination may be disguised and enforced under some other pretext.

Birth categorizes a person into a particular societal class. It is an immovable heritage that is practiced in those societies. This determines a person's social standing and their line of work. It particularly impacts the underprivileged and the disadvantaged because they don't have the means to do otherwise. Those that have had the good fortune to own a business and accumulated wealth have more choice, but they will still not gain the full acceptance of the upper castes. The law does not control the public's psychology, prejudices and habits. This legacy can only be reformed through a positive change in worldview of the entire population.

Deprivation of human rights means less choice in life and this infringes on people's ability to exercise freewill i.e. they have the freedom to do certain things but not the resources. They cannot indulge in normal thinking and are forced to live under severe restriction. The affected group has no alternative but to accept their lot in life. Hinduism dictates that the lower caste groups have to strive for virtue in the current life in order to move to a higher station when reincarnated.

While the caste system has been illegalised in most countries, there is a group that is below the caste system, called 'untouchables'. This is an 'outcaste' group called the *Dalits* in India, *Burakumin* in Japan, and *Baekjeong* in Korea. They are still the most discriminated against and continue to be unfairly prejudiced. Despite laws to the contrary, untouchables remain the most dispossessed peoples in society in which the caste system is still enforced at the social level. The lack of opportunity stunts the exercise of freewill and that leads to unhappiness. Freewill is eroded where a person's lifestyle is determined by the actions and whims of another. This is a human devised cultural problem that is abhorrent and unthinkable in the western countries. Where freewill is severely restricted, there is no joy of personal gratification. However, God who is impartial will judge fairly and take into account their disadvantages.

The spiritual purpose is to replace self-will with God's will. It means to become a slave to Jesus Christ. Since Jesus knows what's best for each one of us, there's no need for self-direction. The aim of freewill is transformation into a conditioned instrument for God's purposes. Freedom from sin allows us to direct and channel our freewill to submit to the Holy Spirit and to live for God. This is when freewill undergoes a metamorphosis from self-centredness to Christocentric. On the one hand, the ability to reject God is still present but the desire to humble oneself and elevate God invalidates it completely. The progressive believer knows that there's no going back. The once indomitable drive for self-determination takes a back-seat, and the urge to know the will of God becomes overpowering. Freewill actually becomes un-free. Once we become un-free, the Holy Spirit can freely do something in us. Freewill is no longer a correct term because a new partnership comes into being where the Father is the sole manager. Freewill becomes surrendered and controlled by the Lord's will and it replaces the old order. The will is no longer free and it voluntarily changes to dependent-will.

Adam applied his freewill incorrectly by choosing to sin, whereas the correct usage of freewill is to apply it in holiness. This was the case before the fall, and Adam used his freedom to do everything righteously in the garden. God intended it this way and Adam only had dependent-will under God's guidance. Freewill has the propensity towards selfishness and is strongly advocated by those whose main focus is self-benefit. Selfishness is not always spurred on by wealth, it may also be driven by pride, recognition, status, fame, egotism etc. The regenerated have a secondary will that is not free but dependent on the Spirit. This is the reason that we have to pray constantly because we rely on the Lord for everything.

The purpose of dependent-will is to draw near to Jesus and maintain a close fellowship with the Spirit. Scripture gives guidance on how to do this. We are called to be holy in our walk with Christ (1 Corinthians 1:2). The Lord desires us to be sanctified so that we may avoid sin (1 Thessalonians 4:3). The Spirit sanctifies us so that we may learn to be obedient to Christ (1 Peter 1:2). God works in us to will and to do his good purpose (Philippians 2:13). Jesus equips us and works in us to do the Father's will that is gratifying to him (Hebrews 13:21). A point must be established where a change of mien must occur to rid self of worldly passions and to live the rest of one's earthly life under God's will (1 Peter 4:2), verse 6 exhorts believers to live according to God in our spirit. The body in respect of the old life is dead and the spirit must now lead the way forward in righteousness. Jesus considered self-will as worthless and only came to do his Father's will (John 6:38). The renewing of the mind transforms a person from worldly habits to holiness and this enables a person to conform to God's will that is perfect and a joy to him, and to us (Romans 12:2). We have to be very careful how we go about life and every opportunity must be maximised. Decisions must be made wisely and not foolishly. It's imperative to understand the Lord's will and to maintain close contact with the Holy Spirit who will give you the most that he has to offer (Ephesians 5:17). Work to increase personal sanctification in the truth as God imparts it to you. Then you can go into the world as an ambassador for Christ to reflect his righteousness (John 17:17-19).

These are multiple sub-tasks that all go to form a coordinated whole to serve the Lord's purposes. The outworking of dependent-will may be summarised into the following sub-processes: do away with sin or reduce it to the barest minimum; renew your mind from materialism to sanctification; learn and practice obedience; be equipped by the Spirit to execute the Lord's will; exercise due care in daily life and make the most of every opportunity; be spiritually wise and discerning; in essence, relate to God through your spirit; build a close relationship with the Spirit and take in all that he supplies; nurture and increase sanctification through the truth; and live the rest of your life under God's will as disciples of Christ in holiness. Reform is not a one-off process but perpetual remodelling one's spirit after God until you get it all.

The aim of dependent-will is illustrated in the words of Jesus found in John 14:31 that he loves his Father and does exactly what his Father commands. Similarly, in John 5:19 where Jesus does nothing on his own, and he only does what the Father is doing. The Father loves the Son and will show him all that he does. This is the benchmark for all believers especially those earnest followers who want the agape that Jesus demonstrated. It takes enormous effort to get close enough to our Father to understand his will and to hear (assent) his commands. Then, self-will must be suppressed so that you do only what the Father instructs. The possibility of getting to this stage may appear out of reach, but it is no excuse to stop trying.

The worldly understanding of freewill encompasses an elevation of self and a devaluation of the lofty concept of humility. Freewill makes you feel exalted to be on par with God and you forget completely that you are in truth a humble sinner before a Holy God. Humility in spirit is an essential requirement if we really want to become more like Christ. Humbleness entails reliance on the Spirit and dependent-will is secondary to the Lord's will. Every believer seeks this high ambition, but often the actions lag far behind the aspirations.

When asked to wholly surrender to Jesus, we raise all sorts of excuses. It's a simple request but we have faith in tangible assets as opposed to intangible promises in the hereafter and the right to self-determination that prevents us. What Jesus went through at Calvary compared with what we are asked to do is grossly disproportionate. An honest assessment will render a person humbled and eternally grateful. We know what we ought to do. The decision-maker alone is to blame and you cannot say that God predestined you to choose what you did – that's just passing the buck. God does not manipulate a person's freewill. Unsanctified freewill on the wrong side of God is purely an encumbrance that you are better off without. God wants the individual to volunteer to make freewill unfree. Dependent-will shows people clearly that there is a preeminent authority that exposes the fallacy and sinfulness of freewill. The path of righteousness is what every Christian ought to desire and pursue and the only way to get there is to abandon self-determination and have God's will take the lead in our lives. Self-will has carnal roots and is negative; dependent-will has God's interests in mind and is positive.

Chapter 13
The Focus of Dependent-will

Faith

A person may undertake a course of study and then apply the relevant parts to satisfy a need. Confidence grows when the procedures work and the correct result ensues. If it is employment related, then the aim is to do the job properly and get paid. You don't have to believe in that information or understand the detail processes of how it is constituted or proved. The ordinary person will only have to know the convention and apply it correctly. Besides, going into the fine detail is cumbersome and uninteresting. There are a few people that really take it to heart and they like to know everything about their subject. They will transfer the information from the brain to the heart. Very few people are like this because one has to be fanatical and passionate to go into such intricate detail for the sake of personal fulfilment. The subject becomes part of their psyche and is the centre of their being. Those that worship sports or any hobby have similar inclinations.

In the Christian walk, the bulk of our knowledge of God comes through reading, listening and exchange of views. That bank of knowledge stops at the mind in the same way that secular information is retained. We may not be aware of it, and that is spiritually hazardous. A person accumulates a certain amount of faith in the mind by being satisfied and accepting of the spiritual information, that it makes sense and is credible. As the Spirit interacts with the believer, that faith takes up residence in the spirit (heart) because it's the communication channel that Holy Spirit uses. This is the beginning of the training process in sanctification and it must be the focal point of life on earth.

The outworking of the human will is always linked with some kind of habit, emotion, desire or trust. Generally, a person will do something because they believe it to be right. Prior to conversion, secular forces establish self-will in a person's spirit and actions will always defer to self-satisfaction. After becoming a Christian, we have this tension within as Jesus competes for our attention.

Dependent-will relies on the guidance from the Holy Spirit and the focus is on Jesus and faith in him. He said that we ought to trust him and then follow his example. It goes further and states that a person will do what Jesus was doing and even more (John 14:12). It connotes a compulsion on the part of the believer that is driven by an external force. This is the sovereign will of God directing the dependent-will in a believer. All the spiritual knowledge that we have in the mind must be transferred to the spirit (heart) so that faith may embrace all that the Spirit teaches. When faith covers every single word of the truth, then sanctification becomes real, progressive and workable to the Spirit. This is a true change of personality. Dependent-will puts belief into action so that we can prove our faith outwardly. The indispensable element is spiritual faith in Christ to act accordingly and not mere brain knowledge.

Where self is still resident in the spirit, it has to be totally vanquished and ejected so that the Holy Spirit may be unimpeded to do his work through us. Faith may lead to greater works, but that's a bonus if the Lord wills. Our task is to nurture our faith to the limit of what we are capable of. The James passage tells us that there is a gap between faith and action. Such faith is still only in the mind and it has not been permeated into the spirit because Jesus said that a person with spiritual faith in him will of necessity be doing outward actions that glorify him. Memorisation of Scripture that is not converted to works represents faith that is useless to God's will (James 2:17-18).

The early stage of victory over self is a major step forward. However, even mature Christians may find themselves still capable of making wrong decisions in kingdom work. It's useful to bear in mind that ninety-nine percent is not good enough and you must get it all right for Jesus and go the extra mile. The secular notion is to do the very best for self; and the spiritual motivation ought to be the same for Jesus. However, there can only be one winner. Jesus deserves the very best that you have to offer and you shouldn't be happy with anything less. The need to maintain faithfulness can never be relaxed. Spiritual growth demands that you stay in tune with Jesus all of your life. The word 'believes' used in John 3:16 is applied in the present continuous tense. The requirement is that you believe and you never stop believing and trusting in Christ. In this way, you will always be faithful.

Over the course of your Christian walk, there will be encounters where the situation from a common-sense viewpoint appears incongruous with faith. Often when we are torn between the spiritual and physical elements of an unclear situation, the material habits tend to prevail. Old habits may override our sanctified common sense and we are guided into the wrong choices. The risk of failure, financial and other loss, diminution of reputation, self-esteem etc. loom larger than life in the psyche. This is the heart of the problem; we over emphasise self and the possible hurt that may result and this unduly influences our volition. When majority opinion prompts a course of action, it's very difficult to break loose from its momentum. Whatever challenges your faith, a decision must be made and the result will prove whether your faith is correctly placed or whether it is in opposition to Jesus. However, failure is not the end, and resilience will take faith to a higher plain that is the hallmark of a faithful soul.

The reassuring thing is that the progression of faith will reach a point where doubt has minimum or no influence anymore because trust and regenerated common sense will prevail. This is one of the glorious milestones in the sanctification walk but you have to resolve and make incisive efforts to get there. Challenges can be capitalised on and turned into faith building tools that get you closer to the nature of Jesus. The Holy Spirit nurtures healthy relationship with those that he has made to conform to his requirements because he knows that he can use and rely on their ability to achieve exactly what he wants.

Adam's experience on freewill provides useful insight. It was endowed upon Adam and Eve at creation. This means that God saw it as a good thing for humankind. Freewill worked in harmony with the rest of creation and with the Lord's plans for fellowship with people. Adam and Eve were very familiar with the Lord's habits in the garden. They knew the time that he would visit them and they knew his walking style (Genesis 3:8). This would have been a pleasure as the Lord was the only being who could give them new knowledge and meaningful conversation and they must have looked forward to their frequent meetings. Adam's spurious executive freewill was tested in the command not to eat from the tree of life. As long as they complied, nothing could go wrong, and they enjoyed a state of euphoria for a while. Their freewill on the operational level was just a matter of course in their daily routine. There was no danger of transgression because ordinary decisions were subordinate to the sovereign will of God. Everything that they decided on and did was in conformity to God's plans for the world. It was a fine display of perfection on how the human will ought to interact with

God's will. Freewill was working perfectly with the Lord's wishes – unimaginable today, but true then.

Freewill was supposed to work within God's framework and direction but sin broke that harmony. Adam and Eve must have hankered for the good life prior to the fall and done everything in their power to get back to the previous lifestyle but to no avail. We are not told whether God ever met with them afterwards. Probably, it would have been a one-sided plea towards heaven with little or no response from God. At a guess, I think that God may have given them bits of encouragement here and there but nothing appreciable. Their banishment from the presence of God was final and the garden was off-limits forever. Outside the garden, it was a different life altogether as the seasons changed and winter came. All of their time would have been spent on survival. They had to work the land and store food supplies, but wild animals may have been the biggest threat because they were living amongst all of them. Suffering and death came after the curse and dangerous animals learnt to kill. Perhaps some of their offspring may have been injured this way. As the children increased, the scope of freewill would have expanded correspondingly because the people would have had many different ideas about certain things. Adam and Eve would have taught their offspring all that they knew about the Creator-God, which wasn't much. Hence, the nature and manner of sin would have increased fairly rapidly.

In the absence of personal experience and response from God, mere words don't have a great deal of substance because it all depends on faith. As broader thinking patterns emerged with the corresponding liberation of freewill, the people became self-centred. They had no fellowship with God and they began to think about many things that they had never conceived of before because they had the knowledge of good and evil. This made the Satan's job much easier as humans had progressed from mere doubt (in the garden) to an array of sin options that affected other people as well. You can imagine the thought processes that gravitated towards self-determination from the events in Genesis chapters 4 to 10. Ever since the Lord severed relationship with humans, it didn't take long for idolatry to set in. God had to limit the progress of sin in the human race through the great flood in chapter 6, and shortly after, the judgment at Babel separated the people by creating the different ethnic groups. At that time, there was no knowledge of other gods so the people were just accountable to one God, but self-deification had already become an issue.

God's denial of his immanence and his withholding of a means to bridge his transcendence left humans defenceless against Satan's temptations. Both of these elements were operating harmoniously in the garden prior to sin. The former being the regular visits and fellowship that God had with Adam and Eve; and the latter was when God was away and Adam had to work the garden on his own. All of creation reflected the presence of God, and Adam and Eve unknowingly revelled in it because they were holy and unaware of sin. The moment God was away, there was a visibility vacuum in the relationship and Satan filled it immediately. Maybe he didn't know it but God was omnipresent and Adam could have called out to him at any time. The evil one became human's close companion. Unmistakably, the proliferation of sin came in so short a time and was devastating to human development, so much so that the Lord had to bring down the two great judgments that followed the curse (the great flood and the confusion at Babel).

Faith subordinates self-will to a superior being. The executive decisions are in God's hands so there is no need for the individual to resort to self-determination. Since the operational decisions are elementary, it is not necessary to think up elaborate schemes and to self-indulge in creativity at the executive level. However, self-expression is allowed at the operational front. Faith places a person's freedoms under the Lord's will. It entails submission to conditions that a person believes will result in infinite value. However, inherent sin has caused changes to our thinking patterns and it is very difficult to change to righteousness because we are most comfortable with sin and totally unfamiliar with sanctification. The Lord has to give holiness to a person as there is no other way to obtain it.

A non-believer assumes freewill to be their personal right and they are ignorant of where it actually came from. On this basis, a person thinks that they can do as they please because they are not accountable to a superior authority. Since secular law protects their rights, a person would normally obey the law. People would readily uphold a system that they have had a hand in creating, but they are averse to God's commands where they have no authority or contribution. The old saying: 'when in Rome, do as the Romans do' is just a means to get along temporarily in this world. It has no significance outside of Rome (in eternity) where the majority of time will be spent. The Bible tells us to prepare for eternity, so people must not do as the Romans do, but as Jesus does.

The conscience of the non-believer is the only guide in exercising their freewill, as they are only accountable to self. Where God is not revered, then anything goes. If accountability is self-determined, the actions can range from trivial moral violations to the vilest crimes. Sin removes and destroys faith in the Lord, so God's transcendence left humans susceptible to faithlessness. The human race did not know God at all (except for Israel) and this is the reason faith is such an alien concept to heathen people and God has to give a person faith in order to develop a relationship (Romans 10:17, Hebrews 12:2, Luke 17:5).

Truth.

Truth comes to a person via a sound relationship with Christ (John 14:6). Untruth is the ex-life that does not know Christ and sins without conscience. Jesus frees you from the bondage of inherent freewill and brings about a surrendered will that is obedient to God. When Christ teaches you the Biblical truths, you will realise that unsanctified freewill is unhealthy for your spirit. From then on, you will not want to trust your own judgment anymore. You will have an openness to explore the goodness of God's will and all that he wants for you. Jesus had always expressed that he had no freewill and only did what his Father was doing. This must be our primary goal in life as well. If not, then we must question our motives and our position in relation to God.

Jesus is the truth that we must understand and develop. A good bonding with Christ will automatically connect us to the Father because our relationship to the Trinity is spiritual and not physical. We have to see the Father through spiritual vision and this comes by knowing his character. It goes even further, in that we adopt godly traits and are renewed and transformed after God's nature. The indwelling Spirit links us with the Trinity and we know our way to the Father. The entire family of God is related in this way. It stands to reason that the more a believer builds up the character of God in spirit, the closer we will draw to God. The desire to know more and the magnetism of the Spirit will make it impossible to be lost. This is the surest way to know of one's salvation because Jesus Christ is with you. It's a personal assurance that nobody can know except you (John 6:39, 10:27).

We don't always practice the truth as we ought to. Even more disconcerting is that all those mountain-top experiences and godly confessions just seem to disappear when faced with hard spiritual decisions. It takes great determination to break out of the old mould, to stop and reconsider and to seek the direction of the Lord. The problems at the coalface have this uncanny way of suppressing one's confidence and all the accumulated learning from Scripture. History has shown that in some instances, the majority can be wrong. The majority will always be wrong if they are outside of God's righteousness. It is never a simple thing to stand alone when going against majority opinion. When the mob thinks differently, it is sound policy to trust the truth of the Creator-God who has complete knowledge and understanding. Nothing in creation can match or even hope to challenge the omniscience of God. This is a faith-based approach and is not too difficult if you give it a chance to work. Practice makes perfect.

God's truth is absolute, pure, unstained and impervious to contamination by anything in creation. People may misrepresent it; reinterpret it; misapply it; translate it through relative propositions, but they can't change the immutable Word of God. Dependent-will submits to the truth and Jesus imparts righteousness to our character. As we grow in renewal, the power of sin will gradually diminish or fade away. Holiness will establish itself in our spirit as the Lord empowers. Our allegiance to the truth must endure forever and our duty is to keep on the side of purity despite the temptations that may appear from time to time.

Chapter 14
The consequences of freewill

If the purpose of freewill is self-fulfilment, then the consequence is contentment. A person feels good after doing something beneficial for themselves. Good decisions will lead to a sense of elation/confidence and also elevate self-worth. Since we attach importance to such decisions, we develop a feeling of pride through achievement. It's all your own personal production, and satisfaction is the result. People make a name for themselves and it shows through wealth, fame, status etc. Most people can't help showing off the opulence of their success for others to take note. Sometimes luck and good timing – being in the right place at the right time gives an opportunity that wasn't anticipated. Nevertheless, the privileged minority have it and most don't. When a poor decision is made, a lesson will be learnt and hopefully a better outcome will be achieved the next time. This reasoning only pertains to the secular environment.

If you consider that everything that you do requires a decision, then this is a serious business. Granted, the majority of decisions are mechanical and things work out in the ordinary course of life or they may have little or no effect on your important activities. However, there are some that require careful consideration because the results are not trivial and those decisions should not to be handled loosely. We are all individually responsible for the decisions that we make because we know what is right and wrong. The path that we choose leaves a trail of evidence that is captured in history and may be evaluated at a later date. There may not be any material evidence, but God knows.

Making a better life for your self is no crime. The most common pursuits are education, wealth, and position. In a competitive society, it is not easy get ahead of the pack. You have to adopt selfish attitudes and also be prepared to overlook morals to a certain extent. Since your peers are operating in this fashion, the person that ignores it could lose their competitive edge. Conscience has to yield to misbehaviour in the secular world. However, the Christian lifestyle calls for the highest adherence to ethics and morals. Care and restraint have to be exercised which means that either self-gratification or comfort has to be foregone.

People who have achieved something in life gain the respect of their peers and they make their family proud. Higher achievement brings deeper respect. Some people value fame and respect more than financial wealth. To gain the admiration of the people that you know and esteem is greater than the fame with the unknown masses. Respect affords a person dignity and pride to move about in social circles, and it enhances self-esteem. An informed person knows that respect has to be earned, and it does not come with a title or wealth. This makes veneration a valuable commodity because associates will also attach a certain degree of trust to that person. This is a common phenomenon in the armed forces; the troops respect and trust their commanding officer and they will follow him into battle no matter what happens.

Leaders and managers will not win the respect of their subordinates if they are not competent in their core duties. In the case where a new direction is taken or where there is a necessity to alter work practices, it may be that even the top-level management doesn't know the full implications. In the face of uncertainty and inexperience, all would be engaged in a learning curve. However, the leaders still have an onus to find out all that is relevant to the matter and to train their staff appropriately. Then they have to package that information to be passed down to the staff so that they can do their work properly and efficiently. This requires careful thought to ensure that the process runs smoothly (least disruption) from start to finish. Leaders are there to give direction, and a good leader builds the morale of the staff. A stubborn boss may insist on doing things their way which may be inefficient. The staff will follow instructions because it's their job, but it doesn't mean that they would necessarily respect the boss.

In the movie 'Cinderella Man' Russel Crowe plays the part of Jimmy Braddock, a retired champion boxer during the Great Depression. He was broke and was behind in paying the heating bill so that was going to be cut off and his three children would have to be allocated to foster homes. Braddock was a man of dignity but even he swallowed his pride and went to the Emergency Relief Office to collect social security payment. As he was still short, he went to the member's bar in Madison Square Garden to ask for charity. This was the hardest thing to do because he was a retired champion and he didn't want to be seen as a beggar in front of his peers. He had to do it as this was the only place that he knew would help him. Crow played a moving role that depicted humility and desperation. There were about a dozen men in the bar, a few were unmoved, but the majority dug deep and contributed towards the $18.38 that was required. The donations were given out of respect for Braddock because they knew him as an honourable person. Braddock remained humble even after he retook the world title later on, a truly remarkable character trait for a world champion. Humility is what we must develop in our personality because it comes from the heart of God and is an indispensable component in personal sanctification. If worldly people see it fit to be humble, then all the more for Christians.

Freewill is submitted to God at the executive level, and once the direction is revealed then rational thought comes into play at the operational level. Rational procedures must comply with righteousness because God does not bless illegitimate actions in his kingdom work. There may be different ways to do a job but it's still the Lord's work and requires much prayer to Jesus in seeking direction. There is the real danger of non-compliance with the Lord's wishes where an option looks attractive but is driven by personal appeal. People may appear to be getting away with it, but they never do. This error was made by King Saul in 1 Samuel 15 and the moral is: obedience is far more important than sacrifice because the former is personal to God whereas the latter is mere ritual. Obedience to Jesus is a command that relates to righteousness and it must not be broken. Central to this matter was Saul's self-seeking tendencies. He thought that he could be creative by deviating from the Lord's command and doing things his way. The Word of God lays down exacting standards for believers and there is no margin for error. This is where the greatest care needs to be taken as freewill may throw everything in disarray. The proper application of rationalism is merely using the most efficient manner to get the job done while still adhering to instructions. Bad decisions can lead to dire consequences when risks are not adequately assessed. Everybody applies rational thinking because it's logical and common-sense. A mental check-list helps to cover the steps necessary to reach the objective and it is comforting knowing that all the boxes have been ticked.

The Lord gave the executive instruction and it was only the operational procedures that had to be implemented. The timing of the attack had to be prompt and he had to destroy everything because that was the essential instruction. However, Saul could have used different strategies for the offensive i.e. less infantry and more chariots and tactical weapons, part ambush and part direct offensive, siege, etc. The execution style was left to Saul's discretion. Saul's failure included the delay in killing King Agag and keeping the best of the livestock. His rationale in sacrificing the livestock was an act of rebellion against the Lord's command in the same way that Adam faltered at the fall. Saul's self-driven motives made him do things his way.

Christians will only be judged for their works because their sins have already been dealt with by the blood of Christ at Calvary. The judgment may sound insignificant because entry into heaven is already secured, but any loss will be acutely felt. On that day, the desire for reward will be such that any diminution will be grievous and hurtful. On the secular level on earth that reward has no apparent attraction, but this is a spiritual benefit that is going to last ad infinitum.

Backsliding has negative implications and the point may be reached where one's salvation comes into question. The warnings in Hebrews are not to be taken lightly. Bear in mind that salvation is a process – faith, sanctification, relationship development and glorification (new spiritual body). This is a building-up process and we have to stay in close touch with the Lord all the way. Any form of reversal is dangerous, even stagnation. It shifts the primary focus away from Jesus and back to self. If there is any hint of a split-allegiance in faith then self-will ought to be isolated and arrested.

It may be that a person has crossed the Rubicon and no longer believes and does not display acts of worship to God. It's clear-cut, you either believe or you don't. Once faith falters then sanctification and relationship will be fruitless and unproductive. Rejection can deteriorate to the stage where a person becomes an unbeliever once again (see explanation from Hebrews on page 137). It's very dangerous to take risks with God in this very sensitive area as there will be heavy loss. Alternate faiths are very attractive and widely propagated in the world today. It is wise to stay as far away from them as possible as they are just not worth the risk. The grass is always greener on the other side and one has to keep careful check on self-seeking motives.

The first warning sign to lookout for is stagnation in one's spiritual growth. Being happy with yourself is comfortable and it leads to over-confidence. Normally we set an objective and then set up some procedures to get there. We may compare our progress with other people or apply some other means of measurement. We assess our position and values and relate that to the environment that we are in. Herein lay a warning because self is used as the gauge for achievement instead of Christ. We are to examine ourselves and our motives. Jesus is the standard that Christians must aim to achieve. Having peace in your own mind/heart is insufficient; rather you need to be in a state where God is happy with your progress. Unlike the secular measure, contentment must come from God and this requires determination to do right.

Obedience and the renunciation of self are essential for a healthy spiritual life. It's hard to keep a restraint on the attraction of material things; forcing yourself to do things that you don't consider the most appropriate; controlling and overcoming selfishness; mastery over fear; concentrating on the unseen over what's visible and the list goes on. There must be a fundamental movement out of the selfish mindset and to become rooted in God's worldview. It's an even greater challenge to stay there and never revert to the comfort of self-gratification.

Spiritual excellence is the goal for all Christians to work towards (Matthew 6:20). Righteousness is not an easy virtue to pursue and accomplish because its values are not based on material gain. The materialistic people will acquire the best for themselves because they have the finances, but the pilgrim would have to be satisfied with the bare necessities. It's a difference in lifestyle but the follower will have enough of the basic things to get by in life. Much effort will be spent on consistency and staying on target towards excellence in righteousness.

Often people don't see results quick enough so they lose interest or give up trying. Distractions hamper spiritual growth and that may cause one to lapse into spiritual neglect. This may be habit forming because all attention is directed towards pleasurable things. Time that is spent on extraneous things equates to robbing time from your spiritual devotion. The purpose is to break away from the old routine and to form new habits. It's easier said than done as the initial transition is the hardest to make. For ordinary people, the sacrifice of comfort and custom is a daunting consideration and distraction to the material things will vastly slow spiritual progress. Spiritual growth is not an instrument for financial gain, so people tend to pursue this as a part time or side-line activity. You reap what you sow. Head knowledge is merely theory in the mind, and some people take a long time to make spiritual progress in the heart.

On occasion, we may regret that we could have done things better for God. This is mainly due to a lack of attention to detail at the time. It's a good observation and keeping it in mind through recall and strategizing will help one to do better on the next occasion. I have had this after thought before and have resolved to improve. Under different ministry conditions the strategy and procedures will not be the same. Hence, the desire to do better depends on the situation at hand. Devout prayer is standard procedure, sincere commitment and close fellowship with the Holy Spirit are necessary ingredients for spiritual development. The actual work depends on the Spirit's guidance. The worker may only plan an approach once the task is revealed. Since reliance on the Spirit is vital, not too much can be done in advance, unless it's systematic routine type work. Often, the worker's only option is to do their best at the time. Preconceived ideas may not apply and it will be wrong to force them to fit into a job when there is no need. Be on guard that self-will may attempt to sneak in at times. A person's best effort on the job comes from character. All the godly traits that a person has accumulated, where relevantly and competently applied will be what the Lord expects. One has to be cautious that self does not intrude to diminish or reduce the quality of the effort. If the procedures are performed accurately and uncorruptedly, it would be similar to God using his personal character qualities to do his own work. The worker is merely a channel to put the motions in place. Then whatever minor reservations that may come up later may be dismissed because everything is under the Spirit's control. The will to do one's utmost in humility is the best attitude that a person may bring to the Lord's work.

Repentance is not only a complete turnaround of actions regarding particular sin, but it has to be reformed in the inner will that causes the fault. More significantly the will has to be remodelled towards righteousness. Once a person is geared up for renewal, then the real work starts. Spiritual progress can only be consistently maintained by the death of self-will and embracing the Lord's will in every aspect of life. Repentance is a resolution not only to banish the old ways, but to grow in the light. The greater task is to reform character and progress in sanctification.

Obedience pleases God, and it's the will that decides this. The degree of employability depends on a person's level of competency. Souls are not won every day, especially when a worker has less outreach activity and opportunity. Benefit is freely available in personal service to all those around you and it takes on a maintenance role with the regular people that you are in contact with. In Luke 22:32 Peter is encouraged to pass his experience on to other believers for their benefit. Jesus calls Peter to teach and to foster other Christians (John 21:15). Individual development is just as important as outreach because God wants good quality sons and daughters. Peter had become a usable instrument that Jesus could rely on to build his church.

Seasoned Christians have fewer problems with the obedience process because they have dealt with their personal issues and have those mostly under control. Nothing is too much to sacrifice when it comes to obedience to Jesus because that is driven by love. Old habits may take years to undo before you may embark on and assimilate the renewed way of thinking and acting. Generally, Christians will walk the road of regeneration and slowly get rid of the obstinate remnants of their old ways and simultaneously practice and grow in holiness. Submission to God's service entails a different train of thought and learning process. You have to get into the habit of praying for everything every day. It's not so simple when you are not accustomed to it. The spiritual consequences are infinitely more significant than the ego or personal creativity and self-satisfaction at the time of the decision. We hardly think about the eternal ramifications of our choices and that is disadvantageous. If we were shown what would happen at the time of making any decision, no doubt we will act exactly the way God commands. God only gives us faith and obedience to work on when doing his work and we have to choose the right path.

Some may feel that surrendering executive freewill would alter a person's nature or make up. This was never God's intention for human beings and it will never be. Some may fear that subordinating control over their lives would make them less of a human being and more like a robot. The reality is that you will still be you; your character, style, appearance, personality, preferences etc. will still be self-regulated. Adam and Eve were unique beings before and after the fall. You will still enjoy the same things that you used to but without sinful motives. Life would be just as pleasurable as before, but even more so. There will be a major improvement in moral behaviour and character flaws will be corrected, reduced or removed. On the other hand, the positive moral elements of love, goodness, kindness, patience, fairness etc. will be enhanced. There will be an overall improvement of a person's outlook in life that reflects the goodness of God. This is real joy.

Your direction in life (priorities), worldview and approach will conform to high morals. You will be striving for different values in life. Doing another line of work and work style does not change a person's uniqueness or individuality. Spiritual change will improve a person's attitude and it will downplay selfishness and afford maximum consideration to others. Godly character will make you a better person while still maintaining your uncompromised personal traits. Once you have sampled the new way, you will conclude that your old ways were unacceptable and that change was vital and inescapable. This turnaround is not objectionable and it must happen.

The consequence of self-will is punishment and the result of dependent-will is reward. Even after a person has professed dependence on the Spirit, self-will may still be a problem. Self-control is a means to get the desired results of a subordinated will to the Lord so that a person behaves as Christ would.

Chapter 15
Caution

The Book of Hebrews tells us much about a person's position regarding salvation and it unfolds in a series of warnings. It was written for the benefit of Jewish Christians and the caution is relevant to all believers.

CAVEAT	RESULT	REMARKS
2:2-3 Pay more careful attention; do not drift away; there is no escape if salvation is ignored.	Every violation and disobedience will be justly punished.	A departure from Jesus is taken as disregard for salvation
3:7-8 Do not harden your heart (rebellion); a sinful unbelieving heart that turns away from the Living God; they disobeyed; not able to enter because of their unbelief.	They shall never enter God's kingdom.	Their hearts were always straying away from God. Encourage one another daily so that none may be hardened by sin's deceitfulness. Hold firmly till the end in confidence.
6:4-6 It is impossible for the enlightened, if they fall away, to be brought back to repentance.	They cannot experience repentance a second time.	Because they have tasted the heavenly gift, they have tasted the goodness of the Word of God, and the powers of the coming age. To their loss they are crucifying the Son of God all over again and subjecting him to public disgrace.

10:26-27 If we deliberately keep on sinning after we have received the knowledge of the truth, no sacrifice for sin is left. How much more severely do you think a man deserves to be punished who has trampled the Son of God under foot, who has treated as an unholy thing the blood of the covenant that sanctified him, and who has insulted the Spirit of grace?	Only a fearful expectation of judgment and of raging fire that will consume the enemies of God. The Lord will judge his people.	It is a dreadful thing to fall into the hands of the living God. Remember those earlier days after you had received the light, when you stood your ground in a great contest in the face of suffering. Sometimes you were publicly exposed to insult and persecution; at other times you stood side by side with those who were so treated. You sympathised with those in prison and joyfully accepted the confiscation of your property, because you knew that you had better and lasting possessions. Do not throw away your confidence; it will be richly rewarded. You need to persevere so that when you have done the will of God, you will receive what he has promised. But we are not of those who shrink back and are destroyed, but of those who believe and are saved.

12:25-26 See to it that you do not refuse him who speaks. If they did not escape when they refused him who warned them on earth, how much less will we, if we turn away from him who warns us from heaven? Once more God will shake not only the earth but also the heavens.	The created things that can be shaken will be removed, so that the unshakable may remain.	We are receiving a kingdom that cannot be shaken, let us be thankful, and so worship God acceptably with reverence and awe, for our God is a consuming fire.

The admonitions increase in severity in the following manner: take great care not to backslide; do not harden your heart and fall into unbelief; there is no leeway for the fallen to be brought back to repentance; severe punishment for those who have treated Jesus with contempt; and, the final consuming fire will totally destroy all those that have refused Christ. The progression moves from a warning while there is still time to make corrections, to the final judgment when it's too late.

At first glance the caution appears to be directed at immature believers, but the progression targets all Christians regardless of what level of regeneration they have attained. It highlights the power of self-determination whereby a person may turn away from God at any time in life. The writer is a true spiritual carer who has observed the wiles of the world and loves God and fellow Christians. He has taken the time and effort to explain the dangers of backsliding in a caring and personal way so that the reader is left without any doubts.

Paul admonishes the Corinthian church not to take pride or boast in their works as some of them had grown arrogant (1 Corinthians 4). It signifies that they still kept some bad behaviour from their old nature that was causing problems in the church. A further warning against impure Christian living including hatred, discord, jealousy, fits of rage, selfish ambition, dissensions, factions and envy are unacceptable to God (Galatians 5:19-20). I Thessalonians 5:14 cautions people not to be idle because unwholesome thoughts can enter the mind. A divisive person should be reprimanded twice and then ostracised because they are self-condemned (Titus 3:10-11). These are just some of the things that bring disharmony to the body of Christ. The Spirit will warn a believer appropriately, but they still have to keep watch over their own minds and spirit.

These warnings are only for believers because unbelievers are already lost. They will only qualify when God draws them to Jesus. The bottom line is that you make the decision yourself and you have to bear the consequences. If you yield to misinformation, then you are responsible. The Lord will deal with the misguided source appropriately, but you are wrong because you did not follow his commands. Freewill is only good if it is unconditionally submitted to the Lord. The warnings caution us to rein in self-will and to stay within the bounds of God's rules. It's about stopping to love self and growing in love for Jesus.

Chapter 16
The turning point

Routine life habitually causes us to separate the material from the spiritual. The physical world is where our priorities are naturally inclined. We favour it because it's what we are able to act on and do something about and the results are measurable. Self-worth propels life and gives it meaning. Until we experience Jesus, we derive pleasure in life through our own making. Christians need to constantly make the paradigm shift from the world of sight to the invisible spiritual realm. To replace the natural with the unnatural requires us to be immersed in the spiritual dimension totally such that we are able to keep close relationship with the Lord and have the mind of Christ. The degree of relationship should be such that we automatically consult God on everything we anticipate, think and do. In our little world, self-preservation is everything. When we encounter an Almighty God who is perfect, we realise that self is so insignificant. The mind of Christ needs to be embedded in our spirit so that we will make the correct choices every time. Spiritual pleasure is the new goal in this life.

It is a struggle to diminish self and bring freewill under submission to the Father. Why was it so easy for Jesus and so hard for us? God is outside of creation; He is Spirit and is at home in the spiritual realm. We still have to get there and we are severely handicapped by bodily instincts that funnel our thinking into the material world where we place all attention and importance. It's a kind of birth defect. Is it then fair of God to demand that we rid ourselves of our bodily priorities and transition to the spiritual dimension? The answer is unassailably yes, because that is the real issue. The Creator created humans and knows what is best for us. Jesus thought nothing of his body and everything that he did had a spiritual reason and purpose. This is something that human beings don't know and we must understand that our spiritual health is infinitely more significant than our physical body (and what we think of ourselves).

The blockade is none other than our naturally bestowed self-will. It's such a major struggle and is the top priority that must not be ignored. Jesus knew this secret before his incarnation and he grew in spirit into adulthood. He had no self-will and it was only the Father's will that enabled him to go to the cross and take on the sin of all humanity. We can start by denouncing self-importance until we are nothing. Most of us will start off and yet still stay there for a very long time – hopefully not until it's too late.

God views the physical world as unimportant. What if you gain the whole world and lose your soul? As believers we have no fear of losing our souls, but the next vital thing is to lose our reward. Simply because we cannot see it or quantify it does not diminish its significance one bit. The Bible tells us that these rewards are eternal which means that they will accompany you forever or they will be denied you forever. These spiritual objects are viewed by God to be the most desired things that all believers should be striving to possess. He is always right.

Spiritual maturity signifies that everything revolves around God. It is only the Creator's personality and intentions that are significant in this life and for eternity. I have found this a most frustrating assignment in life. It's not an easy thing to place God first in everything, no matter how diligently I have tried. On the other hand, it is very easy to forget and leave God out. My shortcomings were always there to warn me. It reminds me how far I still have to go and so I keep on trying. Paul said that he had not considered himself to have arrived there yet. Even at this educated stage of my Christian walk, I still feel that I am way, way behind where Paul thought he was at. How does one get ahead? We all have different personalities and each is called to a different work because of our gifting. We merely have to be faithful in the work that has been entrusted to us. Each person has to chart their own course to Jesus and monitor their own progress. Obedience to the Holy Spirit's guidance is vital as this will relieve you of any uncertainties that may come up. You can only do so much, and God doesn't expect you to be superman, he desires humility and self-deprecation. He expects you to be meek and lowly.

Spiritual high-achievers are few and far between. Only a select few are destined to be spiritual giants. Generally, God works through ordinary people and it is the mundane things that require much patience and plodding. On the home-front, kingdom work is usually of a maintenance nature where all the church programs are set and people just have to keep them running fluidly. Outreach work is always slower and harder to achieve results. It's quite obvious as the people that we are trying to reach usually require a long time to come to their senses. Even if nobody ever comes to accept Jesus in the area that we are ministering, our work has been done because Jesus has been made known to them. It is out of our hands and it's their personal account that they have to settle with God. Ordinary workers are an integral part of kingdom business. There are no praises, no public recognition, no gratitude expressed, no material success or remuneration but the Lord sees it as very important and we can be sure that an appropriate spiritual reward will be forthcoming.

The strain and toil go further once we take Christ seriously because the bar is lifted after each successive achievement. It is simple in the initial stages to turn over a new leaf and purge most of the old bad habits. Conditioning yourself to take on new proclivity is not so easy, as it requires us to embark on a different learning curve. Without the involvement of the Holy Spirit this process of renewal is impossible as only he knows the will of God for each individual. It is only after years of striving, self-talk, stumbling, re-doubling your efforts and edging ahead, that you eventually feel content with the level of your spiritual achievement. It is not perfect, but you have put in your best effort. The majority of Christians take a while to get to this stage and regretfully, some stagnate. There are countless others who get distracted and stumble along the way. However, there's always more to gain no matter where you're at and every little bit of ground won is energising for self and a pleasure to Jesus.

A scholar of sanctification must be trained in godliness that copies God's personality and follows after God's own heart. It is ludicrous to assume that a new or developing believer that has all the intentions and willingness to be like Jesus but has not been adequately spiritually educated and tested, for God to just take them into his confidence. A disciple has to prove their desire and sincerity to pursue holiness before the Holy Spirit will engage in a constructive way. Character development after God is not difficult; it is not a vast amount of new knowledge that a person has to acquire. However, it is self-gratification that makes it hard to attain. God intended believers to adopt a childlike stance with innocent faith that will trust the Spirit to give all that is needed. We limit our growth because we don't do as God desires. Self-will is not faithful and courageous enough to follow simple instructions. If this is done God's way, then even a very young believer may become a mature Christian in a very short time because we all have the same Spirit who is sympathetic and impartial and more than willing to help us attain our full spiritual potential.

Unproven words are baseless; you know that and I know that. Fortunately, we have the Word of God to work from and we have the means (Holy Spirit) to turn that information into spiritual assets. You may become consciously and shamefully aware that living the Christian life is by no means easy. It should not be a discouragement, but an added motivation to reach for the Lord. Although we may rejoice and give thanks for our privileged position in salvation, our good health, our financial freedom, and a myriad of other things, they are not the things that God has as the ultimate prize for his children. They are mere accompaniments for us to get by in this life. If you can't see further than those things then there's something wrong with your evaluation technique, and the spiritual priority has not been grasped or understood.

Sacrifice and commitment just seem to move up a notch each time we reach our immediate goals because the urge to progress will stretch us even further each time we improve. The essence of sanctification is to transition into perfection in Christ. Although we may do even greater things than these, it is the spiritual unity in Jesus, the Father and the Spirit that we must aim and toil towards constantly. Those greater things will come if it's the Lord's will, and he will equip us for the task. What is it like to keep straining yourself up to an improved position? You can only try and find out. In hindsight, I don't want to go back to my formative Christian years but I want to keep pushing towards the next level. A vibrant rapport with Christ brings about an incredible sense of freedom, peace and joy. It is the comfort of your vegetative state that is the most shameful sin, and that must be avoided at all costs.

This pivotal decision has to be a personal choice as nobody can make it for you. After overcoming this hurdle, spiritual stature will continue to challenge you for the rest of your natural life. Self-examination is a hard and cold reality that is essential for advancing your spiritual bank. Invariably, your biggest enemy is not Satan or temptation or any other external force, but your own freewill.

Chapter 17
The transformed life

Freewill does not naturally obey God because it inherently tends to sin and this is why God has to draw believers to Christ. Jesus had the distinct advantage of being born perfect. He didn't have to start a new spiritual life since he was already in it. However, humans are on the opposite end of the scale because we are born into sin. We have to admit our sin, repent of it and then be educated in holiness. Jesus had such a tremendous head start over us because he knew no sin. Life to him was merely a matter of maturing in the things of God. He had no problems understanding the mind and will of the Father. There was no difficulty in discharging the instructions from the Father despite having a human body. Even the abhorrence of Calvary didn't deter him from the Father's will. Jesus didn't have to be transformed into 'new life' because he had never sinned and always been with and known his Father intimately.

New life to human beings is an alien concept. We are so far removed from God and our will and old desires are so deeply entrenched within our minds and hearts. Initially, we have to get down on our knees and confess that we are wrong and in desperate need of the Lord's grace. Somehow, pride and self-worth will always to be lurking in the background. If you don't welcome constructive criticism and get on edge when approached on a sensitive subject, then most probably pride is still an unresolved issue within. Now that we are faced with this mission of nurturing a new life, we find that it's so hard. Imitating Jesus is only possible when we are in submission to the Holy Spirit in every aspect of life. The principal impediment that just won't leave us is freewill. It constantly seeks to move in different directions to what the new life dictates. Living out the sanctified life is a series of stops and starts. Needless to say, it can get to the point where it's discouraging because we know what to do, but we just can't seem to get there.

Self-will has to be remodelled to embrace agape. This is fundamentally sacrificial love and this means the final end to the old nature of freewill. Agape transforms the human nature completely from the inside and is displayed by action. The love of God that imbues a person will directly answer the sacrifices that are called for. It is not coerced in any way and no returns are expected. Agape puts an end to the last things that self has been holding on to. The love of God that grows within the spirit will prompt concern for others. Self-will will meet its final match and be vanquished forever. After the last valuables have been sacrificed then there is nothing left to live for, except Jesus. The point will be reached where even martyrdom is no longer a deterrent. A substandard vessel will turn into an effective tool in the hands of the Master.

In the early stages of Christianity in China when the believers were severely persecuted by the Communist government, there was a strong sense among them that the body was merely a shell and it didn't matter what happened to it. Eternal life was more important than earthly existence. The authorities discovered that they could persecute the body, but they had no control over the Christian's spirit (faith). No hardship or cost was big enough to upset their relationship with Jesus. Persecution and death just meant glory to Jesus and to go to their heavenly home to be with the Father.

Unfortunately, as China gradually developed and modernised, the economic attractions started gaining prominence and began to play a part in Christian life. Self-benefit interfered with the childlike trust that the previous generation enjoyed. Economic benefits are good for the physical person but bad for the spiritual because it diminishes dependence on God and hinders relationship development. People are people and even believers compare themselves with other people. The desire for a better lifestyle and to have what others have is constantly threatening their spiritual advancement. In many ways it cannot be avoided because they see the attractions the moment they walk out of their home.

How do we get agape ingrained into our beings? Freewill occupies the spirit and it must be permanently ejected. When this is successfully accomplished, a vacuum appears and something must fill that vacancy. It may either be Jesus or the evil one. Self-abnegation will invite Jesus into a person's spirit and a new life of spiritual excitement will be nurtured. God's will in Christ becomes yours thereby opening the door to intimate relationship and the pleasure of sanctified service. It is God who has to put agape in a person's spirit, but we have to invite him in to do it and keep him interested. The love of God will reside in the spirit and it will direct the mind to do anything that God commands. It's not rocket-science but we have to ask ourselves 'why am I not there yet'? After submission it's unsettling to realise that there is still such a long way to go. Remember that it's your old nature that make the changes burdensome. The Lord's purpose is to make everything easy (Matthew 11:28-29).

1 Thessalonians 4:3 states that God's desire is for our sanctification. All balanced minded followers know that the starting blocks for regeneration are not hard to get off. We work on the areas that we think we need to revamp. Usually, they are the easy adjustments that need to be put in place. However, as we progress then it gets harder because we are left with our weaknesses. At this point, the weaker believers face the danger of regression. The captive weaknesses are not easy to surrender. Furthermore, these shortcomings are peculiar to each individual and there's no one-size-fits-all solution. Individuals that are subject to similar debilitating traits may be able to offer useful advice but their circumstances are not the same as yours, so your emotions and tolerance make your situation unique. When all is said and done, it's really up to the individual's determination, willingness, and exertion to get the process under way – nobody can substitute for you. After years of wary toil and countless self-assessment sessions, you finally reach the stage where you feel that you have gained valuable ground. Well done, your effort has brought about transformation, but it must be proved in real life. It is Christ that has to show himself through your new behaviour – actions speak louder than words. Many may quite justifiably say that they are far better people than they were before the process began, and they would be right. However, it's not what you have done to yourself, but rather what the Holy Spirit has done in you. These are God's characteristics and not your own, so there's no basis for pride or merit, but humble gratitude to the Lord.

The foregoing passage speaks of the will of God that desires our regeneration. Since the subject is completely dependent on the Lord, one may only absorb and not contribute. Sanctification is the leading testing ground for dependency on God and the deliberate suppression of self-will. The Lord decides on what to teach and a program is tailor-made for each believer. The candidate that truly and faithfully follows the Spirit's teaching will attain the quality of Jesus' personality. I doubt whether any of us can be entirely transparent while going through this process. It can only mean that self-will still has a seat reserved somewhere in the psyche. The cause may be as innocent as caring for family and only slightly neglecting to put others before self. As a consequence, a bit of selfishness may creep in here and there. Partial/selective pride is equivalent to manipulating humility. A person may be truly humble before a selected audience but less so before others that they deem as less worthy. Each person has their own obstinate weaknesses that persist despite efforts against them. You must to be brave enough to confront your giants and overcome them.

The transformed life does not mean immunity to sin, but it does have the ability to enormously reduce the tendency to sin. The prevalence of sin will be in the world as long as Satan is allowed to rule. All the temptations will still be around even for the most sanctified soul, but they won't have much impact. The heavier type sin wouldn't be too troublesome to suppress but the lesser sins are the hardest to deal with. Peter's error in supporting the circumcision group is one example to learn from (Galatians 2:11). Popularity, the desire to please influential people, and customs can sway a person's judgment and force on mistakes. The remedy is to be firm on principles the way Paul reacted to this situation.

The goal of the transformed life is to reach perfection or to become fully mature through teaching (Colossians 1:28). It is a process that we have to walk through with the Holy Spirit that moulds us to conform to the nature of Jesus. It leads to developing a harmonious Christian life with the Lord and fellow believers. This implies two things: getting rid of the old ungodly ways (if this is ever fully possible) and to take after the God's personality (this is an achievable reality). Perfect personal regeneration is beyond the reach of any human being and no person will ever obtain it in this life. Both parts will only be mastered by the diligent soul to a certain degree. Sins of the mind and heart are somewhat uncontrollable as they tend to appear at the most unexpected times, and they may negatively influence one's actions at the time. It's a weird situation where the goal seems to be pie in the sky. This is where harmony and intimacy with Jesus is vital for forgiveness and to keep encouraging a person to move forward. The method is to persistently and constantly walk with Christ and improve our spiritual attitude at every level that he takes us to. We must understand our obligation to Jesus that drives us to keep on trying and not to fall backwards.

Giving up sin will result once we control the real task of abandoning personal rights, independent behaviour and self-will. Taking care of the latter will vastly assist in reducing the former. This is where the rubber meets the road and the stakes are high. We are encouraged to give up everything in this pursuit. Self-will causes damage to the spirit, yet at times we follow personal preferences without estimation of the eternal effects. That being said, it is not easy for the human being to just switch over to God's ways at the drop of a hat because of our background, it is always an uphill battle. We have to stay close to the Spirit and not give in to self-will and personal prejudice. You may know of a person's unpleasant side but there is also the need to treat them fairly and lovingly. You know that they will gladly accept help but still continue in their old ways that you disagree with. You are forced to make a judgment-call. A righteous call will not be disturbing as long as you are willing to give up your prejudice. Paul's words in 1 Corinthians 4:4 may be of some assistance. Your conscience may not accuse, but it doesn't mean that you are right. This dilemma shows how much we have to depend on the Spirit's discernment. Our natural lives are not spiritually inclined and our judgment may be skewed to towards selfish purposes despite wanting to do right. The only way for the physical body to be in sync with the spiritual is to sacrifice self-determination. The void left by the vacation of freewill must be filled by God's will.

Individuality may be viewed as that part of a person that seeks to be different; to assert its own style; and to stand out from the masses. It doesn't take much public attention after which pride, egotism and self-assertion will come to the fore because self likes the prestige. Humble people are not prone to this vice, but great care must still be taken. Personality is an inherent quality and it makes each person different. Sometimes it may take many years for a person to understand themselves. Then again, certain people go through their entire lives thinking that they know their personality but in fact they don't. It's disconcerting when we all read the same Bible and some practice the relevant precepts but others don't. The difference is in each individual's personality because we are supposed to be growing in character. The brain knows what is right, yet a person may allow bad habits to repeat themselves so they keep doing the same wrong things. A third party may point out the error, but after a while that advice is set aside and the old pattern repeats itself. It's a kind of mental-blockage in the personality. These lapses can range from simple typing errors to habitual undesirable behaviour. The former are inadvertent or involuntary actions whereas the latter actions are forced on by self-will (desire/idolatry), and they require a basic correction in the will.

The saying goes that you have to get married and your spouse will tell you about yourself. Such advice may appear sound but it still relies on another fallible human being's self-will and judgment. The Creator is the only being who knows everybody clearly and completely. If you know Jesus truthfully; you will know yourself. However, will you be strong enough to make the hard changes? You can go through your whole life without a spouse but you can't do the same thing without Christ. Eternity is too big a cost to be taking silly risks.

After you have successfully walked with Jesus and remodelled your personality to absorb and integrate the Holy Spirit's habits, the changes will be reflected in your new character. This renewal will be noticed by all those who know you because your behaviour will show the difference. A regenerated character does not destroy individuality. God can work with varying personal styles in the same way that the Bible was written by various writers with different personalities in various parts of the world and at different times in history. You don't lose your individualism when you allow God to assume control of your life. Your unique personality will define you as an individual to the outside world forever. Even in heaven, you will still be your own private personality but immersed in God's righteousness.

One matter that is sensitive to most people is that of money. Generally, attitude towards money is at the centre of this tug-of-war between self and God. If you get your spiritual inclination wrong, it will insidiously diminish your spiritual priorities. Rationalisation of personal action is often if not always, on the wrong side of God's direction for you. Biblical maxims are truths that don't need to be reasoned out or explained. The Spirit's leading often appears illogical, unsafe, acutely risky, and there's a strong aversion to go that way. In the majority of cases, this dislike has something to do with money whether directly or indirectly. The Lord usually challenges a person in the area that they are most sensitive to. For some, it may not be financial but pride and fame. The unregenerate soul inherited a selfish nature to covet things. This driving force is not limited to finances but everything that appeals to self. It's bad enough that we put ourselves in opposition to God, and it can get worse where we defer to immoral and unfair means to satisfy selfish motives. The boundary between idolatry and ethics can easily be ignored resulting in sin. The further one gets into this perilous territory, the harder it is to break free and get out. We bring these hardships on ourselves and then want a magic bullet from God to repair the damage. Self-gratification is toxic to one's regeneration plans. Innocent people that have suffered because of unjust actions will see justice done at the Judgement. When sin is finally put to rest, that is the time when God will assess each believer's work for merit or demerit, there's no escape.

Regeneration brings joy to the spirit. Superficially, there's nothing to show for it but it brings peace and comfort from God. It's a gift from heaven to be able to ignore the material and have the propensity to hunger after righteousness. As you get to understand and know Jesus better, it enables smoother and rapid development of the spiritual things that really count. A person's motive quickly switches from 'wanting' to 'giving'. The willingness to sacrifice starts with minor things until it reaches the highest stratum of generosity where nothing is held back. Christian giving does not emanate from the world. Naturally, finances are always limited but expenses are not limited. Unwise spending can create problems that adversely impact a family and can cause break-up in relationships. However, the regenerated person will make an effort to give more than the tithe. Our Father is not a kill-joy. He knows exactly how much we can take because he knows our spiritual strength and tolerance limit. Making things easier and happier for the follower is God's idea of relationship. He will never push you beyond what you are able to bear. Part of spiritual enlightenment is the realisation to give back to God. True awakening is the point where you are ashamed that you can't give more.

There may be so much to be done and so much that you want to do, but there's no direction from above. Persistent petition is met with hollow silence, and it can be quite frustrating. This is especially hard on the mission field where the target group does not lend itself to the Good News. The worker's best intentions just seem to be picking at the edges and the results are not promising. Our Father knows when the timing is right and when the target is ready to accept the Gospel. There's no need to panic, your availability and willingness to work is good enough for God.

Transformation cultivates and tests the fruit of the Spirit. Peace, patience, kindness, goodness, faithfulness, gentleness and love will be encountered in life situations. God wants the fruit to mature in a person's spirit and careless actions can thwart all of one's hard work in an instant. It is our duty to condition our mind and heart to receive the Spirit's teaching and to steadfastly implant it in our character. Peace enables us to approach difficult people; patience helps us overcome frustrations and criticisms; kindness paves the way to better relationships; goodness enables others to see what Jesus is like; faithfulness is the primary ingredient for our sanctification development; and gentleness makes people responsive. Demonstrating the love of God make these things work together and it lubricates our dealings with folk who don't know Christ. All these elements are vital to our spiritual wellbeing and they require more thought and attention than we actually give. The seemingly unimportant may just be the key to opening up to deeper levels of fellowship. It's definitely something worth mulling over. Boredom, stagnation, frustration and lack of progress can give rise to thoughts that are not in line with God's initiatives. The intelligent worker ought to lookout for the warning signs.

Love implies sacrifice and Calvary proves it beyond doubt. Every Christian has to face up to and make a decision about this love and deal with it in positive ways. The depraved nature of humans separates us totally from God, but once we find the love of God, sacrifice is a necessary ingredient of the agape framework. There must be appropriate sacrifice on our part in order to comply with Jesus' teachings. A healthy relationship with Jesus will include sacrifice of one kind or another. As a person gets closer to Christ, their skills and talents will be developed for effective application in kingdom work. The good part is that once you have abandoned the most stubborn vestiges of your worldly nature, the rest becomes easy (Matthew 11:28-30). There will no longer be the conflict within your spirit of allegiance to Christ and selfish motives.

After we have personalised the death of Christ in our mind and heart, we must play it out in our lives through a conscious clearance of sin, worldliness and self. The whole point of living becomes Christ alone. Death of the material motives must be replaced by spiritual growth. The spirit is the main focus in life and we want to be as closely linked to Christ as we could possibly be. Without transformation of the spirit, it is impossible to grow in Christ. If it were possible, then the Holy Spirit would be redundant. It requires uncompromising obedience to start off correctly with Jesus followed by a determination to stay there. Then a wonderful thing takes place and we find that the fellowship of the Holy Spirit enhances our ability and desire to obey the directions from Jesus. It's the foothold that trumps potential renewal and simultaneously thwarts the urge of self-will.

Normally when a person becomes a Christian, we tell them that they have to read the Bible; join a church; pray and do other godly things. We hype up the initial joining of the kingdom as the pinnacle of a Christian's life. You were once lost to all eternity, and now that you are saved, heaven is going to be a bright eternity. In the overall scheme of God's realm, this is one critical part of our Christian walk. However, discipleship demands far greater effort on our part than a simple assent to Christ as saviour. The wider purpose of God is to configure a believer into a state where they can be trusted in the spiritual things entrusted to them. Our Father's desire is to get you into the kingdom so that you can understand and seek after what is means to be personalised with Jesus Christ. This is hard work. I was never taught to think this way until many years after I gave my life to Jesus. All the while, my self-will was doing its own thing and freely opting in and out of God's will. I trusted the Lord when I was about twelve years old but I only really started to grow many years later when I was in my late thirties. I look back at twenty-five wasted years. However, I am also very grateful to be given the grace to make it all up now. We err gravely when we fail to inform any new believer that the fundamental target is to nurture a personal relationship with Jesus from day one. This must be their main ambition in life. Kingdom work can come later. The disciples went through this sequence and so did Paul. It is rapport first, followed by kingdom work.

The transformed life seems so very far out of reach, but it isn't. We prevent and hamper ourselves in regeneration, not God. It necessitates giving up the things that the body esteems, and most of all, our freewill. Self-will opposes it, but your spirit knows the right thing to do.

SECTION TWO

Chapter 18
The way forward

Christ must be established in my spirit (Galatians 4:19), so the Holy Spirit can have a free hand to lead and teach my spirit the ways of the Lord. Jesus purposefully came into our world because we were pervaded by sin and death and in dire need of a saviour. Humankind (Adam and Eve) didn't even know the magnitude of the predicament. The Genesis record revealed the in-roads that God had made into the human experience and the subsequent prophets revealed the nature of God to human beings and this told us about the nature of our relationship with him. Jesus did not attach any affiliation to this world (John 17:16) because Satan is the prince of the world. He also stated that believers do not belong to this world. This passage amplifies the necessity for believers to be constantly directed towards heaven just as Jesus did. Everything good on earth suits the lifestyle of humans because it was meant to be this way. Yet, we don't have that craving to be with God. We revel in all the fine pleasures on offer and forget about providing for our spiritual wellbeing in eternity. Over attachment to this world and our biological family connotes affiliation to Satan and detachment from the Lord. Jesus came from purity into his own creation – a demeaning act for the holy to mingle with the unholy. Yet, it had to be done. That was God's in-breaking into the human epic. By the same token, we need to be broken into by the Holy Spirit. This is our personal illumination from God himself, and it is his way of separating his people from the world controlled by Satan (John 15:19).

He is the only means to equip our spirit for our heavenly future. The open heart and willing mind allows Jesus to immediately bring about change. The evidence of God's work can never be hidden and will be evident to others. Walking in the light is something that only the Holy Spirit can enable. This renewal process empowers a person to understand the true nature of sin in relation to the Lord. As God hates sin, likewise the believer will grow to hate sin as well. Although sin will not be completely eradicated until the Judgment, it will become increasingly repugnant that we want to keep as far apart from it as possible. The flip-side promotes the drive towards holiness. The nurture of holiness makes a person's spirit attracted to God. It's a wonderful mechanism that the Spirit puts in place that allows a sense of peace to prevail that gives encouragement and assurance that we are in a benign position with the Lord as we accumulate spiritual wealth.

This road has to be travelled by each person alone with Christ. The initial stages of sanctification are the hardest because the tests will involve acting against the things that we value most in life. Although God created freewill, he desires to conquer it by revelation of himself to people. Freewill was distorted by sin and has been misused to keep humans away from God instead of working with God as originally designed.

God wants the best for each individual and giving up self-will is the best for each person despite how detestable the idea may seem. This doesn't mean that you must live like a robot, but rather that your intimacy with the Lord constrains you to conform to his will. Freewill has been grossly perverted and Satan has ruined a perfectly good endowment that God has given. Yet, God put it there because he wanted it so. That doesn't solve our dilemma. How do we work it so that it fits in with God? The mature believer will come to hate freewill. I want God to put a tangible restriction on me, but he won't. Surely, if I overcome this persistent heinous threat, there must be an enormous prize waiting for me in eternity.

Freewill stands in the way of God's will. It is one-sided because we see our earthly responsibilities every day, and we are naturally drawn to make decisions in favour of those first. Yet, God views earthly things as secondary. The average Christian is further hampered by not being able to see the spiritual values that God has set up for us. It may seem unfair, but that's the way God has worked since time began. Everything depends on faith and trust. The visible items induce responsibility and we always view the material risks as being bigger than what they warrant. Yet, the spiritual values are vital and the risks are far greater.

Our spiritual walk is an invisible road that we have to trust God with. We can only guess at a possible outcome, but we do know with a fair degree of certainty that it won't make us financially wealthy. Fear, uncertainty, lack of confidence, discomfort in moving into the unknown and the lack of financial gain appear to be larger than life. The prospect of not having enough to live out a reasonable lifestyle and retirement is always there. The financial and economic news reminds us; the marketplace encourages us to save; friends and neighbours constantly bring this to mind in one way or another; and the government superannuation laws keep it fresh in our minds. We are just swamped with the "what if's" and it's very easy to be partial towards what we are used to and to our comfortable disposition.

The drive to satisfy the material life is greased and emboldened by rational thoughts. There's nothing wrong with doing all the good things such as caring for your family's future; earning enough to live comfortably; being available to participate in church programs etc. The invitation to serve in kingdom building goes out to all followers of Christ, but some exercise selective reasoning and never make that pledge because their priorities and circumstances are not in the right place. The mind tells one to play safe and follow the visible trail.

On the other hand, God calls a person to take a risk and venture out into the unknown where only he knows what the conclusion is going to be like. Contrary to human nature, the Lord does not make known the entire process from beginning to end and we are called to trust him. The critical element is God's will for you as an individual. Since he has the blueprint, he can engineer the details perfectly. The confidence that God inspires ought to lead us to surrender to his leadership. Those with the right spiritual posture will find that assurance.

In the day to day things, we have to overcome personal conflict, negative thoughts and the taunts of the material world. For the uninitiated, the initial stages are always the hardest. Faith has to be at its strongest and perseverance will be tested by upsets. Getting over those hurdles will raise your faith to a level that you have never imagined, and it keeps getting better the further you progress. Your spiritual eyes will be opened and there will be a serenity and satisfaction knowing that you have overcome your greatest enemy – yourself (something that you thought was beyond reality). Self-will will still be there but it won't be the dreaded nemesis of the past. After that, the tough decisions won't appear to be so fearful anymore because we begin to see life the way our Lord did. Then we will be truly on the road to sanctification. The holiness walk is not merely a set of do's and don'ts that we have to ritualistically comply with. Sanctification prompts spiritual reform that is bound by a solid and ever-growing relationship with Jesus. The renewed personality will display the glory of God (John 7:38). Ritualistic compliance will be superseded by the desire for holiness.

We need to copy the life of Jesus and that entails suffering of some sort. I thank God that it is not crucifixion because I won't be able to handle that. You can be certain that whatever difficulties or challenges that may arise, they will be equal to your tolerance and ability to cope. Nothing's easy and they will go against the very fibre of your being, but the Spirit is there to help you get through. It's a must-do and now is not the time to waste that opportunity.

Bonding with Jesus is like a marriage that has to be worked at continuously. The evil one is always there to disrupt the relationship. Sometimes I feel that even after going through all those mentally taxing times the new obstacles still seem to be impassable. If your relationship with Jesus is healthy, then you need only pause and think back to all those victories where you had conquered self and the joy that it brought, and the rest is easy.

Billy Graham's devotional 'Unto the Hills':

'God knows us, how we work, and what is best for us. If we will only relinquish the controls to Him, He will see us safely home. What about you? Who or what is in control of your life? Are you still holding onto the controls or have you allowed God to take control? What are you waiting for?'

Ps. 48:14 assures us that God is always there for our benefit and he will guide us to the end of our natural lives. The pertinent issue is 'who or what is in control of your life?' It takes colossal courage and nerve to face up to your intimate stronghold. Personal secrets and ambitions are kept behind an impregnable wall of privacy. These desires are what feeds and makes self-identity thrive. Once we commit to trust Christ, we have to surrender everything to him. The inevitable collusion between personal privacy and God's sovereignty must take place at some time or another. The question: who or what drives my thinking and decisions must be honestly dealt with. Whatever that dominant force is, it has to be eradicated and replaced by Jesus. It all comes back to a question of whether we worship the Almighty Creator or the creation. It is sad when self-will dominates and leads onto the path of self-centredness. This is a clear statement that we place personal desires above the Lord's ownership over us.

At times, we attempt to postpone selecting God's will until after we have finished our business or when we retire. You are only fooling yourself because God generally calls at the most inappropriate times when you have all the material things going your way. We may also rationalise the situation by saying that God put our secular situation in place and that is where we must continue. However, honest introspection will reveal God's will and we are left with a choice. He wants our total trust and full commitment – anything else is not good enough. Fear of the unknown and the uncertainty of the future as well as financial insecurity together with other negative thoughts tend to overpower our thinking. Sometimes Christians dwell on the matter of not being sure of what God is calling them to. This then leads in to a protracted state of procrastination and hesitation and nothing gets done. Such situations place a question on our true relationship and faith in the Lord. If a person is unwilling to make sacrifices then it suggests that there's one faith for self and another faith for God. Many may not have a clear calling and this is a bane and not a boon.

When believers begin their walk with Christ, it is a time to nurture faith. We don't know what to expect and we start by praying. Usually, we see God's hand in the minor things and that gives encouragement so we move forward slowly. As we see answers to prayer, our confidence rises a notch. The specific needs that are met, the timing of events, things that appear to be coincidental, and other ordinary daily things that need to be done that just seem to fall into place, add value to relationship with Jesus. It makes us aware that God is involved in our ordinary lives. This is a personal walk and each step that we take is faith-building. The Lord is well aware and he meets us in that situation at the right time. The realisation that it was the Lord that put events in place sparks a quick flash of happiness. We know that he is interested and he is watching over us. The answers that come during times of uncertainty and trouble leave us without a doubt that the Holy Spirit is with us and actively participating in our lives. Trust grows with the strengthening in rapport.

It's easy to draw closer to the Lord when everything is running according to our desires but life is not all roses. It is critical that when things don't go our way that we must continue to grow in spirit. In fact, it is in the darkest times when our faith may genuinely grow stronger. If you have been through enough of these down-times, an amazing thing happens. Faith no longer needs to be borne as though it were a burdensome task and the desire for value-added relationship takes the lead. Faith becomes mechanically embedded in all our decisions because we would always seek the Lord's direction in prayer. We don't even think of faith as an essential ingredient in our association with God. It is automatically assumed and nobody has to remind you to have more faith. When a problem persists and there's no answer from the Lord, we don't question our faith and we trust that God has everything under control. Healthy fellowship with God enables us to trust him to do the right thing, even if it takes a while to get an answer or when nothing happens at all. Faith grows in tandem with the reinforcement in relationship.

Fellowship is the focal point. You don't want anything to harm or upset your relationship with Jesus and you would do anything to preserve and strengthen it. You may even go so far as to entertain the thought of dying for Jesus. However, very few Christians are called to this end. Martyrs have special enabling by the Holy Spirit to stand by their relationship with God and what they believe. The ordinary believer may never have to contemplate this fearful happening, but if it does come, you can be sure that the Spirit will provide all that is needed to handle the situation faithfully. The kingdom of God utilises normal people to build and maintain it, so the majority of Christians will be serving in their own people-related situations.

One fine day you will find yourself doing things that you never wanted to do in your early Christian days. It's an odd state of affairs where your mind tells you that this is not what you want, but the spirit moves and self-will acts upon it. There is no conflict because acquiesce of the mind allows it to conform to the spirit's will. Where fellowship has reached a mature state, the Spirit will move a person to do something that they don't like. At this stage, self doesn't have a say anymore and the renewed personality does what God wants because one's character follows after him (John 21:18).

This passage had a notable impact on my decision to give up a good job and join the mission field. It was a hard decision to make. I never thought of myself going to the field; that was for someone else, not me. I was happy to pray for missionaries and to give financial support, and that was where it stopped. I purposely skipped the visiting mission meetings because I didn't want to get involved. However, a friend encouraged me to attend, and then I never stopped and even looked out for where I could fit in. At the end of the talk, they always finished with an invitation for more workers. At first, I ignored them but gradually a change of mind came over me. There was a need and I had the skills and no commitments. So, I assented in my mind to change careers, and it became very easy once I made that decision.

The hardest part was to leave my dream-job. I knew that once I quit, there will never be another like it ever again It was now or never. I started looking out for possible destinations and waiting for the Lord to lead. I didn't want to go to one particular country because I wasn't interested and there were others that appeared much more exciting. However, it took several years before the Lord disclosed my destination. I was at a conference and asked one of the representatives and he suggested this country (the one that I had previously discounted) and I was disenchanted, so I left. A year later I went back to the conference and asked the same representative in the hope he may have forgotten me and that he would suggest something else because they had eight other alternatives. To my dismay, he suggested the same country! I went home and gave it a bit of thought and much prayer. I concluded that this must be the place that the Lord wants me to go to. Shortly after, I contacted them and what transpired is encapsulated in history.

After your relationship with Jesus builds up, the spiritual state moves from theory to practice, and you will actually want God to lead you to participate in building his kingdom. To submit to someone else's direction is a sure sign of victory over self-will. The idea of going to where you do not want to go requires an authentic move away from your old values. This can only be achieved through relinquishing freewill otherwise the act will merely be driven by self-fulfilment, for reward or some other ulterior motive. In the absence of coercion, I can't think of anything that would compel a person to take orders from somebody and to do things that they never wanted to do, except for the love for Christ. Everybody who has had the proper education and exposure in the west is fully aware of human rights, freedom of thought and self-expression, and a host of other things that oppose the above passage of Scripture. To follow a concept that is counter-culture and that goes against the grain can only be brought about by a superior Being. However, the act of surrender still requires a decision to be made on our part before we can get into the play. Jesus works in our spirit to free us from anxiety. They are not random or impulsive prompts but preconceived and fluidly executed with certainty. A person will know indisputably that those motions came from the Lord.

Impulsiveness stems from our background and that has no part in God's plans. It indicates a lack of patience. We want to look good in the presence of others, so we will always attempt to vindicate our actions in one way or another. Impulsiveness must be changed into sanctified intuition through discipline, training and sensitivity to the Holy Spirit. Discipleship is a gift from God and we are not naturally attracted to it. It's something to be treasured, nurtured and passed on to other willing believers. Humility in a student greatly enhances the absorption of the spiritual training received. We must have the constant fellowship and grace from God to live out our convictions every day. It gets easier with practice. Sanctified instinct must override impulsiveness.

Kingdom work usually takes a long time to accomplish and in the mean time we have to go through the monotony of uneventful daily life. At times we wish that God would hurry up and get it done but that's not the way that he works. The old nature tells us that we have to be doing something noticeable for God. As long as God notices our obedience, that's good enough and nothing has to be forced. We are required to show grace and patience amid the drudgery. Our efforts often go unnoticed and that adds to boredom and opens the mind to wandering thoughts. However, the element that keeps a person intrigued and willing is a reactive relationship with the Spirit.

Jesus never had to go through a transition from self-will to the Father's will because he knew what the Father required of him and he obeyed. We don't have that privilege and must undergo a paradigm overhaul however distasteful it may appear. The relationship that Jesus had with God was the most intimate and most critical thing in his life. He was determined to fulfil God's will even if it meant the cross. If your relationship with Jesus is flourishing then you are blessed and there's nothing to worry about but everything to look forward to. Self-will must die a spiritual death, never to interfere with the will of the Father ever again in our lives. The fruit of the Spirit – love, joy, peace, patience, kindness, goodness, faithfulness, gentleness and self-control all blend in and operate seamlessly under the umbrella of our association with God and people. You take in the other moral aspects of God and become more like Jesus. Since we are born into sin, we can never get away from the temptation. This relationship requires that we make serious efforts every time to reduce and eliminate the possibilities of sin because God has no place for waywardness. It's a great position to be in; one that substantially resonates with the Holy Spirit.

Serving for a limited time and then reverting to self-interest is a sign of dominance by the old self. All of humanity gained from Jesus' sacrifice, but it was God's will that Jesus had to obey relentlessly. Partial obedience equates to unfinished business that produces fractional rewards, if any. The way forward is not as simple as the mere utterance of the words. Each process presents a different challenge that calls for perseverance and responsible decision making. After all the easy adjustments are made, the hard ones will be waiting. These stubborn personal interests may hold you up for a while, and each time that you don't correct them, the Spirit will remind you the next time. The Spirit has an agenda too and he won't leave until you submit. Self is to blame for the lack of progress in renewal. However, grace abounds and the fellowship of the Holy Spirit will enable us to do those greater things when we are in the right standing with him. The greater things are not described in the Bible and those depend on God's discretion.

Freewill is a powerful tool but it can never outwit God and it never will. The best foot forward is to win the Spirit's favour through steady spiritual growth. If you don't pay the price now; you won't get the rewards in future. When you do the arithmetic, there's only one choice. It's quite simple; or is it?

Chapter 19
Cycle

Personal prejudices are the scourge of spiritual advancement. Regardless of how hard we try and how much we improve, prejudices are never truly extinguished from the subconscious. They seem to appear at the most inappropriate times. God does not tolerate bias because this is not in his character. The new creation seeks to stamp out bias completely so that the moral attributes of God can be appropriately fostered to function the way God wants it to. It is fallacious and unnecessary to compare one's spiritual personality with others. You will notice that some people behave in a way that you do not approve of. This is no cause for criticism because this is their own business and they have to get their spiritual standing right with God. Instead, you ought to keep raising the bar in pursuit of Christ (John 21:22). The converse is also true, where you notice that another has better morals than yours, then you should learn to convert your weaknesses to strengths. The Holy Spirit will help you get there if your attitude is correct because he is the healer of the spiritually ill; more so he is the benefactor of invaluable spiritual assets. The rejuvenation by the Holy Spirit in one's life cannot be hidden. It will stand out and people will take note because it points them to Jesus who we reflect through our sanctified life.

The Lord is not interested in what we can do or bring to him. It's what he can do for us and the use he has for us. God can only transform us after we have made the determination to enlist the Spirit's assistance. There must be no reservations, and no turning back. The implications are startling. How are we going to change to a lifestyle that has no envy, no lust, no self-interest, no sensitivity about negative comments etc.? Disencumbering yourself from inherent and habitual prejudices is the only way forward. The training process is not easy either. Admission of one's faults, writing them down, and talking about them are essential but meaningless if not followed through by genuine renewal in attitude and behaviour.

To break out of old habits, thoughts and speech is an ongoing work that seems to have no end. The moment we move a step forward, the next hurdle is there before us. Christians must live up to their 'new creation' status (2 Corinthians 5:17, Galatians 6:15). It's a spiritual make-over that comes out in physical reform. Jesus reconciled us to God and now we have a message of reconciliation to others to point them to Christ. Reconciliation is our personal continuous business with God. It follows after the Lord has been pacified through our faith in Christ. The believer must change from the old nature to the new and harmonise their spiritual characteristics to conform to God's. No amount of learning can be considered as too much. Instead, one ought to guard against complacency as it tends to encourage laxity and stagnation. This is the time that the believer is the most vulnerable and should be alert to the evil one's tricks. Usually, it is just redirecting attention back to self. However, spiritual reconciliation to holiness is vital.

The secular idea of 'looking back' has a reminiscence connotation and in the business world it usually is a reflection on past error or poor decision making. There's a positive implication that indicates success if a person never has to look back. The Bible takes a different view and keeps exhorting believers to look back. We have to remind ourselves where we were before we became Christians. It is God who drew us to Christ in the first instance. Then we have to recall the special moments when Jesus came to our assistance and got us out of our darkest moments. Reliving those precious times will bring gratitude and joy all over again. The power of God to change lives and build a spiritual bond ought to inspire us to greater faith and closer fellowship with him (Ephesians 2:13). This system of recollection concentrates our attention on God as our most trusted companion in life. Introspection applies the same principle to correct mistakes and to move forward.

Jesus will never change and he will be there for all our future challenges and sorrows just as he had in the past. Simple faith, basic trust and mature reliance on the Lord are all that is required. Will you be deterred if the Lord allows all blessings to be withdrawn? Those that have a mature relationship with Jesus will never allow any conceivable hardship to interfere with their trust in and allegiance to him. The accumulated evidences of God's hand in your life and the proximity of the Spirit living in you are compelling influences to continue in faith.

The aspiration of every believer must be to reach the highest level of spiritual discipline that we are capable of attaining. It would be a shame to aim for anything less. A static target for spiritual growth is not defined as only the Spirit knows how far we are capable of going. The Christian life consists of a lifetime's striving to get to that higher position. When we think that we have arrived, it keeps pointing to an even higher level that goes beyond the boundaries of personal comprehension and perceived capability. Only the Holy Spirit can provide us with the ability to reach beyond. However, we have to want it so badly and we must put in the motions to solicit the Spirit's initiative to make it happen. The decisions that you once found so hard to make and always wanted to avoid become so easy afterwards. Human opinion ought not to be misconstrued and it is God who must be satisfied with one's progress.

Relationship.

When we get our relationship to the Lord right, we get our meaning and purpose in life correct. It's normal for people to conceive an aspiration and then work towards its accomplishment. Human life is only meaningful if it is managed by God. Failing this, a person may be trying to force something to work into God's kingdom that he didn't intend, and that will count for nothing (Isaiah 64:6) because the effort is self-generated. The human mind is driven by ego, personal reasoning and the desire to be recognised by others. More often than not, it does not conform to God's desires. We can only get on the correct path through reading the Scripture, prayer and sensitivity to the Spirit's advice.

The Holy Spirit prays in our behalf to the Father. I have always been curious as to what he prays for. Is it for the things that I am immediately aware of and concerned with; it is for things that are yet to materialise; is it for things that I have no knowledge about; is it for the kingdom work; is it for what God wants and expects of me or is it something so simple that it has caused me to be unconsciously blind? Is he interceding for the things that I'm praying for? These questions give rise to some interesting scenarios. We could work through all the permutations and emerge with a different set of questions every time. Whatever it may be, our primary concern must be to stay in line with God's purposes and be aware of the spiritual meaning behind ostensible things that occur. The Spirit's help comes when we are weak and in need (Romans 8:27). It is God's will that the Spirit prays according to and we may not even be aware of the connotations and should pray for illumination.

Once a sound relationship with the Spirit is in place, our prayer-life ought to be stepped up. Prayer is the quintessential act of our submission to the King. It is our way of showing dependence on God.

Since we cannot see the invisible God, prayer is the only positive way that we are going to get his attention and it is the lubricant that puts our relationship with the Lord in good working order. Non-communication kills a friendship. Despite God perceiving our thoughts from afar, personal prayer is an individual's attempt to connect and fellowship with the Lord. Its very nature elevates God to the high position that he rightfully occupies. Your offer of prayers must be as regular as breathing and that demonstrates your sincerity and zeal in wanting to know God. If you are walking close to God, your prayer life would be complimentary.

After the seventy-two disciples returned from their mission, they were amazed that even demons obeyed them at the name of Jesus. However, Jesus told them not to celebrate over that but to rejoice because they have a place in heaven (Luke 10:20). Successful completion of kingdom work only calls for thanksgiving to God for the results as the glory belongs to him. Works have to be done appropriately but they should not be elevated unduly and this is a humbling thought. It's an easy mistake to make because self is involved and the temptation to express personal style and interests are ever present. Rather, the emphasis should be on the priority of relationship to Jesus that the work is performed with Christ as the centre. We must follow him and serve him in the place where he is (John 12:26, 21:19) and God will honour the servant in this regard. Following Jesus requires us to be patient and to wait for him to open the doors. In the real world, this can get very boring not to mention the frustration when it is apparent that so much can be done. Blind faith is invalid because fellowship with Jesus Christ has been proved to be reliable and trustworthy. The fact that we can't see where we're going does not amount to blind faith because Jesus sees everything clearly.

All kingdom work is created and given by God alone to whom he chooses to use. The worker is unimportant and obedience is the key. People are so powerfully drawn to the visible results and we incorrectly conclude that the greater the material outcome, the higher the elevation of the individual's spiritual status. Do great works and achievement enhance intimacy with Jesus? I think not because intimacy with Jesus and spiritual development is based on a healthy bonding and not on works. Drawing closer to the Holy Spirit is a personal learning process and cannot be achieved through works.

It is incorrect to get so involved in the work that relationship with Jesus becomes secondary. This may happen unintentionally when the work becomes time-consuming. We cannot make our mark in kingdom work by our own exertion, unless God approves. There are certain people with particular skills that will fit certain needs in God's kingdom. It is an insult to the Lord to come before him offering all your skills and intelligence for his work. An omnipotent God needs nobody let alone puny human talents to get his kingdom built. A servant is a person who follows instructions from the Master. If you were to think that your creativity was the main driver for the success of any spiritual achievement then God is relegated to the background and pride is projected to the fore. It is the undertaking that God does through us that is paramount and not what we do for him. The danger comes from within as people like to see something produced by their own talents and exertion. It elevates self-esteem and this may be a subconscious hidden agenda or it may be unintentional, but its presence lends itself to temptation.

The verse in 1 Chronicles 29:11 describes the sovereignty of God as being above all creation. There is no match for God but the liberty of free-thinking allows people the choice to believe that human beings are able to do anything that glorifies self. Everything in creation belongs to God and when a person invents anything noteworthy, they are only using the tools that the Lord owns and has provided. Human ingenuity falls far behind the wisdom of God. The work of human hands must be submitted before the Lord in humility; but self-aggrandisement encourages pride and the desire for personal acclamation. Glory is only attributable to God alone. Idolatry, skewed scientific arguments, humanistic postmodern thinking etc. rob God of his glory. The Children of Israel departed from God and followed the practices of the heathen nations all around them. They glorified their own thinking and handiwork and this angered God greatly because Israel was supposed to reveal the glory of God to all the nations around them. God will never allow His glory to be shared with anyone or thing.

An important part of relationship is to seek after God. A good habit to develop is to frequently inquire of the Lord every time a decision has to be made. Fellowship is enhanced at the same time. There are several passages that describe how the Israelites and David enquired of the Lord and the favorable results that ensued. This shows faithfulness, dependence, trust and obedience to God and it keeps in interactive fellowship with the Lord. There are cases where the people did not enquire of the Lord and the outcomes were calamitous. Normally, we will not hear the voice of God in answer to prayer, but he will enlighten our path. The avid follower prays often so as to draw closer to Jesus and thereby reinforce the spiritual bonding with God. If prayer is relaxed, a person's thoughts will drift back to self. People that constantly admit helplessness before God are the ones that get the most benefit, and they are the ones that the Lord delights in the most. It is the humble that moves the heart of God.

The disposition of being wise in the ways of God and foolish according to the world is not acquired overnight. Spiritual wisdom only comes from the Lord and the world doesn't understand it. It is of no financial value, so the uninformed consider it worthless and foolish. The noble trait of humility brings wisdom, discipline and understanding from the Holy Spirit (Proverbs 11:2 James 3:13). The wisdom from Christ will take you where you have never been before.

God's purpose.

Earlier on in this book, I posed the question as to what the meaning and purpose of life is. By now, Christians should realise that life is not about ourselves but all about God. Are we going to make this real? Let's go through a brief recap. Life itself originates from God, thus, all life belongs to God. When the body dies, the soul/spirit will return to the King for reward or retribution. Once this fact is understood, the purpose of life becomes clearer. If God owns my life and everything else, then the next question has to be: what is God's will for me? We can only know his will if we are in the right standing with him. God will only reveal his will to people that he can use as they will have a part in kingdom construction and reward.

As new believers, we participate in the body of Christ. We participate in the church programs and that is our introduction to kingdom work. There are various outreach activities and we try to do our bit. Once a routine is established, it's easy to fall in line and work methodically. Somewhere along the association, one may ask what God's purpose is for one's life. Most will be satisfied to maintain a routine in church life because that may be planned to synchronise with their secular interests. It's a stable and controllable lifestyle. However, a few will venture further and come closer to God because they feel the need to do so. The Holy Spirit will respond by dropping a series of leads, but nothing concrete. It's all encouraging so we keep going along as the path unfolds.

In the early 1990's, I wasn't really interested in God's will because I had many things on my own agenda. I was always afraid that he would call me to do something that I didn't like or that would take me away from my hobbies. After accumulating more Bible knowledge, my spiritual bank grew in the early stages of renewal and the Bible became more interesting. Several years went by and routine Christian life became monotonous. I wanted something more and made the commitment to seek after God's will. It took great courage and this time I was serious about it. I continued with Bible study and regular prayer. My daily prayers always included a plea for God to show me his will, but there was no answer so I stopped asking. He does not react to my timing (no matter how sincere my plea) but only when he has things in place. This was proved many times over and it didn't disappoint but rather encouraged me. The progression eventually led to service on the field.

I didn't realise that God's purpose was to break my self-will. Despite resolving to sincerely obey God, there was still a bit of self-interest that I had reserved in my heart. However, he did not force me to do things instead he used my Bible study times and indicators in life to reveal his personality. During my studies, my self-will was gradually being eroded and replaced by the willingness to accept God's will and direction. My interest grew rapidly and eventually when I had to leave for field service, there was no doubt and no hesitation. My relationship with Jesus had reached a milestone. I knew that I only had to ask once and then wait for his reply, and sometimes it took a lot of patience. Over time, patience became an appendage to prayer. God's silence never diminished my faith which kept on strengthening.

Discipleship training is part of God's will for all his followers. The more knowledge gained; the better. However, training has limited value and the Lord can only effectively use a person after their self-will has been broken and eradicated. You have to be poured out like a drink offering in sacrificial service where there's no retraction (Philippians 2:17). I did the right thing despite discomfort and personal bias. This made me realise that self-determination cannot be part of God's plan. Service simply demands the death of personal freewill and nothing less. A seed has to die before it can be productive (John 12:24). The disciple has to die to self and render full commitment to God and then the Spirit can use them to work effectively for Christ.

Evangelism is just part of the process of our bonding with the Lord. In spite of how much we desire that all the peoples of the world be saved, spiritually that's impossible because nobody can come to Jesus unless the Father enables. It's plain that there will be the saved and the unsaved. As we grow older we see this reality in life. Evangelism requires a broad approach to the target group in the hope of getting the chosen ones that God brings into one's path. Once meaningful contact has been established, then a narrow approach must be applied to concentrate on the ones who are interested. It is a necessary part of the Christian life but not necessarily the main task for every believer. Some have talents that are better suited for building other parts of the kingdom. A new convert must be told that their primary goal in life is to grow their personal relationship with God. If this leads to church planting then be it by the will of God. It's a misnomer to think that credit only comes via winning people to Christ because rewards apply to all aspects of kingdom work and not just evangelism. Being an agent in this vital process is merely that and no more. Just be satisfied that the Lord has favoured you as the instrument to connect with people. Looking at others that have a thriving ministry is deceiving because it is the Lord that has brought about that success and it was not humanly manufactured. Every worker will be justly rewarded for their obedience.

The ultimate method of glorifying God is to become one with Jesus as he is one with the Father. It is important to understand how God assesses my spiritual status and how I must narrow the gap between God's will and my perception. The assessment criteria are all laid down in the commands in Scripture and there are no trick questions. God's purpose is to have you personally close to him such that his thoughts become your thoughts (John 17:21-22). This idea seems so distant and unattainable. I have tried to discover the will of the Lord in the majority of my decisions but I have seldom thought of reaching the level where God's thoughts and intentions are actually mine. Somehow, it appears so remote because this condition requires a perfect relationship with the Father (which we will never experience in this life). It's easy for Jesus to say because he came from the virgin birth. Is it then unfair for Jesus to want this of us? The moment a believer starts the transformation through regeneration, they begin the process of learning the thoughts of God. Holiness only comes from the Lord and he will teach us how to behave according to his standards. The distance that we have to go will always appear to be out of reach, but it's the resolve to keep growing in sanctification that matters. If you feel that your spiritual association with Jesus is progressing then you are heading in the right direction. Obedience solves this problem because we are doing what God thinks and intends and we don't have to know his thoughts in advance.

The kingdom of God has multiplied exponentially since the first church was birthed. There have been so many obstacles to growth, yet the church has stood its ground. This can only be attributed to the Holy Spirit training believers into the right material that is fit for use by God for his kingdom construction. God brings us into relationship with himself and we merely have to commit to the partnership. Humans can never offer personal creativity that is acceptable in the kingdom. The supreme Creator creates his own holy work and we just link up all the pieces so that the building can take form. If you refuse the absolute direction and authority of God, then you will be of no use to him. Choice is not forced or coerced; I have freewill and I use it to obey God. Regeneration allows me to recognise and admit that I have nothing of value to offer to God. He is right and I'm wrong. Sanctified common-sense tells me that I cannot match the Lord's love and I owe him so much that it bothers me constantly. Obedience is the only course of action left. Nothing that you can do would please God more than this. The process of God integrating his thoughts with the believer is only confined to wisdom and instructions and never to granting executive powers of management, design and creation.

Chapter 20
Invitation

After conversion, when the renewal process gets under way, the next step is to take in as much Bible knowledge as possible. Most of my friends encouraged me to do that and it was wise as the possibility of distractions could hamper the early development stage. There are so many things in modern life that occupy our time and thoughts. If time is not set aside for Bible reading and prayer, then worldly things will occupy that void. The domineering influence of society, work and business often has a unbalanced hold on our decision making. Time is divided between church attendance and ministry, work/business, leisure and family responsibilities. We try to strike a balance but it is never the ideal and we wish that we had more time for relaxation and more money to do the things that we like. These choices are significant because a Christian must act responsibly.

We are living in the end times and the divide between the unbelieving sector of the human race and God is ever widening. Science and technology are advancing at such a rapid pace that human arrogance and pride tends towards self-deification. It's only a matter of time, finances and the correct research and development to discover new inventions that lead to commercialisation. Once scientists know how a system works, the skilled mind will be able to exploit it. Anything is possible with humans as the Lord said in Genesis 11:6.

Prior to the fall, Adam and Eve had perfect memory and thought processes and they were given the authority to subdue the earth. They had no major challenge, no knowledge of the world's resources etc. so there wasn't any need for their intelligence and capability to be stretched. I wonder what it would be like had Adam had all the modern equipment, resources and technology that we have today. I'm sure that nothing would be impossible for him either. Since human beings belong to God, so we have always had a natural enemy in Satan. After the fall, the roles were reversed and Satan became our closest friend and we became enemies of God. This is the reality whether we realise it or not. The Holy Spirit is our ticket back to God and righteousness, and each person has the will to make it happen.

In the first five thousand years when life was simple, the revelation of God was exhibited through the prophets. A person did not have the multiplicity of distractions that we have today. Even believers put their attention in other things first and their faith in God lapses. Christians must apply faith appropriately in order to stay close to Jesus. The secular world is preoccupied with its own developments and God is not important. We must be cautious not to unintentionally fall into the same mindset. It takes determination as there are many interesting things on offer. However, we have the Bible to guide us and the Holy Spirit for companionship so there's no excuse.

The Holy Spirit works silently and this is not very useful at times but it is the way that he has chosen. It seems that God is happy to allow the world to be blinded by the distraction of science and technology. Spiritual truth is being over-shadowed by the ingenuity of the human mind and creative spirit. Jesus relies on his church and the mission effort to fulfil his purposes. It may seem disadvantageous, but it has been like this in the past and the church has still flourished. Whatever happens in the future, God is still in charge.

Monotony and drudgery are a bane in long term ministry. It's most conspicuous when least desired. This is the time when thoughts of change come to mind. You may have been doing menial and uninteresting tasks for a while, hoping that somebody else would take over, but to no avail. There may be many valid arguments for change as well as beneficial reasons for not changing. Petitions for the Lord's direction are essential but sometimes it takes a while before he responds. Those concerned have to be patient and faithful. Routine work in ministry is a test of your spiritual maturity and endurance. It shows whether your self-will is sincerely committed to the Lord or not. Monotonous work is never ideal and it may go unnoticed. It may be tiring, boring and even unpleasant but there's no one to do it except you. At times like these, you need stimulus from God to carry on. The Lord gives meaning to all these daily insignificant and unattractive tasks because he created the concept of work right at the beginning. When you see a job in the light of God's purpose and character, it alters the way you do it forever. Every simple matter in the kingdom is important, not only for expansion but also for personal spiritual enrichment.

The possibility that the Lord may want you to alter your current working environment cannot be discounted. This has to be prayed through thoroughly and careful steps taken when an opening is revealed.

Caution should be the order of the day until certainty is established. The Spirit may alert a person to any changes that need to be made or to alternate courses of action that will facilitate the process. Time and labour will be wasted if the Lord does not approve, and earnest supplication will make us sensitive to the Spirit's guidance.

The Lord's directions are not anything that humans can devise or concoct because we don't know God's blueprint. The kingdom of God is managed by the Lord himself and only he knows how it works, what he wants in it and what its ultimate form is going to take. To this end, Christians can only learn from God and act upon his commission. Self-will is outlawed because self cannot share in God's glory and a worker must only apply their talent and get the job done in the proper manner. This is not as boring as it sounds because your love for Jesus will help doing it a joy. It is only God's will that counts and nothing else.

Partnership with God.

Since people are kingdom business, and people react to stimulus, it is ineluctable that the messenger will attract a certain degree of attention. The admiration and esteem lavished on a talented worker can have negative effects. In a world where people can express themselves through so many mediums, it can be distracting. The messenger is a servant and cannot and must not be competing with God for attention. The attitude of the servant must direct attention to the Giver and not the gift.

Incipient sanctification happens without us even realising the great potential it holds for us. As our spirit matures, we come into a workable partnership with the Holy Spirit. This is a split-level association whereby God makes the sovereign decisions and the worker has to do all the assembly tasks. It is a Master-servant arrangement where the servant must follow orders to the letter. It's nothing new because all the prophets in the Old Testament did exactly that.

Those sent to outreach work on the field know the objective. Once you are on the field, you get on with it. It's never easy, but it's up to the individual to adapt. If you are sent to a disadvantaged group, the advantage is that the magnetism of the affluent lifestyle is not there to distract you. Out of sight and out of mind; you can concentrate on the Lord and always be looking out for the opportunities that he may bring about. Co-workers are equally important because they propagate the gospel and help to strengthen each other's faith (1 Thessalonians 3:2). This is a partnership with fellow believers in kingdom work. It is supposed to work closely after our relationship with God, but it doesn't always turn out well. Disciplined prayer is an interlinked accompaniment and is the means to receive instructions, encouragement, healing, teaching and all the vital things that a worker needs from Christ.

The cross was not Jesus' idea, it was God's decree. He used Jesus for his purpose of salvation for the world. Sanctified workers are no different. Getting to the stage of total abandonment to God is much harder than just reading the words. It's a hurdle that every serious believer has to get over. God is using me for his personal objectives. This is a phenomenal privilege and I must assent to the belief that my purpose in life belongs to the Father and not to me.

Creating a cocoon about oneself is tantamount to building a personal-world within God's world. It's an attempt to hide from God and creates a false sense of security because the Lord sees the deepest secrets of the heart. There's no place to hide. Self-determination is idolatry and it hates taking orders. Your freewill prevents the Holy Spirit from remoulding your personality after God's. Children of God must take after their Father. It will be a disgrace to those who have made scanty attempts or not tried at all.

The Bible never refers to Jesus as having faith, it's assumed. On the other hand, Jesus always associated faith with people. Faith is a concept for people to grasp and master. Jesus is God and it is people that need to place their faith in him. Belief, trust, dependence, reliance etc. are all faith-based concepts that are directed at something or someone that is able to satisfy a need. Jesus didn't need faith because he and the Father are one (John 10:30). Humans must have faith so that a connection to God and the Spirit may be made. Everything that a person links to God requires faith. Christ didn't have to learn obedience; it came naturally to him. The greater a person's faith in Christ, the stronger the fellowship with him will become. Faith's other noble function is to support a person's dependence on the Spirit to cultivate sanctification.

Unswerving faith assists in the metamorphosis from the worldly self to regeneration. The life that is synchronised with the Lord's leadership will find assuring tranquillity and peace in every situation. Random occurrences won't catch you by surprise. The shock and fear factor that accompanies certain situations and helplessness won't overshadow faith and dependence on God anymore. Your faith won't allow them to interfere with the priority of God's work. Thus, the Holy Spirit may go about unhindered in making you an effective instrument for service. This is where you want to be.

Deep sincere personal convictions should always be checked for authentication with God through prayer. Devotion to the Lord is the sole purpose of the maturing spirit, the commitment to maintaining and strengthening one's divine relationship first ranks above actual field work. This reinforces the habit of obedience. The wonderful realisation and feeling that comes from the sanctified life that receives prolific wisdom from the mind of Christ is pure joy. Fanatic pursuit of work is easy to do, but it may not always be trouble-free because skewed thoughts will introduce personal purposes into God's work. A worker may be complying with all spiritual morals but the urge for better results may introduce self-interest to do more. Unknowingly, the drive for greater yield is fuelled by personal ambition. Humbleness before God combats self-will.

The Lord invites believers into his family to enjoy personal relationship with him and to do his work. This is not our initiative and we have no right to input personal desires and ideas. God sets the rules and we have to comply. We normally dislike being confined to boundaries because we have been spoilt by freewill. Compliance is really quite normal, for example when a host invites you over for a function, the host sets the rules and all attendants have to abide by them and also maintain an acceptable level of etiquette. People usually have no qualms about this because the arrangement has visible benefits and it's only for a short period of time. God's demands are always long term and sometimes the rewards are invisible and people have big problems with that.

Chapter 21
Self-control

God is acutely aware of each individual's fundamental weaknesses. The means and avenues for sin are all around us but generally, it only materialises when we choose to carry out the action. In a world where there is no visible moral policeman, it's really up to the individual to decide on what course they want to take. Naturally God holds us accountable for our actions.

Self-control is the ability to reign in self-will so that a person will refrain from self-gratification and choose actions that focus on Biblical morals. This disciplinary process has its ultimate purpose in Christ. It's a preventative measure suggested by Scripture for our benefit. It goes further; once in place, it takes on a spiritual attribute that is part of God's character. It's a quality that Jesus wants all his followers to have. Self-control enables a person to do the things that God wants, and it's a simple way to fall in line with his will.

Throughout history there are countless cases where people have mastered self-control and accomplished some remarkable things. In the secular world, these people were doing things for personal gain. They disciplined themselves in a particular way that brought success. In these stories, we glean many useful motivational strategies, quotes and sayings. The stories move you to admiration and sometimes to envy. The reader is often left with the persistent after-thought: 'If only I could do that'. Theirs was a limited form of self-control because they would indulge in other things. The wealthy like the high-flying lifestyle and the others have their hobbies.

In the spiritual realm, self-control is to be exercised in holiness under all conditions. It is no simple task to get hold of a bad habit or an obstinate mental thought and make it into something that has virtue and is of value to self and others. It's ironical to regulate self for somebody else's cause unlike the secular sense for personal gain. The Lord requires believers to do things in a certain way and that requires discipline and training. The ambit that the discipline of godliness covers is too broad for the ordinary people to master, and they cannot do it by themselves. This kind of self-control can only be taught by the Spirit.

Control over self is a restraint on how you would normally tend to act. The idea is to set aside impulsiveness and meditate on God. In our struggles to stay focussed on Christ at all times, we are invaded by so many contrasting thoughts and those distract us so that we lose sight of our spiritual relationship with God. We fall into the error of meditation when we should be implementing self-control measures. Potential courses of action may come to mind but after appropriate preparation it must be followed by action. Action points ought to be laid down to counter-act bad practices. Likewise, concrete steps are to be taken to enhance godly behaviour. Prayer and obedience to the Spirit's leading are essential for lasting change to personality.

At times we may be over-cautious and we wait for the Lord, and we keep on waiting, so we end up doing nothing. A friend shared this point and he felt that after waiting so long, he may have missed the opportunities that were placed before him all the time. We really want the Lord to put something before our eyes so that we know that it's truly from him, but things don't happen that way in real life. We ought to take a risk and do something and then monitor it for authenticity by the Spirit's guidance. All too often we ignore self-control and move ahead through instinct. Sanctified prayer will prompt the Holy Spirit to alert you of error and you can always change your mind and go the right way. It is no shame to admit personal mistakes as this will open the way for a second chance. This kind of situation takes quick thinking and a careful ear to the Spirit's advice or sometimes his silence. The latter is an indicator not to rush things and it will test a person's patience.

The Christian life must be aimed at surrendering to God's control. You do all the hard work to conquer self just to hand it all over to the Lord. It definitely doesn't make sense if you are looking at this from the angle of self-gratification. Self-control aims at removing self-determination and having God at the helm. It reaches beyond self as it grows in regeneration. This paragon of self-control is not easy to master and is only open to those who have faith. It's a training process and a constant battle for many that are starting their walk with the Lord. External influences have a strong hold on a person's mindset. Picture the following scenario. A talented man has a family plus there's an urge to do something for the Lord, but that path will lead to grossly reduced income and social status. The initial urge to serve may be very strong, but secular temptations cause a person to hesitate and procrastinate. The person makes allowance for the delays and the necessary actions are postponed for another time or simply forgotten over time. This is analogous to the parable of the sower in Matthew 13 and it relates to obedience to God. In the same way, a believer's resolve may be positioned in rocky places where the urge to be obedient rises up very quickly but the sun scorches it and it equally rapidly comes to nothing. When trouble or hardship arises, failure will result because the fundamental principles are not firmly in the heart. Even seasoned believers may have personal fancies where the Word falls on hard ground and stunts the sanctification process.

Mountain-top experiences and godly intentions are great, but they have to be followed by positive commitment, otherwise a person would fall back into their old routine and there will be no spiritual progress. The mindset that is posited among the thorns allows the worries of life and the deception of finance and status to undermine faith and the opportunity to practice new regeneration morals are ignored. Secular reasoning strangles obedience and faith and sanctification will stagnate. You may have accumulated a bit more head-knowledge, but this does not add to growth in your relationship to God. James 2:26 warns that faith that is devoid of the appropriate action is worthless.

Success is measured by fruitfulness. The meaning goes beyond initial faith at conversion and alludes to sanctified productivity and behaviour. Committed believers may be used by God to grow in personal sanctification and to yield a harvest of spiritual fruit. This crop is the fruit of the spirit in Galatians 5:22 – 24 which is a personal benefit. It may also mean evangelism whereby believers are won to Christ or where a believer applies the spiritual fruit that he has gained to encourage other Christians to enhance their own fruit of the spirit. Bear in mind that no person is able to infuse another in the ways of sanctification, only the Holy Spirit can do that – it's a personal thing between you and God. All we can do is urge and guide believers to the general steps that people take to seek improvement. Everybody has to decide their own path. This can only be achieved by denying self-will and allowing the Spirit to teach because only he is able to give the increase.

Self-control is not confined to a dull process of submission to God's direction at every turn. In real life, the Lord is not constantly standing over you and issuing instructions so that life becomes mechanical and a bore. Normally, a Christian takes up the calling and then moves into position for the task. God allows the worker to express the work in their own style and would lead the worker on to do what he intends. Submission at the operational level is crucial and requires a close walk with the Holy Spirit and much prayer. Personal creativity is inappropriate. If things don't appear to work out, there needs to be patience and fervent prayer for direction. If after a reasonable time of prayer and still nothing happens, then there's a strong possibility that the Lord does not want to proceed further with this matter and a change of direction ought to be considered. Never-ending prayer brings God-control into action. We chase after the Lord and not vice versa.

In my experience, I have always had indicators to my way forward. A few choices were not to my liking but I went along with them anyway because my conscience bid me do the right thing. My conscience was at rest in that I was in the Lord's will. In cases where there were conflicting conditions or where I wasn't totally sure, I would proceed cautiously but keep looking for signs that I may have taken the wrong path. Things are much easier to correct during the early implementation stages. To date, I have had peace and confidence that I have done what the Lord has asked of me. Poor worldly decisions have nothing to do with the spiritual. These are not the high-level spiritual decisions that need to come from God. We just have to learn from the results and improve our secular decisions in future. God does care for our material needs.

There is no middle ground in responding to God's call; you either accept your assignment or you reject it. A person cannot negotiate the terms of employment with the Lord. It is invalid to argue that: 'I will do it if I can gain that' because God's terms are peremptory. You can be assured that you will be given all the spiritual tools necessary to carry out the task. In the secular business environment and regarding cultural issues, careful study has to be made in the matter at hand. These areas have their own pitfalls and even after careful investigation, errors may still be made. At the same time, we ought to become astute in worldly ways and to handle matters wisely (Luke 16:8-9). There will be things that you learn while on the job, but with prayer and due planning you will get through. Inadvertent errors may arise, but the Lord will guide. Remain prayerful and you will learn to be wiser for the future.

Self-control in the low-level decisions in daily life is best kept as simple as possible. Try not to create problems that weren't there before. The individual has complete freedom to do as they please. Naturally, health is the criterion that determines the balance and mix of our choice but economics and personal preference are also relevant to these decisions. I remember in my late teens when our family was planning to buy a washing machine. It was a sorely needed item as we were doing the washing by hand and this would save a lot of time and effort. We didn't pray about this and just went ahead to the different shops to make enquiries. It was exciting to discover the various makes and models on the market and the prices. After much deliberation, we finally decided to buy the best model that we could afford and it was most satisfying to have to it delivered to our home. We were very happy and felt that we had made the right decision. It performed to perfection and never gave any problems, right until the day that we gave it away. Common-sense measures are sufficient to keep out of trouble but be aware of any decisions that may adversely impact the spiritual.

One of the hardest disciplines to absorb and practice is that of emotional control. Anger containment is an art that few are able to master. Normally, people are averse to unjust behaviour and it requires self-control to keep heated emotions in check so as to avoid over-reacting. Trivial words, gestures or unwelcome actions stir the emotions. When a person feels insulted, they may react calmly or emotionally. It is best to remain collected and to think carefully before saying anything. Strong words lead to quarrels and reconciliation may be difficult.

Road-rage is rooted in a person's mentality. The driver is on a public road, and the driving space changes with every turn of the wheel. Personal space (right of way) keeps all drivers in sync with one another. If that space is infringed upon, the driver has the right to warn the offending party. Normally it's just blowing the horn. However, some people add so much emotion to it and the right of way is enforced with zero-tolerance. The infringement (normally accidental) gets blown out of proportion as the temper rises. Road-rage is an expression of personal justice and is specifically linked to a motor vehicle. The encroachment of personal space should not culminate in anger, revenge or an urge to settle the score. If it happens, it's best to stay calm and allow the offender to go on their way. Unintentional occurrences ought to be forgiven. People don't behave this way outside of a motor vehicle. The way to avoid unwanted behaviour is to keep control of one's faculties and that's pride and egotism. Let the police take care of the idiots on the road.

The art of refraining from anger is a virtue that any serious-minded Christian must develop. Jesus set the example at the cross when he was executed while innocent of any personal crime or sin, and yet he made no defence to protest his innocence. From the human standpoint, it was a miscarriage of justice. From God's view, the punishment for sin was justified. Jesus never displayed any sign of anger and merely accepted his lot, yet he had every right to be angry.

Righteous indignation is to express anger that is substantiated by moral principles. Usually in people relationships, things are said and done that inflict emotional injury. If the offender is not informed of their error, then they will continue doing it and thinking that there's no harm, yet the victim may be in torment. Controlled anger is the correct way for the aggrieved party to vent their disapproval otherwise they will leave themselves open to future abuse and unnecessary pain.

It's one thing to train yourself to refrain from anger in public situations where the disputes may be legally resolved. You know that there will be a high probability of a fair hearing. It's another matter to reign in the feelings that have been hurt through private dealings where the parties are insensitive to other's needs. Offenders are usually only caring for selfish interests and there is no impartial third party to administer arbitration. It normally ends up that the aggrieved has to bear with the hurt in the absence of a resolution. Sometimes, verbal apologies are not enough to heal a relationship.

Where people harbour grudges, it suggests that they have not taken proper hold of self-control. Petty offences in inter-personal dealings can cause certain people to harbour deep emotional bitterness. Usually these transgressions are not physical, and they may have arisen through inappropriate words, actions, body language or other attitudes. The perception of that personal offence gets magnified beyond it's face value. This is extremely regrettable as the offender may see it as a minor incident (passing joke) that was never meant to be taken negatively at all. Good relationships can turn sour in an instant. Those that have strong views on particular matters ought to be wary of the possible grievances that self may cause. Opposing views must be taken as a challenge to their ideas and not a personal attack on their character. A little self-control will be of great value to one's personality in deflecting potential upsets.

Self-control requires a person to be re-trained through sanctification. Self has to be educated to overcome itself through self-control in righteousness. It would be sad when the corrections are only done in the mind and not in reformed behaviour and attitude. The art of personal control is a character related tool that strives to rectify poor personal attitudes and to gain better morals. A mature believer will reach the point where they can dispense with it altogether because God controls their spirit and their very being. Self-control will always work out well when agape is extended towards others because malicious actions will be avoided.

Chapter 22
Knowing and walking

Humans are designed to embrace something greater than ourselves. We have a massive void inside that we have to fill, and that element is God. Knowledge of oneself is critical in the renewal process. Knowledge of God urges us to recognise our lack and then to correct the wrong. The extent of our understanding of God's revelation is dependent on our worldview, perception and character. The Bible is the complete revelation of God yet we can read it over and over again and glean very little fresh insight from it. Why is that so?

There is a list of things that recur in our lives that seem to be problematic and yet we haven't attempted to straighten them out. They do not result in physical injury, financial loss or anything that requires immediate resolution, so we tend leave them on the back-burner. Some of these festering malignancies may be:

- wandering thoughts have a bearing on inaction because it diverts attention away from the immediate spiritual needs. The mind wanders because we have too much time on our hands and there are other things that attract our interest. Awareness will reduce the time wasted, but it's relaxing to have a short break when busy. Be aware not to allow such thoughts to impinge on our walk with the Lord.

- a stagnant relationship with the Lord may point to boredom or interest being diverted away from Jesus. Employment or other demands may be encroaching upon quiet time with the Lord. The reasons must be ascertained and steps taken to allocate time due for fellowship with the Holy Spirit. Extended periods of silence from the Spirit may also allude to problems. It is always some action or abstention on the believer's part that quenches the Spirit.

- monotonous prayer life is not a true indicator of any fault on the believer's part. However, one must recognise when prayers are mere ritual without a desire to have a meaningful relationship with the Lord.

- continuous distractions in life that unduly occupy our attention are the most common occurrences in western society. It may be caused by hobbies, friends, new innovations, the internet etc. Interesting things appear and there's the temptation to follow them up because they are the current fad. A faithful follower must adhere to a discipline and give time to God for spiritual development.

- a feeling that you are content with your circumstances in life that forms a safe enclosure. There is no will to stretch one's ability and various reasons are posed to decline the Lord's call. The peace that your physical world is safe and you don't want to rock the boat because change is too unsettling. A lack of interest in the Lord will evoke the same treatment back to the believer.

- lack of fresh spiritual ideas and Scriptural enlightenment is a deliberate withholding by the Spirit. This usually happens to intermediate Christians that have a fair knowledge of Scripture and are at a point where they feel comfortable with their Christian walk. There must be a drive to keep wanting more spiritual intelligence from God. Sincere action will receive a response from God even though it may take a while. It almost seems as if the Lord wants a person to prove their commitment and patience before he will reveal himself.

- no spiritual goals or desire to advance spiritually. Salvation in Christ is the most important thing, so a believer just takes it easy after that. Spare time and energy is spent on personal interests and not in the pursuit of God. This will become habit forming and more time will be invested in secular things and worship will be confined to Sunday mornings only.

- self-gratification is always a major challenge to the Lord's interests. It encourages selfishness if not consciously guarded against. As the standard of living rises, many new things can divert attention away from God. The need to keep up with friends that have the latest technology and equipment becomes a status symbol that is popular with the clique.

- lack of introspection for various reasons. It may be just through pure neglect; interest in other things; not wanting to examine self for fear of what might be discovered; procrastination etc.

This is an important control to keep check on the bad points and it attempts to reduce/eliminate them. In addition, the positive points ought to be enhanced and improved until you can't go any further.

- limited understanding in service and relationships particularly in outreach work. Culture and social customs must be understood in terms of Biblical standards. Practices that are religiously neutral are acceptable. A study must be made of all the adherences with religious links to ascertain those that are definitely off limits. One should beware of the danger of syncretism when working with cultural practices. Social customs that are neutral ought to be respected. The worker must understand the Bible clearly so as to know how far to venture into their practices. All Biblical principles that are unalterable must be treated as such. The worker should not attempt to replicate their own home church structure into the local mindset and setting. Instead, they must be allowed to follow Christ in their own social way.

We may ponder over why the forgoing keeps appearing from time to time, but we dismiss it equally quickly. Contentment is good for mental and emotional stability but it focuses too heavily on the material state. Mature believers must look beyond self and the physical situation. One ought to strive for spiritual improvement and never be satisfied with each bit of ground gained, but to keep reaching higher. If you persistently vet and adjust the matters above, you will know yourself a great deal better than before. For one thing, it's going to lay bare all your faults. It will show clearly the things that are preventing you from getting closer to God. You will have to apply your will and have the courage to make the relevant corrections. Freewill must not be viewed as an all-powerful human tool that nothing can tame or obstruct. It can be reined in through self-control. God will not prepare a training program for you, and you will have to make the adjustments and corrections yourself. This will show that you are genuinely in pursuit of a solid relationship with God.

The will to give up self becomes easier as your spiritual state improves. However, there may still be some skeletons in the cupboard. A glitch in the sanctification growth process may point to certain issues that have been allowed to linger while walking the renewal road. This gives a distorted understanding of your spiritual growth and in reality, you may not be where you think you are at. No doubt, the festering malignancies are a direct product of those favourite desires within. The highway to sanctification cannot be compromised and pet fancies must be cleaned out.

Once the Spirit is willing to form a sound bond with a follower, a wonderful flow of knowledge will come. This wisdom opens up the simple things in Scripture with a whole new eye-opening perception. The Holy Spirit is the lateral-thinker that gives profound description to the ordinary things in life. It's more precious than economic wisdom because it will take you into eternity where money has no influence. Yet, when this occurs, it merely ignites the realisation that you are so puny before an omniscient God. It can only lead to honest humility and dependence. The older you get, the more you become like a child before the Father. This is the right relational position and you will be well on your way to knowing the Father in the manner that aims for maximum spiritual intake.

Knowing yourself is essential to correction and promotion of your spiritual wellbeing. Our secular and Christian friends have an influence over us in one way or another. Keeping up with the Jones's is an insidious concept even though we may manage to convince ourselves that we don't fall in that category. It is satisfying to possess the things in common with or better than our peers. Scripture does not encourage us to compare ourselves with others (Galatians 6:4). We can't even compare ourselves with Jesus Christ because it's a no-contest. All we can do is to shoulder our own burden and follow God's character. Each person has to keep track of their own progress.

We like to see ourselves as following and trying to be like Jesus, but the very thought of comparing ourselves with Christ is incomprehensible. He is perfect and we are imperfect, and it will just show a string of deficiencies on our part. Comparison is not the aim but transformation to Christlikeness is our objective. He will only show how far behind we are lagging and this makes it a life-long project. Jesus is bad for our self-confidence and self-image, yet these two items are exactly the problem. We are to subdue self- confidence and trust in Christ to lead and teach us to become like him. Self-image and pride must be obliterated so that we may revert to the sanctity that places God first.

When we get on the right track, we will find that Jesus is not there to put us down but to build us up. We may cling to our pet values jealously, but after experiencing the new light that the Spirit shows, we will get rid of those vices quickly. After this spiritual life-changing process, you will never want to go back or even look at the old person again. However, self-centredness does not just disappear through mental assent, and there will be many internal struggles before a satisfactory position is reached within your spirit. Self-cleansing may be a noble target that you have set for yourself, but it's God's opinion that matters most, and the wonders that he can do for you.

Knowing yourself does not stop there; the joys and changes stemming from the same old body are now under the control and influence of the spiritual fruit imputed from Jesus and is propelling you forward. You derive a reassuring sense of affirmation and confirmation that your relationship with God is promising and sustainable. The assurance is in knowing that the Spirit communicates with you daily. It's something deeply entrenched in your spirit that nobody can take away. The works and circumstances that the Lord engineers in your life attests to what the Bible says. Relationship moves from a general nature to one that is specially tailored to your particular needs in this life. Once you get on this high, you don't ever want it to stop, and who can blame you. You realise that you are honoured because it pleased God to work through you to uncover your unique latent spiritual potential and to have it developed to the maximum.

Know your character and understand how you tick. Consciously or subconsciously, your character will disclose your intentions to the world. Some people try to project the right image by quoting the morally and ethically correct things, but if there is an underlying flaw in character then the true motives within that person will be displayed in their decisions and actions over time. This will be clearly evident to impartial people who have close or regular dealings with them. For others who interact occasionally, it will take a bit longer to discover but the conclusion would be the same. It is normal to give the perpetrator the benefit of the doubt, in particular, where the association is one of common purpose, shared beliefs and mutual trust. When inconsistencies emerge, it is up to the observer to act. It's better to correct your own faults first before it reaches public scrutiny. Outspoken people will state their observations bluntly and that could be embarrassing.

Trust makes generous allowances for incompatible mannerisms. However, there comes a point where you are forced to call a halt and re-examine the principles. The circumstances have to be treated at face value and the connotations clearly distinguished. Care ought to be taken so as not to view the situation through tainted glasses. What ensues is quite intriguing and honest evaluation will suddenly uncover several things that don't match your original expectations. Familiarity is marred by the benefit of the doubt, but independent unbiased evaluation shows a completely different picture. An alternate viewpoint rapidly emerges through logical thought, and you have to adopt a new set of criteria to evaluate a longstanding relationship. Honesty and impartiality is absolutely necessary in arriving at a correct assessment. The startling discovery is that you never really knew this person until after your findings. Discordant behaviour kills trust. Doubt raises caution and often scepticism, and cooperation slows down tremendously or may even come to a grinding halt. Character is the truth-teller because it exposes the superficial niceties.

The lessons learnt will be beneficial for future dealings. It is a higher priority to ensure that you don't fall into the same pitfalls. Pride coming from new discoveries can easily and unwarily set up a pedestal in the enthusiastic mind/heart. Self-examination will ensure that the same problems don't exist in your own mind and that you never give them a chance to manifest themselves in your character. If you resolve to stick to the straight path, you will never go wrong because the Holy Spirit will guard your mind and thoughts. Isaiah 26:3 exhorts us to keep our minds riveted on God and perfect peace comes to all who trust in him.

A good friend once told me that nobody is able to control their mind. Irrespective of how advanced you may be on your path to holiness, the loose thoughts that come to mind can always upset the apple cart. This is exacerbated by the society that we live in as there are too many secular things that impose themselves on our lives. It's so easy to fall victim because of peer pressure or self-interest. Earning a livelihood and tending to future financial resources is normal. However, they can quickly turn counter-productive and unspiritual in our relationship with Christ. Self-control is a gift from the Lord. Impulsive thinking has no place in the process of sanctification and especially in kingdom service. However, mind-control can play a positive role if structured in the right way (Romans 12:2).

One of the best aids to spiritual success is to condition yourself to associate all things with God. Good things come directly from his blessings and unfortunate things pass through his permissive will.

Everything is there for a reason and they may help us know more about ourselves and about God. We should learn from our own mistakes and maintain a positive attitude towards Christ. Even suffering has a spiritual purpose and it behoves us to learn from those trials. Blunders may be caused by an error of judgment, ignorance or some other reason. If your trust is genuine, misfortune will always lead you to a deeper trust in God that will draw you nearer to him. Developing a good habit of constantly consulting with Jesus will reveal the good that we can learn from the results of mishaps. On balance, there are far more good happenings in daily life than bad. Keeping God at the forefront of our daily thought processes will open up the realisation that he is a loving and beneficial Father despite the trials.

Most people want to be recognised by others for having done something creditable during their lifetime. When I was quite young, I used to hear adults say: 'when I die, nobody will know that I have been in this world' or 'I have left nothing behind for people to remember me by'. At that time, it meant nothing to me. As I moved on into adult life, it still didn't strike any chords. I would surmise that those people had some sort of hang-up with self-esteem or pride. In the Chinese culture, the term 'face' comprises a mixture of pride, self-worth and self-esteem. People always act in a manner to save face because shame is disgraceful and must be avoided at all costs. From the poorest to the wealthiest, face conveys respect. It's all about acceptable behaviour amongst peers, as well as increasing one's respect from others. However, the Bible never supports actions that condone peer-pressure (Matthew 22:16). There is no basis for making a name or mark in the spiritual realm either, so spiritual-peers will never pressure young followers to excel in spirit. This is a personal matter between you and God, where nobody can interfere. Worldly values are heavily slanted to self-image and worldly opinion; whereas Scripture emphasises the servant role, humility and the Lord's approval.

We are disadvantaged from the moment of conception. Inherent sin has an excessive sway over our freewill and we will always tend to do the wrong things first. You are born into the world as a partner and intimate associate of Satan. If God leaves you alone, you will have no chance of ever knowing the salvation of Christ (John 6:44). The customary family view to a new born child is that the baby is so sweet and innocent and so helpless. We cannot help but shower love and affection on the baby. We carry the preconceived notion that there's not a mean bone in that infant's body. The concept of sin is not associated with any new born and we never think that way either. In truth, this is a conscious and deliberate human error because every baby is a victim of inherent sin. Babies grow up and it's the parent's duty to teach and train them in righteousness. Parents are mere stewards of their children's upbringing because their souls belong to God. Thus, the parent's duty is towards God first and then to the children (in fact, they are God's children first). If all parents adopted the view that their biological children are really God's spiritual children, then they will be very careful to find out what the Bible commands in regard to raising children.

Jesus pointed to those seated around him and said that whoever does God's will is his brother, sister and mother (Mark 3:35). As such, we will share in his glory and inheritance (Romans 8:17, Colossians 1:12). Jesus did his duty as part of an earthly family member, but he never attached undue intimacy to biological ties. His full allegiance and dependence was always on his Father in heaven. Jesus said that his purpose was to bring division in a family (Luke 12:51, Matthew 10:34). If a Christian loves father or mother more than Jesus, then they are not worthy of him. These are very strong words. Many years ago, when I first read these passages, I thought that they were quite cruel and insensitive. Now I can see that Jesus was addressing the spiritual family of God that endures for eternity, where the biological ties count for nothing! For this reason, Jesus added that everyone who has left family for his sake will receive a hundred times as much and will inherit eternal life (Matthew 19:29). Our Father rewards his spiritual children generously. No earthly family can match an offer like this. It's clear that a biological family means nothing to God and obedience is everything to him. In fact, he wants your fidelity to his spiritual family first. This is a very unorthodox policy and positively unsociable. You may think that you are doing everything right, but it's God's opinion that counts (1 Corinthians 4:4).

We over-rate and over-stress our biological family who are powerless to prepare us for eternity. The material comforts that the family provides are necessary but temporal. Biological ties only assist us through this life and yet we place all our energy and interest in the earthly family and ignore our spiritual ties. Caring for loved ones is a moral obligation, but God's spiritual family supersedes the material. All believers must pay maximum attention to their spiritual obligations and their biological ties rank a distant last. This is the meaning of loving Jesus above all. Everybody is going to be judged individually and nobody can assist any friend or relative in any way. A person's accountability before God cannot be shared or divided. This is how God has created human beings. If you get your priorities wrong, then you are not thinking the way Jesus is.

As odd as it may sound, a person may go from birth to death without fully realising that they have been siding with the evil one for part or most of their natural lives. It's a sobering thought and this ought to be dealt with early on in Christian life. Every person is an enemy of God until they give themselves over to the headship of Christ. Christians in their early years may become wayward children that displease God, but this can be reversed where they are obedient and progress in developing spiritual maturity. You only become a friend of God after you have surrendered self-will to him because this is when the relationship really starts flourishing. Believers that have remained spiritually undeveloped or under-developed truly don't know God intimately and personally. The greater the fealty to Jesus the stronger the friendship will become.

This decision involves truth and a complete exposure of the deep recesses of a person's heart that still guards self-will jealously. Progressive regeneration gradually exposes and lays bare the insignificance of self in the light of the majesty of Christ. The crucial role of your spirit over your body will be manifested over time. It is vitally important that your spiritual personality grows under the enlightenment of the Holy Spirit. This switching of sides over to God brings the kinds of rewards that only a spiritually minded person can appreciate. God's joy is not measured in material possessions. It seems strange that a Christian can experience overwhelming joy in apparently invisible things.

Mark 9:7, John 6:45 and John 10:27 emphasise the need for us to listen to the Lord's leading and go to Jesus. Listening must be followed by obedience but contempt amounts to rejection. Refusal and disdain must be admitted for what it is: disobedience and self-gratification. I think that this is the fundamental reason why God doesn't communicate with us. Sometimes, we don't like what we hear or see and hence it's easier to disobey. This mental-barrier hardens over time and must be broken down by thoughtful prayer and to reinstate the priority of God in our lives. If this matter is not rectified, you will become a person of split personality. The minor part yielding to God and the greater part reserved for personal satisfaction. It's just another way of reviving self-will and there's nothing spiritually profitable about this one.

Sometimes, when we hear an admonition from a fellow believer, we invariably apply the 'two-sided argument' to it. It may be the Lord speaking through you but it may also merely be your personal opinion. Hence, it is only necessary for me to take the parts that I feel are pertinent or I can refuse it entirely. Usually, people always take uncomfortable comments as that person's personal opinion; they hardly if ever, view it as a reality check from God. It then becomes a one-sided view. The aggrieved party becomes upset with the offender and unaware that they are actually being agitated with the Lord. This is especially so where the offender sincerely believes that they never meant ill will of any sort. Everything good emanates from God, even harsh discipline for our correction. God's goodness is a spiritual concept but we often view it in terms of material benefit. This is a grave error because the goodness of God is unseen (2 Corinthians 4:18). Our obstinacy and lack of self-correction disappoints our Father who wants the best for us.

There are times when we have an internal debate as to a choice for God. Self has no power or bargaining chip to bring before the Lord. We are all still sinners who have been redeemed by Jesus. All people have been bought at an indeterminable price. If you think that the calling is not suitable for you or that it's too burdensome, think again. The privilege of choice is not yours because your life is not your own.

The hope of an ordinary life made extraordinary becomes a reality through intimacy with Jesus Christ. In our daily existence there may be nothing that remotely compares with the great deeds that some of the renowned Christian folk have achieved over the centuries. There's a spiritual transformation that is within the grasp of every human being who is willing to affix their relationship unconditionally with Jesus. Knowing the way is distinct from walking in the way. If you are still struggling with certain stubborn glitches in your later Christian life, then perhaps you don't know Jesus as intimately as you think you do. You are still holding back something vital from Jesus. All you have to do is just follow what he says, it's easy. Once Christ takes hold of you, spiritual life becomes extraordinary. There may not be much outward signs of it, but inwardly there's a supernatural outworking that nobody can interfere with, and it's all yours alone. Your move will bring about a reaction; Jesus will come to you if you go to him as Paul intimated in Philippians 3:12. It's a determined motive that comes from the heart that will persist in reaching its goal. More significantly, this ambition aligns a person towards maturity. In this life, maturity has no fixed completion point and Christ was motivating Paul to keep reaching for more. Even the experienced godly people cannot afford to rest on their laurels.

Self-deceit barricades self in a protective cell within. Usually this kind of person has to keep to a careful list of do's and don'ts in support of the conceptual directives that they have set out to pursue. The protection of personal intentions is at odds with the truth of God. Fear of exposure drives people to odd behaviour. There comes a point where they will do anything in order to maintain the charade. The game develops into one of false pretences in keeping the façade immaculate for the outside world. The Holy Spirit will expose those faults and the patient must take remedial action against those impediments. Self cannot be permitted to have its way but, you could also keep playing the fool with yourself.

The hardest thing about walking in the light is that the maxims are set by somebody else and not by you. You don't dictate your own pace and you are accountable to a higher authority. The alternative is to serve the Lord under your own terms or according to somebody else's guidance. It's the comfortable route because you have choices and you may choose between options. On the other hand, God does not give any alternatives. Sometimes what happens before you is not the ideal and they contain things that you don't feel at ease with. I don't like the way God works because the initial directions are just a hint and I often have to wait for confirmation.

In hindsight, going through with it in trust has resulted in much satisfaction and a stronger desire to get closer to God. This is easily said in a few sentences but going through those hard times wasn't pleasant. Knowing Jesus in theory is a mere shadow of knowing him in his suffering. After going through several experiences, I have found that first impressions are never exciting but it's wise to exercise patience, bite the bullet and go through with it. Every result brought a spiritual benefit and deepened my trust in the Lord which made me very happy. I know what I have to do and it will be easier the next time.

Waiting.

A major part of the Christian life is centred on re-training in spiritual development. The Bible is so rich in knowledge and so profound that nobody could ever hope to know it perfectly. If it is so time consuming just to get the information into your head with reasonable clarity, then what about the assimilation process into the spirit and then the physical outworking of the transformed life? Accumulated knowledge no matter how abstruse, if it is not integrated into your spirit is useless to God, and it merely remains in the memory. Renewal targets the rebirth of the spirit that demonstrates the fruit of the Spirit outwardly with absolute integrity. All our moral preparation usually does not immediately translate into work or application and we usually have to wait for the Lord to open the doors.

During this equipping process, there's also a lot of waiting. These hollow times just seem to drag on and on, but they are not meant to be wasted and fellowship with God through prayer and quiet times must be productively employed. Quiet times help consolidate the newly acquired knowledge and that gets us into oneness with Jesus in fellowship and understanding. The closer our intimacy with Christ, the easier it is to relinquish self-will and for him to take over control.

Waiting should not be seen as a form of chastisement (although sometimes I tend to feel that it is), but rather as a time to examine self and to nurture patience. In a world that is increasingly developing the instant-satisfaction expectation, Christians have a real hard time learning to be patient. To sit around waiting for God is not something that any of us like at all, particularly when the waiting room is empty and our hearts are filled with enthusiasm. It takes maximum restraint and submission to wait quietly before Jesus. The impatient part of your character must be subdued and be re-taught to wait, even when it doesn't make sense. It is better to wait a bit and be reasonably clear on an issue before making a decision. Impulsive actions give rise to unwanted consequences that are frustrating and take up more time and effort to correct. Impatience is a cohort of self-will whereby a self-devised course of action spurs an urgent desire to implement it. Patience waits for God to direct and removes control from self-determination. Faith is bolstered when the Lord reacts in response to our situation.

Patience is an essential quality for achieving success in the kingdom business (Genesis 21:2, Job 30:20, Acts 1:4, Romans 8:23).

The Lord's plans are known only to him and he calls for the work to be done as he considers appropriate. God does not have to wait for people to decide before he can act, rather, he constructs his plans based on foreknowledge. Human beings make decisions to reveal their intentions to others but for the Lord every move is a foregone conclusion. This is the reason that prophesy is fully accurate and there is nothing that anybody can do to negate it. God is omniscient and he is outside of time, so time presents no difficulties. Humans like to exercise their intelligence, we like to have a plan of action before us, we prefer certainty, we like to prepare ourselves beforehand, we work better with full or reasonable information, and we like to have a certain degree of control over the task at hand. Usually, God gives scanty information, so a degree of uncertainty is always present and each stage has to be revealed as we progress, and we have no say in the matter. This makes people uncomfortable and reluctant to obey the Lord. For the faithful there is no choice and patience is a part of the renewed life.

Waiting is virtue that we must work through and develop. As our trust develops, we learn to restrain personal impulsive behaviour. God knows what he is doing, he is responsible for the outcome and he will give instructions when the time is ripe. Thus, workers must learn to be patient and be occupied with other kingdom business while waiting. It is a terrible mistake to do things that are not authorised by the Lord. This is mutiny and it just makes things worse for self. Learning to be patient doesn't come overnight, but it is worth developing as part of our character. It is better to wait for a while than to anger the Lord.

Working.

Secular work is usually career oriented and employees live on their remuneration. It's normally what a person has chosen to do and it lasts until retirement. Some people change their careers for various reasons, but it is still their means of earning income. The workplace is a competitive environment and the employee must apply their mind and talent to the best of their ability in order to gain promotion and for longevity. Gifted employees will have no problems because they will show their skills naturally and get ahead in their career. The lesser talented staff will have to work harder because they may feel threatened by others. Unscrupulous staff will resort to unmannerly conduct, bullying tactics, nasty ways and unethical practices so as to keep their positions and to get rid of competition. A worker has a limited degree of freedom for personal creativity, intelligent design, innovation and other skills that will bring efficiency or generate more income for the employer. Senior management make the executive decisions.

Kingdom work is not of our own creativity but the genius of God's design. Our bodies are the means through which God shows his morals to the outside world. The willingness to serve is a commendable gesture but the work must be done in God's way. Doing work according to our own standards and aims will jeopardise our standing with God. Our views and methodology will compete with Jesus' plans for us. By doing things our way, we fuel our pride, ego and self-importance. The priority will be on our procedures instead of on Christ. If something goes against us then we retaliate in order to defend our position. Great care must be observed in this situation because we are capable of committing some horrible actions that could hurt others. We may not be aware of it, but at that moment we place self-will in a lead position and disregard Christ as head and personal bias will force bad decisions.

When the Lord calls, the job ought to be done properly by following his directions. A worker cannot add personal ideas or any self-generated intentions to kingdom work. This is not the secular environment where freewill is tolerated as a personal right.

Chapter 23
Servant and serving

Servant.

Servants of Jesus have to condition themselves for service. It's getting the mind ready and desensitizing the body to the comforts and habits that it previously enjoyed. The servant has to prepare themselves for the conditions that they are called to work in (John 12:26). Our Father will honor the worker that obeys Jesus. It's reassuring that our Father is watching over us as we do the work. His presence keeps us honest and accountable and it's all for our own benefit because of the reward that awaits the faithful.

John 15:14-17 exhorts us to be loyal and Jesus will disclose the Father's business to us. Moreover, Jesus chose us to serve him and we did not invite ourselves in. Servants are chosen to bear fruit. It is both the fruit of the Spirit and fruit from our labour in the kingdom. The latter is the assistance/guidance that we may bring to the spiritual lives of other believers. Both of these are the kind of fruit that will last forever, and our Father will help in whatever way that we need to achieve this. Obedience is reinforced in a close association with our Father (John 14:31), and it is a deep love for God that makes us compliant. Christ wants us to be successful, to do as commanded and to receive our full treasure in heaven, and he will guide us so that we do not deviate from his wishes (John 16:1). A faithful servant is highly prized by God and we ought to live up to all that he expects.

God is unreasonable in the sense that he wants all of you. You can't bargain with God. He will always allow you to follow your own interests but don't mistake this for his approval. At times, we are split between two directions and trying to find justification for what we desire. Personal fulfilment is always in opposition to the Lord's objectives. Jesus said that people who do self-motivated good deeds for public applause should enjoy their temporary achievements because that's all the reward they will receive (Matthew 6:1). Similarly, apparent righteous works that are done to please self will not be rewarded by your Father. Christians that only think short term are treading in dangerous territory because the spiritual loss will be very costly. It is plausible that some will get to heaven with very little or no spiritual award at all. They will be the odd-balls and their loss will be noticeable. Those that were not obedient, who did not follow instructions, who sort self-interest before God, who valued the material over the eternal, whose love for Christ was limited, will be poor in heaven. It will bring a sense of shame because God's agape was so generously given and yet they spurned their opportunities.

He knows what's best for you and the full blessing that's perfect for your eternal existence. It's something that you will like, enjoy and cherish for all time. On earth, we can't form an idea of what is going to make us happy and fulfilled in spiritual terms because we exist in the body and material things act as our main if not sole benchmark for satisfaction. The Lord has spiritual entitlements prepared as remuneration for our obedience on earth. It's going to enhance our spiritual existence and make us whole and will bring us closer to be more like God in character and personality. The rewarded ones will have a spiritual extasy resulting in an internal thankfulness that erupts with such unspeakable joy, that they will forever be grateful to our Father. If followers are willing to sacrifice their lives on earth (Romans 12:1-2) based on faith which is invisible, then what is it going to be like when they see that faith materialise in a reward that they will be able to feel and enjoy forever?

Choosing to serve the Lord is one of the hardest to master particularly if you have status in society; an elite education; marketable skills, gifted intelligence or where you have built up a sizable wealth. These things carry the joy of belonging, recognition (perhaps even fame), and in most cases financial freedom. The most painful and soul-searching task is to honestly lay out how important is 'self' to you. If you get it right, then none of the foregoing matter. I don't think that we get it right most of the time. If you find yourself in this position, it could mean that the Lord is still knocking and extending a further opportunity to you. The same vices keep on bugging you because you have not risen above them. It's prudent to bear in mind that God's invitation doesn't last for very long. After I took the decision to place God first, nearly all the material elements pertaining to self never bothered me again. There are still odd concerns here and there but they never commanded the fear and anxiety as in the past. This freed me up to concentrate on what I was called to do. Partnering with the Lord is the most spiritually fulfilling place to be. Some may be fortunate to be working in safe locations, but there are those who don't have the comfort of a non-threatening work environment.

The servant that has placed the interest of others before self, will humble themselves and not mind hardship and degradation (1 Corinthians 4:13). Unkind words really fire up the emotions but humility brings self-control. Workers have to be very careful not to fall into the pride-mindset when serving Jesus. This may come about in a very subtle way i.e. where their services and talent are much sought after in their ministry. Self and bodily comforts are not determinants where the servant has resolved to be poured out like a drink offering (2 Timothy 4:6). It implies giving your will to Christ with no possibility of withdrawing it no matter where it leads. Above all, our love for Jesus constrains us to follow him because he died for us (2 Corinthians 5:14). The servant has a power from God that nobody can understand, and it is only obtained experientially.

Serving.

> 'I believe firmly that the moment our hearts are emptied of pride and selfishness and ambitions and everything that is contrary to God's law, the Holy Spirit will fill every corner of our hearts' – D L Moody.

This statement briefly describes the unregenerate person who is governed by intuitive personal will, and who needs to be commanded by the Holy Spirit. It calls for resolute and genuine alteration of one's outlook. The old way of doing things must be eradicated and replaced by the Spirit's management. Nothing in a person's entire make-up can be more radical than this. One thing that you have to settle in your mind is the nature and scope of the concept of work. The human definition of secular work and the Biblical definition are poles apart. This variance lies in the essence or intention of the person. Is it going to be self-gratification or self-sacrifice for God?

Angels have a servant function that is limited to specific things that God sends them to do. These tasks are often unrelated and are of a one-off nature. Christians are servants in kingdom construction and the phases are inter-related and on-going, until all those chosen for redemption have come in. A point to note is that only chosen human beings are approved to work in the kingdom, and no angel or spirit can participate. However, the Lord on occasion may allow an unbeliever to assist in a need, but no recognition or reward will be given. Angels don't have the luxury of applying their own style to the job and they just have to carry out their assignment with clinical precision. The biblical description of the 'angel of the Lord' is taken to mean that it is God himself speaking, so whatever the angel says is to be taken as divine authority. Their power to do things comes from God; so the work is really sanctioned by God. If angels are mere messengers, then it implies that they don't have superior permanent power and it is only given by God at the time to accomplish a specific task. After that they revert to servant status. Assuming that angles do have fixed embedded divine might; then there is a possibility that the combined strength of all the legions may be a challenge to God. I very much doubt that this is the case because God is still the Creator and they are the creation. The might of each individual angel is limited by the Lord. We do know that there are certain angels that rank higher than others, for instance, special assignments were given to the angels Michael and Gabriel (Revelation 12:7, Luke 1:19). Satan was the most powerful angel in heaven, and he chose rebellion but even he and all of the demonic world are no match for the Lord.

A theophany usually occurs in the form of an angel, but in Genesis 32:24 we see this phenomenon in the form of a man. Jacob asked him his name but there was no answer, just a blessing from the man. We know that God does not have a name and that he calls himself 'I AM'. The man was real and Jacob saw God face to face in the form of a man. A theophany affords this wonderful benefit to the people in the Old Testament who have encountered God in a visible form. It's a vehicle that God applies to serve his purposes directly.

On the other hand, the Lord in pure spiritual form and holiness is off-limits to human eyes. Moses was hidden in the cleft of the rock and was forbidden to see the face of God. From the human standpoint, the concept of 'seeing is believing' does not compute with God. Philip asked to see the Father but was denied. The Father is not a material entity that can be seen by the human eye. People emphasise seeing, but this is not important, and people are concentrating on the wrong aspect of God to prove that he exists. The phrase 'seeing is believing' only applies to the material world. Believers have to look at the metaphysical through the eyes of faith and change the words to 'faith is believing'. Faith is proved experientially and each person will know the Lord personally, although this cannot be shown to another person. The manifestation of God's character and outworking are the only spiritual evidences of his existence. God the Father was doing his work directly through Jesus' physical body. Jesus was the servant of God on earth, and he claimed that his actions shows that God exists in his personality (John 14:10). Jesus did better than a theophany because he was the incarnation of God. His entire life was an exemplar of obedience as a humble servant of the Father and he received the highest spiritual rewards.

From the secular standpoint, work is predominantly associated with a cash nexus. We don't apply the terms master and servant but choose the words employer and employee. Both parties have rights, so the boss may terminate the employee's services under given conditions or the worker may resign voluntarily. The employer pays the wages and has the right to demand the employee's dedication and loyalty. This is of greater significance in the 21st century where key-staff hold sensitive information and work with valuable intellectual property.

Salvation cannot be earned, but the perk comes in the kingdom work because it will demand personal sacrifices, and it is compensated by rewards in heaven. This is the bonus that will differentiate all those who have obeyed God's calling. The spiritual composition of those rewards will place them in a distinct position in heaven. Heaven is a spiritual place and the spiritual elements pertaining to God will be the most attractive and desired treasure. In our earthly state we can't imagine what form it's going to take, but the Bible has promised that this will happen. When it does, we will see the full value of what the Lord said. The biggest drawback is that we can't relate this in earthly terms because we can't see it and we can't quantify it. Spiritual entitlements can never be described in material terms. Paul's words in 2 Corinthians 4:18 firmly place the priority on the unseen. There are too many worldly distractions in the ordinary course of the day that it's easy to dismiss the Lord's advice and make light of our spiritual priorities. Christians have to outlay their services upfront and the remuneration is delayed but it's pledged by God.

Chapter 24
Paradox

2 Corinthians 4:7 tells us of the marvellous treasure that we have in our being. It's a benefit of unrivalled worth that has been given to us by God Himself. We have to work out what this treasure means and gain all the benefits that are available. Normally a treasure is there to make us wealthy and prosperous, so we lock it away in a safe place. God's treasure is a living fortune comprising of spiritual elements that we have very little knowledge about. Very few people have truly managed to get the most out of it but that shouldn't discourage you. On the contrary, it should spur you to strive harder to unlock its secrets. Only the Spirit can serve its full potential, but we have to urge him to do so. The spiritual assets that we are endowed with comes from God and must be refined and given back to Jesus in the form of service. We can't create or manufacture our own spiritual gifts and Jesus is merely using all the gifts that he has given to you in order to build his kingdom. Believers must obtain this know-how from God and it's a personal asset that remains forever.

2 Corinthians 4:10 is the objective that must be at the forefront of our existence. The death of Jesus must be in our bodies and then the life of Jesus may be played out and displayed to others. It depicts the final removal of self-determination and followed by spiritual resurrection into holiness. This paradox of life and death in the same body is a spiritual thing as a physically dead body is useless to God. Thus, we share in Christ's sufferings when called to service so that the intended audience may understand the love that Jesus has for them. The reason why Christ died is our motivation in new life. Death to self-will paves the way for accurate service and Jesus can apply the follower's talents to show the way to eternal wellbeing. A certain degree of hardship will always be asked of the servant but their spirit will be enriched and the mind of Christ will direct all that they say and do.

Without the death to personal-will, new life cannot take root and grow as the Holy Spirit intends. The two forces are constantly vying for dominance within a person's spirit. The life of Christ is the key feature because it's what we must imitate now on earth. We must strive to be a living example of Jesus' personality and to be an agent for change in the area that we are called to minister in. The dead person in me gives way to the living person of Christ ruling in me.

The Holy Spirit is trying to teach and train us in righteous living. If we fail to grow then it can only be our own fault. We disrupt this teaching process through our desire for other things that we consider as more pleasurable. Poor judgment leads to poor decisions and we fail to eliminate the trifling things that damage our spiritual bank. These trivialities keep the Spirit from advancing because they will always resurface to lead us astray. God's requirements are truly stringent and he works best through a sincere obedient person who maintains a progressive regenerative life. The Holy Spirit is a silent spirit and he does not handle competition well. He will always withdraw when a person chooses self-gratification too often. Freewill opens or closes your heart to the Spirit.

All who have received Christ as Lord and saviour are sanctified for salvation and cleansed (John 13:10). Believers are justified in Christ but are yet to grow in spiritual renewal and this is the second phase of sanctification. It is a personal task to clean out persistent poor habits and to displace those with righteous practices. We have to keep cleaning the inside until the Spirit is comfortable enough to develop a deeper fellowship with us. God works through all believers that are justified at conversion. However, those that are advanced in regeneration have a far more meaningful and rewarding experience than the immature. God can use any mature or immature Christian that is at the right place and time to fulfil a task in the kingdom. Christians have to be humble in order to serve others in less fortunate circumstances.

A sinner trying to live in God's holiness is an anomaly. This is more pronounced in the mature Christian life. It's a time when you don't want to sin, but the reality weakens the will and lofty ambitions are stifled and sin enters the body. It's a perpetual reminder that sin will always exist in your body until death. Knowing what you are and attempting to live a progressive Christian life is only possible through the constant urging of the Holy Spirit. It is spiritually dangerous to stagnate or to allow your relationship with Christ to grow cold (Revelation 2:4, 3:16). The growth in holiness is the better way to ward off sin.

People like to be different and to exert personal flair in daily life as well as in kingdom work, but there is no justification for personal creativity in God's design. There is no way but God's way. Jesus is the only way to salvation; yet people want to find a different path to heaven. By the same token, the holiness of God can only be obtained by the method prescribed by God. There is one certainty; the closer we get to God, the further we are removed from self-will. Jesus must be continually elevated in our lives and we must be correspondingly self-deprecating. This is the spiritual reality and the aim of every serious-minded follower of Christ. We all want to get there; we all want to live the victorious Christian life yet we tolerate, guard and rationalise our personal agenda on the basis of our freewill. If Christ is to be lifted up then self-denial must first be firmly enforced and established in our spirit.

God is asking us to exercise faith and to follow his leading into the unknown. It is by no means easy as it goes against common sense and risk aversion. Whenever there is a major uncertainty in any economic, political or other catastrophic event, the world stock markets take a dive because investors dislike the unknown. They can handle normal risk via decision trees and probability analysis. They can handle loss in a rational way as long as it may be reasonably quantifiable. Uncertainty introduces subjectivity as the possible outcomes are volatile, and this makes investors nervous. Objective decisions are the kind that we are amenable with, but God always seems to involve the unknown. He wants us to trust him to lead us through difficulty – something that few of us can handle properly.

Developing believers should be long past this state of indecision and debate. If you are still sitting on the fence, then you have a problem. The aim for all aspiring believers that desire maturity is still the same – character renewal. The difference is in the personal fancies that won't let go of self. It is time to stop fighting with yourself and to do what ought to be done for Jesus' sake and for your personal eternal wellbeing.

Chapter 25
Spiritually

Human beings are innately spiritually unnatural and this has to be turned around. Adam and Eve had a natural spiritual affiliation with God in holiness. Our primary motivation should be to get our spiritual nature heading in the right direction towards Jesus. Self-will resides in the spirit and that needs to be replaced by God's will, so that the Holy Spirit can operate freely. The Spirit will automatically work to remake a person's spirit after God's personality. This is changing the spirit back to its natural state towards holiness.

Jesus was holy from inception and his spirit was clean. He spoke directly about his spiritual state in regard to his ministry. The vital things that mattered most were already implanted in his spirit. The primary goal was his Father's will, and this was his guide in all that he did on earth. He never did anything that the Father did not approve of. Therefore, he was able to fulfil all prophesy that related to him in the Old Testament, and God's purposes were carried out precisely. He spoke of his relationship with his Father as being so close that they were one person (John 10:30). The very words that Jesus spoke were God's words and the Father was living in him and using him to fulfil his objectives (John 14:10). This was a spiritual state that was invisible to the public eye, but so real and powerful in Christ's spirit. This was the perfect means for the Lord to operate in because it was a holy environment, and God could do anything at will. After Jesus proved his worth by triumphing over Satan's temptations in Matthew chapter 4, there was no other obstacle to bar him from his path to the cross.

When humans deal with God, the crucial interaction is spiritually based. People first have to get their spirit right via regeneration and this is a struggle on its own. It's the personality alteration in the spirit to conform with God's character. Humans will never arrive at the perfect state that Jesus was in, but we have to get as close as the Holy Spirit will take us. Easy to say, but not so easy to get there but we have to keep at it. Only then are we vaguely where Jesus was at, but our wilful nature is another big hurdle to overcome. The target is to reach the obedience level that Jesus was at. This will posit our relationship with the Father as Jesus had. All the values that Christ possessed will flow through to the believer. This is the ideal that we must work towards and it will come as we reach closer to regeneration fullness. The ultimate position is for our spirit to be in sync with the Holy Spirit (John 14:20, 23, 17:21). We ought to dream about it and desperately desire to get it and then to keep striving to retain it. Inherent sin will be in the body until death, but being obedient is enough for the Lord to reward the believer handsomely hereafter.

How do you do it? Answer: a living intimate association must be in place with Jesus (Revelations 3:20). This interaction is the closest fellowship that a person can ever experience. Your spirit is the real you that will never die despite the body being replaced by a new heavenly body. This fellowship exists at the very heart of the human will. It is repentance in its pure form – you used to run things your way and now you banish it forever, and Jesus takes full command in the new you. As long as you are living in this world, the physical nature will be attracted to the sensual attractions in life. It's going to take all the discipline that you can muster to realign your regenerated spirit to assume the lead in living out your new life. The major drawback is that your spirit has to make decisions relating to the unseen. This requires sound faith and a mature relationship with Christ that is able to consistently bond with the Holy Spirit and be led in total trust in him. Whenever we falter and err in our decisions, the problem will point back to our inconsistent bonding with Jesus that causes us to choose personal-gratification over the spiritual.

All the holiness teachings in the Bible are meant for our spirit to be rectified and put on the right path towards seeking after God. When this concept is operating in the proper manner then God can really start using you. The discordant, vacillating self may only be used in small tasks here and there - if it pleases the Lord, but never in solid foundational work because this requires obedience, self-disciple and a required level of spiritual competence. Self-seeking mannerisms are opposed to the Lord's purposes, while comitted followers are in favor with God and the Spirit will impart Christ's knowledge to them (John 16:15). This ensures that one stays on the right path. If and when such information is withheld, then the worker must ascertain the reason and proceed to remedy the situation before going any further. This makes it easier to correct any mistakes before they get out of hand.

There are many works that may appear relevant but the Lord's approval must first be sought through prayer so as not to go astray. If not, then God will not reward the effort in eternity. Personal creativity is a total waste of time and God will not bless anything that is outside of his plans. There may also be works that were earnestly commenced under the Lord's instructions, but somewhere along the line it went adrift. It is debateable whether such works would be subject to a partial reward.

Assume a fresh cross-cultural work that will take a number of years to establish and to bear fruit. A half a dozen people join and each serve a year or two and then return home. Compare this with a person who spends ten or more years consecutively on the job. There is an immediate disparity between the two ministries in terms of effort and results. Spending a short time on the job is only enough to familiarise yourself with a fundamental approach to the work and doesn't allow enough time to build a viable working model. If workers act individually and do not ensure transferability, then all their experience is unlikely to be usable as building blocks for future workers. So, there may be a dozen short term workers whose collective effort amount to very little due to insufficient foundational grounding and lack of continuity. Relationships are personal and once the worker leaves the field, those are also left behind or lost.

Teamwork could act as a cohesive agent but this works best where all members are working in the same area and with the same target people group. Where there is a change of staff, the incoming worker and the local believer may not have the same harmonious working association as the outgoing member. People perceive their parts in ministry differently despite all having the same goals. There are a host of reasons for this and there ought to be guidelines that workers have to adhere to so that there is an integration process into the same objective. Ministry is personal and not akin to a company where everything is regimented and nobody is allowed to step outside of fixed procedures and systems. Outreach is a personal effort and personal attitude and style goes into building relationships. It lends itself to individual flair, where personal freedom of expression may be applied to advantage.

History will show how relationships have developed and you will know what works and what doesn't. It's better to have long term workers to establish a base of operations. Once a system is in place, then short term people can be more productively employed to maintain the ongoing processes that are vital to a healthy ministry. Progress is never accomplished overnight and this makes the cross-cultural outreach work so hard because it requires years of dedication.

We cannot create God's work because humans don't have God's power and blueprint. The overarching plan is God's right alone and governed by his sovereign will. Believers may acquire the mind of Christ through the Holy Spirit. It does not have executive power to design new plans. Self-will is an outlawed activity in God's kingdom. The ever-present threat of complacency and freewill can always appear when we are spiritually weak and off-guard. Even the most faithful saint can't rest on their laurels (1 Corinthians 9:27).

God conceived the whole process of salvation and he carried it out himself through Jesus. It is self-will that adds redundant work to perfection because it wants to draw attention to self. The perfect mechanism has already been completed and nothing that you can do will change it. When the Spirit introduces a new vision, we must be faithful and wait for him to lead further. Over enthusiasm tempts us to add our own ideas and this subconsciously becomes our hidden agenda. We ask the Lord to bless our work and disappointment is inevitable.

Uncertainty may be a bad thing in the material world, but it is a standard phenomenon in spiritual matters. Our spiritual walk is based on certainty in Christ and then everything is to be taken on a step-by-step basis. Once an assignment is known with certainty, then all the necessary plans and strategies ought to be put in place. Large and complex projects require more thought and planning. It would be silly to leave things until the last moment or to assume that everything will happen merely because we know that God is with us. Faith pertains to our relationship with God, but physical work in the material world must be done according to the principles of good workmanship. You receive instructions from Jesus and then you use your ability and skills appropriately in the physical world to get the job done effectively.

In the face of the unknown we feel a palpable aversion to the situation at hand and confidence fades. The spiritual life calls us to look forward with eager anticipation and faith in the Lord. New information comes to light only after the previous step has been completed. It takes some getting used to. You need to go through this a few times and confidence will grow as you see how the Lord works, so that you may be ready for the spiritual maturity phase. Conversely, if you don't apply yourself, you'll never know and you will be the big loser – God never loses. On the flip side, it will make you aware of how destructive freewill is if wrongly exercised. Don't think that you are doing God a big favour by your obedience; you are doing yourself a great service and that will be appropriately rewarded in due course.

For ordinary mortals, God's work is open-ended and anything can happen, necessitating a close walk with him. If we are able to settle our minds on the omniscience of our Father, our approach to everything in life will be transformed from trepidation to joy and peace. When you get to know God better, these gaps don't scare you anymore. The child of God concept is perfectly suited to our education process because children trust their Father explicitly and they don't fear the unknown (Matthew 28:18-20). This is exactly what God expects of us, but we allow circumstance and our minds/emotions to play tricks on us.

Spiritual laxity and indifferences are silent killers. One cannot expect to grow strong if one keeps on taking time off from the spiritual training. Going from one uplifting convention to another and neglecting to practice the principles and the meditation times in between will not enhance growth. Carelessness in this respect will bring about complacency and regression. Seeking after God must be consistently kept up at a brisk pace until life ends; it's only a matter of the will.

Intentional blank page

Chapter 26
Vexation

'We have no right to happiness; only an obligation to do our duty'.

- C.S. Lewis

You reach a stage where you know your spiritual state and you know what you ought to do. The memory of the right direction and actions that you have taken in the past gives you peace of mind. You keep on walking with Jesus towards holiness. You have done everything in your power to be a regenerated person. You don't fall for the comfortable option under difficulty anymore as you know that God has proved himself in your past trials. You know that you must be under the direction of the Holy Spirit at all times, yet the circumstances in life never allow it to be so simple. Nevertheless, you manage to get by. Personal expectations are not as high as before so disappointments are proportionately less hurtful. Although many decisions become easy to make, but there are always some hard ones lurking about that could cause you to err. Past lessons and intuition assist in graceful self-control so you live at peace with yourself. Life should be great but things still happen to cause anxiety.

Negative feelings malign a person's mood. If you continually suffer from uncontrollable mood changes, you may have some baggage hidden in the secret places of your mind that has not been dealt with. This could lead on to neglect. Uneasiness comes from external matters - bad news that upset your plans; unanticipated events that abruptly appear; economic upsets etc. that cause an avalanche of pessimistic thoughts to break your comfortable disposition. Praying does not help much as the underlying problems still exist in the mind. Moods are personally generated and not reality as nothing has really happened yet. Pessimistic thoughts based on probability linger in the mind. You can choose to be positive or negative and react accordingly. One way to overcome this is to put your feelings aside and examine the reality of the situation. See what you can do immediately to relieve the stress. If the potential problem is contingent on some other future event, then don't think further about this and wait until that event occurs. Issues may be lingering in the mind and each person's problem is different because we prioritise things differently. It may be that certain past events have led to psychological issues in which case professional help ought to be sought. Material things cause depression and anxiety.

I have gone through this kind of mental problem before. I was a worrier. It started off with minor matters, and I always imagined the worst-case scenario. As I kept thinking about them the problems grew bigger in my mind. These were all different types of secular and social issues. The potential problems were all dependent on other events. One day, I felt that the burden was just getting too much for my mind to cope with and I decided to forget about them until those critical events actually happened. It was the best advice that I ever gave myself. My cloud of worry just disappeared and it brought tremendous relief. I could think about other pleasurable things and enjoy a bit of peace. I always looked back and none of the negative events ever happened or they were minor matters that were easily dealt with. All my past worries were in vain and a waste of time. I had made the imagined problems real in my mind and they were blown out of proportion. The more you think about them, the bigger they become and it's all in the mind. A useful technique was to think about the potential issue and quickly think of a few points to handle the matter. This was reassuring as I now had some form of contingency plan. Sometimes, people would raise some future issue that may become problematic and my reply is always: I will cross that bridge when I get there. Worldly mental torment comes from Satan and it should not be allowed to overwhelm any person.

You must resolve not to succumb to irrational or impulsive actions that are prompted by negativity. Playing mind-games with your-self can be very destructive and it is not reality. Sanctified common sense will inevitably lead back to Jesus, but you have to set your mind to do it. It is true that you should take charge of your own soul; but it is wiser that Christ takes charge of you. It is also helpful to listen to good advice from reliable and trusted Christian friends. It is imperative that you try doing the things that they suggest. I have known people that have sought advice and been given useful information but they have never acted upon it. If so, then why seek advice at all. Remember that they are also acting on the Holy Spirit's leading. It is worthless if you just treat it as a good Christian pep-talk session and not try the remedial measures. It's like having an uplifting mountain-top experience and not attempting to work the goodness into your spiritual life. Concentrate of the parts that are easy to do and the way to healing will come because God wants his people to be healthy in body, mind and spirit. Never shrink back into old habits because the way forward is to do something different. This will get your mind working on alternate counter-measures.

Stable Christians normally don't suffer mentally from worldly worries because they have placed the spiritual ahead of the material. Their faith in God is sound and they pray often and take their problems to Jesus. They have a stable mindset regarding the secular environment and they apply Biblical truths in problematic situations. This is the first course of action for all believers. Their spiritual wellbeing is more important than their material concerns. However, some still suffer from depression. Personally, I feel that depression may be handled by taking the problem head-on and doing something concrete to resolve it. I have found problem-solving techniques and meeting dead-lines to be helpful in maintaining a stable disposition. Under time constraints, a person has to push themselves to the limit. The mental exertion that goes into the task is demanding and exhausting. However, there is enormous relief and satisfaction after the job is done and the timeframes are met. It gives one solid confidence in proven personal ability and a belief in self to overcome difficulties. Where possible, it is preferable to convert your mental problems into material form and this will help you think in concrete terms instead of abstractly. If an issue materialises, I will follow pre-determined steps. You will be dealing in the real world instead of in the mind. This is a self-help technique that encourages a person to meet the challenge. Doing things with one's hands to solve a problem can be wonderfully therapeutic and it lifts one out of helplessness. If things still don't work out then professional help is the last resort.

In cases that you have no control over, you should never shoulder the burden on your own (in the mind) but share it with Jesus in prayer. People's problems may cause concern but you have to understand the limit of your Christian responsibility. Help should be extended where possible. You may even share in their suffering but be careful not to venture into the bounds of their personal privacy. It may be an entirely faith-based matter and you just have to leave the outcome to him. Praying with trusted believers for encouragement and healing is free therapy. If the initial problem was caused by spiritual attack, then God can bring about spiritual healing (1 John 4:4).

CS Lewis mentioned that we have no right to happiness; only an obligation to do our duty to Christ. This statement shows a spiritual maturity that has put self-interest at the end of the queue. Is Jesus my constant concern and have I completed my duty to him? This is the question that ought to be on every Christian's mind until it has been appropriately answered. Our obligation is not an optional matter as the liability is so great. A lacklustre approach will never attain spiritual maturity. Not everybody is called to martyrdom or to missionary work in distant places. Each person's obligation is personal and Jesus will give you something that is doable and all it needs is a loving heart (Matthew 11:28-29). Once you build up rapport with the Holy Spirit and overcome your hesitation by obedience, you will be heading for a better relationship and volunteer to do more and more for Jesus. Sound spiritual ties with the Lord will settle the mind in that nothing else matters in life except Christ. Jesus' death at Calvary overrides our right to happiness. He carried out his duty to his Father and we ought to do the same for him. The interference by self-will is real but each person is capable of dealing with it correctly. Many believers will attest to the joy that comes from completing a task that the Lord had given them and the upliftment of their faith to the next level.

In the past, I found that living the assiduous spiritual life was so laborious and torpid. I would do the right things and suddenly go wrong again. This caused some distress because I knew that God is watching. Furthermore, I couldn't profess allegiance to him and then double-cross him at the drop of a hat. I felt like a hypocrite. Anyway, I would undertake to do better next time. When that came around again, I would do the right things and then sin again. Then I would confess and profess to do better in future. The cycle just kept going around. On a particular occasion, I promised God that I will never do that again. This was a grave mistake – never promise the Lord anything that you cannot honour with absolute certainty. Of course, I did it again!

Self-interest was my main priority because there were several things that I really wanted to do in life. My faith in Christ was just part of that package. Nobody told me about the obligation that I owed to Jesus (1 Corinthians 6:19-20), so freewill was there for my enjoyment. This split-interest between Jesus and self was untenable and it bothered me a great deal. However, freewill got the better of me and I did my own thing. The Lord didn't intervene so I thought that everything was okay. Things were going normally and over time I became desensitised to the Holy Spirit. I was happy that he wasn't bothering me anymore and that left me free to enjoy myself. Even so, I was aware that God is watching.

Years later when I started to read the Bible seriously, I changed my habits and spent more time pondering the things of God. It wasn't as monotonous as I had previously imagined and I kept on doing more. The above passage in Corinthians was an eye-opener and it made me think about Jesus in a holistic manner in my life as opposed to him just being my saviour. Even my friends in the fellowship never mentioned the obligation that each believer has to Jesus. Only once in a Bible study session did it get a mention in passing but there was never any solid discussion. Now that I had a better grasp of Scripture, I knew that the party was over and I had to deal with my liability to Christ. It haunted me constantly and I was praying for answers. Eventually it led to my missionary endeavour and that (mission) was something that I had always avoided in my Christian life until this concern was dealt with.

If this or other passages do not prey on your conscience, then you have to re-examine your sensitivity to Christ and to the Holy Spirit. The best gift that we can give back to God is found in Hebrews 10:7, 9. This will settle your conscience and set you up for an improved association with Jesus. Living the Christian life won't be as toilsome as before and your conscience will be at peace. Self has been the cause of all this frustration and now it has been brought under control. Vexation in spirit will be replaced by pleasure in Christ and the things that he asks of you will not be an infringement upon your personal rights but a pleasure. It's the accumulation of small changes that sets up the growth of one's spiritual account. This newly found joy will keep you coming back for more. The contest between self and Christ will be permanently put to rest.

Chapter 27
Intrinsic Nature

God is the only true free being because he is perfect and without sin. Absolute freewill only functions in holiness. Human freewill is a mere speck of its infinite counterpart because it's severely restricted. An improper understanding of this will elevate self unduly.

Although Adam could do as he deemed fit, there were rules. They were forbidden to eat of the tree of life. Therefore, human will is placed below the sovereign will of God. Before the fall, we see God's will and human will interacting in perfect harmony. God used to walk with Adam in the garden in the cool of the afternoons and have fellowship. We don't know what they talked about, Adam probably told God all the new things the he had done and all the new things that he was discovering each day. Notably the Lord was not bored with Adam's small talk. From other parts of the Bible, we know that God delights in fellowship with believers. Adam was the epitome of a holy relationship with God. Since then, only Jesus has had that experience in human form.

So why was freewill given? God wants meaningful companionship with people. He wants independent, personal and emotional response of our own volition and style. This is the primary goal of freewill and everything else that people do is secondary. The Lord only allocated human freewill for one purpose, and that was to serve his own satisfaction.

The second question: what value does freewill really have? I wish that the conversations in the garden were recorded because that would give us a clue as to our approach to fellowship with the Lord. The reason for the omission is that fellowship is a personal thing and God treats it privately for each believer. He doesn't want a procedure manual where everybody ticks off the boxes and the relationship become a mere ritual. This is intriguing because there are over a billion Christians in the world today and God is dealing with each one separately and simultaneously day or night! The earth is a dynamic environment and the decision-making process is equally enterprising. Human thinking is shaped by worldview and this allows an array of outcomes, and each person is as diverse and creative as the mind allows. The essential value of freewill is in the difference of expression. A class of students writing an essay on the same topic will inevitably vary from student to student. The teacher may not necessarily like what's written, but the variety demonstrates the distinction. God views our development and output with even greater interest and concern. The Lord is never bored with anyone despite sin, and always seeks to draw closer. It's truly up to us to respond appropriately.

Freedom from slavery to sin enables us to live and walk closely with God and to live under his rules. It is ironic that freedom from one thing (sin) only leads to captivity into another (Jesus Christ), but that is where you want to be. Inherent sin forces self-will to sin and Jesus wants self-will to be redirected to him (Galatians 5:1, Romans 8:2). This doesn't just happen in the mind, but we must be resolute and not revert to the old ways of self-direction. Human freewill was created by God to serve his purposes and it is the duty of every Christian to be educated in holiness so that God can do what he originally designed humans for. The true role of freewill is to voluntarily exist in holiness with God. The Holy Spirit imbues freedom to the believer that is willing to learn from Jesus. Obedience will change that person into the Lord's likeness and his glory will be displayed through them as well (2 Corinthians 3:17-18). Righteousness is freedom from sin and it is more important than life because it is partaking in God's personality. Once you have earnt the right to the Lord's attention, it is only a temporary victory and you have to stay close to Christ and thereby keep his interest in you booming. The evil one is always waiting close-by for the chance to get back in to break your intimacy with Jesus. A momentary lapse of attention will usher in the Dr Jekyll and Mr Hyde caper that will undo all your painstaking work. It is easier to regress than to progress in righteousness and a close bonding with Christ is not an elective.

Freewill has to be used in the way of God's personality and that is love-service (Galatians 5:13) and freedom applied to live as servants of God (1 Peter 2:16). It's a far cry from the secular understanding that freewill is a human right for personal satisfaction. Spiritual freedom does not give the follower a choice at all. The more intimate your walk with the Spirit, the greater spiritual freedom you will have. The more we submit to the Spirit; the wider we will delve into the domain of sanctification and the proper application of self-will. It's only within the realm of the Spirit that freewill has meaning. The Lord gives a person freedom and as such, freedom is limited by God's rule, therefore, there is no unrestrained freewill in the kingdom of God.

The question immediately following is: what is freedom? It's certainly not the freedom of self-determination. God wants us to learn the way of holiness (1 Peter 1:15-16). It follows then that the more one is saturated in the Spirit, the greater the probability of making decisions that please God. A strong walk with the Lord ensures doing the kingdom work appropriately and learning righteousness progressively, but one is still capable of making bad decisions in the secular realm. This is a fact of life. Deep spiritual nous does not equate to secular astuteness. These are two different spheres and both have to be learned and nurtured. The idea is to be deep-rooted in the Lord and then allow him to live out your life in your vocation and your social engagements. There will always be a conflict between the worldly priority and the spiritual, but the latter is the leading imperative.

Freedom is only obtained through in-depth sanctified alteration. Attitude has to fit the mould and mimic the nature of Christ in every human way. With this in mind, freewill ought to be automatically subordinated to Jesus' control. This should not be any shock to Christians because we want to be morally renewed under our Teacher. Freewill is actually dependent-will under Christ.

Human rights and the freedom to make different choices are awarded by God. Both are constrained by the will of the Creator because he created them. God did not purpose human rights and freewill to have unlimited freedom. The fact that the human body has limitations attests to this. Freewill is merely a decision-tool with which to get through this life. The worldly system has made freewill an absolute right, whereas sanctified freewill only operates under God's authority in holiness as it was before original sin. Freewill is a misnomer and it ought to be dependent-will under the Lord's guidance.

Risk is an inevitable part of every decision that we make in the affairs of the world. Some carry higher risk and others are lower. However, we tend to view risk in negative terms i.e. danger or loss. In contrast, God deals with spiritual outcomes. God's procedures are perfect so there is no spiritual risk. A person with a weak relationship to the Lord will not see the spiritual advantages. Usually, a material advantage means a spiritual loss. For instance, a believer may be called to ministry, but there is a secular choice of earning more money. If the job is taken, then the spiritual benefit will be lost. Forgoing the material benefit and choosing to do God's purpose will yield a spiritual reward.

A believer that is intimidated by material risk at the expense of the spiritual choice will actually be taking the biggest risk to their position in the hereafter. The standard of measurement that we will be weighed against will not be as casual as the decisions that we sometimes make on earth. It won't be imaginary or wishful thinking that a good outcome will result; just a cold assessment of whether it's right or wrong. You have the freedom to choose how you run your life, family, private affairs, business, career etc. but you have to be aware of any spiritual gains that are competing with your secular affairs. There is no freewill in God's framework because every task must be performed exactly the way God intends. Style may change from person to person but the essentials don't. The God who knows and maps out our path in life also warns of suffering and harm (1 Peter 4:12-13, 19). Scripture points out that persecution and martyrdom for the sake of the kingdom is possible. There may be physical harm, but there is no spiritual risk in obedience because the work will be rewarded if the outcome conforms to the Lord's wishes.

The cross demonstrated that God loves humanity immeasurably. Life is precious and people must love and care for their bodies because we are made in God's image. We do this as a matter of instinct. God loves humans because we are the pinnacle of his creation. Human life is worth everything to God, so much so that he resorted to self-sacrifice, he couldn't give any more than that. Our family, friends and social habits condition us to care for self. It is abnormal to knowingly engage in activities that carry higher risk of injury or loss; after all, who in their right mind would want to purposely bring suffering upon themselves?

It appears to be a contradiction that God would want harm to fall upon a believer. The calling here is to endure suffering according to God's will. It's an honour to participate in the sufferings of Christ. It suggests that the will of the Lord is the over-riding principle in life. This dilemma can only be reconciled via spiritual terms. God's emphasis is on the spiritual and not the material because the spiritual rewards are the ultimate prize. It is usually your parents/teacher who teaches personal-care and hygiene in your formative years. After you have grown up and come to know the Lord, self-preservation falls under the Lord's disposal. It's a change of direction to submission to God and to learn spiritual hygiene. Even though we may have to undergo suffering and hardship, it doesn't dispel the duty to care for one's physical wellbeing under normal circumstances. Believers have to engage in the kingdom work strictly according to God's blueprint. This makes the spiritual elements the priority because it's God's will. Christ demonstrated that the material body means nothing and it's to be used for his Father's purposes. Sacrificing the body is only a material loss for a very short time compared with the associated rewards in perpetuity. It's counter-culture to consider giving up personal values for God in return for something that we have not seen and don't even know what it's going to be like in heaven. Mature faith is hard to attain but easy to live by because mature believers will always place the spiritual above the material. It's simple to understand that the meaning of love is sacrifice; and so much harder to sacrifice self-will in order to demonstrate that love. Agape is something that we speak freely about but lack of execution doesn't carry any value either.

Self-esteem and an undue preference for self-preservation will lead to self-centredness. Despite having the knowledge of God, the priority will shift from the Creator to the creation. It all happens in the physical world and it is simple to forget that the spiritual is what counts at the end of life. Idolatry may be psychologically held at bay in this self versus God contest. We appease our conscience by partitioning our fervent desire to seemingly want to know God zealously but be self-centred at the same time. You know that you should be doing the right thing by God, but you emphasise the merits of the alternative and take the more comfortable line. This fickle state of mind can easily be accommodated over time because we choose to see things in a certain way, thereby making them acceptable. An honest examination of one's actions and habits will bring out the true intention.

Take care that you don't get too used to the material way of thinking and living, otherwise, choosing God's calling will be very hard and maybe verging on the impossible. This is surely the bane of the Christian purpose in life. We end up in an unenviable position where we have to take secular risks for the Lord yet knowing that there's no spiritual risk to our souls. This is no easy feat and may only sensibly be performed by those who have a confident relationship with Christ. It's very difficult to choose the path of the unseen because the world and peer pressure urges conformity and is unsettling for most.

Jesus had secular freedom but he subordinated his right to self-determination to his Father. In so doing, he chose spiritual freedom that is constrained in holiness. In God's realm, there is no unlimited freewill or freedom because it's restricted by holiness. The Bible only refers to freedom from sin i.e. freedom to do righteousness. Freedom encompasses a spiritual connotation and is opposed to the worldly definition. Thus, by being candidly associated in spirit with the Holy Spirit results in freedom for the soul. It is only intimate fellowship with the Lord that one is able to discern the boundaries and will of God that carries the freedom to do all the spiritual things. Freedom from sin is the passport to holiness; it liberates the soul to follow the mind of God. The Spirit of the Lord sanctifies you for this very purpose.

> Martin Luther: Therefore, faith is far another thing than free will; nay, free will is nothing at all, but faith is all in all.
>
> He goes on to add: It is not so much faith that is the decisive factor but obedience. Even with a little faith you may be saved. But, obedience often challenges faith and the fear of risk. It is obedience that overcomes self-will and drives you to unity with God.

No matter how hard we try, our earthly bodies will never be forged into holiness because we are inherently sinful creatures. However, our spirit is justified through Christ. Our dependent-will only has value when we obediently follow the Lord's directions and he confers holiness through our actions; we fit in with his kingdom goals and he will pass the eternal blessings to us.

Since God created everything in the universe, freewill is posited in the system and rules that are already in place. Human freewill does not have originating creative ability. It cannot create any material object or alter the tenets of Scripture or restructure the conceptual framework of the Lord's spiritual dimension. This is beyond human understanding, capability and control. An atheist may assert that the supernatural realm is imaginary and mythical, and he may choose to deny the Bible or any other religion but it doesn't make them disappear. If they don't make any attempt to understand it, they will never know. Every field has its own jargon, and the Word of God is the same except that it is it's spiritually discerned. Freewill is not infinite and it is not a law unto itself. Generally, self-will cannot persuade a reluctant person, therefore, it is simply a personal right and nothing more.

National laws in general are there to protect the activities and rights of the citizens. Some are more fairly enforced than others, but the aim is to benefit society as a whole. The free actions of society have to act in accordance with the law, otherwise there will be legal repercussions. God intended human self-determination to operate in a similar manner. All the rules are contained in the Bible and the emphasis is placed on the moral aspects which are governed by spiritual laws. It's an honour system as there is no physical policeman to hold people to account. However, there is a coming Judgment where all secrets will be revealed.

Chapter 28
In the Beginning

Adam and Eve didn't know the full implications of freewill. Unfortunately, they were oblivious of their honour and privilege, and they made a great mistake. Up to that point, they just knew the good things about their Creator and suffering never entered their worldview because they were holy. The general authority for freedom of action was given to people in Genesis chapter one. Humans received the right to control all living creatures that moved along the ground, in the air and sea. Note that humans were not authorised to control the rest of creation. Humans are not endowed with the capability or power to manipulate nature and the ecosystem.

Scientists may be able to develop ways to benefit from nature i.e. solar, wind, tidal energy etc. but they can never master nature because this is the exclusive domain of the Creator. The Lord has put the laws of nature in place (Genesis 8:22) because he owns everything in creation (Psalm 24:1). Freewill does not apply to interfering with life and nature. Cross-breeding and cross-pollination ought to be limited to enhancing the original species and not to change it into a different or new classification. It's not human's work to attempt to create new species of plant or animal. The Bible does not support evolutionary theory that is mere human conjecture and fanciful freewill (1Corinthians 15:39). All life, both animal and plant were created to reproduce after their own genus. The idea of putting an animal gene into a human being is not in keeping with its own grouping and goes against the image of God.

The eco-system was precisely and delicately created and introducing an alien element into normal environment can cause damage that cannot be controlled or reversed in certain cases. The release of the American cane toad into the Australian cane fields is an example of a pest that was originally thought to be a solution. It ended up as a far greater problem that wasn't there before. In these problem-solving situations, the greatest risks are uncertainty and the unknown. Scientists should never go ahead with large-scale change just because the immediate benefits are very attractive. The potential outcomes, both benevolent and malevolent must be thoroughly understood and the associated cost and benefits weigh up. Stem cell research and genetic engineering ought to be treated with great caution because the risk of abuse is extremely high for those with curious minds. God created a perfect world, but he cursed it with death and decay. Now humans are trying to stretch their freewill to interfere with the laws of nature – something that they were never authorised to delve in. Human beings are attendants of God's creation but pride covets a much higher status.

What is the definition of 'rule'? Does this include freewill to do as you please? Freedom to act is confined to Genesis 1:26; any attempt to go beyond that is tantamount to rebellion against God's design. Stewardship is the best way to define 'rule'. This responsibility carries accountability because the whole world belongs to the Lord. Humans exist on earth to take care of it as good custodians and not to misuse its resources or interfere with the mechanism of nature.

Adam's first job as ruler of the living creatures was to name them all. God brought all the living creatures to Adam to see what he would name them. Adam had the privilege to exercise his judgment unconditionally. At that point, Adam knew that he had responsibility; and with responsibility comes accountability. It was all good because there was no sin. God did not use unfair means (e.g. warn Adam by foretelling the future) to protect the creature that he loved.

God commanded them not to eat from the tree of life (Gen 2:16), and this was the first hint of self–determination in the human history. Where there's a law in place, there's a choice to comply or reject. Laws are enacted to enforce a system of order and justice that is fair for all, and for the protection of the people. Therefore, under normal circumstances, freewill is limited and everybody must comply with the law or there will be penalties for violation (Romans 13:1-2). You are free to do anything within the law, but not free to break the rules. Likewise, you are free to do anything in holiness but not free to exceed its boundary.

Adam and Eve were created as adults with perfect rational brains. They were free beings and God did not and would not have coerced them into doing anything that they did not like. By the same token, Satan and the rest of the spirit world had no power to force them to do anything because they had freewill. Adam and Eve had enough knowledge to exercise their judgment and to think and act correctly and independently. This is where Satan saw his chance. He applied manipulation and half-truth to achieve his objective, so he was the culprit using unfair tactics.

Humans were not created to be autonomous and independent of God. Instead, God created humans for his pleasure and fellowship. This throws a completely different light on a person's priority in life. The original intention was that people belonged to the Lord and not to themselves as we wrongly believe under the right of freewill. Freewill has been distorted by Satan at the fall to give us the misconception that we can govern ourselves and exist without God. The reality is that God made people to be totally dependent on him for life and without him there is only spiritual death. Self-determination was and still is the plight of humankind.

The exercise of freewill is not only a personal consideration but all related factors must be taken into account. It's a grave error to think that freewill is confined to a personal right to do as one pleases. Adam was applying his freedom when he fellowshipped with God in the cool of the afternoons in the garden. Adam had the independence to behave in his own style and it was in harmony with the Lord. The Creator allowed his creation freedom of expression, but not the option of self-governance and independence of God. Freewill was given prior to the fall and it was functioning correctly in Adam's relationship to God. Self-determination was meant for humans to work with God in the stewardship decision-making process. To this end, it also applies to consideration of others that may be affected by personal decisions. Self-determination must be applied with the broader community in mind. Freewill may have communal implications and we are all accountable for our actions.

Chapter 29
Heaven

The previous chapter was about the beginning, so let's see what the end may be like. For the unsaved it will be the end of their existence with God, but for the saved it will only be the start of a new beginning in the true sense of the word. The Bible doesn't describe the spiritual conditions in the heavens where Jesus is presently sitting at the right hand of the Father and where the angels are. We are told in Revelation chapters 21 and 22 about the Holy City, the New Jerusalem. John saw it coming down out of heaven from God, and the saved will reign with God for ever (Revelation 22:5). The Holy City/ New Jerusalem is a name given for a perfect place, and it is heaven because God will be living there among his children.

The New Jerusalem is a material place where people will live in. Revelation tells of the size, walls, gates, streets etc. Furthermore, the river of life flows from the throne of God and of the Lamb down the middle of the city. The tree of life is situated on each side of the river and it would bear fruit every month. It's the same tree that's connected to the river of life. We will know how it works when we get there. The city is extensive and there will be no night and no sun or moon because God will give the light. The curse will be removed for ever, so everything in it will be holy and God will be stationed among the people. There won't be any need for a temple building either. This is consistent with 1 Corinthians 6:19 that our body is a temple of the Holy Spirit (believers are living worshippers), and the Spirit of truth will testify about Jesus (John 15:26). The temple is a spiritual concept and we will worship God in spirit and in truth (John 4:24). We are not told whether the Holy Spirit will remain in us for all eternity. It's not essential as God will be there for all our needs. He structured the foregoing that points to personal holiness as a key ingredient to be part of his family. God's ideal for believers places an inevitable duty on us to labour in sanctification, there's no choice.

Revelation 21:5 states that the voice from the throne said that he is making everything new i.e. a new heaven and a new earth. Since the new entities have to endure for ever, all of creation will be remade for eternity.

The obvious feature is the absence of sin. God saw in his creation that it was very good, but whether there will be a similar place as the Garden of Eden is debatable. The dinosaur debate will be settled once and for all. Everything is going to take on a new appearance because they won't be tainted by sin (death, decay, pain and sorrow). There is no indication that things will be created into new species that we don't know of. Everything that we are familiar with will be there. If the Lord were to restore all the animals since creation, then there will be some kind of garden where these animals will roam. We will have fuller knowledge and will recognise fellow believers that we knew on earth.

Isaiah 65:17 mentions new heavens and a new earth and the existing system will be erased from memory. This is an indication of a new experience for all God's family. Isaiah 11:9 tells of the complete absence of dangerous behaviour and the harmony in creation that existed prior to the fall will be restored. What is a lion that never roars or kills going to look like or a wolf that never snarls and bears its teeth? There will be no more killing so all animals will revert to eating plants for food (Genesis 1:29). There's a strong possibility that people won't be eating meat either. The wolf, lion, leopard, bear and cobra will be just as tame as domestic animals. No mention is made of the creation of new species and people will recognise all the animals that we know, except for the reintroduction of certain extinct life-forms. The absence of destructive behaviour in all animals will be a new concept. The make-up of the new earth is going to be similar to what it was prior to the fall. We will see the beauty of creation that far surpasses anything on this earth. The Lord called his creation very good and we will see exactly what he meant by that.

Sin had so defaced the original creation that its removal will present nature with a very new look that humans have never experienced before (after the fall). All things animate and inanimate will have a different look, although their form will be the same. Certain animal's behaviour pattern will be radically altered and this is going to be a whole new experience for us.

Revelation 21 give an idea of the new heaven and earth:
- Dwellers will be his people and God himself will be their God.
- God will live with them.
- There will be no more unhappiness, death or pain.
- God will give the water of life to all.
- Father gives his new creation as an inheritance to all his children.

These few intimations already point to a future experience that is unprecedented in the human experience. Since everybody will be holy, they will see God face-to-face. God will be there instantly for any need that we may have. Think back to all the times when your prayers apparently went unanswered and the Spirit was silent. Our loving Father will never let that happen again. This together with the holy appearance of the new creation that the Lord will bring about is going to be mind-blowing and it will well up in rapturous joy. We can only imagine the situation from our tainted human worldview that is distorted by sin but there are still the spiritual connotations that we have no idea about. Things will be far better than we could possibly perceive. The surprises, pleasure, atmosphere and aestheticism will amaze and delight a person to no end. It may seem like a surrealistic mixture but our spirit will be entirely harmonious with it.

This will be a place that humans have never encountered before. Humans greatest desire is to be with God. The Father will put the entire system of social behaviour in place. It will be suited to the people's existence and needs. It will be the perfect place for the new spiritual body to thrive in. There will be work, but it won't be burdensome but more like a pass time. Jesus will be able to resolve any issues immediately so there will be no possibility of making a wrong decision. The Holy Spirit will return to the Father and God will be omnipresent for each individual.

Everybody who enters the Holy City will come in at a particular status depending on their reward. In broad terms, rewards may be classified as full, partial (at the Lord's discretion) and zero. All the saints before Jesus' time will receive their reward for obedience to God for the related work done. Those who have rejected God/Jesus until the last minute of their lives will have been disobedient and therefore earned little or no reward. I have heard certain Christians say that they want the best in this life and are not interested in obedience to God's calling. They would be satisfied to get into heaven with just the bare minimum; and indeed, it will be as they wish. The thief on the cross (Luke 23:43) would not have known about Jesus' teachings, so at face value he would have no reward. However, all the saints before Christ will be judged according to their faith and their heart. This thief admitted his guilt and he feared God. There is a possibility that he may have had some godliness in his past that may warrant a reward of some sort, but that's only speculation.

The highest distinction will be given to those that have been meticulously obedient to the Father and have received their maximum reward. There will be a kind of spiritual status but there will be a total absence of boasting (pride). People will notice those that are spiritually rich and those that are poor. I think that the distinction will be in the merit system because everybody will be equally holy as the Father is. The spiritual poor will intimate that they have not loved God as much and not been as obedient as they ought to have been on earth. It will be a sign of shame on them together with those that have lost their reward through negligence or other reason. The material value that believers have gained while pursuing self-interest on earth will be burned and only the spiritual benefits to all the obedient will remain. There's just no comparison between the two and the loss will be sorely felt.

An individual's style, personality and character will never be interfered with by God or anyone. You will be uniquely you and not forced to imitate another human being, except Jesus. A person's entire existence will be in perfect harmony with everything else. As a result, there will be no need for personal executive freewill and we will give it up in order not to unbalance the harmony. If a person has tasted submission to Christ on earth, it will be second-nature in eternity. Most of all, there won't be temptation so the possibility of another fall will be impossible because Jesus will be our joy and defender for all time.

This only leaves simple dependent-will that is relevant to one's personality and fancy. A person will be free to choose their own hobbies, lifestyle and preferences to satisfy their own tastes and wellbeing. The exercise of self-determination will be limited to a person's style and personal preference. It will deliver full happiness and fulfilment in life. There will be a respect for every individual's choice. Harmony with God and all people will never be broken. There are still many unanswered questions, but we will know it all when we get there. That's the least of our worries right now.

Chapter 30
Always a child

Nature.

God views all believers as his children (1 John 3:1). The adult mind has difficulty processing this concept and that is an obstacle when we fellowship and when we want him to teach and respond to our communication attempts. The kingdom of God belongs to children (Matthew 19:14). Furthermore, a believer has to learn as a little child or they won't enter the kingdom of God (Matthew 18:3). This passage says that adults must change their attitude towards God and there is no choice but to alter their mindset and adopt a childlike posture before God. Childlike dependence and humility will afford a person outstanding recognition in heaven.

Children accept what they have been taught because they trust that the teacher has pure and benevolent motives. They say plainly what's on their mind and they don't adopt double standards, so there's no need for guessing or mind-games. Kids are transparent in their faith and they believe what they are told. Under the care of a beneficent guardian, there's absolutely no reason to object to anything that the benefactor offers or requests. Adam was an adult but also an impressionable child in spirit which was ideal for God's purposes.

Contrast.

This is particularly hard for adults to adjust to because they are so accustomed to making informed decisions. People grow up and have families of their own and new responsibilities. Their childhood memories are long forgotten and now they view themselves as the provider and protector of the family. The responsibilities are onerous and every aspect of life has to be weighted up in terms of benefits and hinderances. Parent life is one of continuous giving, teaching, guidance and caring/worrying about their children. Once the children become adults, they would normally leave home and fend for themselves, but some parents still cling to the idea that they are children. Adult children are free to make their own decisions and assume responsibility and this signifies that they are no longer dependent-children.

With so much baggage in the background, adults first have to readjust their thinking and worldly tendencies. A good habit in the worldly sense may actually be a vice in the sanctification process. For example, a person would always keep their problems and shortcomings secretly in their heart for fear that the opposition will discover it and take advantage. People keep their private matters to themselves and actively guard against any leakage to the public. On the other hand, Jesus wants you to bring all your difficulties and struggles to him (Matthew 11:28-29). Intimacy does not keep secrets and private matters from Jesus in fellowship, and sometimes we don't open up to him as much as we ought. These are the things that retard our rate and pace of renewal. If you hold back on Jesus, he will hold back on you too, and it's all your own doing. You are your own biggest hurdle to spiritual progress.

Despite having an unmistakable understanding of the meaning of being a child of God, adults find it hard to fully undertake the Biblical guidance on this. The result is that the task is not properly done because certain Biblical requirements are ignored. Part application will bring little benefit and one's development in renewal will be compromised. We will explore this further in the next section.

Learning Process.

How does an adult learn as a child? This requires an attitude of humbleness in line with a childlike nature. The foremost quality is trust in everything that the Spirit leads you to (Hebrews 11:6). Allied to that is humbleness and this requires the adult to set aside all their academic and secular achievements that have helped build up their lifestyle. This implies that all management or executive freewill and adult ways must be set aside. A child absorbs knowledge without question, and the secular reasoning as to cause and effect do not apply when the Spirit teaches. God does not reveal the outworking and results before or at the time he gives a command. Sometimes his directions appear to be baseless, and may even seem unreasonable, but the child's duty is merely to assimilate the information and do as requested. In an academic situation, it is natural to question authority, and to formulate a logical understanding in one's mind, but all of this is invalid in God's agenda. It takes a great deal of humility to step down from such a high worldly position to the childlike status. Humility leads to spiritual greatness because God makes things happen through the follower. Adults have to weigh up whether they value future eternal riches more than self-reliance and personal satisfaction.

Jesus invites us to learn from him (Matthew 11:29). We are children of God and Jesus was also a child of God (who gave up equality with God), so we have something in common. Christ was gentle and humble in heart, but we have to learn that first before we may be given teaching of substance by the Spirit. The absence of self-effacing will render the lessons on character development only partially efficacious. Jesus grew in wisdom and stature, and in favour with God and men (Luke 2:52). You cannot say that you are following Jesus or that you have progressed in sanctification if you are not true to this verse. You may gain the accolades of men, but you can't fool the Lord and the internal change must be genuine.

The teachings of Jesus are fairly familiar to us because new converts always start with the synoptic gospels because that is where they find out about their saviour. The stories and parables are the easiest to remember and we commit them to memory without really probing the depth and worth. Over time, complacency closes out the exploratory side of the Christian mind and there is a propensity to stagnate. However, Jesus merely gave the essential parts to the Christian walk i.e. a summary of the Christian's objectives. He didn't say much about how we are to go about reaching those goals. Everything is based on faith and trust. However, the contemporary hurdle is how to personally overcome trust in the secular domain and shift it over to the spiritual. The digital age is producing more new applications every day in all walks of life, and those require time to study and absorb. This takes our time away from God, but we have to give up some of the worldly essentials and follow our spiritual needs. The secular worldview requires knowledgeable adult thinking but Jesus wants us to be childlike.

I suppose, this childlike adjustment process was purposely omitted because sanctification is an experience that each individual must go through personally with the Holy Spirit and the learning experience will be different. The Father's motive is to reveal his knowledge to his children and not to the wise and learned individuals that always have their own opinion (Matthew 11:25). Humility attracts the Lord's attention but even seasoned Christians may fall out of favour with God due to pride and self-determination. The starting point is to be right with God before the Spirit will actively engage in fellowship in a person. Luke 10:22 says that Jesus gives the knowledge of God to the ones that he deems worthy. John 17:17 states that we are sanctified by the Word of God which is the truth, therefore, a certain amount of

Bible study is a prerequisite before proceeding to the detail. The Spirit's advices don't come cheap, and you have to prove your sincerity before he will react. However, the primary requirement is still to submit in childlike humility for the Holy Spirit to take hold of us. Everything that we learn and do must be from a child's disposition before the Father. Childhood trust and obedience is mandatory in attaining spiritual greatness because God will reckon you as worthy to be groomed.

When I became a Christian, nobody told me or taught me about discipleship (Luke 14: 26, 33). Friends merely encouraged me to read the Bible. Since no emphasis is placed on discipleship, we pass over it as something only for super-Christians with noble ambitions. However, Jesus spoke of it as relevant to all his followers, right from the earliest Christian conception. Thus, we start off on the wrong foot and the real priority is sidelined or never mentioned at all. After a few years when we decide to pursue God earnestly, we find that the years of misdirected thinking and worldly conditioning becomes a sizable obstacle. We want to be Jesus' disciples, but the cost is holding us back. Secular values obstruct our need to give up everything and to put Jesus first. This is what Jesus demands, and it's an unconditional surrender to follow everything that he requires.

Years ago, when I decided to seriously embark on Bible studies, I accumulated as much knowledge as I could muster. At the end of the exercise, it was all just memory work. I wondered about John 14:26 that the Spirit will teach me all things but he never did. It made me distinguish clearly between knowledge and wisdom. I often wondered how some of the gifted pastors and speakers were able to present such insightful sermons. I knew undoubtedly that it wasn't just a matter of memorizing numerous Bible passages. I also considered why I didn't have that ability, but then dismissed it as the Spirit's prerogative. Although the ball is in his court, Jesus may be impelled to respond if we comply with Luke 14:26.

When I was working on the Gold Coast in the mid-1990's, the company had several distributors for its products. One particular agent was a German Christian and we got talking because I controlled all the accounts and finances. I got to know him a bit more, and one day he informed me that he was disposing of his shares in our company. I told him that this wasn't a wise move because the company was doing well and heading towards higher profits and bigger dividend payments. He replied that he understood, but he wanted to dispose of all his business interests and go into ministry (didn't say what part) because this was his calling. Anyway, I carried out his wishes, but thought that it was a very short-sighted decision.

This was true commitment on his part in giving up monetary value because he had a good business. It told me of his firm trust in and love for Jesus and willingness to give up all. I was touched because I was not prepared to do it myself. I never saw him again and he faded from memory. After a while, I seriously thought about my own aspirations of ministry. About five years later, I resigned from my job and went to the mission field (for the next twelve years). The resignation was a very difficult decision to make as this was a 'dream-job on the Gold Coast' one that I knew will never come my way again in this lifetime. I thought about my German friend and now I was doing the same thing.

Without the discipleship concept active and working in our lives, sanctification and maturity will never be satisfactorily accomplished. God's favours cannot be bought with money or anything else, he has to offer them to a follower as he considers suitable. The starting point is to sacrifice personal independence for the Lord's sake, and for our own benefit. Even then, things don't just happen at the flick of a switch, and we may have to wait a while before we see an initiative from the Spirit.

The learning processes commences with correcting personal deficiencies first. You have to take steps to rehabilitate yourself according to Scripture, and then the Holy Spirit will step in to assist. After this is successfully done and under control (not a simple task) the Spirit is free to take over and do his sanctifying work. The latter is much easier than the former because the Spirit will prod you on to obtain maximum benefit in the areas where you need it most. The main ingredient to success is humbleness. In the absence of humility, the learning process will be severely hindered because the Spirit does not work with the proud (1 Peter 5:5, James 4:6).

Servanthood and discipleship work in tandem, and the Holy Spirit is partial to those that are sincerely committed. The wisdom from the Spirit is not a one-off learning process but a lifetime interaction. In this way, a believer will never depart from the Lord. Seekers have to pursue this higher education from God only to deploy that great learning in their role as a servant. God equips a person firstly for his own purposes and the individual's personal academic record and achievements are secondary. This is definitely not accordant with secular logic. Today, minor services that were ex-gratia in the past now carry a service fee, especially in the banking sector. In God's realm, the servant pays the price and the beneficiaries receive a free service. Jesus did that for all of us.

Some Specified points.

Self-control: Titus 1:8 encourages people to avoid being overbearing, quick-tempered, drunk, violent, and dishonest, and to nurture hospitality, self-control, righteousness, holiness and discipline. It takes self-control to master all of the foregoing. This list is not exhaustive and each has to search deep within themselves to find their vices. Self-control is our escape route from temptation, provocation, prejudice, unfair dealings and anger. These are the most common areas that weaken our spiritual bank. They appear in various forms in life and may cause hurt to sensitive people. Self-control requires a person to keep their mind/actions in check at all times and not just do what is easiest or to satisfy personal preferences. Quick thinking and balanced judgment is needed in any given situation to avoid self-interest and to do what is fair and righteous. There may be specific things that cause us to sin and self-control will help counter-act those because we want to grow in righteousness. Pride and envy are hidden emotions that need to be controlled, and then attempts made to have them eliminated from character and replaced with humility. This is an onerous undertaking. A modest external appearance may be hiding an excessive ego and unwholesome pride within. Over time, outsiders can see through a person and it becomes a burden because frank comment can't be made outright for fear of offending them.

On a positive note, self-control works to promote renewal where a person is able to discipline themselves under the Spirit's guidance. Control applies mainly to the sinful nature where the bad habits have to be forced out and replaced by good. Self-discipline in obedience to stay on the path of righteousness will allow the Spirit to make compliance easier with the passage of time.

Selfishness: James 3:16 says that selfishness gives rise to disorder and every evil practice. Fights and quarrels come from your desires that battle within you (James 4:1). People will do almost anything to satisfy themselves. It depends on their conscience as to how far they will go, but the self within is still king over their lives. Most Christians get rid of this bad emotion soon after conversion, but somehow, a vestige still remains. It may not be as corrupt or as obvious as before, but under the right conditions, it will surface to take over. If nobody's looking and we feel that we can get away with it, then self-interest comes out to make us do wrong. I was at college and the residents had to do three hours of ground maintenance work each week. I was always allocated the mowing of the lawns. The grounds were extensive and even after three hours I could only finish about 80%. Summer was the worst as my whole body and clothes were drenched with sweat, really hard work. On another occasion, I was allocated the cleaning of the bathroom/toilet. It was very dusty and filthy and the first attempt was the most unpleasant. After that, it was much quicker and easier. I'm glad that I got over personal dislikes and did what had to be done.

Disorder, quarrels and fights are disruptive to ministry and friendships, but self-assertion is so strong that people don't think about the consequences when they speak. It breaks up the friendship and breeds deeper ill-feeling among participants. This ought not to happen in fellowship, but it does. Selfishness may lie dormant for many years until circumstances change. Things may go very smoothly and righteously, then a certain type of person enters the scene and bias sets in. One cannot truthfully say that one is unselfish because there are always petty things that we are averse to and those often prompt us to act selfishly or prejudicially. Each person is entitled to choose their friends and that includes the privilege of personal preference. If one acts fairly, then there will be less chance of selfishness emerging. Self has to give way to others, and even more so, to consider the needs of others before self.

Comparison: Workers should be satisfied with their own assignment/effort without comparing themselves with others (Galatians 6:4). Comparison has a good and a bad side. The beneficial part is to use others as a yardstick to strive to better your own position. Improvements come when people keep lifting the bar and the better person moves to the lead. Others come up with improved methods and they take over the lead, and another does better and the lead keeps changing. Hence the product or service keeps improving and everyone benefits. Competition is healthy and it brings out the best in the competitors. However, if winning becomes an obsession, then comparison is all about self-interest and beating the opposition. Pride will dominate a person's decisions. The aim moves from a simple comparison to a must-win scenario. It's all for personal glory and self-esteem.

However, in kingdom work it is a mistake to apply comparative measures to ministry because the Lord allocates the work and some workers get results faster than others. This does not diminish the importance or value of the slower work (provided the hold-up is not caused by human/personal interference). Besides, the person with the better result may not necessarily receive the bigger spiritual reward because the expansion is given by God and not achieved because of the personal effort of the servant.

Ungodliness: Unrighteous behaviour is the first thing that new believers attempt to clean up. Over time, gradual improvements are made and the renewal bank expands accordingly. Each person has inherent weaknesses to particular sin, and try as we may, there always seems to be a remnant somewhere in our minds and habit. Maturity in sanctification is the only way to get rid of these obstinate vices. It is the stage where Jesus means more than life itself and reformation is a small price to pay.

For some, the issue of pride, ego and self-elevation (praise/popularity) are shrouded in the inner strongholds of the mind. Attempts to keep it suppressed are usually quite effective as people make conscious efforts to do so, but when conditions change, they may readily resurface. I have seen workers that appear self-effacing on the surface, but are self-assertive and quick to make a personal stand. Minor issues often get turned into major personal matters. Ministry, friendships, trust and association invariably suffer diminution of some sort. People who are prone to this problem will find relief in promoting and concentrating on humility and internal reflection, but few take pains to rein in their impulses.

Other.

Charles Price was speaking at the Keswick Convention at Mt Tambourine in the early 1990's and he related the story of his friend who retired from ministry (a fine worker) due to an illness whereby he lost his taste-buds and food was tasteless and burdensome to eat. He lost a great deal of weight and was confined to a wheelchair in hospital. He shared this with Charles (words to this effect): 'Day after day, sitting here in this wheelchair, I'm getting these provocative thoughts of women. Things that I had dealt with thirty years ago, they're all back!'

He was merely alluding to the ubiquitous nature of sin in the world. Whether it came from his own mind, Satan or the surroundings is immaterial because this did not become an outward habit and he was still justified by faith in Christ. This may easily be dismissed as irrelevant to your particular situation or as something that happens to someone else, but it is a dire warning to us. Despite years of successful ministry, we are still open to attack from the evil one. Complacency is a silent adversary. Repetitious work will create a comfortable routine and this is another potential setback to the aspiration of spiritual maturity. Jesus challenges us to take a risk for him and do things that are counter-culture. If we remain in our easy position for too long, it will be very hard to respond to God's calling.

The next question: did this person diminish his regeneration bank in any way? Without knowing the details, and all other things being equal, I would hazard a guess and say that his accumulated sanctification did not deteriorate because his renewed character did not regress. Usually, the degradation of character is outwardly demonstrated in attitude and action. Minor sin does not devalue character unless it becomes habitual. Entrenched behaviour comes from a person's character, be it godliness, carnality or a mixture. Sanctification will only stop or diminish if the Holy Spirit withdraws his fellowship and support (becomes silent) or when we recommence self-direction. The lack of motivation to seek God will cause one's spiritual life to stagnate and self-indulgence will cause one to backslide. Actively reaching out to Christ for the rest of our natural lives is a necessity. Sin has made spiritual growth cumbersome and we have to be alert and on guard constantly. It's always there to make us stumble and this persistent spectre will follow us until we die. If the Spirit maintains interactive fellowship, then this matter will never drag you backwards ever.

A godly grandmother that I once knew said that the human mind cannot be controlled, meaning that unwanted random thoughts from the subconscious can come to the fore at any time. Sometimes they appear when you are unawares or when you are thinking about a completely different subject. These thoughts intrude while studying, at work, reading, solving problems, in unexpected places and times, and almost anywhere. Often, I would pause and wonder where those came from. It feels as if I have no control over them, and in future, they can pop up at any time and place (Romans 7:15). These things make me feel so unworthy – what a wretched man I am.

Over time, I found that suppressing those thoughts and concentrating on the task at hand set me at peace and help me stay out of trouble.

The Holy Spirit has continued providing insight and inspiration into my devotions and growth. It's the will and intention not to follow through with sin that keeps the Spirit in touch with me. This is very encouraging as I can continue moving forward in regeneration. After this new unbroken period of coaching and input from the Spirit, it would be a big let-down to have to start wooing him back to a salutary position again. Prevention is better than cure. I never want to go back to the previous silence of the Spirit in my Christian walk. You stain your character (sanctification) by entertaining those intrusive thoughts and persistence will grieve the Holy Spirit into withdrawal.

Pride is a sensitive matter and authentic self-examination must be carried out to pin-point the problems. We have to devise ways to eradicate bad attitudes and to replace them with godly behaviour (Galatians 6:7-8). Remember that God is not mocked. Whatever it is, genuine action must be made to purge them because they won't go away by themselves, otherwise they will come back when you least expect. Both Titus 2:12 and 1 Peter 1:13 exhort us to be self-controlled when facing ungodliness. Are you going to control self or is 'self' going to control you? Self is stationed in your spirit and does not refer to your material body.

Encouraging words from Paul in 1 Corinthians 9:27 that he controls his body to do what he wants with the aim of retaining his heavenly treasure. Moreover, he does not act randomly, but goes about his business in a carefully determined way. This habit ought to be evident in every follower's actions. In Philippians 3:8, Paul repudiates all his worldly achievements and they are really a deficit when matched with the spiritual reality of Christ. The same applies to all our secular honours and achievements because they mean nothing to God. For anyone to follow Paul's lead is not as easy as reading the text.

Children not only faithfully follow the instructions that they have been given, but are also good at making corrections when told that they are wrong. Adults usually try to rationalize their actions and when faced with self-interest, are slower to take remedial action. Each is responsible for their actions and self-discipline is essential to spiritual progress. The learning process involves learning about self thoroughly, and then learning from the Spirit to bring about effective change. If you have not fully eliminated bad practices, then the Spirit's input will be limited by those elements that you have reserved for yourself. All efforts will be a waste of time for the Holy Spirit and for you.

Father figure.

God created humans for his own pleasure, and that enjoyment is fellowship. Although Adam was adult age, he had to learn about his environment from God. All Adam needed was just a few pointers and he could work out the simple things in life because he had a perfect brain and he was intelligent. There was no death and pestilence prior to the fall so life was easy, pleasurable and in line with the Lord's original intentions.

God was Adam's Father through the creation process. The Lord met with Adam regularly to enjoy Adam's companionship. God may have talked about some of the complex things to Adam but there was so much about creation that he had to learn. The most significant aspect of Adam's studies was that of righteousness. Adam was holy, but he wasn't spiritually mature in that his character was not adequately educated in the fruit of the Spirit and righteousness. This is the primary reason why Adam fell for temptation so easily. God's pet project and pleasure was to train Adam's spirit to mimic his own and fully realize the image of God. Alas, it never reached that stage. Adam was created holy (sinless) but his knowledge about the application of holiness was scanty.

Adam was spiritually under-nourished and he did not understand that he could never survive outside of God's care. He didn't even know that obedience to God was his lifeline. Adam was a spiritual dunce at the time of the temptation. Had he resisted Satan successfully and then asked God to explain why such a thing happened, we would be looking at a very different world today.

On the other hand, if he was capable and mature in righteousness, he would have known the fruit of the Spirit well, especially self-control that would have helped avoid the fall. He would have at the very least hesitated and asked God for advice or explanation before proceeding. It doesn't appear that he knew God intimately at all or else he would have known the might and awesome power of God and truly thought twice about falling on the wrong side of his judgment. He never saw God angry because he was holy and he did everything that God told him to. He had no example of sin until he committed that fatal error. Perhaps he saw God as a good buddy that will excuse minor faults. He needed his Father's guidance forever, and he wasn't even aware of it. He didn't know that his spirit was his most important possession. However, we know better than Adam, but still making the same mistake as he did is discreditable.

Children are relatively helpless and they will turn to their father for help, advice, financial assistance, protection, comfort and assurance. Adults have the same avenue available to them in our heavenly Father. However, adults have their own families and new responsibilities, and they have moved on from their distant childhood memories. It now becomes difficult to turn to Father in all situations, and impulsive decisions are made because we are used to this as adult decision-makers in the secular environment. Yet, God expects us to turn to him constantly and regularly in life. However, the Lord has not neglected humans because the Bible commands believers to teach their children the ways of the Lord (Deuteronomy 4:9, 11:19, Psalm 78:5). This teaching forms good habits that will ease the path of regeneration. The instruction may be as simple as instilling a habit of reading the Bible regularly. The seeker-reader will find the Lord and the Holy Spirit will teach the necessary. It may take some time but the Lord will respond. That's the way I came to a reactive fellowship with the Spirit.

One good discipline is to keep the Lord in mind all day and to be prayerful at the same time. The follower that is habitually consulting God will invoke the Spirit's power to impart great benefit to the soul. Thoughts that flash through the mind ought to be heart-prayers to God to enhance the good and repudiate the bad. People that are in high-pressure jobs, and in tasks that require total concentration, will find it hard to pray continually (1 Thessalonians 5:17). Whenever there's a pause in the work, pray about your needs and it will only take a few minutes. Keep trying until the habit establishes itself. This sets up a personal connection that you will never regret. Heart prayers are personal and relevant and the Lord will answer in a meaningful way. Heart prayer benefits the individual whereas corporate prayer is offered for other's needs. It's better to establish your personal prayer life first and then move into corporate petition. It's a case of getting your own house in order first.

Spiritual children in an adult body must undergo training by the Spirit with the emphasis on practical implementation. There's no other alternative. Like Adam, all believers at conversion, know nothing about regeneration. They may have a better than average knowledge about the theory of sanctification, but their spiritual education is still very much in the infancy stage. It's only after the Spirit has worked God's attributes into a person's character through experience, that renewal manifests itself. However, as children in attitude, we ought to apply our sanctified common sense to learn the ways of holiness. Sanctification has a two-pronged approach and that is in theory and in practice. At the end of the day, the regeneration has to be accepted and appropriated into your spirit of your own volition and in your sound mind and faculties. Sanctification is not a mechanical input like a computer program because it requires personal coaching from the Spirit. This aims to root out issues that are peculiar to that person.

Jesus always addressed God as my Father. He was fully human and he gave us the right to become children of God (1 John 3:1). In my early years as a believer, this statement seemed unrealistic because I was spiritually so far removed from Jesus. Growth in fellowship with the Lord assures a person of his approval. You can now have peace of mind because God is with you. Being a child of God is a personal claim for every believer and the incremental regeneration gains in becoming more like Jesus adds to one's faith.

How do we relate to our Father who is a spirit being? Adam spoke with and communicated with God in the normal human manner. He may even have seen God face-to-face because he was holy. On the other hand, we cannot see God and we cannot hear his voice under normal circumstances. It seems to be a one-way communication process from the human side with no immediate audible response from the Lord. James 1:6 says that we ought to ask God for something and we must believe and not doubt, and Hebrews 11:6 says that without faith it is impossible to please God, and we must believe that he exists and that he rewards those who fervently seek him. God may be silent for a long time, nevertheless, our duty is to believe regardless and keep doing what is right. This is a major departure from the usual human interaction process where proof is required before moving forward, but beggars cannot be choosers. Problems in our association with God always stem from the human side, and we have to do all the hard work to keep this relationship thriving.

Sight plays a major role in our communication process. We cannot see demons and evil spirits. God created humans with a protective barrier whereby the evil one cannot invade or interfere with the human body, unless people invite them in. This protection is connected to freewill and the image of God. People were never meant to have fellowship with evil spirits, and the only spirit that we are allowed to interact with is the Holy Spirit. Demons are very fearful beings and the sight of them would be terrifying. They would dearly love to wreak havoc with human beings, but we must never allow them and never even think of entertaining their presence. Therefore, not being able to see God is immaterial, we still communicate in the normal human way. The omnipresence of God should make us aware of relating to him everywhere we go and in everything we do. If you have a problem relating to the Lord, then it will be your concern and not his. Regular introspection is necessary to discover your shortcomings and to find ways to improve.

Executive freewill.

Adam was learning from God to be righteous each time they met, and God was revealing a bit of his personality on each occasion. He was given limited freewill (routine freewill) to work the garden and to rule over all the beasts and animals. God did not give Adam management freewill, so he had to take his orders from the Lord. Adam knew that he was a subordinate and that the Lord was the master. He depended on God for guidance and knowledge. However, if Adam was accustomed to following God's instructions, then the command not to eat of the forbidden fruit would have been top priority. After all, He was a highly intelligent being. This seems to suggest that Adam's spiritual training was in its embryonic stages. He was a spiritual baby.

The Lord did not warn Adam of Satan and actually wanted this test to go through. If God did, then he would have had to explain who Satan was and what sin meant. Then Adam would be on guard. Maybe the evil one took advantage of Adam's ignorance (meagre knowledge) and played out the temptation. This shows that God was fair in dealing with Satan, because he did not build a protective barrier around Adam and allowed Satan an equal opportunity to tempt Adam. In fact, God deals fairly with everybody and there is no excuse. The sin was disobedience and the enticement to be like God knowing the difference between good and evil. This was the very first incidence of self-determination in the human epic. It suggested to Adam that he had the power to make his own executive decisions (free of God's supervision). Adam was a created being that belonged to God, and he could not make life-changing decisions without reference to God first. This was the hidden lie (the first was that he would not die immediately). The attractions of the temptation were too great – the fruit was good for food, pleasing to the eye and desirable for gaining wisdom. Adam's weakness was self-satisfaction and he didn't know the power of God.

Adam's sanctification was sparse and that's when Satan played his trump card. I don't know why Adam didn't exercise caution and paused at that very moment. He should have broken off and thought about it carefully because a decision didn't have to be made immediately. Adam was so accustomed to meeting with the Lord regularly and asking for advice as normal routine, but this time he didn't. Not astonishing at all because self-will tells you that you don't have to ask for the Lord's permission in anything that you do.

From creation week until the temptation, Adam had only known the peaceful and loving side of God, but now he suddenly saw the anger of God and it was terribly fearful. Rebellion made humans and God eternal enemies because people had sided with Satan. Humans wanted to take control of their own life and make their own management decisions, and this was not how God intended it. Self-management is fundamentally wrong and God views this as a severe sin; revolt against his intentions. People that persist in self-determination are already marked for judgment as they have the same rebellious attitude as what Satan has. It doesn't have to be a clash of arms, and mere disobedience is sufficient to become an enemy of God. This is why obedience ranks above all forms of physical worship and sacrifice. Thus, it routinely rules out executive freewill.

A friend once said that she wanted the Lord to make her do things like a robot instead of having to think and decide. This will avoid sin. This struggle is really about problems with executive freewill. I had similar thoughts as well, but freewill is a personal challenge that God has given to all people. It's the individual's responsibility to set themselves up on the path to reconciliation with the Lord because he has something that we need desperately.

Directive control is a product of the secular lifestyle and it is a normal part of life. Major decisions have to be made in all worldly affairs. People face this from adulthood to death. Young people think about their future and what sort of life they want to plan for, and old folk prepare a will that dispenses all their worldly possessions after they die. This is a person's final parting wish for their beneficiaries. Where there is a sizable estate, the will can become a hotly contested document. Secular decisions whether wrong or right will end on earth, but spiritual decisions have eternal ramifications. The aim of Christian life is to be in the right standing before the Lord. Unfortunately, we have brought executive freewill into our relationship with God and this is so hard to reverse but it must be done.

The most outstanding example of subordination was Jesus as a child of God who submitted his will to his Father at the cross. We are children of the Father and we ought to surrender our management-will to him in the same manner. There is no power-sharing with God because nothing in creation is his equal.

Operational freewill.

Adam's responsibilities were to work the land and rule over the living creatures. He may not have realized it, but his major responsibility was to be obedient to God and to follow directions. This meant that he only had operational freewill in performing his duties and that was to care for the garden. He could not make any substantial changes or any reconstructions without permission from the Lord (even if he had the means to do so). He was just a steward and did not own the land. God gave him limited freewill to name all the animals. God allowed him to choose whatever name he desired and he could apply his creative abilities. Adam could enjoy himself in whatever manner he chose i.e. he had complete freedom to do what was right, and he had no right to do what was wrong because God owned him.

The same rules apply to Christians today. Follow what Scripture dictates, and the rest is left to the individual's choice and personal taste. As more and more new things emerge, there are more issues to consider and following the rules is not as simple as what Adam faced. If you have a family, then additional matters have to be taken into account before decisions are made.

We always approach matters first with self in mind because that is what everybody does as we are brought up this way. We have family responsibilities and so we have to consider carefully what we do. This method always creates division with the Lord and poses dilemmas because we are tempted to apply management control over our own affairs. As a Christian, it is not merely our own affair, but it is Jesus' affair too. If we put God first, then the path is set and it's easy, but we make it hard for ourselves by rationalizing our preferences. When the first hardship appears, the urge to re-take control from God is ever present and our resolve falters and we hamper our spiritual progress. God invariably asks for some sort of sacrifice from us but we hardly see things his way. Our secular judgment always sees more lucrative alternatives elsewhere. Hesitation and procrastination to do what's right seem to get the better of us. The resolution to be childlike must be reaffirmed and we have to give up those things that obstruct our relationship with the Spirit. Each time we confront spiritual decisions that promote self, we must approach it from the child perspective and not as a secular adult.

Children have no concept of self-management and fit the meaning of a true servant of God. They are obedient and will do only as the Father instructs. This is imitating what Jesus did all his earthly life. All the executive decisions are in God's hands, and what children do is not of their own invention (John 8:28-29). Jesus gave up equality with God and also his right to self-determination. He had no supreme freewill, but only elementary freewill. Having been left only with routine decision-making ability, one would think that his life would be monotonous and mundane, but not so. In fact, Jesus' life was anything but boring. This is mainly because his Father was empowering him because of his obedience. Little children will obtain the best spiritual benefit from God's wisdom and his guidance (Matthew 11:25).

Children of God that subordinate their freewill comprehensively to the Father will also experience similar might from our Father as Jesus had, but obviously not as dramatic because Jesus was perfect in his relationship to the father and had universal responsibilities to bear. We have many corrections to make before we get there, but if you never try then you will never know. Jesus being fully God surrendered his executive freewill to his Father, whereas mere mortals have substantial difficulty and are extremely reluctant. It defies logic.

Chapter 31
Spiritual child

Members of the family of God are obliged to follow Jesus and learn from him. The objective is to grow in sanctification and this will start the journey to spiritual maturity.

A friend of mine once said that she doesn't trust other Christians because of the unpleasant things she had experienced in the past. It ranged from worldliness, pride, hypocrisy and showing-off that had a depressing effect. The perpetrators behaved this way for various reasons. However, it shows that they are mere babes in Christ. My advice was to assess the position carefully and consider whether to remain in such relationships. Hurtful comments have to be taken back to the culprit and worked through. If not, they will think that they are doing right and keep repeating those wrongs. Neither the perpetrator nor the victim displayed much by way of sanctified common sense. However, this was a good start for her to improve her understanding of social behaviour in Christian circles. She applied Biblical precepts and did what was right thereby enriching her regeneration experience.

Another friend had the dilemma of the commandment to show love to all people. Unbelievers are usually more scathing than Christians because they don't know Biblical morals and some may be plain rude. Love does not preclude a person from being assertive. The culprit has to be confronted and the brash behaviour appropriately addressed. Love does not mean that you have to keep on taking abuse just to keep the friendship going. If the relationship is unworkable, then it is best to walk away from that person because it's not beneficial. Pray that someone else will have the opportunity to lead them to Christ. In this case, both parties had been acquainted for the better part of ten years and the unbeliever had even attended a church service. After this length of time, I doubt whether a person would ever turn to Christ. How much more grace do they want? It strongly suggests that they trust themselves more than they trust Jesus. Matthew 7:6 is a point to bear in mind.

This situation may provide an indication of a person's level of spiritual understanding of how to apply Scripture in practice. Understand your own temperament and limitations and know when to draw the line. Some people are stronger than others, but each has to know when to pull the pin and preserve their sanity. Disabling yourself makes you unfit to help others that need your assistance, and that is counter-beneficial in kingdom work.

Another Christian friend was so disillusioned by the unbecoming behaviour of fellow Christians that she stopped going to church and had grave doubts about her faith. Self-will caused this damage but everybody is accountable to Christ. Discipleship/worship is centred on Jesus and has nothing to do with the erratic behaviour of other church-goers. It's deeply regrettable that she allowed other people's actions disrupt her relationship with God, thereby strangling her regeneration progress. The evil one scored a double in this respect and she didn't give Jesus a chance. Personal relationship with God must be preserved and not be detracted by the harm that others do (John 21:22).

Secular background and spiritual nurture.

The worldly environment is the perfect breeding ground for human freewill to flourish and the liberty with which people do so puts human beings in direct opposition to God (James 4:4). Human beings are inherently sinful and the world is the ideal environment to drag people further away from God. We do so much to ensure that we thrive in the secular domain, and so little for communion with Jesus. The odds are truly in favour of the dark forces. Human persuasion is heavily swayed towards sin and self and this makes people very insensitive to God. It's small wonder why we are so hesitant when the Lord beckons. However, God is still winning and the enquiring mind ought to take note and attempt to discover why. Sometimes precious spiritual lessons lay waiting to be uncovered.

Children are taught to prepare for adulthood and almost all their education is of a secular nature. They may attend Sunday school and Kid's Club and both provide some spiritual input. Some may have godly parents that set aside time for Bible reading and prayer, but the deeper teaching is limited. Some grow up to be worldly-wise and self-confident. Kids that attend pre-school are usually taught how to build up assertiveness and confidence. After they graduate from high school, they are prepared to hold their own upon entering society. The learning process continues in the workplace, and they strengthen their self-confidence and capability. The Uni. graduate has an even wider outlook and greater self-esteem. Personal talent, achievement and broad-thinking promote self-worth and pride. The best academic preparation affords the best chance for success in one's career. Successful business parents groom their children to enter the family business with the aim of taking over when they retire. Parents may also help their children set up their own business. It's all about looking after self for believers and unbelievers alike. This is the world that we live in.

Young adults get married and have children of their own. The mindset shifts from being dependent children to guardians of their own kids. The cycle repeats itself and parents put a lot of effort and money into their children's development. The adult mind is focused on responsibility and self-enrichment. They do whatever they can to give their children the best opportunities. Society sees them as able parents that have a stable family. Commendation from neighbours and friends give rise to pride and self-worth. Each person is conscious of their social standing and some try earnestly to better their status through higher education, business or other talent that brings higher financial returns.

The average person perceives self in the following manner: I am a capable adult, I have achieved certain things, I have my own opinion and values and I have a right to express them, I do as I please, and I reject everything that is outside my ambit of acceptance. I have my pride and I deserve respect. I want others to recognize what I have achieved.

Rene Descartes' philosophy had a wide influence on western thought. His flagship statement: "I think, therefore I am" emphasized himself as an intelligent individual thinker. It's a statement of self-identity for everyone that exercises their mind to think as an individual. Thinking brings out the character and essence of who you are and what you value. He employed logical thinking processes in a cause and effect scenario, and this later developed into scientific method. It brought out the importance and the need for people to think for themselves. However, if you dwell on it long enough, the words could focus on self ('I am') and this will lead to pride, self-importance and self-aggrandizement. Self-elevation may not be acute or obvious but self-esteem will be present to promote it in some manner. It's human nature. Adam was self-seeking when he sinned and that put him at odds with God.

Status-wise, human beings are nothing compared with the Almighty. Being valueless and worthless is a bit hard to accept, but the Biblical tenor is that a person must get down to despair (self-hate – Luke 14:26) before the Spirit will help them rise up to renewal and spiritual magnitude in God's holiness.

Peter's confession in Luke 5:8 is a blunt expression of the truth about every human being on this earth. Peter confessed these words to Jesus who is the 'I am' before Abraham was born. God designated himself as 'I am' in Exodus 3:14 and this is the only name that God said of himself. 'I am' in the secular context points to selfish interests and self-conceit. This is a long-standing habit that God wants to change in his children as it stands in opposition to his majesty. The pronoun 'I' has to be redirected to them, and others, who are to be afforded consideration before self. Self-denial means that 'I' has no status or significance because the humble servant is the person that God loves and wants to train. The appropriate place for 'I' in the Christian life is self-immolation as a suitable reciprocation to Christ. Believers must view 'I am' in the context of God and never to self-interest. The personal pronoun may be applied in ordinary things that do not attract uncalled for attention to self (e.g. I want to help him out or I'm going shopping).

Towards the end of his life, Paul mentioned that he wanted to know Christ and the power of his resurrection, and he also wanted to attain to the resurrection from the dead (Philippians 3:10-11). All the saved will experience the resurrection when God gives them their new spiritual bodies. Scripture say that we are alive in Christ and alive with Christ (Ephesians 2:5), but the physical body is dying each day as we get older. Therefore, the life from Jesus is not for the body, but specifically for the benefit of our spirit. For years I was under the impression that Jesus was in me to help me (in bodily actions) to stop sinning and to love God in return. I never thought that the root cause of sin was my self-will that is embedded in my spirit. Real death pertains to one's spirit and the same with true spiritual life in Christ.

Paul was not speaking about the future resurrection experience but to know the fellowship of Christ's suffering in his present life on earth (verse 10). The sensible analogy is the resurrection of one's spirit after the character of Christ and the related hardships that a follower has to endure so as to gain continuous spiritual growth. This resonates with the teaching and training by the Holy Spirit. It seems like a precursor to the ultimate endowment of the new spiritual body. The power of the resurrection from the dead can only be explained by God.

Sanctification is the core of one's relationship with Jesus and it goes on for the rest of one's life. Kingdom work may come and go, but renewal must be absorbed until death. It makes sense that a Christian must commit a lifetime to Christ in order to be like him in character and to bond as closely in fellowship as is spiritually possible. It's all in the spirit and the body only expresses the internal values. The spirit that is alive in Christ will live eternally. We have our own spiritual resurrection on earth that needs urgent attention while we still have the time. This applies to all those areas of our character and personality that lay dormant and waiting for the Spirit to impart new insights into. There is so much yet to experience and life is short.

Christians must try to accord with Paul in the satisfaction that we have done what God expects of us (2 Timothy 4:7). On that day, you will be over-joyed to face the Father knowing that you have attained the fullness of his character traits that he has planned and allowed you to grasp. Kingdom work has a set time and place to be completed, but personal holiness has no limit. Humans are only allowed the time of their lifespan to grow as much as they can. Christ is our spiritual limit.

Western independent thinking is focussed on individual capacity. This makes it hard for people to think about society and more importantly, their neighbour. The dog-eat-dog mentality promotes self-centredness. However, many western countries now have social responsibility regulations or ethics that force corporations to consider their position in relation to the community in which they are operating. Environmental protection, fitness programs, beneficial social activities, community support programs etc. are detracting from corporate selfishness but executives merely find other ways to benefit their organisations. Social responsibility is forced onto corporations by law, whereas Christians are bound by the self-regulated morals in Scripture. In God's realm there is no choice, but people have their own way of interpreting and practicing Biblical principles. We ought to develop habits that direct our self-will for the good of others and still keep a moral balance of self-care.

God gave humans intelligence, so thinking was part of that gift. Innovation and creativity are the hallmarks of human ingenuity and global progress would not be possible without the passion to invent and discover new things. Bitcoin (BTC) was in its early stage of expansion in 2017 and was based on blockchain technology. Banks and governments were very concerned. The former was facing a new type of money in the form of cryptocurrency (non-fiat money) transacted in cyberspace. They have no control because each owner controls their own private digital keys. The public need for a banking institution will be vastly reduced. The encryption built into the mining system of BTC makes it impossible to be counterfeited. Governments were fearful that they had no control over monetary policy (collection of revenue) as all the transactions by-pass all international sovereign borders and laws. The main drawbacks were the fear of financing of terrorism and money laundering. At the time of writing, cyber-crime was an issue, however, cyber-security developers were also hard at work to come up with better systems to counteract hacking and strengthen the safety of all users in cyberspace. Negative publicity and resistance to cryptocurrencies played havoc with market prices, but protagonists were confident that this will replace fiat money in the future.

Cryptocurrency is the ideal way to avoid theft, forgery, and other forms of financial crime because it's based on blockchain technology. If there was only one cryptocurrency for the world, then the control of financial and commercial activity would be greatly enhanced, and so would the power of the person that controls it. No doubt, the world is heading that way inevitably. This will usher in the prophesy in Revelation 13:16-18. Saudi Arabia's Islamic Development Bank (IDB) has also started using blockchain technology to develop new financial services and products. Islam is a major player in a unified financial control system and now the way is open to world domination by a single entity or person. However, China (world's second largest economy) was still resistant to cryptocurrency, but they will be forced to change if they want to keep trading with the rest of the world. At that time, the world supply chain will be on the blockchain system and private bartering outside of the system will be severely curtailed.

This technology is far ranging and includes financial service, payments processing, logistics, biotech, entertainment, business services, websites, medical activities etc. Every piece of data has the potential to be collected, analysed and monetised, and this has birthed the term Big Data. Every day, more Internet of Things (IOT) are being embedded with smart-chip capability and the future roll-out of 5G technology. However, certain information is still restricted by privacy laws, but there are ways around it. Enigma coin was working on a system that has powerful analysis features that enables the sharing of information without disclosing the identity of the source. The integration of the IOT and cloud computing into the blockchain system will ensure that the information for every essential service will be contained in one central data base. Blockchain technology can be applied to almost every conceivable industry, and every day more organisations were getting involved. It will have a strangle-hold on all nations that are reliant on cyber-business. An article mentioned that Microsoft, IBM and Maersk were already working on incorporating blockchain technology into their systems. Walmart was developing a version of blockchain technology to track the millions of goods passing through its business. Food sold to consumers will be able to be traced along the value-added chain right to its source. These things are all beneficial, but it will become a major problem if a single entity or person is able to seize control. The benefits of blockchain technology on which BTC is based is far too wide-ranging for any business to ignore. The attractive commercial and personal advantages considerably outweigh the disadvantages. Anything that is this powerful becomes a very strong incentive for political purposes and the genie will be out of the bottle for the one that takes charge. Human nature is selfish and domineering and certain people may already be plotting ahead to vie for the top job. World supremacy doesn't have to be won through war and bloodshed. Self-elevation will have its greatest showdown with God for ultimate command.

Although God did not limit our thinking, we have to be very careful that we don't conjure up thoughts that antagonize him. Since we are inherently sinful, unbridled thinking will portray self as more important than God. Christians must maintain spiritual vigilance at all times and be sensitive to purity. When an adult becomes a believer, the mindset has to change. They have to learn to be spiritual children. Even sincere Christians carry baggage of some sort that the adaptation to learning and practicing Biblical ways is not going to be easy. Those that come to faith earlier in life also have a few kinks to straighten out, but they know the way and are able to get on the path to renewal much quicker. The challenge is to stay there and to keep on improving. On the other hand, kids from Christian families have been known to ignore the faith and go their own way when they reach adulthood or earlier. The unpredictability of freewill is colourful but this is not a game.

A believer is expected to grow in regeneration (1 Corinthians 3:1, I Thessalonians 4:3 and 5:23-24). Babies require constant care as they are helpless. They take up somebody else's time and productivity is scaled back. This is all because they have chosen to concentrate on worldly values and not on godliness. Paul accused them of jealousy and bickering and not behaving as he expected. Spiritual-wise, they were well below the sanctification maturity grade expected from people of their length of time as believers. It is shameful and a stain on their character.

Wealth, status, pride, egotism, selfishness and self-fulfilment are all secular ills that the world reveres. However, they reflect infamously on Christian character and are obstacles to progress in holiness. All believers start out as babes in Christ and have to learn to become spiritual children, and the objective is to become a mature spiritual child-adult. There must be a change in a person's value system and resolute persistence to keep heading towards the goal. Words can be vacuous and self-satisfaction can lead you off the rails, so vigilance is to be exercised at all times. Self-control not only acts to reduce the tendency to sin, but also to practice good habits. Failure is not only a disappointment to self but also to the Lord. The child concept is a standing policy before the Father and the distinction is whether one is a babe or a spiritually developed child.

Normal adults want to get ahead in life and better themselves, in this regard, selfishness is implied. Carnal thinking dictates that an opportunity has to be grasped or else someone will take it away. A person first has to look after self and too bad if others miss out. Some show it openly through their behaviour while others tend to keep it down (but it's still there). The aim is to get ahead of the competition and everything must be done to ensure that. A person would grab all that they can and leave others with nothing. Self-will shows up strongest under limited choice situations. People only think of themselves and would choose the easiest jobs and take the best for self. There's nothing wrong if viewed as a 'first in, best dressed' in a payment situation, but over time, it becomes ingrained in character. People would behave stealthily and uncaringly until they have all that was available. The late-comers are seen as having run out of luck.

I was visiting a country town in north-west China where the villagers were dependent on a common pump to draw water from a well. It only operated at certain times, so the people would bring their containers and share the water on an honour system. Over time, those that lived close-by took more for their own convenience, and when the others arrived, the water was all gone. This caused upsets and allocations had to be regulated. Self-interest breaks trust and makes bad friends.

It's normal to want to better one's position in society. Kids growing up would usually have one talented person standing out from the crowd and that one becomes the leader. The rest may be just followers or there may be ones that wish to challenge for the leadership. Bad feelings could emerge if personal attitude gets out of control. Petty matters can be blown out of proportion. Nevertheless, the drive to reach higher is always present and it's all to do with finance, status, popularity, respect etc. because self is king. In the business world, unscrupulous businessmen would use and step on others just to get ahead. The thinking is: they don't like me and I don't care. These people are devoid of feelings for others.

Christians who are in this position have a lot of soul-searching to do because God demands humility, self-sacrifice, a servant heart and putting others before self and all this has to be done in love. These elements oppose self, and this calls for radical changes in personality and practice. It will take time and determination to keep on doing right. It's no place for the faint-hearted, yet, I would encourage all to have a go. You won't know if you don't try. It will turn a new page towards spiritual betterment as there are always new things to learn. Many would only achieve this in part for various reasons, but nobody ought to give up. Spiritual honour is a personal matter with God and it is not measured by physical effort but in one's moral quality. Although results may allude to a person's spiritual state, only God knows the precise position of where you're at.

Some workers may carry their worldly habits into ministry and it may be inadvertent or due to negligence or carelessness. They may not even be aware of their own competitive nature. Things are done and said with the view of keeping an edge over others. Competition may emerge in various areas such as work, music, connectivity/relationships, extent of ministry, nature of profession or trade, popularity with the local leaders and people, number of converts won to Christ, the accumulation of local friends etc. With the passage of time, distrust will develop and there wouldn't be any real benefit coming through to the participants. At some point, it would be appropriate to breakaway and move elsewhere to seek a better work environment where all may gain and grow in harmony.

When a person guards their feelings and values obsessively, anything that appears confrontational would automatically be met with opposition. Most times the remark is unconsciously or mistakenly taken as a personal attack. I have been in this situation several times in my early adult life and have learnt to handle myself in a gentler and calmer manner after each experience. The assertive party wants to make their point known. The pulse rate rises, voice tone increases, defensive remarks are enunciated, people get keyed up and the mind prepares for all-out defence. This tinder-box situation may also quickly turn defence into offense.

When the Rubicon is crossed, people are likely to speak out sharply and say hurtful things. Those in the western society are expected to voice their opinion, and they have been trained to do it since their school days. Biting remarks are usually made on impulse. It just requires calm level-headed thinking to keep the peace. Tempers should be defused and order restored before things get out of hand. A tit-for-tat bout can be embarrassing for both parties. In addition, an innocent observer may also feel very uncomfortable for just being present in a private altercation. Self-control has to come from both parties, and this will put the brakes on further deterioration. People ought to keep in mind that where emotions are high, self-will must be restrained and humility brought to the fore. Comments that cater to the opposition's situation would help avoid ill-feelings. Ranking the other person first does wonders for reconciliation provided that there is compromise. The critical point at the height of the argument should prompt a person to pause and think. Placing self last and the opposition first requires enormous self-discipline. The Bible is infallibly right when it requires us to be humble. The person that is able to successfully negotiate all the foregoing will have demonstrated commendable spiritual discipline and maturity in righteousness that will be pleasing to the Lord.

In the world system, comparison is good as it provides a means to gauge personal performance. Improvement will only come if you aim to reach a higher standard. Following those that have reached a better position will bring improvement. People apply the act of comparison in business, education, sports, social relationships, standard of living, remuneration and anything else that people are interested in. In my school days, I found that playing against the top table tennis players was daunting because they would rout a novice mercilessly. However, the hidden gain was experience and after a short while, personal skill would be lifted and new young potential players would emerge. The goal is to gain a benefit for self but in the process it encourages selfishness too.

In the large corporations, 'climbing the corporate ladder' is the goal of every aspiring employee that has managerial skills and ambition. It's very selfish conduct and unconscionable staff will use any means to get to a higher level. They will use others for self-advancement and at times it may involve hypocrisy and back-stabbing tactics that are hurtful. Even in a general office, employees will have this competitive streak and that is based on a ranking system. A dominating personality will often resort to office-bullying tactics that can make working conditions most unpleasant. Aggressive and nasty attitude give rise to hatred, and all this started out as innocent competitive behaviour!

In God's domain, there is no competitive structure and no corporate ladder to negotiate. Since he rewards us only when we get to heaven, we don't know how much credit each person has accumulated. Hence, we can't compare and compete against one another. This is a good thing as it takes envy out of our effort in pursuit of God and his holiness. Each person has to keep in step with the Spirit and expand their regeneration as the Spirit leads. In the back of our minds, we know that we are improving, but we don't know the exact extent. Since God rewards a person's work according to his own plan, it is useless doing anything that is outside of his will. Good works must be motivated by the Spirit and be in the Father's will to be of value, and personally driven works will have no credit (Matthew 7:21). Competitiveness is accompanied by self-exertion; whereas sanctification is found only in the Spirit's interposition.

There may be some that try to do more work than their peers. In most cases the motive is to be seen to be doing more work than others or seen to be working harder. The correct attitude is to do it solely out of love for the Lord. Generally, people serve because they have the talent and time and they feel called to that position. People don't work specifically for future reward (and don't even think about it), but because there's a need in kingdom work and they can fill that post. Most do the work because they love Jesus and want to please him. It's so different from the secular employment process. Selfish personal worldly habits should not be brought into God's work. However, constructive business and other systems may be applied where they bring control and benefit to the body. Kingdom work ought to be done as efficiently as possible by utilising the best tools available.

I have seen people use secular methods in ministry with negative outcomes. They seem to forget that this is God's work and not their own. As an observer, it is sad to see how their actions go against Biblical morals and normally accepted convention, and even sadder that they persist in their ways. Trying your best while still remaining inefficacious is no excuse. Recognition of the responsibility of the office and accountability to the stakeholders ought to be clearly delineated and adhered to. Where necessary, a knowledgeable third party should be brought in to help put the correct procedures in place for the proper operation of the system. It may require a member's meeting to decide on remedial action, but poor workmanship ought not to be tolerated. Staff may not have the competence and they may rationalize their reasoning and appease their conscience, but the fact remains that it is God's kingdom work, and they are creating more problems than solutions. Taking one step forward and two steps back reflects poorly on self and severely undermines the quality of stewardship. It tells of the strong inclination towards self-direction and little of desiring the highest quality workmanship for the Lord, and disregard for accountability.

Some people cling to their posts because of self-image or for some other selfish reason. If they had put the stakeholders first, then they would admit their inadequacy and implement corrective procedures. This admission is respectful and highly honouring to God. Even though the Lord remains silent in these situations, it doesn't mean that he is happy to see the errors being perpetuated and left unchecked. He is a God of order and not chaos. Doing your best for God means doing it right according to accepted convention. A worthy servant will produce good quality work that shows respect to peers, members and other interested parties. In this way, the duty of accountability is fulfilled.

Servanthood and humility go together, putting others before self, and doing the job acceptably for the benefit of all interested parties so that there are no repercussions. It's helpful to pause and meditate on how Jesus did everything in obedience to his Father. A good servant will always do a good job for their master. When people in ministry call themselves a servant, but do not have the competence or training to fulfil their post, over a reasonable period of time, it becomes indefensible and even borders upon contempt. They ought to examine their motives in the light of what Christ would do. I knew a person in ministry who admitted that he wasn't competent to do his job, but there was nobody else available at the time. As soon as a better qualified candidate appeared, he stepped down. That's doing what is morally correct by ensuring that the Lord's work is kept at the best standard available.

In daily life, Christians have to consider three worldviews: personal, third party and God. The personal level is where a wholesome godly perception ought to be established with accountability in mind. This is the place to make productive changes as well. It is vital to clean out all unfair and prejudicial tendencies otherwise mistakes may easily be made. Operational objectives ought to be clearly established and carried out consistently. The main issue is to keep personal worldview neutral and in-check so that it does not interfere with servanthood principles. Our actions must glorify God in the hope that unbelievers may be attracted to Christ. Simultaneously, believers may be assisted in their spiritual guidance or aided in doing their part in kingdom work. Humility, third party priority, obedience and sincerity must undergird personal operating policy and this will be pleasing to God. Proper self-control will keep one's focus correct. Personal worldview may change over time, but it must be grounded in Scripture at all times to minimise wrongs.

Kingdom business is about interacting with others. In order to properly fulfil personal responsibilities, you have to understand their worldview before acting. This has to be done in humility. In non-compatible situations, objectives and methods will be unworkable with no realistic prospective benefit, so departure may be the right course of action. Christians are to be used by the Lord and not by people. Some people will take advantage of a meek Christian and they will misuse their kindness, goodness and time for selfish reasons. Unconscionable people may even do it for fun and self-elevation. I came across a case like this and my advice was to pray about it and then decide whether to continue that relationship. Love has its limitation where there is no intention to change for the better. Even Jesus had a limit with the unrepentant cities (Matthew 11:21).

In this case, the friendship was affecting the believer's mental and physical health (sleep deprivation over the problems). Enough time was already put into that relationship and it was time to move on so that friendship was terminated. This brought tremendous relief, peace, and normality to the aggrieved. It was clearly a case where the offending party's worldview was not adequately understood, as it was rigid, unalterable, selfish and incompatible in a Christian relationship. Awareness of the Lord's leading and general enquiries of third party's values and interests will indicate whether to continue or abandon a relationship. Understanding a person's (unbeliever/believer) worldview ought to be supplemented with prayer to see if the Lord has any specific direction. In the case of believers, it is hoped that they will learn from the interaction and enhance their own walk in regeneration. All people are capable of playing mind-games and one has to consistently seek the Spirit's guidance and wisdom.

God's worldview is the lead feature. God's criteria cannot be altered whereas the previous two are always subject to improvement. It's loving God first and loving your neighbour as yourself. The practice of godliness, justice, fairness, grace and humility are essential parts of God's personality, and we ought to take those into account in our methodology. Helping others with advice in their spiritual development and building up the kingdom of God are part of Christian duty. Servanthood, third party priority and personal sacrifice will have to be worked in appropriately. After this, the hidden by-product is progression in regeneration; nobody sees it but the Lord knows it. Personal improvement means that the servant is better equipped for service and the overall quality of one's work will strengthen accordingly. Most of all, it fulfils the Lord's requirements and personal relationship becomes stronger and closer. Specific tasks are meant for particular people. Therefore, it is necessary to stay in close touch with the Lord so that his will and purposes may be readily ascertained in any situation that he has placed you. God has a particular view and approach to his work and the Spirit's help will give you the discernment that coincides with God's worldview. Self-generated decisions have no place here and meticulous care needs to be taken to ensure that self never interferes with God's policy.

After due consideration of the three worldviews we will be in a better position to be used by God in whatever he calls, and we need never be afraid of committing to his will. Each personal obstacle has to be identified, purposely worked through in detail and the finer problems rooted out through personal resolve. At some appropriate point, the Holy Spirit will assist in making those corrections and then he will take the lead into new hope, fellowship and he will illuminate his secrets for your personal joy and benefit. This personal connection is with God and the realization that 'God is with me' will be authentic and not mere wishful thinking. It seems like a fairy tale that God will come alongside a sinner, but Jesus promised it in John 17:20-21, 26. Your spirit will know the Holy Spirit's intervention when it happens because it's not from your own brain-storming, but something that has come from outside of yourself of which you have no control over.

Repentance.

Sin is ingrained into the human character and psyche since birth. We will remain in our sin unless change is introduced. This alteration of attitude and action is called repentance. It's not regret in the secular meaning, but a refinement of character in the spiritual dimension. It seeks to make a person do things that are out of character with a sense of permanency. A person would repent of past sin and not only stop those sins, but also proceed to do the opposite in future. It is a move away from doing wrong and turning to the opposite direction of righteousness. In this way, you change from being an advocate for sin to a supporter of holiness. The objective is to habituate sanctification. This warrants a complete change in personality and worldview, and we have to work to make that happen. Once we show good faith, the Holy Spirit will take over and make the spiritual life-change much easier.

Peter was asserting himself and only thinking of the physical circumstances (Matthew 16:21), and Jesus said that he was merely looking at the human perspective and not at God's intentions. Later, on their way to Jerusalem (Matthew 20:18), Jesus explained his fate to the disciples again and still Peter did not register. We are the same and the Lord has to tell us several times before it sinks in. Hopefully, our obstinacy won't be too testing for his patience. Peter had been with Christ for a while now in terms of the length of Jesus' public ministry, and yet his spiritual understanding was still at the fringes. His impetuosity led to his next indiscretion when he denied Christ.

He was a self-confident and strong-willed person. Peter said that even if all desert Jesus, he will never. He added further that he would die rather than disown Jesus. Peter was expressing strong personal feelings, but he had no idea of the weakness of his spiritual state. However, Jesus knew him intimately and predicted his denial that very night. He also said that Satan had asked to sift Peter as wheat. I wonder what Peter was thinking when Jesus said that to him. He probably dismissed it as a comment in passing and just continued in his own unregenerate worldview. At that stage, Peter was just living in hope. He still had great expectations that Jesus the Messiah was going to over-throw the hated Roman regime and establish his kingdom on earth. He probably expected Jesus to call down an army of angles to wipe out the Roman armies. No matter what Peter thought, his actions were purely driven by his flawed human perception. He was thinking in secular terms and not in the spiritual. He should have coordinated what Jesus said to them with Zechariah 13:7, but perhaps he wasn't aware of it.

Peter's regeneration had not reached maturity yet. However, he had all the spiritual knowledge that Jesus had taught him, but it was useless in human hands. It was only at Pentecost that the Holy Spirit raised him up to his full spiritual understanding and potential. His spiritual transformation was accomplished and his denial of Christ became self-denial and death to self. This is intriguing as it tells us that despite having extensive Biblical knowledge of Christ, it's only when the Spirit enables, that we actually activate real spiritual growth, understanding and discernment in our soul. Sanctification only happens at God's will and this is his initiative and is not of human origin. The only way to renewal is for a person to do things God's way, in the hope that he will enable regeneration and disclose himself in a personal way.

Even after Jesus was arrested, Peter was still hopeful that something dramatic would happen and followed at a distance. He was still trying to be closer to Jesus. He probably still thought that Jesus would not die, and hoped for a turnaround. After the rooster crowed, Peter knew the truth of his spiritual weakness – he couldn't keep any of his promises to Jesus. Repentance came when he gave up, went outside and wept with great remorse. He knew that he was spiritually inadequate and all that he said and did was just out of his frail human nature. After Pentecost, Peter was a renewed man and discarded his old ways and did everything God's way. His spiritual training was complete and the Holy Spirit gave him boldness and power to carry out his work in the body of Christ. It goes without saying, that Peter had completely surrendered his executive freewill to Christ and became a true servant of God. A transformed mature Christian will never make the same mistake as Peter as the Holy Spirit won't allow it. An encouraging thought is that God changed Peter's nature and he was the rock on which the church was based. Self-gratification is not invincible and the Spirit can give you the ultimate remodelling, if you only invite and urge him to do it.

Repentance puts us firmly on the road to regeneration, and this is what God desires of us. We have to repent and walk with God so that regeneration may be fully worked out to alter our personality towards purity. Repentance also implies giving up self-determination and surrendering to the Spirit as our teacher of righteousness. It is silly to think that repentance is just feeling deep remorse for sin, and never doing that again and hoping that our moral lives will improve. Satan will introduce other sin at the opportune time and we end up back to the same old repentance cycle. It keeps going around and we can't seem to extricate ourselves. Is it a particular type of stubborn sin or is it merely self-will?

Grow and Growing.

The spiritual child after exiting its infant stage, must move ahead to the development stage and ultimately to maturity. Having resolved to escape the clutches of secularism, effort must now be invested in learning from God fervently. Having understood how our material background affects our thinking and choices, we have to take firm action to reform the bad habits. Honest self-examination will go a long way to aid this transition.

Selfishness mirrors self-indulgence. Usually people can't quit a habit that has been there since childhood. A child gets spoilt either partially or substantially and it grows up to expect self-satisfaction. This is not always possible, but it will grab the opportunity every time it appears. The remedy is to delay satisfaction. This is only a temporary measure, but it gives you time to think things through in terms of self-denial, humility and putting yourself in the other person's position. The Spirit will help you get used to thinking this way over time and it will meld into character with experience as renewal gets going. Self- will becomes less prominent, but it's not the time to sit back and relax. The next phase is to consider personal sacrifice to God's calling and ranking people's needs before self. This is much harder to get pass as there are certain things that we hold dear and this will take more time to deal with.

One self-help process is to study the nature of a genuine servant, and repeatedly walk through the conditions in your mind and spirit. The leading text is Philippians 2:6-8. It demands that a servant disregard personal values and give up all rights to status, title, wealth, power and everything that pertains to secular nature. Obedience is the primary ingredient together with loyalty, humility, and reckoning the benefit to others before self. This is the hardest part because you have to follow the commands precisely even though you may have strong opinions regarding your duties. It is highly likely that you will be called to do something that you detest. The cross was so troublesome for Jesus that he needed an angel from heaven to strengthen him (Luke 22:43). We will never have to face anything as despicable as the cross, yet we still shy away from the small things that God asks of us. Very few workers face true hardship in ministry today, and I was one of those. Upon reflection, I feel that I didn't do enough for Jesus. Self-sacrifice will be part of the calling, and the servant has to be prepared to handle decisions righteously. Giving up the small things first will get the mind and self-will facing the right direction. The Lord will test you to the limit because he wants certainty (Genesis 22:12). Personal regeneration progress is decided by your own hand.

Adam was a servant of God and he got his job description from the Lord. Adam knew nothing about creation and his surroundings, and had to learn everything from God. He must have picked up the basic knowledge very quickly, but there were many things that he didn't know (in the same way that scientists today still don't have answers for). However, he didn't have other people to contend with so his job was very easy. At this infancy stage of his sanctification career, Adam wasn't properly prepared. During the temptation, Eve was the weak link and the evil one approached her first. Adam was standing by as an observer. If he had solid understanding of servant concepts, he would have put his loyalty to God first, and questioned the serpent's motives. Secondly, he would have been concerned about Eve's welfare and thoughtfully worked through the dangerous path that she was treading. Thirdly, he should have weighed up his own position and responsibilities and stopped before it was too late. In short, he failed miserably as a servant of God. He just didn't have it in him. However, one may argue that Adam was not groomed for servanthood and that he was more akin to a friend (child) of God. Even though we are children of God, brothers in Christ, heirs with Christ, friend of God, we are still expected to adopt the same attitude as Christ, and that is servanthood. This is a vital part of sanctification training and there's no easy alternative.

Maybe Adam knew all this in the back of his mind but decided to do nothing (complacent). The temptation of self-determination was the most lethal weapon in Satan's arsenal. It was nothing that Adam and Eve had ever experienced before, so they had no guidance. Of course, Adam broke the cardinal rule and disobeyed God by exercising his freewill. The punishment may seem harsh, but God deems it as justice. Sin is no trifling matter.

The kingdom of God works on an inter-related help system for its members. If everyone shows restraint, courtesy, and selfishness is completely absent then this will produce a good working system that is trouble-free and fully harmonious. Each person will care for the next and the welfare of the whole is maintained. Every member is a team-player with the group objective as the priority. That is the theory, but personal ideas and self-interest place individuality first and that upsets the Lord's model.

I was on a group tour to a popular destination and there was a middle age couple in the group. We stopped at a restaurant for lunch and the place was small and a bit cramped. This couple sat in a manner that took up more room than allocated by the number of chairs (for better comfort). When the last person arrived, she had to sit alone on the opposite table. The couple continued talking as though everything was normal. I was disgusted but said nothing as I had already formed a negative opinion of them. I feared emotions may get the better of me and that I might speak out too strongly. Anyway, my good friend did the right thing and gently asked the couple to move over so that the lady could join the group.

I couldn't believe it. This couple were educated people from a developed nation (the husband was a lecturer and the wife held an administration position), and they behaved in such an inconsiderate manner. There was no apology, no respect and no etiquette displayed and they continued dominating the conversation without the least sign of embarrassment. It was a good lesson for Christians to learn and witness as it highlighted the selfishness and utter disregard for anyone except self. The Lord's protocols do not promote fragmentation but cohesion, inclusiveness and harmony, and the humble servant must act accordingly.

Sooner or later, the spiritual oriented child must conclude that self is spiritually bankrupt and unreliable. The confession of faith in Jesus may have been echoed many times in the past, but this is a turning point where one's spirit has experienced the goodness of the Lord (Psalm 34:8) and there is a strong desire to attain sanctity in him. The urge to follow Christ will adopt a revolutionary aspiration. The genuine step to accept God's rule unconditionally is taken and we want the Lord to act immediately because we are sincere, whereas in the past, we were hesitant and intermittently wavering between God and self. However, the surprising or disappointing thing is that God does not instantly react to work on your renewal. The reason may be that he wants to test your patience and authenticity or his timing may not be ripe. It takes much resolve to persist when nothing is happening, and it's easy to throw in the towel and revert to old ways. Some may be fortunate to receive the Lord's response promptly and that is a blessing, but I had to wait a fair while before things happened.

I had already taken the decision to give it all to Jesus about three years prior to leaving for the field. At that time, my thinking was: Lord, I have given you everything, now please reveal yourself to me. Unfortunately, I heard and saw nothing particularly interesting from him. The silence of the past was still continuing as usual. It was disappointing, but I left it in his hands. However, I knew with certainty that I was doing the right thing. Ten years later, when I was with a team in the last city that I served in, suddenly things changed. My spiritual life was given a boost by the Holy Spirit.

Whatever situation that I faced, be they major or minor, I was given hints or pointed towards the solution and life was good, easy and a joy. It was a revival in my walk with the Lord and this was the happiest, the most satisfying and rewarding time on the field. It was also the most memorable time of my entire spiritual walk. The bonus came in sermon preparation. I was reading familiar passages of Scripture that I had read many times in the past (but merely seeing the words), and suddenly ideas would come to mind. It gave me fresh insight into old passages of the Bible that had become dull over time. It was clearly evident that those thoughts came from outside and were not from my own thinking. I would do my devotion and a thought would come into my head, then another and another until it became a sermon. The outline was the easiest part, but the typing and logical presentation took the bulk of my time. This was revolutionary as it had never happened before. I gave up doing devotions as it was so interesting and I would get energized and it took up too much time. My priority was to do well in language studies as that was the basis of my visa. The magnetism is in the relevance of the inspiration that struck me at the time. Steve and Lindsey Williams were missionaries in Irian Jaya (now Western Guinea) for many years and he remarked that the sermons that he prepared before his field service lacked substance and that he would never use them again because he had better insight after his field experience. I can relate to that.

My language studies took up eight hours each day plus a bit on Saturdays. I couldn't afford spending hours every day on devotions. Immediately following on, was the accounting teaching post and that took up a great deal of time preparing the examples, teaching program, assignment research etc. I would try to sneak in a portion of a devotional in between, but time was limited. Astonishingly, the Holy Spirit kept feeding me with useful information even when I thought that he would be silent. Despite neglecting my devotions, the Spirit was always there to spur me on whenever I opened the Bible. I did regular daily prayer-walks and that compensated for the absence of devotions. This kept my relationship fresh as I would bring all matters before the Lord. Those walks were about an hour-and-a-half and I really valued those quiet times and the exercise. I would immerse myself in prayer and it was delightful.

God is honoured when outsiders see that a Christian fulfils their responsibilities regarding their secular work. This country is one that observed and monitored Christians closely, and non-performance on the job would have been a smear on the Lord's honour. We ought to obey the government who maintain order for the benefit of the community (Hebrews 13:17) and also be salt and light when appropriate. I put in my best effort and fulfilled my duties. God was with me and he hasn't stopped prompting, hence my renewal career has been progressing steadily ever since and the Lord is still responding to my spiritual curiosity from that fateful day when I gave it all up for him.

Short continuous prayers were fitted into my daily routine. Self-awareness of this was the key to consistency, except for when I had a heavy workload. Sometimes a lapse of concentration would break the prayer link, but I made sincere efforts to keep at it. During my daily walking times, I would be praying about the day's activities, the issues that I was facing and generally praising him for all my blessings. Often, more useful thoughts would come to mind as the Spirit moved. It was exhilarating and uplifting for my overall wellbeing. My happiness index was always at the high end and since then, I can't recall a low point yet.

Matthew 13:52 tells of a teacher of the law who learns about the kingdom of heaven and displays new knowledge as well as old. In this context, Jesus asked his disciples whether they understood the parable of the net. It's reasonably easy to understand the principles. However, there is a notable difference when the Holy Spirit moves. He takes the old knowledge and makes it come alive in refreshing ways. The application and enlightenment of the relevant text makes one marvel. It's still all the facts that you already know, but they are put in a way that you have never thought of previously. I wonder why I didn't think of this before, and why didn't I see the application in this way? It's as though we have tunnel vision and the Lord has to open our minds to new insights. This is not an eureka moment. I did not find it, but God found me suitable to be entrusted with new treasures. This in-breaking is by the Spirit who passes on invaluable information that cannot be obtained from any other known source. It's not a case of how much you know, but how you wisely use what you know, and this certainly rings true when the Holy Spirit imparts. It's invaluable to me because it's personal whereas the same information may mean very little to the next person. I see a likeness with the road to Emmaus in Luke 24:25. When the Spirit speaks to you, there will be an intense passion for the Word in your spirit. Despite knowing the Scriptures, Jesus will expose the hidden treasures to you and give spiritual depth.

The Jews were amazed that Jesus had such learning without having studied the law. You will be astounded when the Spirit reaches out to you even if you have studied the Bible. Close friends will know that there has been a notable change and that something special has happened in you. You will be in a position to glorify God through relating your own story and to encourage others to seek their unique path to renewal. It's not easy because self has to be wholly subdued before the Spirit will disclose those treasures.

This sums up the basic development path of a spiritual child. The Holy Spirit will do something to a person's spirit in a permanent manner. No tangible evidence is available but the internal workings and joy is real and inexplicable. Every Christian ought to take great pains to get the Spirit to react in close fellowship, otherwise Christian life would only be partially experienced and great eternal loss would result. A spiritual child needs the assurance and encouragement of this sort of training. It won't be the same for each person, but the excitement will be just as intense, if not greater. The relentless quest for spiritual growth is true satisfaction.

Chapter 32
Spiritual child-adult

This depicts the life of a developing believer and it encompasses both the secular and metaphysical realms. The process that we have to go through will place us first as spiritually educated children of God and then as renewed adults that are able to deal with the world in godliness. In the kingdom of God, a Christian is a child first and adulthood is secondary.

Dilemma.

Secular adult background has many encumbrances. From childhood to teenage to adulthood, a person's worldview changes with the times. Adults have children of their own and new responsibilities. Their childhood dependency is a thing of the past and now they have to provide for their own children. Parents do their best to advise, direct, encourage and render the most financial assistance that they are capable of. It's a process of giving and it never stops. Even after the children have left home and have their own families, the grandparents think about their children and grandchildren. Should any form of assistance be required then parents will usually oblige. The adult mindset must adapt to handling worldly affairs, but the Lord requires us to abandon secular perception and to resort to childlike dependency on him for our spiritual growth. It's not an easy switch because adult minds are obstinate and set in their ways. The secular adult psyche just won't let go and keeps butting into the metaphysical where it is not wanted. When people are accustomed to exercise their own judgment in the world, they will also struggle to subjugate it when trying to learn from God. Fellowship with God must be conducted in a childlike manner, except that we may exercise our intelligence under regulation. It is only on earth that we have to live out this dual role, and in heaven we will just be children of the Father. Everything will be so much simpler in the absence of the secular dimension that is a necessity for life on earth.

Adults have to set aside all the experience and skills that have brought them so far in life. They have to give up self-effort, intelligence, creativity and pride in exchange for humility as a primary school student in the subject of renewal. All control over self-direction is to be set aside and one must depend solely on faith in Christ and be obedient to God's will. The change from the tangible to the intangible is just too much for some to accept. This demands total commitment and a person has to make a firm resolution in this respect. Half-hearted attempts are a waste of time as the Lord does not work well with partially faithful children. Christ gave full dedication to his Father and he is our teacher and example. Many may choose to delay making a decision and just carry on in their old ways. The problem doesn't wither away; rather it shortens your time on earth to foster spiritual growth. People may feel comfortable going this route, but understand that the time lost is actually spent in self-fulfilment and this detracts from the time for spiritual nurture in the Lord.

The spiritual priority ought to be preserved. The choice to delay and pursue self-interest is a shadow-price (cost) in terms of the time lost. This effectively becomes a double-loss because you have to make up the time lost due to selecting self-interest in the first place and then catch up to where you ought to have advanced to. The longer that a person delays; the harder it is to make up for the spiritual loss. However, the grace of God can save the day and if it pleases the Lord, any loss can be made up. But, I wouldn't gamble on that. It is always safe and correct to choose wisely in the first place and thereby remain in the Lord's good books from the outset.

Sanctification.

Jesus sanctifies a believer for salvation at the point where they trust him as Lord and saviour. This is a one-off event just as Christ died once, for all the world's people. It is granted by grace as a free gift from God. On the other hand, the Holy Spirit's on-going work sanctifies a believer to become like Christ in this life. However, renewal doesn't come for free and the follower must put in adequate effort to gain in holiness. Works are merely a by-product of the core attributes of Christ's character and this is the main objective. John 17:23 alludes to believers being one with Christ and one with the Father. This is a challenging passage that applies to seasoned believers that are spiritually mature. Jesus is in the believer and the Father is in Jesus, so that believers can be brought into complete unity. The way to be one with Christ/Father is to be sanctified by the truth. I dare say, the average Christian is going to take a very long time to reach this momentous state. It changes a person to conform to Christ's personality and that alone is very satisfying. However, it's very easy to falter along the way and those people will never get there if they don't have the will to do so.

Jesus is one with the Father and our direction is clearly to get to the state where we are similarly in tune with the Father. It appears to be an impossible goal for any believer. Yet, Jesus talks positively and realistically that if you love and obey him, he will lead you to glory (John 14:21). This is not symbolism and it is attainable. Jesus' disciples had this relationship with the Father because they gave up everything and followed Jesus to martyrdom. It is fair to say that all those that have been martyrs for Christ have also reached the state of being selfless. The conditions are simple. They had understood Jesus' precepts and they obeyed them. This demonstrates their love for Christ and so the Father gave them his love too. As Jesus revealed himself to them, they were able to do anything that God required of them as the Spirit empowered.

God's imparts his character to the seeker. This is only worked out under God's rules and humans cannot add to or do anything of their own devices to speed up or advance regeneration. Self-determination can only cause it to degenerate. We are obliged to seek after God relentlessly for sanctification to mature. God controls this solely for each and every living person that merits his attention. People have no say or input into the teaching process, and freewill is invalid and must be renounced. The seeker has to do exactly as led and any deviation will retard growth. Self-directed work is a waste of time, and people may even fool themselves into thinking that they have made progress, when in fact they haven't. Sanctification is an education in holiness and if you have not learnt the lessons then there is no gain. This renewal process is a fair footing for all because it's individually tailored.

Sanctification develops our nature to become as close to God as we may possibly be. In the regeneration process, holiness does not mean that we are to become totally sinless as this is impossible. It implies obedience in striving to be as close to God as the Spirit enables. This includes the development of the fruit of the Spirit, all the morals of God, plus humility, grace and other traits that he uses in human relationship. We learn from God and then apply those morals to personal relationship with others. It is character-based and personality changes must be permanent. It's akin to the new creation mentioned in Galatians 6:15 and 2 Corinthians 5:17. Holiness may be viewed as the new career that the saved will be occupied with in heaven. It will be what we live with for eternity. There will be work in heaven, but that will not be laborious and distasteful, but enjoyable. There won't be any careers in heaven because we don't depend on that for living. Striving for holiness is a must-do for all believers. It does not mean attaining the perfect state as Jesus is, but to labour with the Holy Spirit to reach the purest spiritual form that our capability allows.

Human beings cannot create their own holiness. Sanctification only comes from God as he is the source of all righteousness. It sounds ludicrous, how can a born sinner become holy? The impossible for people is made possible by God (Luke 18:27). It is a process that the Lord initiates, develops and assesses for each individual and he has to be satisfied. All we have to do is follow instructions and God justifies us through obedience. Many will find that the initial decision to allow Jesus to take over our lives is too uncomfortable as self-management (self-gratification) is strongly opposed to it. Once we submit self to his leadership, Jesus will make it easy.

His yoke is like a partnership that we have entered into. It is wrong to think that we are doing kingdom work on our own. Jesus is partnering with us and he knows our feelings. In this way, one must be careful not to introduce self-initiative because we are tied to a senior partner. It's a good way of keeping workers accountable and to shield us from error. Jesus did not promise to take suffering away, but he did promise to be with us always (Matthew 28:20, Hebrews 13:5-6). I force myself to go through with it and afterwards it doesn't feel as burdensome as I initially thought. Jesus doesn't break his promises.

Pride hinders the sanctifying work of the Spirit because it wants self to be first. If pride occupies a dominant area in your spirit then you have to work harder to eject it so that the Holy Spirit may take his rightful position and help you make the necessary changes to personality. Some will have to search deep in unexpected places to expose the problem. Pride may appear unawares and one has to be vigilant to remove it completely. Modest and quiet people won't have as much difficulty as those that like to have people around them or that like others to look up to them. Humility learns holiness easily but pride doesn't because selfishness has great difficulty submitting to the Lord.

Believers are justified by faith on conversion. This entitles a person entry into heaven because the blood of Christ sanctifies the believer and covers over all sin. At this point, their personal regeneration bank is quite empty, and they need to learn righteousness and to raise their spiritual character to be like Jesus. On conversion, one does not automatically or instantly change into a mature spiritual person. Christians are obliged to seek renewal in personality transformation (1 John 3:3, 2 Peter 1:8, 1 Peter 1: 15-16). The more ground gained in holiness, the further away we remove ourselves from the tendency to sin.

Every believer opens a blank sanctification account when they first believed in Christ. The sins that convicted them are the first to be dealt with through repentance. Those sins are usually fully eradicated or they become minor issues that do not bedevil one's life as before. The real matter is learning to be like Christ. Sin will always be lurking, but the temptation does not have the vice-grip that it once had because our spirit has tasted holiness and we do not want to sin as before. However, if you keep on vacillating between self and holiness, the journey to connect with God will be a long and tiresome one. It need not be this way, but tendencies to self-gratification and hesitation will keep the Holy Spirit from making your journey easier. The goal is to please God and improve our spiritual standing in order to get closer to him in fellowship and to win his favour.

Regeneration has no human measurement mechanism. Hence, there is no element of competition amongst believers. God imparts renewal education to each candidate and only he knows the sanctification level that each person has the capability to reach. One minister made the comment: 'I don't know where you're at' and I took it to mean regeneration grade because this is the true position of a person's standing in relation to God. Nobody knows where the other stands, only the Lord. This is a good thing because it eliminates competition amongst believers. If this was known or readily accessible, then the human mind will brew up all sorts of schemes and ways to out-do their neighbour. It will merely generate more chaos and sin. Jealousy normally comes as a by-product of competition. I have come across people that were envious of another person's sanctified wisdom. It's really superfluous because they can likewise reach the same level of sanctity and bonding with the Lord if they commit to doing it the right way.

The Lord in his wisdom made renewal a non-human interference work, what a remarkable God! Sanctification is immune to human interruption, personal score cards cannot be manipulated and corruption cannot enter the process. The Lord treats everybody fairly and equitably. All spiritual children start at the same level and there is no favouritism. Achievement is obtained solely through self-discipline and self-conditioning in association with the Holy Spirit's guidance. Those that have had their knowledge successfully tested in life are the progressive children of God to whom more will be given (Luke 8:18). The Lord maintains the regeneration system and it is completely accurate, immutable and inaccessible to human intrusion.

Renewal is an individual process as the person interacts personally with the Holy Spirit. This is a one-to-one tutorship system because its purpose is to target the particular weaknesses and character traits that need to be changed in that believer's spirit. The degree, extent and nature of the faults are different for each person. If you genuinely desire change, you must identify your weaknesses. The Spirit is an expert on this because he knows you far better than you know yourself. Admit that these vices are displeasing to God, and then you have to direct self-will to change your mannerism. The Spirit can never decide this for you due to the privilege of personal freewill. Once you have committed to righteousness and proved your bona fides, then the Spirit will give his assistance generously.

Jesus is teaching you and that's the greatest personal joy ever. It tells you that the Lord cares and makes the effort to reach you. The crucial part of fellowship is to know him in a personal context. He is not an invisible being who is so far away in heaven but is omnipresent and living in you. The immanence of God through the Holy Spirit is his connectivity with all believers. It's amazing and gratifying to know that amongst all the hundreds of millions of Christians in the world today, you matter so much that God takes a personal interest in you and wants to give you good things. It really makes a person feel special, and is further motivation to maintain a thriving and stable bond with the Holy Spirit.

On the contrary, if a Christian is hesitant and unwilling to let go of self, then despite the Holy Spirit resident within a person, the distance from God will be protracted. Under these circumstances, head-knowledge of renewal principles is likely to fool a person into thinking that they are growing in sanctification. This is a most precarious situation because self could be driven to do a fallacious 'good work' and the deception would be perpetuated. Sometimes we may do works and afterwards feel that God wasn't in it. This undermines the very purpose of sanctification which is to get closer to God. Although the transcendence of God is nullified by the immanence of the Holy Spirit, yet we don't do the right things to engage the Spirit's beneficence.

In my early Christian life, I was rather undisciplined and the Spirit seemed so far away. Most of my decisions were taken without reference to prayer and I was just doing my own thing. I was mentally aware of the indwelling Spirit's presence, but never consciously felt his guidance. I did what I felt was Biblically correct and rambled through life on my own. As I look back, I can see that he was always there even though I was so far away. I have come a long way since those days, but there's still a lot of learning ahead of me. The Lord's goodness had come to me on many occasions. It was a gradual building up phase where each incremental interaction added to my faith. Now the Spirit's stimuli are more inspirational and relevant, and I'm hungry for more.

Each person is a unique creation and whose spirit is able to relate to God. The Lord views a soul as special and wants to interact personally with that person. The Holy Spirit is the only agent that is authorized to coach each individual in sanctification, and he is the person that we have to deal with directly. Each person is accountable for their own sin, and by the same token, each person is responsible to motivate their own regeneration career path. If you don't help yourself, then nobody else can do it for you. Regeneration must enhance your character and holiness must be practiced in real life situations, otherwise there won't be any permanent behavioural benefits.

The Bible gives guidance and we can commit that knowledge to memory. Bible study groups, formal study courses and people can help expand our knowledge and give us a better understanding. However, head-knowledge does not make a person holy. I mentioned earlier that an ethics speaker chose to disregard ethics in preference for a large monetary gain. His reply was: 'what I teach and what I do are two different things'. I hope that this is not true of you. However, financial pressure and peer pressure are snares to be very wary of. Throughout my life I have maintained the policy of practicing what I preach. It's an ethic that I won't give up because God is watching. I doubt whether ordinary Christians will ever face a dilemma that involves a large sum of money, but the pitfall is in the small practical things that we think we can get away with.

Husband and wife always like to do things together. This tendency is stronger in some couples than others. It is a secular social habit that has been brought over into the spiritual realm. I have seen situations where the one partner has a better quality of renewed character than the other. Friends have mentioned that they like Bible studies or other godly pursuit, but their spouse didn't. Why is this so? Small teams and cell groups can only share knowledge, pray, give advice and moral support but they cannot do the work of regeneration. The only way is for the individual to faithfully do what the Spirit is teaching. You must go through the motions yourself and nobody has the capability or authority to substitute for you.

Charles Price was speaking at Keswick, Mt Tambourine in the mid-1990's. He mentioned a person in the UK who God had used wonderfully. One day, this person announced that he was leaving the ministry because he was divorcing his wife for a younger woman. This came as a surprise to many of his peers. Why would an apparently godly person do such a thing? After that, he never returned to the ministry. I thought that it was an unhappy story. However, it highlights the point that a person may be greatly used by God and yet little is gained by way of renewal or no improvement in regeneration after all the work is done. Physical work and sanctification are two different disciplines; the former is personal physical exertion and the latter is a transformation of character by divine will. People may think or feel that by doing a lot of ministry work, it will increase their holiness. It's completely fictitious, and furthermore all works will be examined for authenticity.

Kingdom work has a dual purpose: first to advance the kingdom, and second to enhance one's own regeneration through experience. There are spiritual lessons in all aspects of kingdom work. During and after each segment of work, you should learn something more about spiritual truths and about yourself. It may be some benefit or something that reinforces present knowledge. It may also be a disappointment, and that may provoke thought on any remedial action that is needed. If you don't see them, then you may be spiritually vision-impaired, and you ought to go back and discover why. Over concentration on personal effort may cause blindness to God's initiative/purpose and we must be alert to this. You can do a lot of work and still not prompt the Spirit to teach you the relevant spiritual lessons. The primary reason is that the person is focusing too much on the work or personal performance and not on the Holy Spirit. This is a very easy mistake to slip into because the work may be quite demanding and the worker may be distracted by their personal desire for results. Things take up so much of your time and you over-extend yourself. Some may prefer to have a mental check-list that they consciously bring up on each occasion. It's all good as long as the Spirit is kept central, and he will alert a person of error. However, it's still up to the individual to heed the warnings.

God has the blueprint and he knows how to direct the candidate to fill their part appropriately in kingdom development. At times, the Lord may call a person to service despite not having matured adequately in renewal, but they have the skill and are in the right place and time. This is a privilege but it is also a time of caution in case personal effort is overstated. One ought to concentrate of the lessons learned and see how they may enhance character. If not, then it will just be a lot of work with no personal spiritual benefit.

Kingdom work does not add to a person's sanctification. People may serve in church and other ministry areas, but if it's of their own making then all those works are useless and they will be burned (1 Corinthians 3:13). The kingdom of God is finite and each part of work has been allocated to someone on earth to do. There is a corresponding reward for the worker that has completed their part satisfactorily. The Bible doesn't mention any bonus system for work done outside of the kingdom blueprint. God rewards his own creativity according to what he has pre-planned (Ephesians 2:10). If this were not so, then anybody could devise and add to kingdom work at their own convenience and expect God to reward them. In other words, they will be creating their own reward system. It is human nature (selfishness) to live a comfortable lifestyle and after personal gratification, decide to use the left-over time for God. The Lord does not work according to your timing and incorrect decisions carry very high risk.

The ideal is to have attained a reasonable level of regeneration before doing ministry (Luke 12:35), and maturity will increase as the worker learns from the Holy Spirit while on the job. A savvy worker will see the spiritual treasures in the work whereas the uninitiated will merely see the work. However, it doesn't always work out this way and some are called very early on in their renewal career. When the Lord calls, it means that the timing is right for the kingdom purposes and the work has to be done. A working knowledge is normally sufficient and the Lord will give the necessary information as the work progresses. The worker merely has to follow orders and the task will be successfully completed. However, that person's renewal status would more or less be the same as before the work. Notwithstanding how much work is done, it does not simultaneously advance regeneration. In the absence of humility, self-denial and third part priority, the quality of service will not meet the standard that Jesus set in Philippians 2:8. Some may even show signs of self-esteem amongst peers. These faults curb spiritual benefits that may be derived. The onus is on the worker to identify and select the most urgent sanctification treasures and assimilate them into personality.

There was a couple on the field and a friend of mine used to help them by servicing their computer. They had meals together every now and then. One day, they suddenly started criticizing things that he did for them. Gradually it grew worse. My friend gave them a less than perfect gift (on sale). On revisiting, they unleashed a barrage of criticism and unkind words were said. He was dumbstruck and very disappointed because he was just continuing the friendship and trying to build up rapport. He had sincerely given of himself and this was how they treated him. I felt it rather odd for them to serve on the field in the first place. The field has a mixture of pleasurable and unpalatable elements, and some things are going to rub you up the wrong way. The worker has to have the grace to handle all of it in a proactive manner. This kind of work always calls for sacrifices of some sort and agape is the key to pleasing God and getting along with others.

This friend also looked after my computer for several years and we had fellowship over meals regularly. He was a very amicable and helpful person. I was satisfied with his sincerity and was certain that he did not have a mean streak in his body. When he related this story, I really felt for him. The offender and the offended always have something to learn regarding their sanctification.

Personal restraint is the answer whenever anything untoward occurs. The working space was too small for us (foreigners). It was not wise to make bad friends because we saw one another frequently. If I met an acquaintance in the street, I wanted to be able to exchange greetings and to have an honest and sincere chat. Creating animosity because of personal grievances wasn't appropriate. I had to put my emotions and self-assertion aside and practice the grace given by the Spirit. It worked and I avoided all personal and external strife that is so unnecessary.

Mental assent to Bible knowledge does not enhance the personal regeneration process. Reading and talking about sanctification only gives understanding and guidelines on the subject. Steadfast renewal can only be gained and retained through practice. Regardless of how distasteful the test may be, you have to go through with it to establish the righteousness principles in your personality. Romans 5:3 set the order of progression of our hope in the glory of God as: suffering – perseverance – character – and hope in the Holy Spirit. James 1:3-4 says that the testing of one's faith is what trains perseverance, and perseverance leads to maturity.

The Spirit opens up new learning opportunities, whereby you go through the trial, absorb the goodness, and then apply it in your dealings with others, and your growth in holiness will keep ascending. In this way, you demonstrate to the Holy Spirit that you are conscientious and your character is moving closer to his. The new character is only proven through consistent application in real life occasions where God and people can see it (Matthew 7:16, John 15:16).

It's interesting that I had learnt all these moral lessons from Christians. There's nothing to learn from unbelievers. People are in the habit of speaking out and saying what's on their mind. It takes disciplined self-control not to retaliate when emotions are on edge and there's so much to say. However, the grace of God saves the day. Despite how highly strung a person's emotions are, the Lord will always help a believer humble self and keep the peace. This is further merit to one's sanctification.

When the Spirit remains silent then there must be a problem on your part. Detailed self-examination will reveal the reason, and the causes have to be rooted out and corrected so that the Spirit may continue his work. It may be hard to face up to those issues but it has to be done. The silence of the Spirit ought not to be taken flippantly as it is always convenient to revert to self-satisfaction at the expense of sanctification. This is the time when you must prick your conscience and make the hard decisions.

The Spirit will teach you all things (John 14:26). However, he doesn't just volunteer information but you have to secure his attention by proving your worthiness through action. He may still remain silent for a while, but patience is a virtue and you are under the microscope, not him. You have to show good faith first. Remember that Jesus has done everything and you have done nothing yet. You are in partnership with the Holy Spirit and you have to bring something to the negotiating table. When you have won his trust, and he opens the doors, the rest is euphoria. The joy that comes from small victories in holiness reassures you that God is with you. Real growth is taking the little that you already know and applying it in practical ways that benefit others. The illumination and wisdom that the Spirit brings is worth more than many hours of reading. Most of all, the Spirit's value is in building up your character and every experience keeps adding worth to your regeneration repertoire.

> Never mistake knowledge for wisdom. One helps you make a living and the other helps you make a life.
>
> - Sandra Carey

The Spirit takes a person through a spiritual education process that gives life to the spirit. Spiritual life is the crux of living on earth and not the making of a comfortable material lifestyle. This teaching and wisdom are from the Lord and it lasts forever.

Losing or forfeiting the greater part of our reward is an enormous shame. It means that we have not lived according to God's estimate of our capabilities and therefore have under-achieved as a child of God. When we are called to service, we ought to check whether we are doing it right and whether Jesus would be pleased with our effort. It's easy to please self by claiming that you have done your best, but it is God who has to be satisfied with your progress in Christian life. The manner in which a person has lived on earth will receive praise or humiliation from our Father. Loss of reward is far worse than losing one's entire estate on earth. There may be social security benefits and perhaps opportunity to make up for the deficit. There may even be friends and family that may offer some assistance. Once a reward is foregone, it's lost forever and there will be no opportunity to increase or decrease it in any manner. Whatever a person has, that's what they live with for eternity. Anything that may cause damage to one's reward ought to be the primary fear of all the saved.

Each person's quality of their Christian life lies in their spiritual progress. We are made in God's image and should conduct ourselves as close to his holiness as possible. The Father expects all his children to grow in righteousness and failure to do so will be a great disappointment to Father and to self. Jesus paid the debt of sin for us and we owe him big-time. We should be ashamed that we give Jesus so little in return. Repayment is not in financial or material terms but in spiritual regeneration. As a follower of Christ, we must be transformed to his likeness otherwise we will shame his name. Under-achievement is a disgrace and Christians ought to do everything to reach their best. We will only know the result of our effort on that day, and until then, we have to conduct ourselves before God with fear and trembling (Philippians 2:12-13).

Reverence for the Lord in knowing how great he is and how unworthy we are will keep self-concern at bay. There's so much to learn from God but are we going to get it all? The Lord gives all good things and we receive it in deep humility knowing that we do not deserve it. Only after we are appropriately submitted to God, does he reveal his will and direction to us to fulfil his sovereign purpose. Bear in mind that God will not manifest himself if we retain any trace of self-determination. Self-will contaminates God's purity and he will never have that. We have to earn the right by winning the Spirit's confidence and then his blessings will flow on to us. It is a two-way process; we demonstrate allegiance to God and he blesses because he will honour all that he has promised. Grace is not cheap, Christ paid the supreme penalty on our behalf and this invokes an appropriate response.

The wisdom of the Spirit described in 1 Corinthians 2:6-7 will be understood by the mature as spiritual discernment that comes with the teaching by the Spirit. This is the target for those who value unseen riches. In Chapter three, Paul talks about those that are still immature in Christ. They were adults that had not discarded their carnal habits and their spiritual lives were adversely affected. Secular values and sanctification cannot be mixed as sin and holiness are poles apart. Hopefully, those that have progressed in spirit may give advice to others on how to improve, but self-will is still the focal point that the individual must reckon with. It can make or break a relationship with the Lord. Friendship is a responsibility and a commitment and not an opportunity for self-enrichment. It's utter folly to deal with Jesus in the same way that one would approach a business associate.

The proof of a renewed character is found in consistent obedience to the Lord. Some may submit a bit at a time but when it comes to testing, their obedience is inclined to falter. It's the old contention between comfort and discomfort. It's better to take a strong stance and commit everything to making it work. This indicates to the Lord that you mean what you intend, and he will help you to become obedient. Displacement is never easy when self-satisfaction still has a grip on the spirit. If you are not doing God's will, then you will satisfy personal desires. There is no way around testing and all Christians must face their worst fears. One may refuse the tests but they will remain to judge you at the end. Jesus went through his greatest test on the cross because he was obedient to his Father's wishes.

Sanctification is achieving God's purpose for Adam (humankind) after the fall. Against all the odds of inherent sin and worldly upbringing, those that have the urge and willpower to learn more about holiness are successfully partnering with the Holy Spirit to progress in character renewal. It's only when we get to heaven that we will be clothed in full holiness. God has made sanctification on earth possible and it depends on two things: subordination of self-will to Jesus and the initiative of the Holy Spirit. It must be done is this order because the Spirit does not force himself on anybody. It's a simple way to get out of a horrible mess, and the Lord is winning. The extent of regeneration is dependent on the individual's desire to push forward. The sequence at every level of progression is always for the seeker to submit and then the Spirit responds accordingly. The Lord wants all people to have the maximum that they may take in but this requires full submission to his control. Jesus gave up everything because he loves you. In following his example, all believers have the potential to attain the maximum.

The parable of the Pharisee and the tax collector in Luke 18: 9 was a demonstration of opposites. The Pharisee was proud and conceited whereas the tax collector was humble and self-effacing in admitting his deep regret for his sin. Pride breeds self-aggrandizement that shows non-dependence on God. The tax collector left himself fully at the Lord's mercy as he was powerless to help himself. It was an acknowledgment that he had offended the Almighty and now needed help.

You may implore the Lord to give you more intensive teaching because you see great value in righteousness. Leave pride and self-centeredness aside, and don't settle for second best. Don't be an average Christian, reach out for the Lord's grace and ask for even more to get ahead in sanctification in earnest. Don't be content to live in comfort but take a risk for Jesus (Matthew 8: 20-22), and see God do wonders in your spirit. Every bit of ground gained in regeneration will bring joy for drawing closer to God. Once you get going, the desire for more won't stop. I want the full extent of God's moral traits that are due to me. This sanctified craving has no relationship to the secular connotations of greed, rather it is selling everything to buy a pearl of immense value (Matthew 13:44). To possess the qualities of the Lord's character is the ultimate high. Character is who you really are, whereas reputation is what others think you are. The inner substance of righteousness is what God values and personal fame means nothing.

When I was an immature believer, I knew that the pearl was Christ. My trust in him for salvation was the greatest prize that I could gain but I never thought further than that. Now, the more I look at the pearl, the larger it seems to grow. A developing follower will see infinite value in Jesus because it's his personality that is so highly prized and desired. Eternal riches will be measured in spiritual terms and there is so much to gain.

I want to be the most righteous person of all the people around me, without comparing myself with others. I'm going to keep pressing forward in self-motivation without the need to beat anybody. If you don't impel self, then nobody will push you. The Spirit can't prod you because it's not his job to do so; he is but a teacher and counsellor. He is definitely not a motivational trainer or speaker. If you don't aim for high achievement, you won't get far or hit nothing at all. It will be worse if you regress.

In a world where lifestyle is changing so rapidly, the pressure to maintain and advance in holiness becomes greater by the day due to all the new distractions. As the end times unfold, a believer's sanctification will come under more intense scrutiny by those in power. The spiritual confrontation between good and evil will reach its apex and it will be a harrowing time for believers. The world financial system will be firmly under the control of the evil one and sanctified Christians will clearly stand out as the ones that oppose the system. Only the resolute ones will be able to stand firm under such harsh and extreme conditions. Be assured that the Lord will strengthen you to face whatever you need to get through. Maturity will tell you that the body is nothing and the spirit is eternal and it will be a shameful loss to yield to the evil one at the expense of eternity with Christ.

Train yourself to stay focussed on Jesus and never even entertain the slightest thought of self-direction as it will undo all that the Spirit has done in you. Under harsh conditions, God must have comprehensive control over your executive and operational freewill. He is master of all eternity, and the slightest error may turn out to be the ultimate regret. For those that have grown familiar with denying self, this will be a simple decision. Although the losses of turning away from the material world will be overwhelming, the training of your spiritual eyes will see the enormous value in the unseen. Godly training takes years of close association with Jesus and it is he that will choose for you. Those that have not conditioned themselves in this manner won't make the right choices because self has been allowed to rule for too long. Don't believe in yourself, just look at all the mistakes that you are making right now.

There was a TV program called 'The Biggest Loser' (USA production), about overweight contestants that competed for the most weight lost over a specified period of time. Each week, the players were measured for the most weight lost and were given a new target weight to attain, and a non-performer was eliminated. They were usually in excess of 360 lbs. (about 145kg). Prize money of about $250,000 was up for grabs so there was a lot of incentive. One contestant was 366 lbs. and came down to 210 lbs. It was a noteworthy achievement that took a great deal of hard work. Each player had a trainer to help them lose as much weight as possible in a safe manner. They were put on a special diet and had to work through a stringent daily exercise program. It was not an easy feat and they required much encouragement to press forward with the hard workouts and rigid discipline. As they watched others that had won in the past, their enthusiasm was stoked. It proved that a task of this magnitude could be done. Competition drives people to give their best.

At the outset, the typical comments were: I want to win; I'm motivated; I'm committed; I was lazy, but that's all gone, and now I really want this badly; I want to prove that I can do this etc. It was evident that they were there for a purpose and they were serious about their mission. This program was wonderful encouragement for overweight people and no doubt, and many viewers set it as a priority to watch every week. The amazing thing is the amount of weight the contestants are able to lose in such a short time. Every pound lost is hard work and the competition never lets up until a winner emerges. The finalists work harder because they are within reach of the prize and the losers show intense tearful emotion, disappointment and regret. They had lost the race for the prize money and also weren't good enough. After trying so hard and exerting so much effort, defeat is not an easy thing to accept. The victor exudes joy and pride because of the money, publicity and recognition to have been the best in the competition.

These principles also apply to our walk on the road to renewal, except that there is no publicity, and there is no recognition by peers, but the eternal reward is greater than any amount of fame or financial compensation. God's character is the ultimate prize. There is no competition and only the Lord knows the extent of your progress. We cannot compare our standing with others, so there is no jealousy or envy. Secular competitiveness is driven by selfishness, pride, fame and wealth, but sanctification has no competitive mentality and we learn to be unselfish towards others.

The only losers will be those that have never bothered to commit to obtaining a renewed personality, and that is the true loss. Every born-again believer would have changed something in their lives i.e. stopped particular sins and learnt a few concepts in holiness. Each permanent change is a gain. Thus, the extent of the loss would be that portion of sanctification that they have not achieved during their life-time on earth. God will show the spiritual worth of sanctification and there will be regret as the deficit will be greater than any material loss on earth.

Everybody has the same trainer, the Holy Spirit. Self-motivation, persistence, practice, and hard work are offset by your love for the Lord as your only encouragement. Everybody's in the same boat and all have to go through the same hard choices. You love God so much that you want to imitate him. The Spirit will help you get there once you have proved your sincerity. Unlike those contestants, our sanctification workout gets easier as we mature because we get used to refining the rough edges and practicing holiness as we progress. They are competing for money/fame, but we do it because we are obedient to the Lord. They do it for self-gratification, but we do it because we belong to God. They do it for the thrill of competition, but we do it because of the joy that God gives. Regeneration is a career that must be completed to secure the maximum returns.

The people that will be the most familiar with the Father will be the ones that have come closest to his character and personality. Every bit of ground made up will last forever because righteousness comes from God and it never fades or corrupts. Those that have chosen not to try will surely be the 'Biggest Losers'.

In John 9: 41, Jesus was talking about the spiritual blindness of the Pharisees because they did not believe in him. They knew the law and still didn't believe in him, so they were still unredeemed sinners. In the Christian context, we are not blind or guilty because we believe in Jesus, but in our sanctification development we are blind and desperately require the Holy Spirit's guidance. It's a spiritual blindness that keeps us from obtaining the mind of Christ. Have you ever wondered why you have read old Bible passages many times, and only seen the printed words? Then you listen to a speaker and they present it in a different light, and you wonder where they got the inspiration from? Perhaps some of the ideas came from books, articles, internet or some other source. There is a noticeable variance between book intelligence and spiritual wisdom. The latter will stand out clearly because it comes from the Holy Spirit, and that is what sanctification is all about. The most useful and meaningful applications relate to your own personal circumstances and experience. This is where the Holy Spirit steps in to provide the illumination at the right time and place when you need it most. You will know unequivocally that it was the Spirit's leading that gave you the idea. This has happened to me on many occasions and each reminded me of my inadequacy.

I have never heard the Spirit's voice audibly, but certain thoughts had come into my mind while I wasn't purposely brainstorming. It's clear that those thoughts came from outside and not from my own making. It is the Spirit's initiative that gave impetus to my sermon preparation while I was on the field. I didn't have books that I could refer to and I didn't use any information from the internet or other sources. It was a great feeling to have new light shed on old passages of Scripture and the words were so relevant to real life situations. God speaks to me through his Word. It engenders warmth, assurance and joy to my spirit and I don't want it to stop. Personally, this is palpable evidence that God is with me.

Different people have different needs and perceptions. The salient point is that the Lord meets you at the time and place of urgent concern and need. The Spirit works in personal contact that touches deep within your spirit and you will experience the joy and relief of receiving an answer to some situation that you are facing. It's relevant to what you are doing and it fits in neatly and seamlessly with the unfolding of your circumstances. Enlightenment doesn't have to appear in any spectacular form; it's just the quiet, comforting and firm manner in which the Spirit connects with you. You will recognize it because it conveys a personal touch. If another person were to experience the same thing simultaneously, they would probably dismiss it as just another incidental thought that carries no relevant meaning in their situation. The Counsellor teaches all things and he fellowships with each individual in an intimate manner. However, if we try to do this on our own, we are like blind people wandering aimlessly, going nowhere and achieving nothing, and it is worthless in eternity because God is not leading it.

God made light shine out of darkness, and his light shines in our hearts to remove our darkness and gives us the knowledge of God's glory. This magnificent treasure from the Lord is in us, described as jars of clay because we are unworthy of it and it's only by the grace of God that we are given it. Furthermore, this supreme indisputable power is from God and all glory belongs to him (2 Corinthians 4:6-7). Although our bodies are getting older and weaker, yet our spirits are being renewed day by day. The troubles and hardship that we go through are temporal, but they are not in vain as they accumulate priceless eternal credit for us. We have to keep focusing our efforts on the unseen heavenly riches because the visible comforts of this world are temporary and the heavenly treasure lasts forever (2 Corinthians 4:16-18). An individual's regeneration career is not recognized on earth, but it will be given due notice and consideration in heaven. These words are motivation for all who try.

Daily renewal shows favoured status with the Lord who truly wants you to follow him. This illumination process is not only about a different outlook in life, but its eminent value is in your quiet private times with the Lord. The Spirit is able to probe your innermost habits, the small troublesome bits that are so readily overlooked. The evil one wants you to retain them, but the Holy Spirit wants you to exterminate them; and you want to by-pass them and that's why they are still there. Joy comes when you face up to those little strongholds and eradicate each vice permanently. This personal triumph is very satisfying because you know that God is watching and you have chosen righteously. This is a simultaneous building up of fellowship with God as you ask him to reveal more of the internal corruption that you need to deal with. It is presumptuous to think that you can reach the point where all your imperfections have been eliminated, but honesty will drive you to keep making improvements. During the process, renewal through God's interaction gives warm assurance that you are in favour with him. You face every new day knowing that the Lord is pleased to walk with you, and this is a remarkable happiness that brings peace. If you are not feeling the Lord's affinity, then be warned and take corrective measures.

In 1 Corinthians 2: 4-5, Paul talks about his preaching as coming from the Spirit's power and from God, and not from his own learned and motivational words. He attributes this power to the wisdom of the Spirit that is passed on to mature Christians. Spiritually seasoned believers are going to get the maximum benefit from the Holy Spirit's wisdom. Those in the development stage will gain as much as their outlook allows. This secret wisdom has been kept for each eligible individual to personally experience God's glory. Preaching may not be your forte but wisdom is available and attainable by all. The enlightenment that we are given tells of the glory of God and is a privilege that we are allowed to share in because he preordained it. This knowledge is actually God's wisdom that we express in our personal style. It's an awe-inspiring thought to be drawing closer and closer to our Father as we mature. This is only possible because God has extended the invitation to us through Jesus Christ. For the sinner, learning holiness is a privilege and we ought to embrace it with great yearning. This education from the Spirit is not an optional extra, even though people may treat it as such.

Maturity means to be at your best, and to be at the top of your moral capacity. It is the stage where Jesus has taken firm hold of your spirit in a close association. Sanctification comprises of various elements and each has to be developed to the stage where Jesus is happy to be unfettered and voluntarily linked with that person in fellowship. We will never be perfect on earth. Maturity is being able to do what Jesus did but according to our own capability. Jesus accepts us as mature in our imperfection through our obedience and trust in him. Offering your best must be accompanied by giving up your self-will to Christ. This goes in hand with regeneration where the Holy Spirit stays in constant communication with a person and never leaves them. Even though we can't quantify spiritual maturity, it is attainable in this lifetime. I just wonder how many of us will ever get there? It may sound too hard, but once you have tasted the joy from the Sprit, you won't give up.

No eye has seen, no ear has heard, no mind has conceived what God has prepared for those who love him. Salvation is for all who believe in Christ as Lord and saviour, but the bonus issue is only for those who love the Lord to the extent that he deems worthy to be trained in holiness and character. It is faith-based and is a special gift that carries both present and future blessing. This endowment is not a one size-fits-all because we are all different. The Spirit will probe the depth of God's knowledge and pass the pertinent parts onto the seeker, as required.

The teaching expresses spiritual truths in spiritual words that enrich our inner self. God deals with the heart and not the material parts of human nature. The Spirit will enable one to understand the spiritual truths because his words are spiritually discerned. It conveys a sense of inestimable worth that God has placed on his own people. The mature follower will ultimately receive the thoughts from Christ. The image of God (in character/personality) in a person will be at its apex. The final completion will come when we receive our new spiritual bodies. Most probably Paul was hinting at 1 Corinthians 2:16 when he professed self-deprecation and declared that all his material achievements were unimportant as opposed to the surpassing greatness of knowing and gaining Christ (Philippians 3:8). It alludes to the believer receiving instructions directly from Jesus. This process of gaining Christ is in the spirit. The mature Christian is a delight to God and highly prized. The Spirit transforms a lowly sinner into a holy being that may approach God freely and enjoy close fellowship with him. The regenerated soul will glorify the Lord far better than the immature believer.

Maturity in regeneration is going to cost you everything, whereas salvation cost you nothing. Following and learning from Jesus is a lifestyle that demands everything of a Christian (Matthew 10:37-38). Physical life was already considered as of little value (Matthew 10:28) and it is the spiritual life that is of utmost importance. The earthly body will perish and we will receive a new spiritual body for eternity. This supports the view that 'save his life' is not referring to the earthly body that will die but to the renewal of a person's spiritual life and that is the true life that mimics God's morals. Maturity in holiness is like a light imitation of experiencing heaven on earth as the Spirit trains us towards completion. As with Paul, we will also come to the genuine admission that all we have in this world is senseless, except for our desire and mission to know Christ.

Going through the motions of sanctification is very difficult at the outset, but it gets easier with each improvement. It's the school of hardship for the immature and the uninitiated. The more the Spirit occupies your spirit, the easier it is to attain maturity. Once you are firmly on the road to renewal, then it is God's responsibility to make it happen, and he won't disappoint. Make the commitment and do it for God and for yourself, and you have the right to be selfish in this regard because craving holiness has no limitation. It may even be the best decision that you ever made in your Christian walk, and one that would bring so much fulfilment and freedom on earth and in eternity.

The indwelling Holy Spirit inhabits all faithful believers. However, we never notice him and hardly know that he is in us because we are not sufficiently close to God. At conversion, most of us just accept the fact and we go about our normal lives and conveniently forget about him. We continue in our secular responsibilities and we try to make the best of our living conditions and prepare for a reasonable retirement. Towards the end of our working career, we save as much as possible to reach the target for comfortable retirement. It's pay-back for all the years of hard work. We may not be aware of it, but all our energies are focused on the material. We may attend Bible studies, prayer meetings, do other ministry functions and of course, attend the services on Sundays (morning and evening). In real terms, all of this takes up a small portion of our time, whereas domestic, commercial matters and leisure occupy the bulk. We have to face up to this fact and then implement some measures to put Jesus first. It has to be individualised to find out what works best for each person.

It would be of great assistance if the Spirit spoke and guided us in a clear manner as that would set our spiritual relationship firmly on the right path. However, the Spirit is holy and we are unregenerate and it behoves us to take determined action to reach for and aspire to actively engage the Spirit in daily life. The Spirit will meet you at some point and take you where you have never been before. It's an intimate interchange that must be kept alive and fresh for the best returns.

When we cry out to God, the Spirit remains silent. When we question: where were you Lord when I needed you most - and the Spirit remains inert? We come away disappointed with the Lord, but we only have ourselves to blame. It's always appropriate to blame your own inaction first. Spending so much time on ourselves and so little with the Spirit is stating that he is of lesser importance in our lives. Thus, the Spirit will be grieved and hence the silence. Conversely, the more time and priority we give to the Spirit, the more readily/frequently he will communicate with us. It is impractical for a normal working/family man to quit his job and live as a monk. Jesus wants us to be in the world but not part of the world. Therefore, the only way to get around this is to involve Jesus in everything that we do in the workplace, leisure and domestic affairs. By making the Spirit an integral part of your life, it will reinstate him to top position and give him a consistent portion of your daily time. Certain working folk may not be able to give the Spirit adequate attention during their daily routine. This appears to be a no-win situation, but God is reasonable. Nevertheless, the onus is upon the believer to prove their intention by taking the necessary steps to include Jesus in all aspects of their life. This vital task can be so easily overlooked. The undisciplined mind would defer to old habits because the change is just too cumbersome. The Spirit's withdrawal is all our doing and our question ought to be: Lord, why have I ignored your will for so long? Please forgive me and help me make amends.

God is exalted in a person's spirit and the effects are visible through outward motions. The acceptable form of worship that God expects is in a person's spirit because that's where the truth lies. God is Spirit and all believers must exalt him in spirit and in truth. This concept is repeated and it indicates the significance of a person's spirit to God and to self (John 4:23-24). Jesus was hinting that the physical address where worship takes place is unimportant, but the spiritual address is crucial. Believers offer their regenerated spirits in worship to God who is Spirit. It stands to reason that a mature spirit that is closer to the nature of God will command greater favour than one that is still in its infancy. Maturity in regeneration tells of a dedicated love for God and people, stronger commitment, better experience, total or near complete denial of self-will, proven humility, highest obedience etc. These are the things that God longs for in his people.

Romans 12:1 says that our living sacrifice is our spiritual act of worship. Sanctification is the true continuous worship to the Lord because it is grounded in holiness. It's duplicating God's nature for others to witness visually. It's astounding that God wants to use us to glorify himself to the outside. A living sacrifice encompasses servanthood, obedience, humility, and agape. Worship happens at any time and any place. It is the life that is permeated by the Holy Spirit whereby one offers self as poured out wine in service for Christ for the benefit of others and it's an on-going cycle of worship. Everything that we do must be immaculately offered as a sacrifice to the Lord. It's important to have a high moral attitude and good work ethic so that the offering may be the best that we can give. Worship in spirit is supposed to coincide with the moral bodily motions, but they don't always do because we segregate our spirit's intention from our physical actions. What's actually done is not of the godly standard that the Lord expects. This flaw must be rectified otherwise we will be wasting our time.

Normally, only mature Christians will be able to commit to being a living sacrifice because of their long association with the Holy Spirit and they know what sacrifice is required of them. Immature believers would not have been through the testing and training that the Spirit demands in order to make such a commitment. A living sacrifice is no walk in the park and only the sincere and determined heart will be able to qualify for this role. The absence of love for others, self-denial and humility will render a living sacrifice a mockery. Serving others is really doing a service for God. Nevertheless, aspiring believers have to start somewhere and they ought to work towards and attempt this noble ambition. It will help improve their regeneration bank in the process. Certainly, maturity in holiness enhances the living sacrifice as it is much more meaningful and honouring to God in worship. He deserves the best.

Nobody knows our mind and we indulge in private thoughts during the worship service on Sunday and this is irreverent to God. Although people cannot see into a person's mind or spirit nothing escapes the Lord. God looks at the heart and spiritual worship tells the truth about a person's priorities. Worship that comes from within one's spirit is genuine and acceptable to God. The outward display is of lesser importance than the inner unseen veneration and adulation. The main reason why we divert our attention is because of self and all those material things that we hold close to the heart and mind.

The Holy Spirit is in us for a special purpose. If we overlook him or his purpose for us, then we negate the reason for his presence. The Spirit is the Counsellor and teacher to remind us of all that Jesus had said and to sanctify us to become mature in Christ. The Word of God must be in your personality as an unalterable part of your spirit. A Spirit induced relationship should be our fervent wish and strongest endeavour.

When does sanctification end? God is infinite and there is so much to learn about his holiness that it will never be accomplished in this life. Those that are privileged to enjoy close fellowship with the Spirit will wonder what it would have been like if they had connected with the Spirit earlier on in life. There are so many permutations in life and the Spirit could have reacted in different ways accordingly. Perhaps you would be at a more advanced stage by now. Any assumption is mere speculation, but the important point is that you are in it now and nothing should bar you from seeking the maximum blessing possible.

One of the tangible outcomes of sanctification is illustrated by Jesus' resurrection body. The Lord wants his children to be transformed inwardly first and then followed by the new spiritual body that makes us complete. It certainly is exciting to contemplate. This is an extraordinary situation. Here we have Jesus' closest friends being unable to recognise him. They were the most godly-educated people in the whole world at the time. This tells you a lot about holiness – it makes things appear totally different when viewed from a sin tainted world. Luke 24:16 said that something prevented them from recognising Christ. That obstacle is sin. Jesus told them that he would rise again and perhaps they were expecting to see the same old bodily form (natural assumption).

On the road to Emmaus, the two realised that it was Jesus through his actions (breaking bread) and not by appearance. The resurrected Jesus had a new spiritual body and that included a voice change. Everybody knows a close friend's voice – even in the dark. In this case, Jesus spoke and they had no idea who he was!

John 21:12 Jesus appeared to them and they still couldn't visually affirm that it was him, but they knew through his mannerisms and habits. John 21:14 says that this was the third time that Jesus appeared to the disciples and they still didn't recognise him. The disciples must have been totally perplexed. They knew it was Jesus but he didn't look like the Jesus they knew so intimately for two years. Sin is the opposite of holiness and the material view from each position will be totally different. When God gives a new spiritual body, it will be perfect and inherently sinful people won't be able to identify that person. Holiness transforms a sin marred object into a new creation. A human being is still in essence a human being because we still possess the image of God. The new spiritual body (holy) is still fundamentally human in nature and not another creation that is not human. Jesus' new spiritual body was essentially human and the crucifixion wounds bear witness to that.

Likewise, the new earth will still be composed of the same materials that God used during creation-week in Genesis. The difference is that it will be entrenched in holiness and be flawlessly displayed. The song 'All things bright and beautiful' is not true in the spiritual context because the Lord God cursed them all. We will only see true beauty in the new heaven and new earth. Even Jesus, although sinless through immaculate conception, had to assume a human form that carried the distorting effects of sin and the curse. When the Lord cursed creation, everything that was beautiful/perfect became marred and lost their true elegance. Hence, reverting to holiness will render every existing thing new.

Even Mary didn't recognise Jesus' appearance and voice (John 20:15-16). It was the way he used to call her name that Mary made the connection because it was unique and Mary knew it immediately. If Jesus had not called her name, Mary would be none the wiser. It was only John that had a sharper perception of the risen Christ. It suggests that he paid more attention to Jesus' spiritual characteristics than the others. He had the closest relationship to Jesus on earth, and he was the only disciple at the crucifixion. John had observed Jesus' mannerism and character very closely on earth and was able to recognise Jesus' idiosyncrasies in the new spiritual body when the rest were clueless.

The new spiritual body will fully conform to the image of God. If you have never liked your appearance on earth, there's something to look forward to in the new earth. When God injects his spiritual DNA into a person's spirit, it will only be recognised by the spiritual people that have likewise been transformed into sanctity. This DNA is the regeneration essence after the character of God, in perfect holiness. It has an incarnational effect that makes a believer into a Jesus model that demonstrates the mind and actions of Christ. A person's sanctification education on earth is a precursor to harmonise with the new spiritual body in heaven. It's the perfect match. John did the right thing, and you have to examine yourself. The value and effects of regeneration are not to be treated carelessly or passed over frivolously.

Sanctification makes a somebody out of a nobody in God's estimation. The world neither appreciates it nor esteems it because the Lord has not drawn as intimately to them as he is to you. Matthew 13:11-12 mentions the secrets of the kingdom of heaven being given to you. You understand the spiritual connotations that even the past prophets and God-seekers longed to know but were denied the privilege. However, verse 23 is the objective; are you going to produce a crop that yields a hundred-fold? Not everybody can win a hundred souls to God's kingdom, but every believer has the capacity to attain their full spiritual capacity to grow and produce a hundred times the fruit of the Spirit.

God has marked out the point of fullness in maturity for every believer that has ever lived or yet to be born. Whatever level a person attains in this life is an asset.

> God creates out of nothing. Therefore, until a man is nothing, God can make nothing out of him.
>
> - Martin Luther.

God invites us to draw near to him with a sincere heart, to hold steadfastly in faith to him and to consider how we may encourage one another to practice the love of God and his goodness (Hebrews 10:22-23). This passage effectively sums up the procedures that need to be performed in forming a vibrant regenerated spirit that has lasting effect. Spiritual beauty is the optimal achievement in the Christian walk. It tells the unseen truth about a person's intentions, authenticity, veracity and integrity. Verbal pleas will be superfluous at the Judgment because a person's spirit reveals the truth to God. The good news is that here's still time to get it right.

Holiness is embodied in God's law. This law is enshrined in our hearts/spirit (Romans 2:15) by the Holy Spirit through reading, memorisation and listening. When we practice obedience to the law, we are certified as righteous (Romans 2:13). Our regenerated spirit knows the standard of God's law and the character of God and it will warn us of unrighteousness and defend us when we practice holiness. The renewed spirit will know the wisdom from God and is able to judge properly the steps to maturity (1 Corinthians 2:14). Sanctification is not a great baffling mystery but within the reach of all believers.

Many great missionaries, evangelists and martyrs have been used by God mightily because they had the faith that Jesus had. It allowed God to make the most use of their abilities. They expressed the qualities of God and not themselves. Therefore, they had to possess that required standard of spiritual character that God wanted to demonstrate through their output. They were not ordinary immature Christians. On the other hand, they may not have been ideal in all respects of God's characteristics, but they had enough to get their part done.

Sanctification displaces self with God in a person's spirit. The Lord remakes a believer's personality and his will overrides self-will. Regeneration has nothing to do with self-exertion because the Lord provides the tools, perfects it in the spirit and then uses his own tools to display his morals to the outside world. Once self-will has been expunged for good, the spirit can become one with God. Don't doubt and do, and God will make it happen because Jesus has made this possible. Worldly possessions don't make you happy but renewal does because God fills the void deep in your spirit as was originally planned. We are only a copy of the real thing in God's holiness.

The spiritual child-adult is remade in sanctification on earth and completed in heaven. You prevent yourself from making holiness a reality. God does not criticize your effort no matter how small or slow the progress. However, you must make headway appropriately over time. Sanctification is a command to be holy as God is holy and our duty is to keep trying. In heaven, all will be equally holy. The difference will be in the reward or recognition process for those that have achieved more.

Executive freewill.

The process of surrendering control to the Lord is a gradual one that takes place right from the time of conversion. There's so much that we have to change. At that time, the worldly nature is still deeply ingrained in our psyche. The regeneration journey has only just begun and self-centeredness is still an issue. Selfishness in modest people is the first to go and the believer starts to think about the welfare of others, to show care and patience. However, certain people are obsessively bound to self and such a vice is deeply seated in their spirit, and they have to work much harder to eradicate it. Selfishness in the minor things is easily dealt with, but not for the bigger matters that involve large sums of money, sensitive information, personal goals, prejudice and the like. Self-gratification is the main reason for wanting to retain executive control.

Adults have to subordinate management freewill to God in order to grow in righteousness. Self-image, wealth, prestige, and other vices have to be sacrificed when handing primary control over to God. All the bad secular habits, pleasures and desires must be suppressed and this requires will-power. The Lord will always require sacrifice of some sort and it will be associated with humility. Many people cannot get themselves to do this because it calls for a noticeable drop in lifestyle that they cannot accept. Some may be restricted through practical reasons but there's always a choice. However, prior to the fall, Adam did not know what managerial freewill was. He was created to stay close to God and learn from him all his life. We have to abandon so much first before we even get to the starting blocks where Adam was at.

When facing a particular problem, we often say that God is in control. This term is loosely used as we only allow him control in selected instances and then continue on our own merry way with everything else. If God is truly in charge, we don't even have to mention it and there's nothing to fear. In the back of our minds, we know that the Lord is not master of our lives and we don't want to go into it because it's too confrontational. This matter won't go away, but we just keep on ignoring it. As a person's spiritual renewal becomes more immersed in God's goodness, the question of self-denial inevitably resurfaces because God wants sovereign control. The spirit that has grown in holiness will gravitate towards the Lord because of his great love, mercy, fellowship and the experience of the Holy Spirit's guidance. The sensitive spirit cannot help but want to get closer to God and to know him better. The personal attraction grows because God has taken such a firm hold on a person's life that the mind relents and brings self to face God.

The dreaded showdown that self has been ignoring and avoiding brazenly opens the confrontation. The goodness of God that has been working in the person's spirit has brought about a calming effect to body and soul. Freedom from sin, the advantages of a sanctified life and the future rewards begin to look very attractive. The fear of losing control does not seem so important any more. Self-worth compared with the majesty of God is a gross mismatch and the mind and spirit admits it. The thought that God can do a better job of one's life than self is the final conclusion, and this just leads to one choice. What was previously an impregnable wall surrounding self suddenly breaks down. The spirit has to accept the obvious.

The spirit is willing, but sometimes the mind goes its own way due to a lapse of concentration or extraneous influences. For the developing follower, this is a warning not to relax and slip back to the old ways. This is the point where the richness of the Spirit's blessing has not yet been revealed, and the joy of his fellowship not conclusively savoured. It's a time to be cautious as the magnetism of the old ways play their enticements through the mind. The urge to revert to self-gratification can happen instantly. The key is to maintain self-discipline and keep personal desire under suppression. Next to God, self is insignificant and powerless, in addition, the promise of future blessings are good things to bear in mind. The negative aspect is spiritual loss and this is simple to ignore because nobody knows the real impact on the after-life. If your faith is genuine and you care for your future, then any loss is not worth the present risk.

On one particular occasion, I was told of a person earning big money in a new job. It made me think about what I could have done if I didn't go on the field for twelve years. I would have financial freedom and all the things that I wanted in life. The thoughts really sent my mind spinning in the wrong direction and they were unsettling. Fortunately, it didn't reach the stage of disappointment, regret and doubt. I went for a walk and prayed about this and all the good things (too many to mention) that the Lord had given me came back to mind. It was wonderfully therapeutic and instantly I was back to joy and praise for the God. I had no hesitation that he must continue being in charge of my life. External circumstances may play out unfavourably and that could be very demoralising but Christ has given me every spiritual blessing (Ephesians 1:3) and I am spiritually very well off. God is my wealth manager and he never disappoints. For the seasoned believer disruptive thoughts are a momentary setback because they will eventually choose God.

The Lord comes to your assistance instantly if you keep short accounts with him and implore the Spirit's aid. Temporary faults are no reason for forlorn despair because God looks at the long-term intention. Such sin is not habitual and forgiveness will be extended so that the unbroken relationship with the Spirit may continue. The accumulated love that binds fellowship will always bring us to back to God.

It's a no-contest to the honest soul and the match is over very quickly. The odds are all on God's side and self has no validity. The once unconquerable self finally yields to the one who is indeed supreme, self-direction will be shut out for good. Executive self-will is spiritually stupid and relinquishing ownership to God is spiritually astute. This is the beginning of real sound regeneration and an uninterrupted rapport with the Holy Spirit.

Operational freewill.

Some may feel that surrendering directive control means a lowering of social status, and this is correct to a certain extent because earthly values and godliness are incompatible. On the other hand, submission raises your value and standing in the Lord's view. Although the material values take a dive, spiritual worth increases with the prospect of exponential potential. If you get your priorities right, there's no loss and you're on a winner all the way. Abandonment of executive will does not mean that life assumes the nature of a robot that is devoid of any interest or pleasure. Believers have routine freewill to carry out the Lord's work as the Spirit leads. We may employ our personal style and expression that will stamp a personal note to the output. At the same time, we are doing exactly as the Lord desires. Biblical writers were allowed to employ their own style and way of writing and they undoubtedly enjoyed what they were doing without changing the primary instructions. The prophets were under even greater restriction, and they had to do exactly as commanded (there was no latitude for any form of personal creativity). There's no reason why a person can't attain the same degree of satisfaction in only employing operational freewill to all kingdom work.

Jesus encouraged his disciples to think and plan ahead. Luke 14:28 mentions the construction of a tower and that careful planning has to be made prior to undertaking the project. It would be embarrassing if the builder were to run out of resources to complete the task. Following on, Jesus gave the example of the king who was thinking of going to war against an over-powering opponent. He ought to calculate whether he has the capacity to win, otherwise he should negotiate terms of peace well before any conflict even starts. Planning in such detail requires intelligence and strategy, and these are the things that the Lord values in a person. For instance, the executive command is to avoid war; then the operational duty is to plan and execute an appropriate strategy to accomplish the aim. This shows that the person is not dull, but a vibrant thinker that can take the initiative and be successful in following instructions. Routine freewill need not be boring at all.

The shrewd servant (Luke 16:8) was applauded for using finances wisely to secure friends for the future. The moral is that believers ought to use earthly wealth prudently for the purpose of accumulating eternal treasure in heaven. This ought to be done in a fair and correct manner. Since Jesus did not rebuke the shrewd servant, it indicates that the servant had the authority to do as he did (Wenham, David. The Parables of Jesus, Hodder and Stoughton London 1989, pages 162-165). Shrewdness means astute, clever and judicious and believers are to learn to act wisely and this requires planning and clear thinking. However, it is wrong to apply shrewdness in malicious acts. It would be unethical to use other's possessions to feather one's own nest or apply them in an unethical manner. In the parable, the manager seems to be acting unethically, but he was careful to plan for his future. Jesus did not reprimand him, so there may be legitimate reasons that the servant did things that way.

Only work done according to the Lord's design and approval will be rewarded in heaven. Kingdom work is only for believers and the beneficiaries will attest to the benefits that they received from the wise deployment of resources by the worker. On that day, heavenly residents will welcome that worker into heaven with gladness and kindness.

Routine freewill is not a debilitating option and believers in heaven will have their full capacity to think and act in an intelligent and efficient manner. This may offer some encouragement to those that feel constrained by surrendering their management control over to God. Heaven will be a place where believers will be completely free to practice holiness. This is real freewill. Everybody will do the right thing and there will be the ethic of common benevolence to all.

Those that have management positions in heaven will govern fairly and equitably and all people will expect the same. There will be no opportunity for self-enrichment or corruption. The secular notion of 'climbing the corporate ladder' will not exist as God has fixed all those positions. Managers will conduct themselves in a righteous manner and in good faith, and they will be accountable for what they do. Their role will be purely on a stewardship basis as all things belong to God. There is no further personal gain because all the rewards and accolades were appropriated at the judgment of believers. If there is a betterment system in heaven, then competition and envy would prevail again. It will be all the distasteful secular habits playing out again because everybody or the majority will want to better themselves and be seen as high-achievers. Some may even want to impress God in some way. Self-effort and selfishness will emerge to corrupt the people. This can't and will not happen because heaven is holy, together with everybody there.

When Satan introduced self-determination to Adam, it was just a sham to cut him off from the Lord's fellowship. Satan temporarily succeeded in taking away God's prized possession. Autonomy is sin because humankind was never meant to survive outside of God's sovereign will, care, protection and most important of all, fellowship. It is rejecting God's sovereign ownership of your soul. God created humans for his pleasure. Satan did not create people and yet we are so attracted to his habits and pleasures. Prior to the fall, Adam never knew what independence was, and now we can't get rid of it. Independence means separation from God and he wants us to return to him. Management of personal destiny is a fallacy and is embedded in the secular framework. At the time of decision-making, people never consider the repercussions of the eternal consequences, but yield to self-satisfaction. It's so short sighted.

Chapter 33
Self-denial and humility

Humility.

Humbleness is the second finest character quality that ought to be pursued. It is the opposite of pride that leads to selfishness. Believers have to de-secularize their thinking and habits to displace pride with humility. Humbleness is not a worldly virtue, but it's essential for our spiritual growth. Christians hardly talk about humility and unless you purposely make a study of it, it will be overlooked. Humbleness enhances all the other virtues in Scripture. It is so important to character development because it counteracts egotism and self-elevation.

Humility is a soft-power as it is able to accomplish great things in kingdom work and it rewards the worker lavishly with exaltation and other virtues that accompany kingdom work. It comes with the power of God to attain maturity in renewal. Sanctification is incomplete without character renewal in humility. In addition, the body of Christ benefits from the Christian that radiates humbleness to others while showing the glory of God. Heaven will acclaim the people that have humility in their personality because Jesus is the outstanding representation. The higher the quality of humility imbued in a person, the closer to Jesus that person will be. Love without the impetus of humility is incomplete.

Humility is a peacemaking tool and God uses it for good to promote amicable relations among his people and the wider world. Humbleness enhances harmony as all members treat one another with respect and dignity. As people grow in humility and manifest it in their lives, good neighbourliness raises the regeneration level in all believers involved because the Spirit works to nurture the body jointly and severally. Humility is there for the welfare of all concerned because it carries no trace of selfishness at all. The objective is for the entire body of Christ to grow gracefully in sanctification as well as getting the work done according to the kingdom plan.

On the other hand, pride breeds aggression and disharmony. It causes strife, boasting, envy, self-significance, selfishness, and does not care for the welfare of others. Pride is a relationship breaker and the rebellious nature is always there waiting for an opportunity to stand against God's rule. Even the slightest trace is sufficient to multiply and disrupt the renewal process. Pride must be purged in each individual and it will never be allowed to enter the kingdom of heaven. The simple and only answer is sanctification by the Holy Spirit. When the Spirit is in control of a person's renewal, pride will have no place to go, but out.

Humility is part of God's very nature. It was natural for Adam to be humble because he followed after the image of God. Human beings were created to be humble creatures. They were supposed to be part of God's family where humility prevails. Conversely, Satan introduced self-determination and sin gave birth to pride and aggressive behaviour. Inherent sin has made humility feel unnatural to the average person because pride is dominant. Furthermore, the material world system is primarily focused on self-gain, self-worth, selfishness and self-importance. Under these conditions, we grow up being alienated from God, and everything that he requires of us is a major burden to perform. We can never get close to God on our own and he has to invite us into his domain and help us in re-education to recovery. The state that we were in before conversion is not natural. A non-Christian life is unnatural, yet people think that it is the greatest thing on earth. In contrast, the humble soul knows that life on earth is meaningless without Jesus to accompany them to eternity. It is not a lonely walk and we have the assurance that once we surrender to the Holy Spirit, he will help make the learning process much easier than we think or feel.

Fruit of the Spirit.

It is so named because the fruit derives from the character of God and the Spirit's work in a person will replicate all his virtues. When a person submits to the Spirit's tutelage, training in the production of fruit will automatically be included in the package. These qualities are in God's personality and there is no law that governs them. Jesus possessed all of these virtues and his Father was pleased with him. The Spirit trains a person in these merits because our Father requires it to be done. Jesus humbled himself and we have to learn to do the same. The fruit involves learning the meaning of its merits, absorption into character and then living them out in humility to produce more fruit in whatever the Lord calls one to do.

Love: this is the leading virtue because God is love. The greatest commandment is to love God first and above all, and then to love your neighbour as yourself. Christians have substantial difficulty to stop loving self, and to love God first and then to love outsiders as much as self. Self-gratification is the code breaker and our good intentions are constantly under threat. Agape will always call for personal sacrifice of some sort. It's very hard to give up things that are close to the heart. Jesus demonstrated perfect love at the Calvary, and ardent followers have to follow suit. Humility eases the decision to give up personal fancies because it puts the interest of others first. Humble people embrace agape better as they desire peace with everybody. They care for and love others because Jesus demonstrated such great love for them. The meek person knows that they have an obligation to love Christ as well as to love their neighbour, whereas assertive and self-driven people will have a much harder time imitating the love of Christ. Concern for one's neighbour is still a great challenge for most of us due to the self-enrichment mentality and the drive to accumulate as many assets as possible. Humility deprecates self so that agape can develop. The mere fact that we have to keep reminding ourselves to show agape to others speaks of festering flaws in our character.

Joy: true joy is a right relationship with the Lord. Happiness is associated with material things and it can change with the change in lifestyle, mood and material comforts. Joy is an internal quality that cannot be bought with money. It lifts up your spirit because it is given by the Holy Spirit. Humility classifies self as nothing and joy is enhanced because we are underserving and yet have received so much from God. Humble people have a greater appreciation of joy. It's like an employee receiving the praise and encouragement from their employer that fuels motivation to do better. When we please God as humble servants and not ourselves, it will bring about joy in that we have done what was right. Merely following the Lord's wishes correctly is a joy to the grateful soul. Every bit of merit received from the Lord is a joy because he only gives good things. If we overlook the simple blessings, then we will correspondingly miss the related joy.

Peace: this is an anti-strife measure and humility promotes peace so that life becomes stress-free with others. Christians trust the Lord with everything. The humble person knows that God has their best interest at heart. Life always brings problems of some sort, but the Spirit brings peace amidst turmoil. Believers know that God has everything under control. Humility suppresses self-gratification, so trouble and loss do not hurt as badly because self is considered secondary. Humble people rank self as unimportant and being right with God brings great peace in the heart. Material diminution does not affect the spiritual rewards that are kept safe in heaven. Meek people do not take risks with God as they don't have great ambitions for self except to seek after God. They refrain from actions that will anger the Lord despite the hardships of the material environment. True peace comes to the obedient soul knowing that they have been faithful in all that they have been called to do and they have entrusted their spirit to a sovereign being with the complete confidence that they will be kept safe after death. The fear factor that death could occur at any moment is ineffectual and non-threatening because peace brings tranquillity, assurance and great joy that their benefactor will be waiting to welcome them home and shower them with all the benefits that have been allocated to them. In this respect, the sadness of material loss must always be weighed up against the joy of spiritual advantages and peace with God.

The ultimate joy is to be with the Father for good, but there's also a secondary grant. This is the promise of recompense for tasks that have been faithfully carried out in kingdom work. This puts the spirit at ease knowing that our efforts (obedience) are not wasted. Christians will have true peace, serenity and self-satisfaction that their work and time spent on the unseen will finally be tangible and be enjoyable when they get to heaven. The accumulation of reward is a kind of sanctified self-interest that nobody can share in or take away, and there are no regulations against it. Those awards will be for the follower to revel in forever.

Patience: this makes people pause when confronting trials and to think and pray. Patience to think things over relieves tension over those uneasy issues as a person works through various possibilities. It avoids a knee-jerk reaction and impulsive attitudes when the matter has not been fully assessed. Humble people admit that they are powerless and they depend on God for all their needs. Pray brings comfort as we wait on the Lord for guidance. Patience works to remove the urge to act on instinct and meekness puts God first as provider and leader. Patience is a normal part of life for the humble because they don't insist on having their way. They are content to wait on the Lord, despite the urge to react immediately. This is putting self-interest at the back of the queue. Meek people contain the desire to want instant answers. They understand that the Lord has his reasons and way of doing things and patience with others becomes so much easier to impute into character. Patience with self is the easiest to contain. Patience with others is much harder and we often act on superficial evidence or preconceived ideas. If full information is not available then it's best to wait until more comes to light. Patience with the Lord is the top most concern. He works in his own way and sometimes it takes years before he replies. Faith has to accompany patience when the Lord's timing is delayed. Humility postpones personal gratification and waiting is not problematic because the urgency is removed from expectation.

Kindness: humility prompts a believer to consider the needs of others. Kind people are observant and have a habit of being aware of the needs of others. They can sense when people need help of some sort. Humble people know that if they were in need, they would appreciate some help as well. Even if they had other business to attend to, they would pause and render assistance if possible. This is real kindness. The joy of knowing that the beneficiary did not suffer loss of any sort is sufficient reward. In addition, the appreciation (relief) that they show adds motivation to continue in kindness. I was in a certain city and needed directions to a particular street. I asked a local gentlemen (retired) and he mechanically retorted that he didn't know. I suppose that he could have several tourists asking him for directions on any given day and he just couldn't be bothered. I was disappointed because I was running out of time and merely needed to know which direction to go. If he had assisted me, I would have been so grateful.

Humble people are gentle and they will excuse honest ignorance and do a favour for that person. Unkindness is usually associated with self-seeking people who do not care and will not help, and they would rather see or know that others will suffer loss. Certain people think that it's a joke or they make fun of people that are in difficulty. Meek people are not abrasive because they know that unkindness will hurt others. Kind behaviour is easily adapted into a meek character due to their concern for others. Some would even go out of their way to help others because humility breeds sensitivity and concern.

Goodness: denotes a benefit. Jesus is good to all his followers and that drives Christians to do good works that bring relief to the needy. Goodness demands sincerity and Christians have to be careful not to do good works for public praise. The humble soul that is obedient to God will follow his will and thereby achieve good works according to God's definition. Meekness is not self-seeking and humble people know that they are mere instruments whereby God may use them to do his good works. In all of this, meek followers learn and adopt the Lord's methodology of goodness into their personality. This assures them that they have acted correctly. However, obedience is the primary ingredient and humble followers always stay close to God so that they don't make any mistakes. It is the Lord that gives goodness and not the servant, regardless of what and how much they do.

A good act is characterized by righteousness, fairness and justice. This should be differentiated from respect and good manners as these also seek to be fair and equitable to others. Humble people would carry out a service and not expect repayment, and they also do not expect the beneficiary to bear a debt of gratitude. They are aware that the glory belongs to the Lord, and so they do not claim credit for their efforts.

Faithfulness: trust is often tested in daily life after we have prayed about something that we need to resolve. We remain faithful even if things don't seem to be going the way we expect. The humble soul will trust the Lord's guidance and behave faithfully. It all hinges on taking self out of the decision-making process and allowing the Lord to take the lead. Meek people care little for their physical requirements and more for their spiritual welfare. Faithfulness is a spiritual trait and is vital in nurturing a vibrant relationship with God. Humility gives God his rightful place in a person's life and self-effacing should be part of the believer's psyche. Decisions that affect wealth are problematic for most ordinary folk, but the humble soul does not rank money as a major concern and will wait for the Lord to answer. Faithfulness to Christ means obedience, and it also bears the obligation to have integrity, accuracy and impartiality in all that we say and do.

Gentleness: humility and gentleness are paired, and it is rare for a meek person to be crude. A submissive mentality always leads a person to tread carefully and to refrain from hurting others. Meek people possess a neutrality that tend to be gentle in their approach to others. They care for the welfare of the people around them and they are able to exercise gentleness because it's how they want others to treat them. Humble people consider their words and actions thoughtfully and will not act on impulse. Even if the other party is wrong, meek people will find a way to respond in a gentle but firm manner. Gentleness does not condone sin, and a person will choose the actions that are righteous without being overbearing. However, certain people are hardened and they treat others in an unkind manner. Gentleness dictates that even they ought to be dealt with impartially and with respect. This is much easier for the humble to do as they leave all judgment in the Lord's hands. A humble person is sensitive to other's feelings and circumstances, and will behave as gently as the situation dictates. Others may retort harshly or angrily, but meekness will find replies that relieve tension and settle tempers so that the parties may negotiate in a calm and civilized fashion.

Self-control: if you have a weakness and lack self-control, sin will proliferate. We must restrain self-will and then exercise self-control to combat our faults. Humble people have an easier job because they are sensitive towards the welfare of others. Meek people have a selfless nature and self-control does not present a serious problem. A humble demeanour enables a person to restrain themselves and always inquire of the Lord for patience and direction. They have a far less chance of losing self-control and taking matters into their own hands. Meek people are more likely to obey orders and self-control is easily manageable because the responsibility rests on the decision-maker. There will be cases where sensitive personal interest is involved in a particular decision. In such cases, there's every chance that a person will choose self-gratification. However, humility will always act as a check against outright impulsive actions. It reminds a person that they don't know everything and it's best to gather sufficient information so as to make a wise and an informed decision. Humility restrains self-will from sin and tends to choose righteousness. Heavenly riches over-rule worldly gain and self-control works to choose the former. Self-restraint deposes impulsive behaviour and allows a person to think clearly and correctly. All the fruit are undergirded by love, interconnected by humility and designed to operate interactively to groom a person after God's own heart.

The moral traits of Jesus embrace more than the fruit of the Spirit. Some of the other merits are justice, fairness, grace, mercy, meekness, obedience, discernment, holiness, self-abasement, righteousness etc. If one works through the fruit carefully and fixes them in character, then the other qualities will fall into place naturally. The serious follower will realize what a mammoth task it is to apply the true meaning of all the virtues correctly into one's personality. Inherent sin makes this process very difficult to achieve and to firmly grasp. We have to resolutely inculcate self into those habits. From the outset, the assistance of the Spirit is crucial. We have to strive with the Spirit's help to maintain a forward direction. Keeping self-will on the path of holiness must be monitored throughout a lifetime. For the humble, this is an easy decision as self-abasement is the catalyst in keeping sound fellowship with God. One realises that there is a high moral objective to achieve and there is yet so much to learn and assimilate.

Christian bonding with Jesus has as its immediate outworking to bear fruit. This is conditional on staying in Christ because the fruit cannot be artificially made. Only the fruit that comes from Jesus will have eternal value. The exhortation is to produce more fruit and this paves the way for enlargement of one's spiritual repertoire. This is so important to the life of a Christian and it demands more attention. My first firm introduction to this passage was at a Bible study at church. I thought about its ramifications but kept it in isolation, and then forgot about it. At the time, I thought of it merely in theory and what it signifies. Somehow, I had to establish this fruit in my life, but didn't think about any particular approach. I didn't realise that living a compliant and integrated Christian life is the means of producing that fruit. The moral traits mentioned in the preceding paragraph work in harmony to make a person fruitful. Even when I started practicing the fruit of the Spirit and the other morals, the Holy Spirit was still unmoving and quiet.

The question then is what is this fruit? Initially, I thought that it was good works and winning converts to Christ. But, this is incorrect because a person can do many good works and win many believers to the Lord and still not be any closer to Jesus' nature and his fellowship. The example that Charles Price mentioned (see section on sanctification) about the gifted minister that did so much for God's kingdom and yet broke the Biblical command not to divorce his wife, is a good example showing that works (personal exertion) is separate from sanctification and they do not bring a person's spirit closer to Christ. One's spiritual record can be so easily spoilt by a moment of self-indulgence. However, it is the magnitude of such wanton acts that bring into question the quality and authenticity of one's regeneration. Knowing what's right and purposely doing the opposite alludes to self-first before the Lord.

The fruit of the Spirit is free of human influence. It is Jesus' exertion into changing your character and you have no control over the input. Change becomes permanent for those that have comprehensively dealt with self-interest issues in their spirit. It brings them a step closer to Christ. In the absence of humility, no matter how much effort is put into the learning process, it will always be possible for self-esteem to creep in and interfere with one's intentions. Humility places others before self and this is the ingredient that holds all the fruit in harmony and gives them impetus to be firmly grounded in a person's entire being.

Special Grace.

Christ humbled himself to the extent of his shameful sacrifice (Philippians 2: 5-9). He is our finest teacher on humility and servanthood. This passage exhorts us to elect to be like Jesus in our behaviour. It's a familiar passage in mind, but not in experience. The immense impediments for a believer to overcome are:

- Renounce equality with others
- Treat self as of no status and significance
- Become a true servant
- Be sincerely humble before God and all people
- Be obedient even if it calls for sacrificing your life for others

Give due meditation on these things and don't let negative suggestions discourage you. A positive moral mindset will keep you in good stead with the Spirit. Jesus was a radical because he did and said certain things that were counter-culture and unheard of. He was charismatic in that he drew large crowds but he never showed a desire for leadership. It doesn't make sense on the human level. Contrary to expectations, Jesus the great teacher was also the humblest person on earth and he became a scapegoat for all humanity – even for the vilest criminal. Although he was innocent of violating any law, he died a very painful and lonely death. He did not protest his innocence like normal people would, and it meant that he assumed the guilt of all humanity's sin. He bore the sin of the world but did not admit to committing those sins (he could not sin). Jesus renounced all rights to self-will and became a vessel that was used by his Father. Since Jesus didn't have any of the human issues of pride, self-preservation, sin, doubt, anxiety, materialism, uncertainty etc. he never had the secular ails of freewill in his spirit.

Just thinking about these things is enough to unnerve the strongest soul. Is this really doable for the average Christian? Our reservations are due to the worldly vices that we have grown accustomed to and depended on for most of our lives. This passage is a spiritual statement as all the conditions do not relate to worldly values and principles. They emanate directly from the will of God. We need the power of the Holy

Spirit to comply with it in order to gain victory. This avenue demands total submission of personal freewill, it's an accept-only arrangement that is closed to deliberation.

Grace is one of God's qualities that we have come to expect from him, but we are slow to learn it and appropriate it into our personality. Similar with humility, grace enhances all the fruit of the Spirit. A person will reach a higher level of sanctification if grace is demonstrated and enmeshed in the psyche. How do we learn to become graceful in character? I have given this a bit of thought and found it so hard to love someone that is selfish, uncaring, nasty, oppressive, cruel etc. Due to our fallen background, we need special grace in order to show grace to those that rub us up the wrong way. Imperfection results in dysfunctional spiritual growth. This means that our spiritual bank will always be lacking in some way if the weaknesses are not eradicated. Despite the enormity of the task, we still have to learn to be graceful. The answer is to disregard self and abide doggedly to God's way. Words can be fleeting and don't fool yourself into thinking that you can go it alone. The reality is that perfection comes from outside of the human capability, from God himself who is perfect.

With such stringent requirements, one might question whether it is worth the trouble? Why not just do what you have always been doing – select the part of ministry that suits you and ignore the rest. You reap what you sow. Partial effort only earns partial reward, depending on whether God deems those efforts as worthy of any reward at all. Those that consider heaven as their ultimate home and want to accumulate spiritual assets that are incorruptible will put in their best effort and submit to the Spirit's conditions. God exalted Christ to the highest honour and gave him the highest name. These supreme accolades were given by the Father to the Son for the work that he did, and he performed faultlessly. This sets the precedent for the children of God. We must also be obedient, humble, self-depreciating, self-effacing and adopt the nature of an authentic servant to attain the heavenly treasure that has been allocated to each individual. To be standing as close to Jesus in the top rankings before the Father will be a great honour. Investing your time and energy in eternal treasure greatly favours the very short time-span of effort on earth. Equally so, enjoying earthly pleasures for such a short period is senseless.

Some may be still mulling over their calling and some may have missed the opportunity altogether because they chose to pursue other interests. Their time and occasion have passed and no matter what they do, they will never be able to bring it back. One consideration is the individual debt owed to Jesus. It's an enormous obligation. The least that any Christian can do is to give self to Jesus because he did that for each and every individual for all time. The decision then is how much to give? Maximum reward demands total submission, and God wants you to have the most in eternity. It will be embarrassing what some people have decided. Bear in mind that Jesus gave everything to please his Father. Obedience may be coupled with loyalty – high level obedience equals high loyalty, and partial obedience equals partial loyalty. Loyalty comes about only because you trust in the Lord and believe in his beneficence. It's indefensible to say that a person loves God dearly and yet only submit partially to him. Love and obedience are inseparable (John 14:23-24, 1 John 5:3). You have to give up everything in order to gain everything that is due to you.

Many years ago, I went through times when I acted in a largely discriminatory manner towards certain people that I didn't like or was partial to. I knew that this was unfair and that God was watching, so I reformed my attitude over a period of time. Righteousness and fair treatment became the basis of my dealings. It truly relieves the conscience and most of all it prompts God to deal with you in the same positive way. However, the better approach is from a position of humility. I want to be a just servant who is mindful of others (friend or foe alike) and take their circumstances into account first before deciding on an appropriate course of action. There's still a long way to go before I get there and I have to persevere even when I don't feel like it.

I served on the field for twelve years with a team working amongst a minority group. My last four years were the most turbulent but also the most rewarding. I enjoyed teaching accounting to my Uni. students. The language learning classes were burdensome yet also profitable. Most of all, the Holy Spirit suddenly imposed in my spiritual life. He gave me so many ideas for sermon preparation and Bible study (this had never happened before). In the past, I struggled and took so much time to do one sermon. Fellowship with the Spirit had stepped up to a new level and he gave me frequent encouragement. During my walking times, thoughts would come to mind. It was definitely not from my own brainstorming because at times, I wasn't even thinking about those matters. If I didn't purposely keep the points in mind, I would get home and completely forget. If I had invented them in my own mind, then I will never forget my own workings. I could honestly say that God was with me. It gave me so much confidence and joy in all aspects of my work and ministry. I could feel that my sanctification account was increasing, and it has not let up since. It brought home the fact that righteous dealings and fair, impartial behaviour is vital in developing a thriving relationship with God and with people. Walk humbly before God and others and serve sincerely and honestly and the blessings will flow.

Humility is divinely enabled. It's a resilient virtue that does not discriminate in any situation whether dealing with people that are likeable or not. People that are still captive to pride may use humility as a tool that can be turned on and off at will. Some people behave humbly in certain situations and not in others. It's not false humility but selective behaviour. However, good works or acts of kindness are no substitutes for humility. Superficially, a person may be humble in appearance, and their behaviour shows the nice-guy personality (done sincerely), yet they may still have deep-rooted pride in their mindset. One person that I came across could not accept the view of others when their thinking did not agree with the other's opinion. They have not even given themselves a chance to place self in the other person's shoes in an attempt to discover why others have come to their conclusions. No matter how much explanation is given, nothing is enough to convince them, and the self within remains obstinately unmoving and dogmatic.

Self-willed people are speaking from their own experience and background and they are making assertions from their own context. Pride and humility are incompatible because the former is motivated by Satan and the latter pertains to godliness. If pride is left to its own devices, a person's mannerism will show inconsistencies as there will be alternating signs of pride and humility from time to time. An early tell-tale sign is disagreement as self-assertion is motivated by egotism. Preconceived ideas, the desire to be heard, the need to be the front-person, attention-seeking etc. may strongly allude to self-elevation and pride. Differences of opinion may be minor to begin with, but further down the line they will get bigger and more pronounced. Stubborn pride usually does not allow for compromise, and working relationships are affected. The spiritual reformer ought to take definite steps to change such behaviour.

In a team situation where the majority is engaged in one particular sector, it becomes very difficult for the outsider to comment because there is an invisible protective barrier amongst those that are commonly-linked. Where group dynamics have been ensconced in a certain way, frustration will appear amongst the minority. Teamwork becomes impaired and individuals do not gain in spiritual growth as they cannot learn from one another (Proverbs 27:17). The learning process is proactive and not merely hearing useful things. In the excitement of their commonality, the majority may not even be aware of the work being biasedly concentrated in only one area. Teamwork within the majority strengthens due to the overlap of certain tasks, and a clique is subconsciously formed.

In addition, the need to defend one's values manifests quickly and members will speak out poignantly and make strong defensive comments. This puts everybody on notice not to venture into those areas. It is counter-productive as the minority is prevented from making honest constructive comments or the response may be mere lip-service with no positive action from the group underpinning the cell. The work relationship would just keep going down the same path as before with no hope of ever changing. This is regrettable as new ministry possibilities may be routinely ignored. On occasion, comments may be made relevantly and in context, and the opposite party may apparently receive it normally, but only on the surface. This just breaks trust and the team spirit down. Outsiders may see their weaknesses, but they can't. When members fall into a comfortable enclosure, there must be a reality-check on the dangers that may be lurking as well as to prompt all-round improvement.

The minority is effectively hamstrung and they can only watch silently. At times, unorthodox suggestions may come about due to circumstance, but the willingness to change is still absent. Once a comfort zone is in place over a period of time, it is very hard to break out of. It's unfortunate as this weakens the overall team effort. Pride may prevent people from looking beyond their own work sector and the benefits of critical thinking are lost. Goals and methods remain the same year after year and ministry progress is very slow. The focus is only in one direction and other real opportunities go unnoticed. Introspection may be partial and frivolous as members are content to keep doing what they have always been doing. Humility and self-abasement would go a long way to injecting new life in the team dynamic and the ministry. On the other hand, if the minority grows in numbers, there will be a polarisation effect in the team due to historical dealings. This apparent segregation is also not healthy for the team as a unit and it requires strong leadership to bring all the members back to thinking and working as a united entity.

An obvious alert signal is one's spiritual rhetoric which shows a lack of illumination from the Spirit. Intellectuals may have been serving for more than a decade and yet not show any signs of God's wisdom (Proverbs 3:13-15). I realise that not all believers place the Spirit's wisdom as the primary indicator of a close fellowship with the Lord, it may be something else that they consider more personal. Nevertheless, I have found overwhelming satisfaction and peace in receiving new insights from the Holy Spirit. They may notice their deficiency, but do not know how to go about fixing it. It's a kind of sanctification dead-end or sanctification-blindness that's holding them back. All this will change if people put self aside for a moment and allow the Spirit to take charge and root out the malady on the inside. Humble consideration of the truth of what others have said will result in remedial action and improvement on their part. This is not easy for proud people that don't like to hear negative things about themselves. It's odd that Christians will accept and admit errors to God, but they refuse to hear it from fellow believers particularly those that they have adverse feelings towards. Even Christians harbour hostility towards fellow believers.

Humility before God and in full submission to his plans allows followers to accelerate the Lord's work for them to be refined as silver and be tested as gold (Zechariah 13:9). God attributes high value on his people that are serious about being holy. A lowly obedient servant that merely follows orders is of great value in God's sight than an intelligent person of great learning but is inclined to self-interest. God who cannot accept sin is able and willing to process and purify the faithful believer's spirit to the height of personal best. A sinner is covered over by Christ and is now a workable instrument that may be regenerated to holiness. Jesus declares a believer righteous before God and the newly ascribed holiness is accepted as authentic and unblemished by sin. The inherent sinful nature in a person is infused with holiness and that is regarded by the Lord as worthy of great reward. This very thought is a contradiction in terms, but it ought to make us very grateful that the Lord is pleased to help us re-learn and be trained to take after his character. Advancement necessitates refining and testing, so we must undergo practical application to prove the permanency of all the new character traits that we have acquired. The end product is the same quality as the holiness in heaven itself. Truly amazing.

Protectionism is a mechanism to shield a country from foreign competition by taxing imports. This theory also applies to situations where there is a close bonding between people such as family, relatives, political cliques, office politics, team cohesion etc. It has the effect of holding the body together through the practice of mutual help. As a rule, the whole unit moves forward together and every participant benefits. However, where corruption enters the system, the unit will be preserving undesirable practices and policy, and the work will suffer. A corrupt government that uses political advantage and military power to remain in control of a nation will always rob the citizens of the proper use of tax revenue. Consequently, the standard of living will decline.

The Bible does not promote protectionism of any kind, instead, it warns of an inevitable judgment and the accountability of each individual. Protectionism is just another form of favouritism and that is sin (James 2:9). God can never show favouritism to any person (Romans 2:11) and that is relevant to every believer. Ministry workers ought to be very careful not to inadvertently fall into this trap. Each participant must exercise their sanctified common sense and seek to do what is just and righteous. Keeping Jesus at the centre will avoid costly mistakes.

Humility is a noble quality but you have to utilize it correctly. Where justice has been correctly meted out, humility does not feature because it does not interfere with the course of justice. Humility does not apply to sport activities where competition is the main focus. All competitors try their hardest to be the best, in a fair contest. The objective is to find the most talented contestant who will win the competition. All competitors give their best and there is no perception of being humble and allowing the next person to win. This defeats the purpose of competition. Education is another domain where humility is not valid. Everybody tries their best to pass the exam and then to see who has obtained the highest marks. It's an honour to be the top candidate and it's not a sin for a person to demonstrate that they are the best in their field. However, after they have received honour and acclaim, then humility comes into play. Christians have to ensure that pride is kept in check and that it does not encourage arrogance.

On that note, God will not share his glory with anybody (Isaiah 42:8, 48:11). At times when a movement becomes popular and stirs the public's interest, the hype and attention may be tantalizing. The worker has to be wary of popularity as that fuels pride. Careful attention to praise God appropriately must be a priority, as it is easy to be immersed in all the interest and not do the right thing. Humility and self-denial are the main elements to assist a person to act correctly. People look to a physical person to relate to and the attention could be distracting. Sometimes it's best to silently fade away into the background, but that's no always possible. Luke 17:10 are helpful words to remember. It seems as if we need special grace to reverence the Lord honourably.

The disciples were debating as to who was the greatest among them. Jesus' reply was the youngest and the one who serves (Luke 22:26). They were all adults, so the youngest was not referring to age, but to childlike attitude. The person that is called to service must assume a childlike manner regarding obedience and an adultlike posture concerning aptitude. The job of the servant is always to satisfy the needs of those being served. Humility is the key element that God is looking out for. Assume a situation where fellow servants from another group got together to form a syndicate. They enlist your services as a fellow servant and friend because of your know-how. During the course of your engagement, you come across vital information that nobody is aware of and would not even discover because of its obscurity. This knowledge will generate tremendous wealth for your employers. If you ignore it and move on, people will be none the wiser. Besides, you may raise the excuse that it wasn't your job to probe into such business and that it requires an expert to delve into that. Servanthood demands that the servant put the interest of others first. Thus, the employee must do the right thing and enrich the employers by all means at his disposal. This will result in his fellow-servants suddenly rising to prominence and the employee remaining or even dropping to a lower social standing. This duty requires high quality humility in a person because it's most unpalatable as envy will divide the mind. However, God delights in humility as one of the finest ethics that befits a worthy child of God.

Jesus said that he was a servant amongst them, and all his life he served the people around him. At the end, he received the greatest accolade from his Father. Commitment to obey God has huge potential spiritual value. All followers of Jesus are servants by association with him. It's there to line us up for maximum merit in infinity but it calls for obedience to make the reward sure.

Jesus' disciples knew that he had no earthly wealth or power structure and he had no status in the religious order of the day, yet they wanted prominence in his future kingdom. Followers of Christ ought to get their aspirations right. This also tells us that the secular mentality of competition has no place in the kingdom of God, and the Father will decide who receives the places of rank and merit. After Pentecost, the disciples got it right, and it guides us to get it right too.

Hardship was not objectionable to Jesus. However, he was very much afraid of the cross and asked for another way, but there was no other. We always tend to ask God for another way (our way) to achieve an outcome. Unlike Jesus, we don't submit to the Father as he did. It's just delaying the inevitable as the Lord will continue putting us through trial and error until we wake up and realise that there's no other way. You will save yourself a lot of time by doing the right thing in the first instance. We look at the draconian effect of our cross and avoid that path and miss out on sharing affliction with Christ. Confession as a believer is effortless, but following his example requires a substantial amount of discomfort. After our relationship with God strengthens to a certain point, we will want to keep positive progress and only then do we choose to pass through the necessary austerity. After the event, those sufferings will not be as daunting as we first thought because our love for God will vastly reduce our preconceived idea of discomfort. Unlike Christ (alone on the cross), the Spirit will be there to spur us along and thereby alleviate most of the unpleasantness. Take the hard decisions now, the earlier the better. Procrastination always carries the real risk of missing out on the primary blessings as kingdom work depends on the Lord's timing and not ours.

God's love is the reason that prompted him to devise a plan of redemption, and Jesus had to do the unthinkable. Jesus' love for his Father enabled him to endure such ineffable revulsion because justice had to be done. Humankind does not have the power to force God to do anything, but in this case our foolishness did. This is the one and only time that humans 'forced' God to do something so extreme. No amount of fasting and praying will ever make the Lord do what we want. We will never know the kind of pain that Jesus endured on the cross, and hence, we ought not to be afraid of the hardship that we may be called to pass through because it will never be anywhere near the pain that Jesus went through. Furthermore, the Holy Spirit will always be with us to aid in going through the hardship, whereas Jesus was all alone. In the true sense of the words, Jesus served all of us and with pure humility.

Did Jesus struggle with executive freewill? He always did as his Father instructed and all his actions were pleasing to his Father. He only had routine freewill and see how exciting his life turned out! Jesus always obeyed his Father, and we have to apply this fine discipline in our behaviour. Our spiritual bonding with Jesus must be as close as we can possibly get it. This will only happen by full submission of executive freewill to God and obedience to follow instructions carefully. The mere fact that Jesus followed through with the detestable punishment of the cross is convincing evidence that he had no sovereign freewill. We are not as fortunate to have such a close bonding with our Father, but we have the Spirit's assistance, so everything that Jesus asks of us is doable. Self-will is the obstacle and it's a kind of spiritual suicide.

As mentioned previously, selective humility makes our behaviour inconsistent. Consider this, Jesus humbled himself before the unworthy, the foolish, the arrogant, the hypocrites etc. Basically, they were spiritual dunces. Jesus asked his Father to forgive them because they didn't know what they were doing. They also included the mockers, the executioners, the proud and the nasty. It took supernatural discipline and grace for Jesus to go through with his ordeal. The mob was guilty as an accessory to crucifying an innocent person. We would humble ourselves before the influential people, the powerful, the wealthy and the learned, but humbling self before idiots is contrary to logical thinking. It's abnormal to be self-effacing before undeserving people – what for? Humility doesn't make sense to us but it makes perfect sense to God.

Humility took Jesus to an ignominious death on the cross. It was such a degrading spectacle to be crucified naked in public. Before that, he was insulted, beaten and mocked as well. How much humility does it take? It's a profound question for all of us because we have such struggles just taking the simple initial step of adopting humility in our ordinary daily routine. What happens when we have to face insults and brash behaviour? Jesus denied self and his physical body was valueless and insignificant and people could do anything to him as it didn't matter in the slightest. Humility gives one unimaginable godly spiritual power, and Jesus had it. The Holy Spirit will give us immense strength to take on huge undertakings with the assurance that there is nothing to lose (in the body) and everything to gain (in the spirit).

He was the obedient servant that manifested humility to perfection. We have a great deal to learn and to incorporate into our lives. Although we may feel inadequate in ability, we have the Holy Spirit to help us. It is only after making a genuine attempt that we know our capability or our limitations. It will provoke the mentality to change and to improve. The worse decision is to do nothing.

True reverence for God only comes after we have largely understood and adopted humbleness. It makes one realize how insignificant one really is before Almighty God. Subordination of self and exalting God to his rightful position in a person's life becomes merely incidental. You have to empty yourself and discard all material merit that you have achieved. Then obedience to the Lord will become customary in normal life and in spirit. It must be part of your inner being. The servant attitude prevails and the Spirit is able to shine out through us. It may not be easy to get it right under all the different scenarios, but identified faults have to be followed up and corrected. Each correction adds to improvement. You will have a heightened personality after a short while. The decision to surrender may drag out but once the resolve to be subservient is made, the goodness of God changes a person's character rapidly as the Holy Spirit takes charge.

Self-abasement.

Jesus said that his disciple has to deny himself (Matthew 16:24-25), and go through the trials that God has set. The primary step is self-denial i.e. to cast away one's worldly identity and achievements and to have fixed in the mind that self is unimportant compared with other people. The associated thought is servanthood and God requires his servant to be humble and to consider the welfare of others before self. The cross is not defined, but in the worker's context, it alludes to a major commitment of some sort. Each individual has different values, and Jesus is asking you to sacrifice what you cherish most for his sake. Jesus demands all or nothing as this brings out the determined followers that have potential for maturity in sanctification.

The cross also denotes suffering. It's prophetical that Jesus should apply the symbol of the cross when describing discipleship because his crucifixion only took place later on. It depicts the gravity of the burden of following Christ. The cross was an instrument of torture and a terrible thing to suffer. The connotation is that the sanctification-walk (to be like Christ) is going to cost you everything. Jesus came to serve, so we as servants ought to share in his sufferings (1 Peter 2:21, Romans 8:17). The sobering thought is that Christ gave up everything specifically for me. My liability to Christ is unquantifiable and he has the right to ask me for self-denial and self-sacrifice. Some may be called to hardship ministry, but the Spirit will empower a person to get through. I have no choice but to follow as the Lord directs.

It makes more sense to take the hardship on earth and secure the unseen wealth in eternity. The judgment will be a pleasant experience for the obedient as they will be congratulated, and a deep regret for those that chose self-enrichment. Material comforts will have to be sacrificed plus the calling will have its particular unpleasant aspects and this is the cross that the worker is to bear daily. Thoughts of the comforts forgone will always be in the back of one's mind, in addition, the work may not be to one's liking. Nevertheless, the work has to be done righteously as Christ would do it. Daily companionship with the Holy Spirit will ensure that a person does not suffer from a lapse of judgment so that the work gets done as God has planned – no more, no less.

Self-denial turns one's attention to God. It's beneficial to take time out with God frequently in prayer and Bible meditation. Interacting with people is the testing ground for the Spirit's input into one's spiritual development. The recipients will have the benefit of your work and also the example to be seeking after God in their personal capacity. The profit from self-abasement is a permanent improvement in one's spiritual outlook. This addition will work to enhance one's approach when the next ministry opportunity beckons. The elation of each portion of gain is something that you can feel and taste that the Lord is good.

Any person that has agreed to become a disciple of Christ will never be so presumptuous as to expect God to fall in line with human fancies. The ardent follower realizes that they have to follow God's criteria. Procrastination is not buying time, but losing time because delays make the self-denial decision that much harder. Getting off the starting blocks will become progressively harder and harder after each failure. Moreover, the specific opportunity at that point in time will be lost. One may only pray that the Lord will be gracious to award another chance as a consolation prize.

The Father gave Jesus the glory because of his obedience and immaculate performance of his duties. God will honour us in due course (John 12:26) if we perform as Jesus desires. At best, it is a lower form of glory than what Jesus has but nevertheless very highly rated for the children of God. This prize ranks above all that the world can offer and it can't be purchased financially or obtained by any other means.

Holiness morals that are enmeshed in a person's spirit will glorify God to the world. Enoch walked with God (Genesis 5:24) and God took him away; Job was righteous and he feared God and abstained from sin; Daniel continued praying openly to God even after learning that the practice was punishable by death (Daniel 6:10); David was a man after God's own heart (1 Samuel 13:14). All these men were fully submitted to God and all their works were according to God's wishes. Self-denial helped them to keep in line with God and their names have been enshrined in Scripture forever. Their lives glorified God to the world. I don't know whether they struggled as much as we do today, but clearly, God occupied first place in their lives. We have so much ground to claw-back just to reach the stage where God is willing to be intimate with us and to impart the essential elements that will transform us. Then we still have to prove our spiritual metamorphosis through application before the principles become permanently grounded in our personality. A Christian is not considered as mature because of a lengthy period of belief after conversion, but rather by their high degree of sanctification. Thus, a relatively young Christian may be more mature than a believer who has been a Christian for decades. Self-worth alludes to self-esteem, and self-abasement implies respecting others first, especially God. The Lord works with people in a personal manner therefore we must reciprocate and give the Holy Spirit our undivided personal attention too.

Material distractions tend to make believers accept some of Jesus' words and ignore the ones that are objectionable. For instance, we like the words of salvation, forgiveness of sin, the love of God etc. but we filter the words relating to the beatitudes, storing up treasures in heaven, selling up everything to obtain the pearl of great value, loving your neighbour as yourself etc. When Jesus speaks of these morals, he refers to them in absolute terms, whereas we self-assess and limit our perception accordingly. This being the case; how hard is it then to become a person after God's own heart? We may profess self-abnegation and indeed earnestly desire it, and yet not grasp it in spirit. Self-deprecation is easily uttered, but no easy feat to perform. It's not going to disappear because every time we wish to advance in regeneration, the Spirit will make us face it squarely. Personal ideas cannot compete with God's wishes and something has to give in. It would be grossly unwise to persist in self-pursuit until death on earth because no eternal riches will be earned. You can't keep on vacillating on the fringes of self-abnegation as it does no spiritual good.

People have openly admitted that they sometimes choose to act on their own judgment instead of waiting upon God. This is a very perilous path to take when engaged in ministry. Self is brought to the fore and that is already the wrong way to approach ministry. A person's intention is the crucial factor that decides whether the outcome is good or bad. Sometimes, the worker has to interact with several locals in ministry. The secular activities demand so much time and the problems are connected to worldly considerations or personal matters. This situation can lead a ministry worker adrift whereby the Lord is unconsciously demoted to the back-burner. Compliance with work policy, meeting people's needs, treatment of relationships etc. requires planning and tactical approach. The time taken up in merely thinking about these things will cut into the quiet-time that ought to be set aside to be alone with Christ.

Intention dictates how a person's goals are met. There are objectives for every task that a worker has to perform, otherwise there is no accountability and it is not classified as work (more like a casual pastime). Once the goal is established, then a plan of action has to be worked out and put in place. Where several people are involved, the action-plan will require negotiation and a procedural approach that may be quite complex. If things don't go according to planned objectives, modifications will have to be made. All this requires a lot of time and effort and it occupies the mind. If a secular attitude is adopted, the task may turn into an obsession. It's a challenge to one's ability and the urge to show that one has the prowess to finish the job under personal intelligence and design is most attractive to self-image. Thus, an ordinary job becomes a personal quest, and the desire to show personal flair becomes a subconscious goal. The objective of the task becomes a personal win-lose scenario instead of a harmonious win-win situation for all to benefit in the ministry. The challenge becomes a hobby-horse. When people are faced with a personal challenge, the Lord will be compartmentalized into the metaphysical part of life and kept at a distance so that self is free to show-off its talent. There is a difference when a person is facing a deadline or a knotty problem and has to devote extra time to it. Once that specific issue is resolved, then the work flows on as usual. In this case, the desire for self-projection is limited. Rather, the employer wants you to prove that you are worth your salt.

Sadly, this sort of blunder happens in ministry as well. The culprit is self-will, and when a worker views any part of the work as a personal challenge, caution must be exercised as attention may very quickly be diverted away from the Lord. Amidst all the time spent in planning and design, it's easy to forget that this is God's work and not one's own. The extent of the error depends on how far the personal ideas have encroached on the Lord's plans. The danger point is when decisions are made based on only one set of criteria. Self-determination will cause a person to rationalize their decisions in a flawed manner and thus make some odd and silly decisions. The decision-maker may be embarrassed or reluctant to admit an error and adheres doggedly to their position. Personal ideas will conflict with concerned parties that have different views, and it becomes a tricky path to negotiate.

A dogmatic attitude is unhelpful as it rules out any consideration of the opposite party's views and this inevitably ends up with unfair treatment. People usual show consideration outwardly, but not give mental ascent to the opposite party's views. There will come a point where the parties concerned have worked themselves to the opposite ends of the scale and there's no way of reconciliation. Thus, one side has to withdraw from the relationship. Whether the intentions are good or bad, any exercise of self-will without waiting upon God is wrong and will lead to mistakes as there is no chance that the person will think/do exactly as God requires. Sometimes we may make our own decisions impulsively or unconsciously, but we are still morally bound to be circumspect about all that we do.

In the distant past, I used to ignore the Spirit's incitements and carry on my own merry way. I was happy to be leading my own lifestyle and enjoying myself. Now that I wish to have a deeper experience with the Spirit for renewal purposes, I want him to respond instantly, but this is not his modus operandi. I just have to wait patiently until he is ready to show me something. After a lot of practice and self-effacing, waiting on the Lord is not quite so frustrating. Doing things correctly the first time is far better than trying to fix mistakes due to poor judgement.

What hinders self-denial? We all know that answer but may be too afraid to tackle it. Its self-elevation, pride and self-importance, self-determination etc. and if these matters are not adequately addressed and corrected, that person will never be right with God. It's a confrontation between self and the Almighty. It's a no-contest, yet some battle to come to grips with this fact and they procrastinate. A nominal Christian will be saved by grace, but they will never have the substance that God values so highly in their personality if they don't exert themselves to attain maturity.

Self-abasement is merited in building relationships with others. It is a catalyst to forming sound progressive friendships. This is a give-and-take situation where all participants benefit as a whole. However, some participants may take advantage of a person's humility and this will create unfairness and bitterness. Self-denial does not preclude self-assertion and the injured party has to address this matter with the perpetrator. If there's no satisfactory resolution then it's better to walk away from that friendship otherwise relationship domination will be firmly established. All of God's morals are for strengthening and building up character and relationships and Christians have to apply themselves correctly in all situations.

Since we are attempting to move from inherent sin to righteousness, and Jesus is the only means to get there, it requires full subordination to him. Any trace of self-determination will disrupt the regeneration program and there will be a constant contest between the Spirit and personal preference. It's a waste of precious time and loss of opportunity to secure heavenly riches. Everybody has their own dilemma about self. It's freewill again, and the ball's in your court.

Reward.

The Bible mentions reward for work done in the kingdom of God. This will probably be something concrete such as a crown and a white robe (Revelations 3:11; 6:11), and it also warns not to allow anyone to take one's crown away, so there is a distinct possibility of losing it. However, in many passages, reward is not defined, so it may also be something abstract. In cases where the Father will honour or praise a faithful servant, it is somewhat obscure how these will work into the reward system and what effect they will have. Certainly, they will not be empty words because the awards will come from the Father. Recipients may be given a higher rank or greater responsibility. Whatever it is, it's going to be a prized item for the deserving because it extends recognition by the Father for the sacrifices they made and their obedience on earth. There won't be any form of envy or jealousy from the unrewarded people but respect instead.

All effort that follows God's will and is according to his plan qualifies for future reward. People cannot do works that are outside of

God's plan and expect a reward for their effort. These are unapproved activities and will be burned, otherwise everybody may merely introduce self-generated activities that they think are good and then expect God to give them a prize. God has set the blueprint before the world began and it cannot be changed. The Lord only acknowledges works done through obedience to his calling. Self-will has no effect and only God's sovereign will carries authority.

Greatness.

Those that adopt a servant attitude are in line for the highest commendation (Matthew 23:11). This is the guideline that Jesus had set all his life on earth and is the key for believers to attain honour in heaven. Matthew 18:4 states that greatness pertains to the humbleness of an innocent child. Adults need to step back and assume the meekness and innocence of a child that places complete trust in the Father. In order to do this properly, there are so many mental blockages to overcome, and most will only reach partial accomplishment (see Spiritual Child). These two disciplines are not mutually exclusive and a follower has to be a servant and to be guileless as a child in service. Honesty, integrity, transparency and impartiality are crucial in this approach.

Greatness is not a material prize but an open recognition of worth that God will bestow upon those that deserve it. It is some kind of title in heaven that will remain with the recipient forever. The disciples were vying for the top position (Luke 9:46-48), and this passage talks about the least being the greatest. Humility is the main ingredient as it relates to the lowest rank and the child concept. A worker has to assume the humblest attitude when serving in order to qualify for the top honour in heaven. A person that has served for over thirty years as the church secretary may find themselves in line for a far lesser award than the one who was doing menial ministry tasks for a far shorter time.

The disciples knew that Jesus was poor and had no earthly wealth, yet they recognized that his future kingdom was going to be majestic. Hence, they ranked spiritual honour above anything the world had to offer. They got it right and we ought to pay close attention. It is not easy for ordinary people to switch from the safety of financial abundance to the unseen and unquantifiable award in heaven called greatness. This takes a change of worldview and strong conviction, and it all depends on self-will.

Are you going for immediate gratification or delaying fulfilment until the establishment of the new heaven and new earth? The material things that are visible hold enormous sway against the future promised benefits. Most will defer to the immediate visible material choice because it's what we are accustomed to and it has value in society. The ones that choose to delay satisfaction must have sound faith to trust in the Lord to make good his word. Besides, we are not told what greatness actually is. This appears all too risky but it is due to weak faith and insufficient thought given to eternity. The fundamental problem is the habit and urge for self-provision and self-help, and trust is built on the wealth created from personal effort. It is necessary to earn a living on this earth, but this is only a temporary measure – until death.

God is in command of all souls and has the power to condemn a sinner to hell, so it's wise to trust him instead of self. If you are working towards going to heaven, then building up treasures there has to be the priority, otherwise you are severely short-changing yourself. Self-direction for whatever reason never works well with God and a believer has to work under God's terms.

Those that have a competitive urge in the secular sense, have an opportunity to direct their energies toward spiritual greatness and to seek after the praise of God rather than people. It's illogical that God would even want to save a wretched sinner and then to train them up; and for their obedience and effort, give them a reward and then exalt them to greatness! The short answer is that the Lord is willing to do so much because he loves us dearly. Then do we reciprocate by returning the same magnitude of love?

Luke 12:47-48 sounds a caveat to unfaithful servants that do not perform according to their capacity and capability. This passage talks about a manager that abuses his authority and neglects his duties, and this attitude is unacceptable and carries stern punishment. The uninformed servants will be shown leniency, but the knowledgeable ones that are negligent will be severely dealt with. Verse 48a affords some comfort in that servants that are honestly ignorant but have to fulfil a role will be treated lightly for their mistakes. Sometimes in ministry there's no suitable candidate and someone has to do that job, so the most competent person gets picked. At that point, they are excused for their under-performance. However, should they gain a better awareness of their duties (responsibilities) and still render shoddy work, then they will fall foul of verse 47. This is more acute where there is a better qualified servant available and willing to step into that role but is prevented from doing so. Accountability is no trifling matter as far as the Lord is concerned and we have to respect that with due consideration. A worker can only get away with honest ignorance for a short time because the work will reveal the responsibilities and accountability issues. An unfit worker that insists on staying in the job will disappoint the Lord through sub-standard production.

Despite having a clear understanding of their role, they follow their own desires and methodology. Servanthood demands faithful adherence to the Lord's instructions and good workmanship. One ought to bear in mind at all times that this is the Lord's work and not one's own, and there is no place for independent self-directed management and self-determined standards of the results. You are not your own boss and ultimately, we are all accountable to our supreme Designer.

Furthermore, workers will be judged according to the grade of the office (verse 48b). The general tenor of this passage concerns rank. It conveys the notion that the higher a worker is promoted, the greater the responsibility. There is no margin for ignorance or incompetence at this level. The Lord will demand a specific standard of output and if this not met then the worker will be guilty of non-performance and punishment will marked for the future. If one is doing the right thing and walking closely with Jesus, then there's nothing to be worried about. The worker will collect all the related information and put in place all the required procedures so that the job will be done just as Christ would have.

This is a warning for workers not to shirk their responsibilities the higher they advance in ministry. The simple way to stay healthy is to be obedient to the letter because God cannot demand more than what he has instructed a servant to do. By staying close to the Spirit, there's nothing to fear in taking on more responsibility. Complacency, status, peer-approval and secular habit can derail a sincere servant's aspirations; these are the trappings of the secular world. However, all snares can be overcome through obedience and the willingness to do the job properly. Renown Christians have achieved prominent works in the past which shows that everything is doable in the light of loyalty to God. Watch out for egotism and self-will.

In the secular environment, abiding by the normal convention, rules and regulations will be deemed as sufficient discharge of responsibility because God has put that government in place (Romans 13:1). The governing body (private sector or government) has rules that all the registered participating entities have to comply with. Religious organizations are not exempt and the administrator in charge must find out what the requirements are and organize their work so as to facilitate the reports specified by that external body. The standard presentation is for all businesses concerned and Christian organizations must realize that ignorance of the law is no excuse, and they must comply like everyone else. If the rules and accepted convention are not being followed, then the person in charge must be made aware. Work that was incorrectly done must be corrected accordingly because the same rules apply to all relevant business entities. Standardisation is a good thing as long as the requirement does not meddle with ministry goals and procedures. A ministry that meets the highest secular standards glorifies God to the outside world. Jesus said to give to Caesar what is due to Caesar.

Christians ought to think carefully before assuming greater responsibility. Each level of office in ministry carries commensurate responsibility. You have to cautiously assess whether you have the capability to meet the work standard that is required. Then you have to do the work accurately. When the Lord calls, he will provide the means to prepare the person for the task. The usual way is to learn from the outgoing officer, attend a refresher course and on the job training. If God calls, then that person is the most suitable for the position. Moses had grave doubts about his ability to lead Israel out of Egypt, but God made him realize that he was right for that assignment. His mind probably didn't register the enormity of the responsibility of heading a nation, and God expected so much of him. According to the passage in Luke, much more will be demanded of such a great undertaking. His secret was that he walked closely with God and he was obedient apart from his error at the waters of Meribah (Numbers 20:12). The Lord expects top leadership to do exactly as instructed. Moses did not honour God when he struck the rock and this simple error cost him the privilege of entering the promised land. God led Moses and trained him on the job. As long as he was obedient, he had no fear of the mounting responsibility and hardships as they moved towards Canaan.

Jesus, the disciples and Paul had burdensome tasks, but they never complained. They all performed their duties to the best of their ability.

They put God first and self was a non-issue, so self-direction had no influence on their work and on God's plans. They gave up their freewill in exchange for God's will, and the church grew. The growing onus of accountability never scared them as they were fully confident of their trust in the Lord and their compliance with his instructions. Self-will is the cause of friction with God (and others) and there will be a reckoning one day. Increased responsibility is not to be feared or avoided as the Holy Spirit will direct us in the correct manner and everything will fall into place because he is the architect and we are merely the agents to fit the puzzle together. There is no fear before God when everything is done faithfully and accurately. The Holy Spirit will make the hardest things and highest responsibilities so easy. It is you that will make things hard for yourself.

The same reasoning applies to any worldly office that a Christian occupies because it must be carried out righteously. Impeccable moral and ethical standards reflect the goodness of God to the outside world. There are so many temptations when money and power is at stake. By keeping Jesus as the head and inappropriate secular behaviour out, the work will be done satisfactorily. God demands the same standard of behaviour in whatever work the Christian does and there are no double-standards. The issues mentioned in this section have a bearing on the quality of a worker's output. The task must be carried out in earnest and done properly because God will inspect all our work.

Exaltation.

God will praise the humble (Matthew 23:12; Luke 14:11). It may be related to status in heaven. Humility is the means for the servant to achieve greatness that the Lord acclaims. The conditions are (Philippians 2:5-9):

- Servanthood
- Humility
- Condescension
- Obedience
- Surrender of personal rights

Praise and recognition will come in due course. It may happen in this life but that will only be a glimpse of the real thing to come in eternity. Exaltation in heaven will be the most sought-after honour that Christians would want. This will be like seeking attention from your boss that you greatly respect. Even a smile or a gesture of approval will be enough to send you into orbit. Attention will be fixed on the Lord all the time just to get him to notice you. Praise from the Lord for humble service will be so exhilarating for the recipient and that would make them so happy. God will honour the humble worker and pay them with an elevation of status that they did not have on earth.

Luke 17:10 describes the reality of the employer/employee relationship. The master would not invite his servant to sit and eat with him but will ask to be waited upon. Afterwards he would not thank the servant for doing his job and carrying out all his instructions faithfully. The same analogy applies to kingdom servants. Whatever task we are called to do, it must be done properly as any competent employee would. Commendation is inappropriate because the servant is merely doing what ought to be done. It's so obvious. Jesus warned of these anomalies because Christians may get their perception of their roles wrong. It's the old-self within that seeks attention, and followers must be cautious when serving in the Lord's work. Popularity may tempt workers to desire favours that are self-elevating and out of good taste.

The employer/employee convention is standard practise all over the world. The worker does the job satisfactorily and gets paid for their effort and both parties are happy. If the work is done in good faith with humility, serving others before self and is devoid of pride, then the Lord will exalt that servant. For most believers, kingdom work is unpaid service and humility and servanthood fit in well. Where possible, ministry work is usually done free of charge because it is an offering to the Lord. If it's a modestly paid employment, the services may still be viewed as a gift to God. However, if the remuneration rises above the average wage in the secular sense, then ministry competes according to worldly standards. If ministry is compensated by a lucrative salary then the services are no longer a freewill offering to God. There must be due caution taken when a high rate of pay for ministry work competes on secular principles. In certain cases, this may lend the worker to temptations that hurt their regeneration. Is the worker's loyalty solely to God or would it be swayed by financial gain? True servanthood means working in a low status position as Jesus demonstrated with the foot-washing.

Sincerely humble servants wouldn't even think of wanting praise or acknowledgement for their work. The exaltation from our Father will be a rapturous bonus apart from everything else. The absence of boasting about personal achievement and position; serving in the low and un-esteemed facet of kingdom work; placing others needs before self; humility and self-deprecation will stand you in good stead for favour in the Lord's sight. Turning attention away from self attracts the Lord's eye and he will turn his attention to you. You don't have to draw attention to self because the Lord will come to you in due course. God's secret wisdom that was destined for our glory before time began and is now given to the mature (1 Corinthians 2:6-7). This glory is from God and is another form of honour given to the humble persistent follower. All these gifts from the Lord are designed to build up to the great honour that awaits in heaven. The Lord makes the obscure worker stand out by giving them particular insight. Others will notice this immediately and all may benefit by sharing in that wisdom. Jesus was given the highest position in heaven at the right hand of God. This is motivation for us to imitate Christ because there's a lot at stake in terms of personal spiritual gain. The secrets of God will be given to the mature follower because they have travelled with Jesus faithfully and consistently. It is really for your own enrichment because you exalt God and he will praise you accordingly. It's a two-way thing. God had thought about our development long before our first thought for him.

Outcome.

Humility in the servant's heart brings reward, greatness and praise from our Father. It is the stand out characteristic that all believers ought to acquire. The greatest quality is love. However, the two go together: if you show love, you will be humble and vice versa. Humility is an indivisible part of agape that will enable a person to willingly make the great sacrifices. We may think that we are doing God a big favour by surrendering what we consider precious, but nobody can do God any favours. We are just doing ourselves a kindness by following his lead. Moreover, if the work is performed accurately, the Lord will praise the worker for it, and that is unmerited grace to unwarranted servants. This shows the value of obedience to God and the glory that awaits the servant that has done well.

Self-abasement has an important part to play in this harmonious whole. Never be satisfied with mediocrity in pursuit of humility; if you are, then God will treat you likewise. It will vastly diminish your rating in greatness. Craving earthly wealth is viewed as carnal, foolish and useless; craving heavenly treasure has no restriction, and is seen as godly, wise and enduring.

Seeking God's favour preclude executive self-will because the tasks have to be performed to conform with his standard. It means that God has sovereign command and disciples have no choice but to comply with his requirements.

Chapter 34
Self-help

Counsellors use self-help techniques to improve people's wellbeing. Self-help, also called 'early learning' starts with toddlers and children and goes right up to adults. There are various life skills that have to be learnt at different stages of life. Young children need instruction on dressing themselves, feeding, personal hygiene, safety precautions etc. This helps them to become independent, and it nurtures personal identity. Along with this comes self-confidence and that is essential for appropriate metal development as they progress to adulthood. Grown-ups have so much to learn in life and personal experience may be fulfilling or costly.

One of the most common places where self-help is encountered is at university and other institutions of higher education. Students have to teach themselves in preparation for the exams and do their own research. The aim is to train and equip thinkers that will contribute to the future of society by way of innovation, skills development, implementing improvements and always searching for progressive benefits. There are also many individuals in the world that have not had tertiary education and have been incredibly successful. These are the masters of self-help because they are visionaries that are self-driven, and they won't stop until they achieve their objective. Failure is merely a delay and not a sign for discontinuation.

In western society, depression and anxiety plague certain individuals. Suffers need to train themselves to handle negative emotions, anger, embarrassment, different types of pressure scenarios and awkward situations. The matter may be approached as a confrontation or retreat. Mental wellbeing is only achieved through handling those problems successfully. Defeat may regress to a position where fear, helplessness and discouragement takes over the mind each time that situation appears. Counsellors can only go so far, and the sufferer must implement such measures to contain those personal hang-ups and improve their lifestyle.

Self-help from the spiritual perspective encompasses all those procedures that an individual must put in place in order to enlist the Lord's initiative in fellowship. The Bible doesn't provide details about God's particular conditions or how to go about reaching that favourable status with him and it's up to the individual to explore and secure it. I must fit in with God's criteria and not vice versa. Even Jesus never mentioned the detail that people must apply in order to get close to the Father. What's the secret? General statements are contained in various parts of Scripture, and I will go through a few that have a bearing on my rhetoric.

The assumption that God is always right points to the premise that humans have the wrong perception of self. We tend to rank the material concerns of self above our spiritual connection with God. All our material habits have to be placed a distant second behind our spiritual development with Jesus. Grace should not be misinterpreted and the Lord will not settle for erratic behaviour and insincere effort. Business with God is by far more important than all the material things that we have ever done in our entire lives for our own wellbeing because God's dynamic input into one's spirit is beyond valuation. Only God can initiate spiritual insight in his unique way.

Self-help is doing the required things that manifest your intention to be obedient to God. The desire to be fettered to the Lord must be true and fervently demonstrated. The Spirit's initiative will bring one of life's greatest joys. Self-motivation is demonstrating your sincerity to the Lord. It is essential that you manifest your interest because God won't just give his wisdom away for nothing.

Spiritual self-help is different from the secular concept. The objective is not to result in psychological improvement, enhanced self-confidence, self-assertiveness or self-interest. Rather, it is to awaken God's interest in you. The emphasis changes from self to Jesus, and it is he that grows one's spiritual life. Naturally, the impartation of wisdom works in sync with regeneration. The Holy Spirit's enlightenment enables a believer to grow into a spiritual intellectual. It's a refinement of personality from the ordinary to a constructive tool in God's service (Isaiah 49:2-3). Spiritual advancement is mandatory and Christians have to align their lives in this vein.

Self-encouragement is not intended to boost self-esteem or ego as in the worldly sense. The purpose is to make a difference in Christ. It's aimed at setting up the right standing in partnership with Jesus. We must assume the correct position because we are the minor partner that doesn't have the resources or capability take on the lead role. My job is to learn from him and excel in spirit.

Self-help draws a person nearer to the Spirit and is not intended to make a person independent of God. This dependence will never fall away even after a believer has attained spiritual maturity. It is only at this happy stage that a person understands that independence or departing from God is totally insane and extremely dangerous.

Drawing near to God is a commitment that sets the companionship process in motion. One way of going about it is to embrace the marriage concept in Ezekiel 23 and Hosea 4. This is the benchmark that Christians must adhere to. The Lord treats his partnership with a believer very sternly and stringently. This is no trifling matter and it must be clearly defined in your mind so that you can consistently put the important spiritual things of God first.

The allegory in Ezekiel 23 describes Israel's alliances with the Assyrians as prostitution that breaks relationship with God. These vile acts were ordinary secular things that any normal person would do in developing social (strategic) relations with others. However, they were done in disobedience to the Lord's commands. Material actions affect one's spiritual standing with God. Friendship with God's enemies makes Israel an enemy of God. They had forgotten their allegiance to God and became attracted to the world. The Bible equates these associations as lewdness and prostitution that had grave consequences for Israel. It's a betrayal of trust that was grossly vexing to the Lord. Even their children that belong to God have been introduced and given over to idolatry. It's a direct infringement on God's personal domain. Forming close links with the unjust is akin to men sleeping with prostitutes. Such adultery makes Israel guilty as though they had killed other people, for which they had to be punished.

Hosea 4 speaks of similar accusations of adultery and prostitution. It highlights the fact that prostitution is founded in the spirit that gives rise to unfaithfulness and leads a person away from God. It also mentions physical infidelity with harlots and shrine prostitutes. The leaders that form unsavoury treaties with the ungodly love shameful ways more than they love the Lord. The nation follows their leaders and perpetuate the wrong that makes the entire nation guilty. These lessons are for all Christians to take note of and to avoid. They are just as relevant to us today and apply directly to our personal fellowship with Christ. We have to think very carefully about what we are doing and how that affects our standing with God.

Marriage between a man and a woman is mentioned right in the early days after creation week. The man ought to leave his parent's home and make a new life with his wife because they are a united pair. They have an obligation to behave as a single unit with both partners working towards mutual benefit. This is a special partnership because God views them as a single entity. Marriages can go wrong because of sin, but most couples get it right. Same-sex marriages are excluded because the Word of God specifically states that this is between a man and a woman.

Newly-marrieds have to adjust and make allowances for their partner's habits and lifestyle. Mutual cooperation, acceptance and understanding will normally straighten out all or most of the disputed areas. A Christian marriage develops best on a level playing field.

If there are no irreconcilable differences, normally the love and affection that grows over time will overcome the obstacles and the marriage will succeed. However, this union brings male and female together that have different value systems, habits, background and possibly culture. Self-determination is a major obstacle if it is not appropriately worked out into the union. I'm assuming a Christian marriage that is based on equality, fairness and mutual respect.

Self-will in my opinion is the primary marriage breaker apart from marriages that just happened without due consideration to compatibility, long term viability and the motivation to do everything to save the union. Mutual agreement and a willingness to compromise will normally repair the solvable inconsistencies. However, persistent selfish desires and a dogmatic mindset will keep eroding the teamwork until it ends in divorce. Ambition that devalues the principles of a successful marriage will be driven by its core value of self-centeredness and self-satisfaction.

Normal couples will try hard to keep their marriage and there may be certain sacrifices that they have to make. Some habits that they were accustomed to prior to marriage may no longer be practical or they have to be acutely adjusted. Both parties must be satisfied as to the progress. Instances where one spouse has to give in disproportionately to the other ought to be mutually agreed on. Unusual circumstances may necessitate such action, but it requires both spouses consent and acceptance as to its fairness. This demands a selflessness that is willing to sacrifice for the good of the union.

In regard to our spiritual marriage to Christ, we come under scrutiny by God. The criteria that he requires cannot be altered in any way. They are easily comprehensible, but often equally easily broken too. The blame is never with God. I must admit that as a male, I find this marriage concept very strange. The conflict comes about because of my misconception of the physical institution of marriage that I'm trying to match with the spiritual integration with God. There's nothing odd here because the human spirit is created by God and is part of God.

In keeping with drawing near to God, a believer must be self-restrained. Biological marriage is a guide to our behaviour in spiritual marriage. This cannot be handled as inconsiderately as people do in biological marriages. This is a far higher mandate because God cannot accept anything lower than his decree. If you're felt that you have striven hard to preserve your earthly marriage, then you must be prepared to exert even greater effort to please God. For those who are single, it may be simpler to comply because there is no spouse to please and responsibility to care for children. On the other hand, some singles still have young children to raise and that may be a setback to developing their marriage to Christ. Either way, we are all so very dependent on God in one way or another.

Prostitution is breaking faith with God. Spiritual adultery is far worse than biological adultery because it leads to spiritual death. We must do all of those things that keep us married to Christ in its purest form. People talk of wanting to be like Christ and they may have different views of what this really means to them. However, a person can only become more like Jesus by being unconditionally bound to him in the first place, and to stay that way forever. The Lord will not impart his precious companionship on a temporary basis. A person cannot expect God to deliver spiritual blessing upon request only to wander off to pursue self-interest and then return to God and expect more goodness. This is not in keeping with the true nature of faithfulness. Self-will must give in to God's will.

Responsible adults nurture love in their biological marriage and they will uphold high moral standards in their behaviour. The marriage may go through many trials, but the husband and wife remain faithful to each other. The benefit of the relationship is such that they won't do anything to jeopardise the bond. Temptations come and go, but fidelity remains intact. It requires firm belief and a willingness to forego selfish pleasures, economic gain, self-elevation, personal desires and many other things that lure a person into sin.

God's approach to his spiritual marriage to believers carry even greater responsibility. People over-value their biological marriage and pay lesser attention to their spiritual ties with the Father. Spiritual greatness will never to attained if Jesus is not posited above all. An aid to this goal is to think of everything that we do in regard to righteousness. Our worldly conditioning and pressures in life make it very easy to decide against the high moral ground. Rash decisions and negligence ought not to be treated casually. Everything must be done to preserve the marriage symbolism to God. If you are so good at keeping your earthly marriage, then why can't you be successful in your spiritual counterpart? This is not a biological union where you have equal authority with the Lord. God demands absolute faithfulness in this respect and he sets the criteria. This is a dependent partnership and a believer has no choice but to comply. There is no right to self-determination in a marriage to God. The spiritual marriage allegory is another way of impressing upon us the importance of having an unswerving bond with Christ that bolsters our status as fully adopted children of God. The essence behind the marriage is being impregnably locked to the Lord in spirit.

In his human form on earth, Jesus was married to God in spirit. It is what all believers have to do in this life. Jesus was inextricably bound to the Father, and it is clearly shown by all that he did on earth. To be like Jesus is to know the Father just as intimately as he did. With God, everything is possible. Jesus told Philip that anyone who has seen Jesus has seen the Father. This obviously is not referring to the physical form, but to the spiritual. It is borne out by the fact that the disciples did not recognise Jesus in his new spiritual body. If Jesus' earthly body had truly looked like God, then there would be no reason to have a changed physical appearance in the new spiritual body. Outward appearances are irrelevant and it is Jesus' spirit before and after that was united with the Father and it will never change. Philip had to apply his spiritual eyes to see God.

Christ reflected the image of God to perfection. He went on to say that it is the Father living in him, who is doing his work. Since the Father is Spirit, we must be concentrating on our spiritual nature to relate to God. To be like Jesus is to have the Father living in you and for him to do his work directly in you and to attain his purposes through your resources and outworking. Jesus had no problems with obedience, but we struggle with it to no end. Business with the Lord demands meticulous care and dedication and this is proof of a person's authenticity. On-going minor careless errors may lead to a stall in fellowship. When multiple matters vie for our attention, it's simple to neglect giving God due attention. It's no surprise that he reacts likewise. The follower is always under scrutiny and this is a good thing to keep in mind at all times as it will remind you to choose wisely. Secularism has entrenched a state of ambivalence in the Christian mind. It is our Christian duty to realign our habits in favour of God.

In simple terms, self-help is to do everything in one's ability that achieves righteousness and maturity in sanctification. Spiritual regeneration is a human being's predominant asset that must be exploited to the fullest. It's never easy, but the pay-off is beyond measure. It is incorrect to applying material standards to spiritual matters and this must be kept firmly in check. Regular introspection will maintain consistency and stability in doing what is right when facing controversy.

After all the necessary personal action is taken, self-help finds its termination point. This is when the Spirit takes control and works his way in your spirit. From this point onwards, God-help takes over. All you have to do is maintain faithfulness and strengthen your new habits in righteousness. Always do what is right. The focus must be fully on the Spirit. Any reservations will just give the evil one fuel to disrupt your advancement. Vacillation between self and the Holy Spirit will indicate a break in goodwill towards Jesus and the lack of sincerity.

A believer has to work relentlessly to overcome self, only to give it all over to the Lord. It's a contradiction in terms that has been caused by sin, but from God's perspective this is a necessity and not an option. The secular driven self is your own enemy in denying you a progressive prolific spiritual life in Christ.

If you have sincerely placed Jesus first in your life and by implementing all the right actions, he has no choice but to respond to you. The Christian status is a privilege not a right because it comes solely by invitation at God's discretion, therefore a sound relationship can only develop on God's terms. The spirit is the real training ground and the flesh has no significance. The flesh does not dictate the terms of engagement with the Spirit. The cohort of the flesh is self-will.

One of the exciting occurrences is when the Holy Spirit enables you to see outside of the box (Psalm 19:7, Proverbs 2:6). God initiates the communication of fresh ideas in ways that you never thought of before. The Spirit brings momentum to your spiritual understanding and he keeps delivering fresh ideas. The beauty of this status is the confidence that you are right with God. Nothing else matters in life. This is the best form of assurance of salvation because you know that God trusts you with the finer spiritual matters that are specific to you. The divine prompts will not be flowing continuously, but they will be there when you need it. We must be constantly dependent on the Lord and waiting for him to lead. This makes us eligible for a great inheritance as children of God.

In John 20:17 Jesus relates his humanity to all believers in that Christ has the same God and Father as we have. It conveys deep sentiment to those who have gained an acceptable degree of spiritual growth and affinity with Christ. The words take on a meaning that strikes at the core of one's spirit. The Almighty is Father to all who belong to Christ. God recognises me personally as a child of his own. This lofty honour of being extricated from sin and placed in holiness as a recognised child of God comes with a correspondingly onerous moral obligation. I must behave in a way that glorifies God. The Lord views parents, siblings, children, grand-children and all humanity as equal. However, those that have nurtured a finer state of sanctification will be closer to the Father in keeping with Christ who is the closest person to the Father.

Everyone has to place biological ties last and tether their spirit to Jesus Christ first and foremost. There is no alternative and I must do what has to be done. If I do not choose correctly, then the reality of the Father's presence will only be an illusion. To get the ball rolling, it must start with a person's basic regeneration and progress to higher levels. God has not deliberately made it hard for us; we are just too far removed from his holiness.

Joseph died at an early age. It was probably part of God's plan. The Bible does not tell of Jesus referring to Joseph as his father. As a child, Jesus would have addressed Joseph as father, but not in later years. Most probably Joseph taught him his trade and the normal worship practices that Jewish families adhered to. On the other hand, Jesus said that he does everything that the Father instructs. All his spiritual intelligence came from God. Jesus never had an intimate spiritual relationship with Joseph as it is not mentioned in Scripture, but he and his Father were inseparable. Christians have a strong relationship with their biological parents, but why is it not the same with our heavenly Father?

The compelling words from Jesus to his disciples are not to call anyone on earth as father because we only have one Father in heaven (Matthew 23:9). There is no mistaking that God is our only spiritual Father through spiritual birth. He was never meant to be a biological Father because he is Spirit. Therefore, a person's spirit was born from the Father's Spirit. Our true father is the Creator-Father. This may be very hard for some Christians to accept, especially those that have strong family bonds. When we meet in heaven, those that have objectively pursued God as Father and matured in their personality will be greatly elated, while those that have not put in sufficient effort will feel dreadfully ashamed. All their time and effort were misplaced in their biological ties and self-discretion is to blame because the Bible is very clear on this matter.

Blood relatives are still family and Exodus 20:12 commands us to honour our father and mother. You as a Christian must respect your parents and call them father and mother but you are not to place them, family, wife, children or even yourself above or equal with God. The Creator ranks above the creation and every soul on earth and beyond belongs to him, and he must be worshipped and obeyed explicitly. Nobody owns you except God and he is also your Father. In certain cultures, the father figure has absolute power over his children. However, this is the wrong approach because it ignores the spiritual connotations. The same applies to any business situation, employer and master relationship. The debtor may owe the lender a huge sum of money, but they don't have any right to their spiritual faculties of faith and worship. God's spiritual laws supersede all material and created things and the judgment will apply fairly to every soul.

Jesus abides in us and he reveals the Father directly to the individual. This is not mere theoretical knowledge and is a real personal experience. Jesus will continue to provide us with fresh inspiration from our Father so that his love will be firmly established in our spirit. The reality is authentic and I have to keep it alive and growing. Once a person has tasted the goodness from God, internal momentum will drive development forward.

The question arises as to one's biological responsibilities. Family, spouse must never be allowed a position ahead of the Father. God is not insensitive and he will not ask a person to do something inhumane. The case of God's command for Abraham to sacrifice Isaac will never happen to anybody these days. He had proved that biological relations did not rank above God and he found great favour with the Lord. I doubt whether that has ever been or ever will come another like Abraham. He was called God's friend (James 2:23) but we still have to get there.

This bonding with the Father is the highest honour conferred upon the saved on this earth and it is a personal matter that you will preserve in your heart and treasure for all eternity. It takes great resolve to keep companionship with Jesus on an upward trajectory. You're got to do what you got to do.

When you think that you have everything under control, self-will makes a wrong decision which you will earnestly regret afterwards, yet it repeats itself in the future. It's vital not to desensitise your attitude towards God. God owns your soul and he will force you to surrender on his terms (Isaiah 45:23). On that day, everyone will know that the personal-will that they depended on so heavily and valued so highly on earth was one big joke compared with God's will. All self-confidence will be destroyed and self will be completely powerless and defenceless before the Lord. The puny and baseless pride and every material thing that a person treasured so greatly on earth will disappear in a puff of smoke. The triumph of God's wisdom over secular human wisdom will be final. Embarrassment, shame and stupidity will be evident all over the disobedient soul. The choice in this life is rudimentary, and God helps those that help themselves. We often pray for God to be with us or to draw nearer to us, but this is putting the cart before the horse. If I endeavour to constantly pursue God, then he will automatically reciprocate without even having to ask. Christianity is not mere ritual; it is a vibrant two-way companionship.

Chapter 35
The road ahead

God makes all the management decisions for the faithful and he directs a person's path in life. It's not something new or strange as the majority of Christians already pray for his will to be done in their daily lives. Obedience is mandatory and Adam's mistake in the garden ought never to be repeated. The Father's directions are incidental to life and easier to comply with as a person matures. It is an escalation of faith to the point where it is immune to any attack. One's trust in Christ is unshakable. Self-determination can never be part of Christian life, and most of us are on this learning curve. The few that have attained self-denial are to be envied as they have a special place in God's favour.

Christians are left with elementary freewill to carry out the Father's wishes according to their own vogue, flair and preferences. They may be as creative as they wish but the management instructions cannot be altered in any manner or form. We are trusted friends of Jesus who know our Father's business and we pledge our allegiance entirely to him. Jesus appointed us to bear eternal fruit, and in return our Father will bless us abundantly. This gracious honour ought to be grasped and fully exploited. Submission brings free and unfettered fellowship with God. Jesus promotes his disciples from servants to friends and this depicts an advanced stage of fellowship. The servant implication is still relevant but this promotion is more for those that are advancing in spiritual maturity and responsibility. It will be insolent for an untrained Christian to think that they will be promoted to a higher standing with God without putting in the effort to get there. There's no free lunch even in the metaphysical, apart from the cross. Preparation, availability and commitment are our responsibility. The multi-role nature of Christian life must be understood and correctly applied to the Father's satisfaction.

The everlasting fruit must be fixed in our character first and this is driven by humility and servanthood. This fruit may then be used to encourage other believers that they may grow as well. It also helps new converts that are hungry for the Word that they may learn from you and then establish their own crop in their spiritual lives. God wants his children to produce abundant fruit and it is the counter-balance to the proliferation of sin in the world. It demonstrates the power of God that godliness will flourish against overwhelming odds.

God desires quality children who are spiritually trained in righteousness that is grounded in their character. He is interested in your personal development and spiritual wellbeing, and he will make his business known to you in due course. For this reason, it is preferable to develop to a certain level of maturity before taking on kingdom work so that you may gain the maximum from all spiritual lessons that may be obvious or hidden in the work. Effort must be put into personal development first, so that our Father may use us effectively in his work. I think that the majority of new believers are already doing this when they first believed. Fresh hungry faith ought to drive them to learn more of Christ and be led by the Spirit to develop in wisdom and in stature. Good habits are readily established at the outset but they must be nurtured and perpetuated. Quality in spirit comes before the work but this is not always possible. High quality Christians will always obey God unquestioningly and perform satisfactorily. Jesus proved this categorically when he prepared himself all his life for Father's work but only spent his final two years in public ministry.

Maturity in sanctification is the ultimate desire for a believer. It only happens when we surrender management freewill over to God because only he has the authority to sanctify a soul after his likeness. The Lord teaches and imparts his holiness to whoever he chooses. There can be no trace, not even the slightest hint of self-determination because God will not share his glory with anybody. God does all the renewal work and self has no claim in any respect. Our task is to learn to live with elementary freewill in a manner that will enable the Spirit's teachings to advance our sanctification to the full. The regenerated spirit in holiness will complement the image of God inherent in all the saved. The spirit world can see very distinctly the holiness that reinforces the image of God in all believers. It will be a personal joy to be a walking-living advertisement that reflects the glory of God to the outsiders. They will see God's representation in our countenance. The ones that have made significant strides in their renewal will be given the recognition that they deserve. All the promises that Jesus uttered about treasures in heaven will be realized. It will be a materialisation of faith in the unseen, that will become palpable.

Self-direction is a bad tendency that humankind should never have taken on. This is abnormal because the Lord made us to be God-dependent. Returning to the Lord now is alien to our fallen nature and extremely uncomfortable to do. Bad genes can harden a person's heart so much that they become totally unresponsive to God. Notwithstanding what God does to help, they will never accept him as Lord. However, those who fear God will know the value of sanctification, and they have the opportunity to surrender their destiny to him and follow in his holiness.

Christians must go back to their roots in Adam to recognize Adam's error in choosing self-direction at the temptation. This time it's making the right choice and inviting the Holy Spirit to help them learn to reconnect with their heavenly Father. It's a sober reminder that self-will is your biggest antagonist because it is attracted to carnality and self-indulgence. However, there's no need to be psychotic about this because the earnest seeker will find favour with the Holy Spirit. Giving up freewill is well and truly a small cost in return for merit from God, eternal treasure, maturity, real freedom from sin and to live with our Father forever. It will rid you of the secular self that prefers to do evil. True freewill in righteousness will prevail once your tenacious quandary has been brought under control. The happiness of carnality will be debunked by the incomparable joy that only godliness is entitled to. Freewill to practice holiness is humankind's authentic natural state and is the true objective and not the freewill to sin. The quest for Christ is only as hard as you make it.

For the regenerate, the commandments of Jesus are not oppressive. People that are born of God in spirit will have victory over the carnal nature to obey the Lord's commands. The Spirit gives the believer the power to overcome self-indulgence which is really the worst temptation. Although all people born of God have the power to avoid sin, it still depends on the individual's resolve to desire and pursue holiness. The spiritually savvy have the mind of Christ that keeps on wanting more of Jesus and none of the world. Those of us that are struggling to grow can take comfort in role models that have achieved more. They may urge us on, but it's the Holy Spirit that gives permanent benefits.

Jesus asked Peter three times: Do you love me? Peter was hurt as he had already demonstrated deep regret. It may be deliberate as Peter had denied Jesus three times as well. I'm not surprised because self-will is such a formidable opponent to God's will. The Lord may be asking us in the same manner. We should also feel hurt but at the same time be moved with determination to prove our loyalty. Firm action has to be demonstrated otherwise there won't be any improvement. Sometimes, we need God to ask us more than three times and pray that his grace will stretch that much further.

John 21:18 is relevant as we know that an immature Christian may still be wayward, but aspiring believers will be led by the Spirit to places where they do not want to go and to perform tasks that do not suit their taste or emotions. Such is the nature of servanthood. I'm glad to have done my time on the field and also discovered the Lord's in-breaking into my spiritual life. This assures me that my calling was right, in addition, the increase in my faith, joy and confidence made it all the more worthwhile. I mentioned unequivocally to my colleagues on several occasions that the Lord is with me, and I'm so glad that he has continued to refresh me. I must be doing certain things right.

It may seem anomalous that freewill goes against the Creator who bestowed it in the first place. This really looks like he is shooting himself in the foot. Freewill was good in its original holy form, but Satan shifted the focus to self-determination. God created humans with righteous freewill and it will never be taken away. There will be sanctified self-will in heaven and it will be a dependent-will. Holiness places a mandatory limit on secondary freewill because there will be no sin, and therefore no other choice. Heavenly dwellers will have no need for executive, sovereign, management or directive freewill because there won't be any more to gain for self after the judgment. Father will care for each person equally and fairly. Sanctified self-will will exist under God's will and be for enjoyment and fellowship purposes. The spiritual family of God will be unblemished and agape will rule in every heart. Harmonisation will bring joy to all. Self-determination only came about because it was introduced by a third party. This will never happen again in heaven. There will be no outside temptation. Besides, Adam and Eve will be there as a permanent reminder of the catastrophic consequences of rebellion.

There will be no executive freewill and personal rights will not be an issue in heaven. People will only have dependent-will because our eternal existence will rely entirely on the Father. The human rights privilege that we value so highly on earth will not exist in heaven as there will be no trace of selfishness because everybody will be humble and caring for the other's needs before self. The spiritual harmony will be immaculate. Father will set all the procedures in place and one will have the freedom to live in holiness, just as Adam did before the fall. There is perfect freedom in righteousness. In fact, nobody would want to step out of line or even think of leaving heaven. It will be the ultimate utopia because there will be no other place to go. Everyone will exercise mutual care and selflessness. It will be a united family that shares fairly in all the wonders of heaven. It may sound overly courteous but Father will be immediately available to clear up any uncertainty so there won't be any doubt or misunderstanding.

The mind of Christ will be available to all and fellowship will be true, open and unbroken. Holiness will prevail and there will be nothing to hide. Privacy will not have the prohibitive constraints as on earth because everything will be open and there will be no need for it as there is no sin. Dwellers will feel the presence and security of Father and be able to communicate with him at any time and place. The angels in heaven have been living like this since they were created and they are only messengers of God. Children of God will have higher status and greater freedom to enjoy the eternal pleasures. The erroneous thinking and temptations that we have on earth will not exist. Members will be able to do anything because everything will be holy including all people's intentions, emotions and actions. Freewill will be replaced by dependent-will and it will be there only to do righteousness.

Furthermore, the childlike nature will be accurately displayed in each person and our Father will protect and provide for all his family. We will be just too happy to have a Father that cares so much for us. Competition will not exist because we won't have to prove anything about ourselves or attempt to better our status in any way. There will be no cause to be boastful and sports activities will be only for recreation and enjoyment. The notion of the biological family will disappear and be replaced by the spiritual family of God. Each person will be a child of the Father. Those family members that looked like their parents on earth will never look the same as they did on earth. Instead, each person will look like the image of God in a spiritual context. The new spiritual body will look very different from its earthly form. Likewise, those in hell will not be recognizable to us either and they will look more like Satan because the image of God will be eternally removed from them. They will be forced to follow after their master. They will exit only in spirit because there's no reason for a bodily form in hell and they will not be human anymore. Biological DNA will not exist in eternity.

Don't put the cart before the horse by assuming that blessings will mechanically come just because a person has repented and placed their faith in Christ. One has to take decisive steps to obey the Lord and prove faithfulness before God will enrich your spirit. It comes at a distinct cost that is disciplined and controlled by the Lord. I once read a book on the blessings in the Bible and there are some marvellous and attractive promises. A friend told me to claim all those that I wanted in Jesus name, but nothing happened. I was perplexed but I realized that blessings don't just come about because I'm a Christian. The other misconception is to think that personal good intentions will automatically materialise. It is contrary to good sense that God should bless a Christian that has not given Christ first place in their life. A redeemed sinner has so many things that must be changed and playing mind-games with yourself does no good at all.

We often look for material blessings, but God puts the more important unseen spiritual blessings as a priority. Obviously, this is to aid relationship development by faith, but we don't grasp it because we are too centred on our material welfare. Most times, our desires are not what God has in mind for our lives (James 4:15). Invariably in our early stages of renewal, what we want and what God wants for us do not coincide. It's only after a certain point in regeneration do we realize that the unseen is far superior to the physical comforts in life. Faith and self-will will be tested and either the former purified or the latter deteriorating deeper into sin.

Our church fellowship and community condition us to be average performers in our quest for renewal. We owe Jesus too much to be aimlessly whiling away our precious time on earth. The repayment is not in legal tender, but spiritual tender. This is what God values most, and so should we. The Holy Spirit indwells a person's spirit and not the physical body. Thus, the body can decay and perish but our spirit endures forever together with the Holy Spirit. When a person accepts Jesus as Lord, they owe Christ everything, and that is the price of their soul. It is a spiritual obligation that is discharged via bodily actions. Jesus questioned his disciples why they could not remain vigilant for one hour to support him (Matthew 26:41), but he already knew the answer. He said to be alert not to make the wrong decision because the spirit knows what is right, but self does not concur.

There's so much to learn from this in our walk with the Lord and for our spiritual wellbeing. Just keeping the Lord in mind constantly is only halfway there, you have to pray that God will test your intentions. Then you will surely know where you stand and what has to be done to improve your character. Mental assent is not proof of change; actions that support the change in character is what counts (James 2:26). Consistent righteous behaviour proves the quality of one's faith and spiritual character. I had some shares on the stock exchange and at the same time I also believed that I was strongly on the path to renewal. Each time the share price went up I thanked God and was content. Each time the price slumped, I put my worries first and God was forgotten. One day while I was jogging, I seriously thought it through and resolved to put the Lord first regardless. I was very happy that I had taken remedial action otherwise I would have continued in a subliminal state of imagined progressive renewal and yet allowing worldly issues to dominate. Godly perception without the related action is mental folly and a hindrance to spiritual advancement.

Human fellowship with God is natural for him but in our unregenerate state, we find this to be most awkward and strange. After we have tasted the goodness of renewal, we can move forward because the Lord opens the way. The destructive nature of self-management must be expunged and redirected to God-will in order to build up spiritual capital. Then the urge for a closer and more meaningful fellowship with the Lord will be rightfully prioritised. It will be a need that you just want more and more of.

Initially, many a Christian will invariably experience a low in sanctification development for a long time (maybe years as I had) before they even get to the stage where they find favour in God's initiative. Each person has to negotiate their own way back to the Lord as this is a non-sharable function. God cares so much for you personally and surely you must be overjoyed and motivated to reciprocate appropriately. It started off very slowly for me being a lukewarm Christian for twenty-eight years. I was in my mid-forties then and was searching for God but only found insane silence. Then I made a firm resolution to do everything righteously and correctly and the rest is spiritual history. As I reflect on the past, the little steps that I took were responded to. Intriguing things manifested themselves in my life, yet most of them came about due to plain, honest and faithful adherence to the basic maxims in Scripture. Even the simplest moral is God's truth and must be respected as such. Cumulatively, they built up to a solid foundation. I put in my best effort to be right with God because I had to prove myself to him. The continuum has yielded good returns and I want more.

Jesus had done all his very hard work for us on the cross, and now it's our turn and the taming of self-determination is imperative. You can't win souls to Christ every day, but you can put your soul in a winning trajectory every day. No matter how close you get to Jesus, it's never close enough.

I used to think that being more like Christ was to reach the stage where I could do the things that he was doing (bar the miracles), and to behave in godliness that others may see the love of God through me. It's like wanting to run before learning to walk. The basic work starts with self-control and self-discipline where you have to master self-interest to the point of repudiating self. This part is the hardest and requires constant concentration to get our spiritual lives in order. The next part is easy because God gives all the answers and we just have to follow his guidance. Only Jesus can teach you how to be like him, and after he assumes the lead, everything else will fall into place. The ultimate satisfaction of being like Christ is his active volunteered intimacy to you and not necessarily in spiritual works. The higher God raises you in sanctification, the humbler you ought to be as a servant who has nothing to boast about. Noble thoughts and moral ambition in the absence of the correct actions will hold you in a state of daydreaming and it will get you nowhere.

Humans were created to have only one command-post with the Lord as commander. I have made earnest attempts to put Jesus Christ in my heart and to keep him there. I know that he is in me because of his responses and the way that he has met my needs that brings stability and peace to my spirit. This connotes that the Lord does not have to be constantly reaching you in a tangible manner as you would like a physical friend to be. It's a spiritual contact that cannot be seen, felt or touched, and yet, the reality cannot be disputed either.

Freewill is not only concentrated on the personal side but also carries implications over from the decisions made by external sources. It would be incomplete to ignore the mechanics of freewill in the world outside of our personal rights and boundaries. The negative effects of self-will on a macro scale may be viewed as unfair on the individual but the authority rank is above that of the personal level and that's life. Large corporations, government and external authorities can make decisions that have adverse consequences for ordinary citizens and if they are acting within the law, there's nothing to stop them. The 2008 GFC revealed the reality of poor decision-making and mismanagement. The austerity measures introduced by the PIIGS economies in 2011-2012 was an attempt to reduce government deficit. Even the stronger Eurozone nations like UK and Germany also passed milder draconian policies. These ranged from pay-cuts for public servants, increases in direct taxes for the wealthy, indirect taxes across the board and spending cut-backs. Hence, the standard of living was adversly affected. Governments acted carelessly and borrowed too much during the good times. The politicians had freewill and acted in their own interests. They didn't think about the repayment of all the money that they had borrowed.

Coterminous disaster also came about because of freewill in the free enterprise system. The ill-effects of self-will is evident in the irresponsible behaviour of the business world and large corporations. The behaviour of the executives of those corporations was downright reckless and there was a blatant oversight of the risks involved. The stock markets took a sharp dive and pension and superannuation funds were severely affected all over the world.

In early October 2018, the IMF had warned of another financial crash. Global debt of both public and private sectors had increased by 60% since the GFC to record highs of $182tn (£139tn). They added that "large challenges loom for the global economy to prevent a second Great Depression". Furthermore, former UK prime minister Gordon Brown mentioned that the world economy was 'sleepwalking into a future crisis' because the risks were not being adequately addressed at present. Diverse objectives in cross-cultural situations and sovereign borders make for a range of problems that have no panacea. If remedial measures are prioritised then hard decisions must follow. Unfortunately, human nature (self-will) ignores rationality and waits until it's too late.

The trade war between USA and China fixes attention of the hazards of self-will. There are valid reasons for this kind of engagement but the fallout affects the rest of the world. The tariff conflict started in June 2018 and the effects dramatically slowed world economic growth. Just months before, the IMF had predicted an optimistic outlook of prosperity for the world economies. However, simple decisions in defence of business can be unpleasant for ordinary people. We live in a global village and everybody feels the pinch in the chain reaction.

Aggressive policies and counter-measures tell of the complexity of all those decisions. People can make life intricate, uncertain and stressful. However, the Lord sees through all the faults and nothing can upset his decisions for the world. Materialism can be directed to yield pleasure and satisfaction but it can also come crashing down through madcap behaviour.

A progressive Christian need not be overly concerned with the macro upshot of freewill and ought to entrust the universal affairs to the Lord. The more important aspect is the micro sphere where self-will is the beast that must be caged. It's time for the people of God to live out their call to holiness because God is glorified in our success.

Our Father/God commands the highest respect and we see that in Exodus 20:18-19 where all the people of Israel witnessed and heard the Lord speak all the words of the Ten Commandments. They saw the thunder, lightning, the mountain in smoke, they heard the trumpet and they were petrified, so much so that they kept a safe clearance from God's presence. They even requested that God not personally address them or else they will die. It's an exceptional honour to hear God speak and it will consolidate one's faith. Yet, sin gives rise to fear and the unregenerate have no choice but to keep a distance from God. The reverse is happening to the sanctified whereby we want to hear more from God but are often denied that privilege. However, a healthy fear will improve our proximity and obedience to God.

The Bible is an instruction manual and the walk with God is private. This can only be grasped experientially. Nothing material can be taken out of this world into eternity but one's spiritual capital can and that has enormous value. The Lord's enlightenment in my spirit is my most prized possession that I have gained. It's the finest favour that I have done for myself on this earth and nothing can take it away because it is preserved and indemnified by Jesus Christ himself.

God's plan for human beings is elementary but human nature introduces so many diversions that foster the illusion that self-sufficiency is the answer to life. The Spirit's companionship is the best way to maintain purpose in your hard-fought pilgrimage. Each encounter with the Spirit will stimulate the urge for the next, it's a powerful incentive. Jesus didn't strain to maintain intimacy with his Father, but we do, and it's really up to us to keep the Holy Spirit interested in us. 1 Peter 2:1-2 succinctly explains the Christian walk i.e. to blot out the old and usher in the new. The attitude is accurately described. We must strive like new born babies for spiritual food that complement our salvation. The final outcome is to graduate as mature children of God.

There isn't enough of the right work done in self-criticism, self-correction, self-discipline and self-control on our part. I think that we are lazy when it comes to self-examination. We don't give the requisite commitment to rectifying the flaws in our character. We capitulate too easily to distractions and we refrain from taking harsh measures upon ourselves. My opinion means little and it is our Father that we have to impress. Heartfelt intentions are one thing, but without unbroken infusion by the Holy Spirit, self-will remains a woeful miserable liability for developing Christians, and perhaps even for those that are ahead in their journey to revival.

Bibliography

Chambers, Oswald. 1992, "My Utmost for His Highest", Discovery House, Grand Rapids, MI.

Cobb, Jr. John B. "Process Theology", return to religion-online.

Douglas, Alban. 1988, "One Hundred Bible Lessons", OMF Literature Inc. 776 Boni Avenue, Mandaluyong, Metro Manila.

Kappelman, Todd. 1998 "The Breakdown of Religious Knowledge," Probe Ministries.

Lane, Dennis. 1996, "One World Two Minds: Eastern and Western Outlooks in a changing world", OMF International, Littleton, CO 80120-4413.

Luther, Martin. 1997, "Table Talk" (Books for the Ages Library, version 1), AGES Software, Albany OR 97321-0509, USA.

Murray, Andrew. 1992, "Absolute Surrender", Christian Literature Crusade, Fort Washington, Pennsylvania.

Murray, Andrew. 1982, "Humility", Whitaker House, 30 Hunt Valley Circle, New Kensington, PA 15068.

Thomas-Top, Donald and Diane. 2003, Ethno-Wholistic Transformation, "The convergence of contextualised evangelism and wholistic development", K. K. Publishing, Northern Territory, Australia.

Tozer, A.W. 1982. "The Pursuit of God", Christian Publications.

Trower, Philip. "The Wanderer 2012". Version: 5th May 2015 www.thewandererpress.com

Wenham, David. 1989 "The Parables of Jesus", Hodder and Stoughton, London,

APPENDIX

Another recent development is the Brain-Computer-Interface or BCI (also called Mind-Machine-Interface, Direct Neural Interface etc.). This involves a chip implant into a person's brain (the host) and that chip is connected to the internet. It utilises augmented reality (AR) and virtual reality (VR) and will render computers, mobile phones, tablets and other personal digital devices redundant. It allows external devices to communicate directly with the host's brainchip. There are countless new experiences that the host may access and it's only limited by the internet. The human brain has been the same since Adam's time except for the regression caused by sin and the curse. BCI can enhance brain capability and experience to uncharted levels where the host may feel superhuman and that they have the power of a 'god'. I will mention a few possibilities but there are countless others that scientists are still exploring.

One of the foremost benefits is in the medical field. Wireless electroencephalo (EEG) devises or Bio Radio attached to the scalp can measure brainwaves and a person's thoughts (no keyboard necessary) can move a cursor on a screen. The host can control another device or a prosthetic limb that has a compatible chip. This opens up a range of opportunities for the disabled. Mind instruction allows communication whereby the brain initiates a few clicks and moves a cursor. Scientists can track signals sent by the optic nerve to the brain and then mark all with colours. This data can be transferred to a blind person, thus giving sight to the sightless.

Mind-to-mind (chip-to-chip) communication can happen all over the world if that information is available on the internet. Education and knowledge will be greatly enhanced. There won't be a need for universities or schools anymore. Cloud computing will enable hosts to download all instructions and operational procedures for anything. They will just know it because they will step into the mind (brainchip) of the person that knows the subject. It's instant knowledge on demand. The system will allow for students to learn at maximum efficiency but at their personal pace.

Memory capture empowers the user to live through another person's experience. AR and VR provides the host with a download of the entire environment and the original experience may be lived out and enjoyed. A subject may pick and choose and literally live outside their own body. However, a user may get lost in the process and won't be able to clearly define which is their real life and which is the borrowed imagined life!

This is by far the most disturbing innovation that scientists have developed so far. This practice is immoral because it introduces a foreign object into the human body that is completely unnatural and it goes against the Lord's design. External forces can communicate with a person's mind. Undesirable information may be sent purposely or accidently to the host. The brainchip can be hacked and that person's identity can be stolen or misused. They can effectively steal 'you'. Personal privacy will be threatened because of Big Data and AI that can work out what you have in private.

A central computer that is controlled by immoral forces will be able to send subliminal messages directly to that person's brain and effectively brainwash people while they are sleeping. Anybody who has Christian beliefs and has received the implant can be manipulated over time. The host may assert their current belief in Christ but as the brainwashing alters their perception, they will reach a point where they don't believe in Jesus anymore. Freewill will not be an inalienable personal right as we currently know it. BCI is open to corruption and hostile forces can manipulate any person they want.

The protection that the image of God offers against invasion by demonic forces will be vulnerable as it can be bypassed. In addition, the absolute right of freewill will be seriously compromised. People will no longer have the personal right to block (refuse) unwanted information or select the things that are good for their wellbeing. They may be allowed to exercise their personal rights but other measures may be introduced to erode their privacy. Personal control over one's life will be limited by those in power i.e. you will live according to how they want you to live. Unlimited power enables Big Brother to enforce full censorship. Freewill will be outdated and replaced by a form of police-will. Conditions may be forced on the host immediately or they may be subject to a gradual indoctrination process. In the coalesce of information from the internet, a subject can lose their individuality and uniqueness. Privacy and personal distinction will be lost through memory inter-change and out-of-body experiences, and individual identity can be irreparably damaged. It's the kind of chaos that the evil one loves. The privilege of a unique personal identity will be severely threatened or even destroyed. This is contrary to the Lord's purpose for each human individual as a unique distinct person.

Once the evil one gets control of the system, then all subjects will be capable of being moulded into their philosophy and way of life. As with all electronic communication, it can be turned on and off by the central command system. This will affect finances, trading and all essential household services and necessities, the most important being food and shelter. The evil one will have complete control over humanity. Despite how stringent privacy laws are framed, they can be circumvented. Residents will be living in a police state. At this stage, it will almost be impossible for ordinary people to turn to Jesus Christ and apostasy will arise amongst the weaker believers. The few that have true hearts for Christ will be in for a torrid time but the Holy Spirit will be in them to assist throughout their ordeal. Perhaps Israel will awaken and recognise Jesus as saviour (Ro 11:25-26, Ze 12:10). Then the Lord will return to judge the world.

During the mid-1990's I was with the Palm Beach Baptist Church men's fellowship and we had access to some material by New Zealand End Times evangelist Barry Smith. He predicted that the chip will be the instrument used for world domination. He advocated renunciation of the chip and many of his arguments are being realised today. However, there are many more apparently useful applications now but bear in mind that the internet had still not gained the momentum that it has today. Furthermore, desktop computers and laptops were out of reach for the ordinary working class. Nevertheless, he was ahead of his time.

Facebook has announced their roll-out of the Dalibra financial system that uses Libra coin. A previous attempt at a conventional framework had failed. This time, the odds are in their favour because the system is based on blockchain. They hope to have all their subscribers, that's over two billion people engaged in cyber business and dealing in Libra coin. It will usher in a new global payment regime. Money can be transferred anywhere at any time from your smart phone without bank fees. There will be no need for traditional banking services. Facebook has partnered with some big players such as eBay, Uber, Coin Base, Mastercard, Visa and PayPal to name but a few. It's a forerunner to wean the world onto cryptocurrency to displace fiat money. ATM's are already on their way out as the younger generation prefer digital cash and cyber shopping.

INDEX OF BIBLICAL REFERENCES

5	Ge 3:12	52	He 11:40	84	Ro 8:28	135	Lk 22:32
9	Mt 7.:13-14	52	Jn 6:44 *	87	Ex 33:20	135	Jn 21:15
9	Is 64:6	52	Jn 6:65	87	Jn 14:8	137	He 2:2-3
9	Ep 1:11 *	55	Mt 7:16 *	87	Ge 11:4 *	137	He 3:7-8
10	Ac 13:2	56	Mk 12:30-31 *	93	Jn 12:32	137	He 6:4-6
11	1Co 12:12	56	1 Co 13	97	Ep 1:5	138	He 10:26-27
16	Lk 14:26-27 *	56	1 Jn 4:10	97	Ro 8:29 *	139	He 12:25-26
22	Ge 1:21	57	Mk 12:30-31 *	98	Ps 8:4	139	1 Co 4
22	Ge 1:31	57	Ro 6:22	98	Is 40:6-7	139	Ga 5:19-20
23	Ge 2:25	59	Ge 2:16-17	100	Ro 8:29 *	139	1 Th 5:14
23	Ge 3:21	59	Ge 2:19	100	Ac 2:23	140	Tit 3:10-11
23	Ro 2:14-15	60	Jn 1:13	100	1 Pe 1:2	147	Mt 11:28-29 *
24	Ge 6	61	Jn 4:23-24	100	Jn 6:64	147	1 Th 4:3
24	Ge 11	61	Mt 12:48	101	Ja 4:13-14	148	Ga 2:11
25	Lk 2:19	61	Jn 19:26-27	101	Da 4:33-37	148	Co 1:28
25	Mt 15:19	61	Mk 7:20-23	101	Ro 13:1-2	149	1 Co 4:4 *
29	Ps 36:1-2	62	Jn 1:29	101	Ja 4:15	152	Mt 11:28 *
29	Ps 39:12	62	Jn 3:16 *	102	Jn 10:28-29	157	Ga 4:19
29	Ps 111:10	62	1 Ti 4:10	104	Ac 17:26-27	157	Jn 17:16
30	1Jn 4:18	62	He 2:9	104	Ge 11:4 *	157	Jn 15:19
33	1 Co 6:19-20	62	1 Jn 2:2	107	Jn 15:16 *	159	Jn 7:38
33	Mt 10:28 *	62	Is 53:6	112	1 Co 7:24	160	Ps 48:14
33	Mt 16:26	63	Ro 12:2 *	112	Mt 12:36	162	Jn 21:18 *
35	Ga 5:22-23 *	63	Jn 7:17	112	Ro 3:19	167	Jn 21:22 *
35	Ez 11:19-20	63	1 Th 4:3 *	112	Ro 14:12	168	2 Co 5:17 *
35	Ez 36:26-27	63	1 Th 5:18	117	1 Co 1:2	168	Ga 6:15
36	Ga 5:16	63	Jn 15:4	117	1 Th 4:3 *	168	Ep 2:13
36	Ro 7:6	63	Jn 15:6	118	1 Pe 1:2	169	Is 64:6
40	Ge 1:26 *	64	Ec 12:7	118	Ph 2:13 *	169	Ro 8:27
41	Ro 8:17	64	1 Co 2:11	118	He 13:21	170	Lk 10:20
41	Ge 11:6	64	Ep 3:16	118	1 Pe 4:2	170	Jn 12:26 *
45	Jn 4:23 *	64	Ro 12:2 *	118	Jn 6:38	170	Jn 21:19
45	Ro 7:7-8	65	Ja 4:1 *	118	Ro 12:2 *	171	1 Ch 29:11
45	2 Co 4:18 *	71	Jn 14:21-22 *	118	Ep 5:17	172	Pr 11:2
46	Mt 6:19-20	71	Jn 5:40	118	Jn 17:17-19	172	Ja 3:13
48	Ep 1:11 *	71	Jn 6:37	118	Jn 14:31 *	173	Ph 2:17
48	Lk 19:17	71	Jn 7:37	118	Jn 5:19	173	Jn 12:24
48	Ro 2:6	71	1 Co 2:14 *	122	Jn 14:12	174	Jn 17:21-22 *
48	Ps 62:12	72	1 Co 7:35	122	Ja 2:17-18	177	Ge 11:6
48	Pr 24:12	72	Mt 10:7	122	Jn 3:16 *	180	1 Th 3:2
48	Co 4:17	72	Mt 28:19 *	123	Ge 3:8	180	Jn 10:30 *
48	2 Ti 4:7	74	Ph 4:6	126	Ro 10:17	185	Mt 13
48	Re 2:7	74	Ep 6:18	126	He 12:2	185	Ja 2:26
48	Re 2:26	75	Co 3:14	126	Lk 17:5	185	Ga 5:22-24 *
48	Re 2:4 *	75	Jn 15:17	126	Jn 14:6	186	Lk 16:8-9
49	1 Sa 13:13	76	1 Jn 4:19	126	Jn 6:39	194	Ga 6:4 *
49	Jn 17:11	82	1 Ti 1:6-7	126	Jn 10:27 *	196	Is 26:3
50	Mt 7:16-20 *	82	1 Ti 4:1-2	131	1 Sa 15	196	Ro 12:2 *
52	Ep 1:17	82	Ac 17:21	133	Mt 6:20	197	Mt 22:16

375

197	Jn 6:44 *	228	2 Co 3:17-18	255	Ja 1:6	295	1 Co 2:6-7
198	Mk 3:35	228	Ga 5:13	255	He 11:6 *	296	Lk 18:9
198	Ro 8:17 *	228	1 Pe 2:16	259	Jn 8:28-29	296	Mt 8:20-22
198	Co 1:12	229	1 Pe 1:15-16	259	Mt 11:25	296	Mt 13:44
198	Lk 12:51	230	1 Pe 4:12-13	261	Mt 7:6	299	Jn 9:41
198	Mt 10:34	230	1Pe 4:19	262	Jn 21:22 *	301	2 Co 4:6-7
198	Mt 19:29	235	Ge 8:22	262	Ja 4:4	301	2 Co 4:16-18 *
198	1 Co 4:4 *	235	Ps 24:1	264	Lk14:26 *	302	1 Co 2:4-5
199	Mk 9:7	235	1 Co 15:39	264	Lk 5:8	303	1 Co 2:16
199	Jn 6:45	236	Ge 1:26 *	264	Ex 3:14	303	Ph 3:8 *
199	Jn 10:27 *	236	Ge 2:16	264	Ph 3:10-11	303	Mt 10:37-38
200	2 Co 4:18	236	Ro 13:1-2	264	Ep 2:5	303	Mt 10:28 *
201	Ph 3:12	239	Re 22:5	265	2 Ti 4:7	305	Jn 4:23-24 *
202	Ge 21:2	239	1 Co 6:19	266	Re 13:16-18	305	Ro 12:1 *
202	Jo 30:20	239	Jn 15:26	267	1 Co 3:1	307	Lk 24:16
202	Ac 1:4	239	Jn 4:24	267	1 Th 4:3 *	307	Jn 21:14
202	Ro 8:23	239	Re 21:5	267	1 Th 5:23-24	307	Jn 21:12
205	Jn 12:26	240	Is 65:17	271	Mt 7:21	308	Jn 20:15-16
205	Jn 15:14-17	240	Is 11:9	273	Mt 11:21	308	Mt 13:11-12
205	Jn 14:31 *	240	Ge 1:29	274	Jn 17:20-21 *	308	Mt 13:23
205	Jn 16:1	240	Re 21	274	Jn 17:26	309	He 10:22-23
205	Mt 6:1	241	Lk 23:43	275	Mt 16:21	309	Ro 2:15
206	Ro 12:1-2 *	243	1 Jn 3:1	275	Mt 20:18	309	Ro 2:13
207	1 Co 4:13	243	Mt 19:14	276	Ze 13:7	309	1 Co 2:14 *
207	2 Ti 4:6	243	Mt 18:3	277	Ph 2:6-8 *	312	Ep 1:3
207	2 Co 5:14	244	Mt 11:28-29 *	277	Lk 22:43	313	Lk 14:28
208	Re 12:7	244	He 11:6 *	278	Ge 22:12	313	Lk 16:8
208	Lk 1:19	245	Mt 11:29 *	279	Ps 34:8	325	Ph 2:5-9 *
208	Ge 32:24	245	Lk 2:52	281	He 13:17	327	Jn 14:23-24 *
209	Jn 14:10 *	245	Mt 11:25	281	Mt 13:52	327	1 Jn 5:3
209	2 Co 4:18	245	Lk 10:22	282	Lk 24:25	329	Pr 27:17
211	2 Co 4:7	245	Jn 17:17	284	Jn 17:23	330	Pr 3:13-15
211	2 Co 4:10	246	Lk 14:26*	285	Jn 14:21 *	330	Ze 13:9
212	Jn 13:10	246	Lk 14:33	286	Ga 6:15	331	Ja 2:9
212	Re 2:4 *	247	1 Pe 5:5	286	2 Co 5:17 *	331	Ro 2:11
212	Re 3:16	247	Ja 4:6	286	Lk 18:27	331	Is 42:8
215	Jn 10:30 *	248	Tit 1:8	286	Mt 28:20 *	331	Is 48:11
215	Jn 14:10 *	248	Ja 3:16	286	He 13:5-6	332	Lk 17:10 *
216	Jn 14:20	248	Ja 4:1 *	287	1 Jn 3:3	332	Lk 22:26
216	Jn 14:23 *	249	Ga 6:4 *	287	2 Pe 1:8	335	Mt 16:24-25
216	Jn 17:21 *	251	Ro 7:15	287	1 Pe 1:15-16	335	1 Pe 2:21
216	Re 3:20	252	Ga 6:7-8	288	Lk 8:18	335	Ro 8:17 *
216	Jn 16:15	252	Tit 2:12	291	1 Co 3:13	336	Jn 12:26 *
218	1 Co 9:27 *	252	1 Pe 1:13	291	Ep 2:10	337	Ge 5:24
219	Mt 28:18-20 *	252	1 Co 9:27 *	291	Lk 12:35	337	Da 6:10
223	1 Jn 4:4	252	Ph 3:8 *	292	Ph 2:8 *	337	1 Sa 13:14
224	Mt 11:28-29 *	254	Dt 4:9	293	Ro 5:3	340	Re 3:11
224	1 Co 6:19-20	254	Dt 11:19	293	Ja 1:3-4	340	Re 6:11
225	He 10:7	254	Ps 78:5	293	Mt 7:16 *	341	Mt 23:11
225	He 10:9	254	1 Th 5:17	293	Jn 15:16 *	341	Mt 18:4
228	Ga 5:1	255	1 Jn 3:1	293	Jn 14:26 *	341	Lk 9:46-48
228	Ro 8:2			295	Ph 2:12-13 *	342	Lk 12: 47-48

344	Ro 13:1
344	Nu 20:12
345	Mt 23:12
345	Lk 14:11
345	Ph 2:5-9 *
346	Lk 17:10 *
347	1 Co 2:6-7
350	Is 49:2-3
351	Ez 23
351	Ho 4
355	Ps 19:7
355	Pr 2:6
356	Jn 20:17
357	Mt 23:9
357	Ex 20:12
358	Ja 2:23
358	Is 45:23
362	Jn 21:18 *
364	Ja 4:15
364	Mt 26:41
365	Ja 2:26
368	Ex 20:18-19
368	1 Pe 2:1-2
374	Ro 11:25-26
374	Ze 12:10

*Quoted more than once

www.ingramcontent.com/pod-product-compliance
Lightning Source LLC
Chambersburg PA
CBHW071853290426
44110CB00013B/1125